ANALYSIS AND INTERPRETATION OF FINANCIAL STATEMENTS

DR. GURUPRASAD MURTHY
Professor - Director General,
Dr. V.N. Bedekar Institute of Management
Thane.

First Edition : 2014

Himalaya Publishing House

MUMBAI • NEW DELHI • NAGPUR • BENGALURU • HYDERABAD • CHENNAI • PUNE • LUCKNOW • AHMEDABAD • ERNAKULAM • BHUBANESWAR • INDORE • KOLKATA • GUWAHATI

First Edition : 2014

Published by : Mrs. Meena Pandey for **Himalaya Publishing House Pvt. Ltd.,**
"Ramdoot", Dr. Bhalerao Marg, Girgaon, **Mumbai - 400 004.**
Phone: 022-23860170/23863863, Fax: 022-23877178
E-mail: himpub@vsnl.com; Website: www.himpub.com

Branch Offices :

New Delhi : "Pooja Apartments", 4-B, Murari Lal Street, Ansari Road, Darya Ganj, New Delhi - 110 002. Phone: 011-23270392, 23278631; Fax: 011-23256286

Nagpur : Kundanlal Chandak Industrial Estate, Ghat Road, Nagpur - 440 018. Phone: 0712-2738731, 3296733; Telefax: 0712-2721215

Bengaluru : No. 16/1 (Old 12/1), 1st Floor, Next to Hotel Highlands, Madhava Nagar, Race Course Road, Bengaluru - 560 001. Phone: 080-32919385; Telefax: 080-22286611

Hyderabad : No. 3-4-184, Lingampally, Besides Raghavendra Swamy Matham, Kachiguda, Hyderabad - 500 027. Phone: 040-27560041, 27550139; Mobile: 09390905282

Chennai : No. 8/2, 2nd Madley Street, Ground Floor, T. Nagar, Chennai - 600 017. Mobile: 09345345055

Pune : First Floor, "Laksha" Apartment, No. 527, Mehunpura, Shaniwarpeth (Near Prabhat Theatre), Pune - 411 030. Phone: 020-24496323/24496333; Mobile: 09370579333

Lucknow : House No 731, Shekhupura Colony, Near B.D. Convent School, Aliganj, Lucknow - 226 022. Mobile: 09307501549

Ahmedabad : 114, "SHAIL", 1st Floor, Opp. Madhu Sudan House, C.G. Road, Navrang Pura, Ahmedabad - 380 009. Phone: 079-26560126; Mobile: 09377088847

Ernakulam : 39/176 (New No: 60/251) 1st Floor, Karikkamuri Road, Ernakulam, Kochi - 682011, Phone: 0484-2378012, 2378016; Mobile: 09344199799

Bhubaneswar : 5 Station Square, Bhubaneswar - 751 001 (Odisha). Phone: 0674-2532129, Mobile: 09338746007

Indore : Kesardeep Avenue Extension, 73, Narayan Bagh, Flat No. 302, IIIrd Floor, Near Humpty Dumpty School, Indore - 452 007 (M.P.). Mobile: 09301386468

Kolkata : 108/4, Beliaghata Main Road, Near ID Hospital, Opp. SBI Bank, Kolkata - 700 010, Phone: 033-32449649, Mobile: 09883055590, 07439040301

Guwahati : House No. 15, Behind Pragjyotish College, Near Sharma Printing Press, P.O. Bharalumukh, Guwahati - 781009, (Assam). Mobile: 09883055590, 09883055536

DTP by : Prerana Enterprises, Mumbai.

Printed at : Geetanjali Press Pvt. Ltd., Nagpur. (On behalf of HPH Pvt. Ltd.)

Course Contents

1. Revision of Balance Sheet and P&L Statement Fundamentals:
   - Indian Accounting Standards
   - Indian Accounting Standard vs. US GAAP
   (This would also cover the manipulations often done by companies to show higher profits)
2. Cash Flow Analysis:
   - Measuring operating/financing and investing cash flows
   - Cash flows and life cycle state of a company
   - Cash flows and financial flexibility (linkages to dividend policy and over retention of profits)
3. Assessing Business Performance:
   - Operational efficiency ratios (Gross profit, net profit margins and various turnover ratios)
   - Liquidity ratios – Current ratio/acid test
   - Profitability ratios, valuation ratios
   - EPS/ROE/ROCE/Total shareholder returns, linkages between ROE and ROCE and optimal capital structure and determinants of PE multiple, price to book value, EV/EBDITA multiple
   - Capitalization ratios – Debt equity, debt to assets
   - Dupont Analysis
   - Coverage ratios and credit analysis and ratings
   (The emphasis will be on correct interpretation and correct measurement, i.e., with necessary accounting adjustments for these ratios)
4. Free Cash Flows to Equity/Firm:
   - From earnings to free cash flows
   - Adjustment from standard accounting to correctly measure free cash flow
   - Capitalisation leasing expenses and R&D expenditure, correct treatment for amortization expenses and deferred taxes
   - Measuring correct ROF and ROC after adjusting for inter corporate investments
   - Implication of the above mentioned adjustment on fundamental valuations/company end PE or price/book value or EBDITA multiple
5. Introduction to Advance Accounting Concepts:
   - Merger and acquisition
   - Consolidation of balance sheets
   - Deferred taxes, minority, interest
   - NOPAT and adjustments to NOPAT from EVA perspective to measure correct concept cash flows
   - Economic value added (EVA) and linkages between value of a company and EVA
   - Equity analysis, stock splits and buy-back
   - Managing productivity of corporate capital
   - Composite index for measuring productivity
6. Forecasting FCFE/FCEF and Security Valuation –

Reference Text:

- Finance of Management for Prasanna Chandra
- Finance of Management for Khan and Jain

COPYRIGHTS ACKNOWLEDGMENTS

- Dr. Vijay V. Bedekar, Chairman, Vidya Prasarak Mandal (VPM), Thane and the authorities of VPM, Thane and Dr. V.N. Bedekar Institute of Management Studies (DR VNBIMS), Thane for their invaluable support and facilities throughout the publication.
- CA Mr. Kedar Nijasure for his invaluable contributions to Chapters 7, 16, 17 and 18.
- Ms Supriya Desai, MMS 2007-09, for the initial spadework.
- Mr Amitpal Singh for his painstaking work relating to Chapters 12 and 14, MMS Lala Lajparai Institute of Management, 2006.
- Ms Simpi Khandelwal for her contribution to a case study of Infosys.
- Ms Suman Mathur for her contributions through the software facilities at DR VNBIMS.
- The library of DR VNBIMS, particularly Mr. Sandeep Bhavsar and Ms Dipali Hindalekar for their unstinted cooperation in making avaibale relevant inputs in record time.
- Mr Deepak Gokhale for proofreading the manuscript.
- Last but not the least Ms. Ketki Mistry for her patience and perseverance in offering all secretarial and related assistance when the book was being written.

CONTENTS

LIST OF EXHIBITS

CASES

LIST OF TABLES

CASES

About the Book

FINANCE - ART and SCIENCE

Financial management is the art and science of managing the resources (physical and financial, animate and inanimate) of an enterprise with the purpose of getting the best possible result-resource ratio to continuously subserve the cause of the expectations of all stakeholders of any enterprise. The idea is to ensure that scarce resources are allocated effectively and efficiently to competing ends and where competing ends are limited and resources are in surfeit, the challenge is to identify the most productive competing ends and also newer productive opportunities, which can absorb the resources in excess **(Exhibit A).** Thus, the end result of effective financial management is seen as efforts which can bring success to any enterprise by making "***two blades of grass grow where only one grew before***". Translating this lofty thought of the American philosopher Jonathan Swift into action, in the field of finance, it refers to the ability to get the best possible output (physical/ financial) for any given input or using the least input (physical/financial) for any given output. Ideally, the rate of output should go on increasing and the rate of input should be on the decline so that the result – resource ratio catapults to higher and higher levels of attainment, above and beyond historic levels, into seamless heights through '***stretch goals***.' In financial terms, it means that the ratio of profit (output)/investment (input), commonly referred to as Return on Investment (ROI) (%) should be well sustained at all times and, of course, always placed above the minimum acceptable rate of return*.

The ways and means of attaining and maintaining higher and higher ROI, open to management, are simultaneously many and limited, a contradiction of terms, nevertheless true. The limited options open can be vividly gauged with the help of the simplest version of the Du Pont ROI chart presented below:

$$\text{Return on Total Assets} = (\text{Net Profit/Total Assets} \times 100)$$

$$= \frac{\text{Net Profit}}{\text{Sales}} \times 100 \times \frac{\text{Sales}}{\text{Total Assets}} \text{ (times)}$$

MAXIMISING SHAREHOLDERS WEALTH: Corporate Financial Policy, all over the world, accepts maximizing shareholder value as a key objective. There have been several refinements to this thought and the expression shareholder value is replaced by stakeholder value, corporate wealth, market value, economic value added *et al.* A study conducted by Pandey and Bhatt (1990) of 57 Indian Companies[1] showed that maximizing the market value of enterprise is not necessarily the key objective of Indian business. According to the study, four important goals are pursued, *viz.*, ensuring the availability of funds, maximizing growth, maximizing operating profits before interest and taxes and maximizing the rate of return on investment. According to another study conducted by Manoj Anand (2002)[2], the important corporate financial objectives, in rank order of importance, are:

**The minimum acceptable rate of return is also referred to as the modicum or target rate of return which is a fundamental standard of financial performance against which the outcomes of managerial actions are assayed. The minimum acceptable rate of return refers to the marginal cost of capital against which the marginal efficiency of capital of various management actions are to be assayed. Incidentally the minimum acceptable rate of return (R) is always defined as $R > k_o$ where k_o is the cost of capital. Depending on the state of the health of business and a host of other factors, R may be pitched at or near k_o or much above k_o. In any case R should never be below k_o.*

---

[1]Pandey, I. M., and Ramesh Bhat. "Significance of Financial Goals pursued by Companies in India: Survey Findings." *Journal of Financial Management & Research - International Review of Finance,* July-December (1990).

[2]Anand, Manoj. "Corporate Finance Practices in India: A Survey." *Vikalpa* 27. 4 October-December. 2002.

(1) Maximizing EBIT/EPS.
(2) Maximizing the Spread between ROI and WACC (EVA).
(3) Maximizing the Spread between CFROI and WACC (CVA).
(4) Maximizing Market Value Added (MVA) of the Firm.
(5) Reduction in the Side Costs in the Form of Conflicts Amongst Various Stakeholders.

EXHIBIT (1)

*Surfeit cash (liquidity), a serious problem faced by enterprise from time-to-time, provides a challenge to the enterprise to sustain profitability in the wake of excess cash or cash-related assets and given the indisputable dictum of finance, viz., '**liquidity and profitability are at loggerheads**'. For example, Infosys has been hounded by analyist and investors to deploy its excess cash, year on year basis, to either invest productively or reward shareholder. For the year ended 31st March, 2011, Infosys had a cash balance of ₹ 129 billion equivalent to USD 3.3 billion (circa). Of course, this is chickenfeed in relation to the huge balances maintained by mega companies in the US. For example: Apple with USD 75.87 billion cash is richer than the US Treasury which has only USD 73.76 billion. Incidentally, Microsoft another US-based ICT company has cash reserve of USD 40 billion (29/07/2011). 40 PSUs in India are sitting on a pile of cash of ₹ 2 lakh, crores. Even capital intensive units BHEL, Bharat Electronics, Siemens and Alstom Projects have huge cash reserves. The total cash pile of BSE 500's Richie Rich has grown to ₹ 128,500 crores, a 14.3% increase over last year's figure. (ET Bureau, 12/07/2011).*

10 Indian companies including RIL, Infosys, Coal India, Cairn India and ONGC are carrying a cash of ₹ 2.3 lakh crores. RIL alone carries 33% of the said cash pile, which is nearly 20% of the company's revenue. Infosys with ₹ 20,591 crores is carrying 61% of its annual sales amount. Cash accumulation adversely affects return on equity and tends to be value dilutive unless a company can continuously and successfully postulate successor projects which can absorb the surplus cash productivity that is to say projects where internal rates of returns exceeds the minimum acceptable rate of return. Otherwise, companies tend to deploy surplus cash into financial assets, possibly gilt-edged returns, leading to diluted return on equity (%). Thus, Infosys is earning just 6 to 7 per cent yield on financial assets against the cost of equity capital at 12-14 per cent. Accordingly, Infosys return on equity has gone down rather significantly over the years due to excessive liquidity. The top 10 firms listed on NASDAQ suffer from a cash pile of $ 117.6 billion (over ₹ 6 lakh crores).

Source: *Naidu, K. B. and S. Shinde. "India Inc., hold on to its cash." Business Standard (Mumbai) 7th May, 2012.*

A contrarian view states that India Inc., which was sitting on a cash pile, is slowing reducing the accumulation. High interest rates are forcing companies to shy from lenders, including banks to meet the working capital needs of enterprise. The short-term financial needs of business are being met by withdrawing deposits using cash accumulation and reducing borrowing as much as possible. Further, excess cash is also deployed for debt-repayment and capital expenditure and also to extinguish borrowings from abroad.

Source: *Saha. Manojit and Somasroy Chakraborty. "India Inc., using up cash for short-term needs." Business Standard (Mumbai) 3rd April 2012.*

EXHIBIT 1(A)

SURFEIT CASH – IDENTIFYING INVESTMENT OPPORTUNITIES

*Philately is an important avenue which can absorb surplus liquid resources and also provide competitive return on investment. It is estimated that as an asset class '**philately**' is very steady and usually offers around 10% return on an annualised basis. It is said that about 25 odd high net worth individuals, in India, are already using philately as an avenue of investments. The minimum amount required for investing in a rare stamp is over ₹ 50 lakhs. Further, rare stamps can fetch upto 1 million USD. It is interesting to note that there is a lot of interest in stamps from India. For example, a "1854 Four Annas Inverted Head' stamp fetched a record price for India. The stamp, which was estimated to fetch GBP 18,000 - GBP 20,000 was sold for GBP 105,390 at an auction in October, 2010 in London. "**This will soon hit a million pounds.**"*

Source: *"Trend spotting philately emerges as high-return investment". The Times of India 30th November, 2008: p. 21.*

OPTIONS TO IMPROVE ROI

The options open to improve ROI are increased sales, reduced cost and reduced assets employed in the business. One more option can be inducted by classifying cost management into two options, *viz.,* managing variable costs and fixed costs.

Within these three (or four) options, management need to identify multifarious ways and means of exploring the same to manage the top-line (sales), middle-line (costs) and bottom-line (net profit) of an enterprise.

IMPROVE ROI – INCREASED SALES

One of the options opened to improve the return on investment is increased sales. Sales in financial terms for any business are a product of number of units sold and the selling price per unit. Usually, high volume necessarily means sacrifice in the margin. Companies which sell limited number of units can afford to have improved or high margins. Essential commodities and consumer good items are characterised by high volume and low margin. As against this, luxury items like Mercedes Car or Rolex watches would enjoy a higher margin and rather low volume. In addition to volume and selling price per unit, the mix of sales plays an important role in deciding the aggregate revenue of a business. Further, there is one more dimension and that is the currency in which the sales take place and the status of that currency in terms of its strength *vis-à-vis* the local currency. All these factors taken together, in addition to cost, result in the profit-volume-cost-mix relationship for a business. Mere increases in revenue do not contribute to the bottom-line of a business though marketing managers, worldwide, entertain an illusory belief that more sales mean more profit. Hence, the theme '***More Revenue does not mean More Profits***'.

EXHIBIT 1(B)

HUL – MANAGING COST-PROFIT – VOLUME-MIX

"Buoyed by a mix of product price increases and volumes, Fast Moving Consumer Goods Major (FMCG) Hindustan Unilever (HUL) posted an 18% growth in net profit at ₹ 754 crore for the third quarter ended December, 31, 2011, compared to ₹ 638 crore in the corresponding period last year, Net sales rose 16% to ₹5,853 crore from ₹5,027 crore during the period."

*This is a good example of sales increase (16%) through better management of price increases, product mix, volumes along with dynamic cost management through "**aggressive savings programs coupled with judicious pricing**". Personal products, oral care, beverages and packaged foods grew in the range of 11 to 14%. However, the performance of Knorr soups was muted.*

Source: *The Times of India (Mumbai) 7th February, 2012.*

IMPROVE ROI – COST MANAGEMENT

Cost management (including cost cutting) is key to sustaining the bottom-line of business.

- Telepresence is a new cost cutting tool. In fact, Tata Consultancy Services has gone on records, in its Annual Report 2008-09 to say that the costs of overseas travel have been reduced after introduction of increased video-conferencing. Further, there is green policy effect – the decrease in the company's carbon footprint. Though the economics of telepresence is not very attractive as of today, Tata Communications has pioneered the public room model to tackle the exorbitant installation cost. "***Customers can access the public rooms by paying just ₹ 6,000 – ₹ 7,500 per hour as part of a special promotional offer.***" Thus, an otherwise cost or expense centre is converted into a profit or investment centre.
- Frugality has to be revered and not ridiculed. Frugality can be promoted if we create a culture where simplicity is respected and not viewed as miserliness. Mahatma Gandhi's ventures in simple living come to the fore, "***Governments must penalise the waste of resources and should create laws to ensure this. People will gradually develop habit of consuming only as much as is necessary.***"
- Tata Motors had posted a net loss of ₹ 500 crores (₹ 5 billion) in 2001. This was regarded as one of the largest losses incurred by any company in one year. A remarkable turnaround took place because of a unique cost management program which was called '***cost erosion***'. Among other initiatives the following were the important moves:
    - Cross functional teams to implement and monitor cost erosion initiatives.
    - e-Sourcing in lieu of traditional purchasing.
    - Rationalising vendor profile. Infact the company moved towards a single vendor policy.
    - Revamped organisational structure from a bureaucratic model to a collaborative, camaraderie-driven mode. The turnaround took 5 years though.
- Bollywood actors, big companies, luxury hotels, BPOs, bankers, socialites, husbands, wives and lovers ... all are tightening their belts to battle the economic squeeze to combat the global meltdown. The Times of India has identified 30 ways and means of cutting cost- atleast one each for every alphabet of the English language that is to say *A* to *Z*.[3]

[3]Raaj, Neelam and Insiya Amir, "A-Z of Cutting Costs." *The Times of India* (Mumbai) 15th December, 2008.

- In October, 2008 following the global meltdown the CEO of Sony, Mr. Howard Stringer, said, "***We are selling a lot of television sets, more than ever, but we are not making money on them, and that's a by-product of a fixed-cost problem that we need to address.***"

EXHIBIT 1(C)

COST MANAGEMENT – MAHARASHTRA

*In several parts of Maharashtra due to shortage of power and labour, in rural and hilly areas, construction labour is difficult to procure and workers are demanding higher wages. To combat the labour shortage the Government of Maharashtra decided (2009) to hire donkeys to perform certain tasks which include movement of '**construction material, such as bricks, metal and sand from one place to another.**' The price of a donkey depends on its physique, height, colour, age and the number of teeth. Donkeys from Kathewadi from Gujarat are the most expensive and are priced between ₹ 10,000 and ₹ 15,000. This price is said to be nearly 50% higher than last year. In Ahmednagar district, in Maharashtra, Donkey Bazaars are held to auction Donkeys.*

Source: Marpakwar, Prafulla. "Donkeys kick-start economy." *The Times of India* (Mumbai) 18th March, 2009.

Thus, the bottom-line of a company depends on a proactive combination of top-line (sales) and middle-line (costs). In Sony to reiterate, cutting fixed cost meant shutting some plants and also cutting jobs to increase profits with a view to bolster profitability. In Japan, in particular fixed costs are an issue. 80% of the sales are outside Japan and a sizeable proportion of production takes place within Japan. Thus, production costs are vulnerable to an appreciating Japanese Yen with a relatively high local labour cost. However, sales are in currencies which are usually weaker than the Japanese Yen. Production activity has to be hived-off from Japan, if the fixed costs are to be reduced. Thus, Sony had to initiate a multipronged attack to sustain its ROI, post global meltdown, which included increased revenue, reduced variable cost, reduced fixed cost and divestment of capital in Japan and reinvesting in locations outside Japan due to the strength of the Japanese Yen.

EXHIBIT 1(D)

IMPACT OF THE SLIDING INR

The rupee has been depreciating continuously and stands at ₹ 55.03 (21st May, 2012) to a USD. It was ₹ 44.42 (5th April, 2011) to a USD. If the slide of the rupee vis-à-vis the USD continues the bottom-line of India Inc., will be adversely affected. In fact, the rupee depreciation has already started adversely affecting corporate profits. Though companies which have large export sales may benefit due to the falling value of the rupee, yet if the import content of the product or service is high on balance the gains are limited. Overall, India is a net importer which would adversely affect the corporate sector profitability. If input cost of key items like petroleum and related products go up, the cost push effects will be seen on the bottom-line of enterprise. Hence, managing return on investment of a business cannot exclude identifying the role of exchange rate variation and strength of the local currency with its associated impact on the financial health of individual enterprise.

Source: "Rupee depreciation may impact corporate profits: Economists." *Business Standard* 10th May, 2012: p. 4.

The myriads of options open and the several permutations and combinations available to manage sales, cost and profits are limited only by the genius of the people in an organisation.[4] However, the challenges before managers at the helm of the affairs of any enterprise are to ensure that "***money works for them rather than they working for money***". Says Edmund Burke, "***If we command our wealth we will be rich, if the wealth commands us we are poor indeed***".

In the context of financial management in an enterprise the question arises as to how to make money in particular and resources in general work for enterprise rather than the other way round. In an exchange or money economy, all business transactions are reported in terms of money. Money measurement is, among others, a universal and cardinal principle governing the financial and accounting process which generates several financial statements. Hence the couplet:

"***Money is a matter of functions four:***

A Medium, A Measure, A Standard and A Store."

Again as Aristotle (384 - 322 B.C.) has said "***Everything, then, must be assessed in money; for this enables men always to exchange their services and so makes society possible.***"

To make money work for business one has to understand the quantified statements expressed in money terms and known as financial statements which usually include the following:

(a) Profit or Loss account for the period ending... .
(b) Balance Sheet as on or as of or as at a particular point of time.
(c) Cash flow statement; for the year ending.
(d) Other supporting, supplementary, statements.

The financial analysts as well as functional managers (line management) need to be well trained in terms of competencies* required to analyse and interpret financial statements. Hence, the need for courses like '***Analysis of Financial Statements***' or '***Financial Statement Analysis***' or '***Analysis and Interpretation of Financial Statements***' in business schools and management institutes in undergraduate and postgraduate, part-time and full-time, degree and diploma programs.

The expressions '***Analysis***' and '***Interpretation***' have been assigned a specific role in the theme underlying this book.

'Financial Statement Analysis' is largely a study of the interrelationships between various financial factors in an enterprise as disclosed by a single set of statements and study of the trends of these factors as shown in the series of statements.

Interpretation is the mental process or conception of a person, with respect to the understanding of the elements of information presented in complicated and compounded financial statements.

Analysis and interpretation are mutually inclusive, continuous and complementary to each other.

---

[4]Improvements in ROI can be derived through a wide variety of options open to management given the said four options. Within these four options there is a mix of several permutations and combinations involving ownership, creditor, income mix, control rights and a host of other factors in varying degrees, with possible permutation and combinations limited only by the ingeniuity of different markets and their stakeholders (factor, financial and output) and of those who manage the financial problems of an enterprise (See Solomon, Ezra. Theory of Financial Management. Coloumbia University Press, p. 28).

**Competencies refer to a composite basket of traits, viz., aptitude, skills and knowledge.*

Managers, all over the world, are expected to develop competencies which help them in the task of analysis and interpretation of financial statements both from the perspective of the requirements of their respective jobs as well as their personal wealth creation, protection and growth.

Developing competencies to analyse and interpret financial statements is a structured well defined process and needs to be developed through systematic learning program/s which act as building blocks leading to the following:

(a) Understanding the anatomy of financial statements.

(b) Knowing the ground rules governing the construction, format and content of financial statements.

(c) Awareness of statutes affecting the preparation of financial statements (the proforma) prescribed by law, followed by convention and designed by managers to meet the needs of existing and emerging situations and problems on hand.

(d) Ability to handle, to start with, simple but a wide array of tools of financial analysis which include comparative financial statements, per cent change over previous year, common-size financial statements, trend analysis and index numbers.

(e) Comprehension of ratio analysis which help to capture the financial health of business with respect to liquidity, profitability, activity, valuation, capital structure (leverage) and any other ratio or set of ratios which help in assessing the health of an enterprise expressed in physical and financial terms.

The nuances and subtleties governing ratios analysis are explored in detail, in this book and in a wide variety of ways through several formats and models by different authors for different purposes in different countries at different points of time. Ratio analysis is undertaken to facilitate, *inter alia*, intra firm, inter period, inter firm analysis.

Since the common language of business is finance most of the ratios are financial based. However, it needs to be understood that the financial numbers are only a mirror image of the actual, physical, events taking place in business. Hence, it is the reality of business operations and not the ratios that needs to be managed. If business operations are well managed, automatically the ratios expressed in financial terms will reflect the same. Further, though there are large number of ratios, trying to get all the ratios simultaneously in one place to address issues faced by business would be a preposterous proposition. The truth is that the substratum of the knowledge base of finance can be presented through a relatively small number of important financial measures through which it is possible to appraise and assess the health of any business enterprise. Such measures are derived from the interrelationships that exist between the key areas of management, *viz.*, operations, investment and financing and the key stakeholders to be addressed, among others, managers, owners and creditors. Thus, in a typical financial model designed to meet shareholders welfare the relationship between overall (total) management performance (return on equity) is literally a physically product of operating management performance and financial management performance. While the former in turn is a physical product of the PV ratio (%) (contribution margin/sales), margin of safety (%) (operating profit/contribution margin) and turnover ratio (times) (sales/total assets), the latter is a physical product of interest management, tax management and management of debt equity. These ratios help to capture the functioning of the entire business to guide management in financial decision making in particular and management decision making in general. The challenge for the learner is not in the computation but in understanding the meaning of the outcomes and how the sum of all the outcomes, taken together, present a holistic view of the financial health of an enterprise. The relationship between different ratios is presented below:

EXHIBIT 1(E)

CORPORATE FINANCIAL PERFORMANCE MODEL

TMC = Return on Equity (ROE) = Profits after Tax ? Owners Funds

OMP
Return on Capital Employed

×

FMP
Financial Leverage

OMP	FMP
◆ P/V Ratio (%) = Contribution Margin ÷ Sales × 100	◆ Profit before Tax ÷ Operating Profit (%)
◆ Margin of Safety (%) = Operating Profit ÷ Contribution Margin × 100	◆ Capital Employed ÷ Owners Funds (Times)
◆ Turnover Ratio (Times) = Sales ÷ Capital Employed	◆ Profit after Tax ÷ Profit before Tax (%)

TMP = Total Management Performance
OMP = Operating Management Performance
FMP = Financial Management Performance

(f) Knowing certain important absolute measures like economic value added, enterprise value, market share (sales volume and value) production (volume and value), number of employees (wage cost) and the like to provide a further boost to the quality and also quantity of information generated and level of knowledge regarding the health of an enterprise.

(g) Exploring other important areas of interest like mergers and acquisitions, deferred tax assets and liabilities, buy-back of shares, stock split and capital reduction, managing productivity of capital and evolving a composite productivity index to enable ranking of enterprise in terms of their contribution year on year basis and that too in relation to similar units in the industry in the country, globally and further in other industries across countries and continents.

The above topics have to be dealt with in the context of the live business environment in which finances are managed so that the power of the tools explored can be established either for their utility (or otherwise).

INTERNET AND FINANCE

In the age of advanced Information and Computer Technology (ICT), Internet is an institution by itself and provides access to an assortment of valuable financial information. Hence, the role of Internet in finance education cannot be ignored. A few clicks on the keyboard of a PC, laptop or blackberry, the information analysts and decision makers can find an avalanche of financial information. Several financial websites have been identified and described in the chapter on ***'Ratios – Different***

Databases'. To mention a few of them – Myiris, Finalaya, Compustat, Standard and Poors and Factiva. Of course, a *caveat* to users of Internet. Many of the websites keep changing their content over time and new websites also get added to the list. Internet is part of life and the process of knowing, understanding and learning finance through the Internet is a way of life. Hence, the special emphasis on different databases which students can have access to.

While Internet is a great friend of facilitators and learners and ICT rules the waves, society should not be hypnotised by the advent of science to the neglect of common sense. The end result of any outcome can be no better than the input fed into the computer. If there is a data entry error then it is as good as '***garbage in and garbage out***'. The tendency to trust computer spreadsheets as gospel truth or ordainments of testaments is the folly of facilitators and learners of current times. ICT is meant for man and not the other way round. Hence, the need to be cautious and circumspect.

The book is supported through live examples, numerical problems with solutions, case studies and a wide variety of supporting data, information and knowledge for a better and deeper understanding of the subject matter of analysis and financial statements. At the end of the book there are case studies which cover most topics prescribed in the syllabus. Solutions to these case studies are available in soft format.

The book has presented details of more than ten databases for the benefits of readers. Of course apart from these databases, CMIE and RBI databases alongwith the *Economic Times, Financial Express, Capital Market, Business Standard* databases are accessible to analysts and interested researchers and scholars of the subject of finance.

This book is tailor-made and customised to meet the requirements of scholars intending to learn how to analyse and interpret financial statements. The syllabus of the University of Mumbai prescribes an exclusive paper – '***Analysis of Financial Statements***' for the two year full-time MMS degree course. This paper is the focus of the book. Yet, the topics explored will be of interest to: various postgraduate courses in business management – MMS, MBA, MFM, MMM, MHRM, MIM, undergraduate courses in management – BMA, BBA, undergraduate/postgraduate courses in commerce, B.Com., M.Com., and also for courses of professional institutes like Institute of Chartered Accountants of India, Institute of Cost Accountants of India, Chartered Institute of Management Accountants (UK) and other similar professional bodies across the globe. Further, this book will also be useful to participants in various executive and management development programs in the area of Finance where '***Analysis of Financial Statements***' is one of the key inputs for study to raise the financial literacy and educational levels and any other individual or groups of stakeholders who are interested in learning the nuances of money management. I hope the book will serve the intended purpose of meeting the requirements of the target audience and their penchant for learning will be duly satisfied. Suggestions for improvement of the contents of this book, from any source, are most welcome.

Dr. Guruprasad Murthy

PROLOGUE

"***Money is the most important thing in the world. It represents health, strength, honour, generosity and beauty as conspicuously and undeniably as the want of it represents illness, weakness, disgrace, meanness and ugliness.***"

– George Bernard Shaw (1856-1950)

The major quantified information in any organisation, all over the world, is financial information. To the extent that quantified information plays an important role in providing the guiding inputs for informed and calculated financial or managerial decisions involving a financial angle, finance is a science. It (finance) has strong links with and even roots in, other scientific fields such as statistics and mathematics[1]. In fact the lingo of modern financial theories is similar, if not synonymous, with scientific nomenclature.

Every branch of knowledge has its fundamental discovery. In mechanics it is the wheel, in science fire, in politics the vote. Similarly, in economics, in the whole commercial side of man's social existence, money is the essential invention on which all the rest is based.

– Sir Geoffrey Crowther (1907-1972)

The emergence of financial models such as the capital asset pricing model and the efficient market hypothesis, alongwith many other financial models, have glorified the role of science as an input in the management of finance at the macro and micro levels. Today there are special courses titled quantitative methods in financial management. These scientific theories, usually based on quantitative techniques, caged in quantitative models, attempt to explain the behaviour of market forces in an objective and rational manner trying to keep emotions aside and also attempting to ignore subjective elements like market sentiments and emotions of players, including '***irrational exuberance***', in the stock and other markets.

EXHIBIT 1(F)

IRRATIONAL EXUBERANCE

*Irrational Exuberance describes a heightened state of speculative fervor. It is less intense than the term '**speculative mania**' or '**speculative orgy**'. Irrational exuberance thus means an abundance or lavish availability of energy and enthusiasm for irrational behaviour. Eg: Herd mentality during scams (Harshad Mehta scame 1992 and Ketan Parekh scam 2001), great crashes including the sub-prime crisis in the US leading to the Sep, 2008 global crisis which Allan Greenspan described as '**once-in-a-century crisis**'.*

Several instances of irrational exuberance can be cited - thanks to the greed, perversion and ingenuity of mankind and of course the erratic and volatile behaviour of markets:

LOUIS VUITTON

Pricing dynamics operates in different directions. Products which are positioned as luxury items and remain unsold are actually burnt. As Albert Bensoussan of Louis Vuitton, says "***Our prices remain constant as we want our customers to feel they've paid the right price for the product. To put the same product on sale would be shortchanging them.***"[2]

---

[1]*Mathematics is the queen of sciences. Incidentally, Physics is regarded as the king of sciences.*

[2]***Source:*** Gupta, Aparna. "We burn our sold products !" *Times News Network.*

ONIONS IN MAHARASHTRA

The volatility in onion prices shows the role of demand-supply factors in affecting the price level. On 18th November, 2011, the average onion prices in Lasalgaon (village in Nashik, Maharashtra) was ₹ 900 per quintal and the average onion price was ₹ 2 per kilogram in markets of Nashik. In fact, in October, 2011, the onion prices crashed below production cost and farmers were not able to recover their cost of production. Suddenly, in January, 2011, the quantities which arrived in Lasalgaon, regarded as Asia's largest market, fell from 50,000 quintals to 2,000 quintals. The prices soared from ₹ 1700 per quintal in the first week to ₹ 6,229 per quintal by third week of December, 2011. It is not untrue to say that from time to time when supply exceeds demand a reverse trend is seen and farmers have to restrict the acreage under cultivation or literally destroy production to sustain farm prices.

FARM PRODUCTS IN EUROPE AND OTHER COUNTRIES

Similarly, excess productions of farm products in Europe are purchased by the European Union to ensure that farm prices do not crash further to the detriment of the farmer. The quantities involved are rather huge – 30,000 tonnes of unsold butter, 100 thousand tonnes of skimmed milk powder and other related farm products. In fact in 1986, the European Union had bought 1.23 million tonnes of unwanted butter. On several occasions these perishable products are eventually dumped into the sea or just destroyed to support farm prices. The same is true of excess production (availability) of any item, *viz.*, sugar in Cuba, coffee in Brazil, other farm products in different countries of the World from time to time. Thus, excess of anything is an unmitigated nuisance. Overproduction lower global demand and falling prices have caused glut in certain '***farm oasis***.' As mentioned in a World socialist website, there is no solution to the farm crisis, however., within the framework of the capitalist market.

"A fundamental contradiction under the profit system is the accumulation of vast surpluses of agriculture commodities which cannot be sold at a profit, side by side with, on a world scale, enormous unmet social needs for food, clothing and raw materials. Children starve in Africa and India while American farmers go bankrupt for lack of buyers. This contradiction can only be resolved when agriculture is integrated into a reorganized world economic system in which rational planning, not private profit, is the driving force."[3]

MONEY IN SWITZERLAND

What happens to products in physical form as mentioned above, happens to money in Switzerland and in few other countries. Interest rates represent the price of money (loanable funds). Money from all parts of the World flows into Switzerland. The bankers are not in a position to absorb the inflow and deploy them into productive use. Hence, the Swiss Government from time to time identifies negative interest rate policy as an effective strategy to tide over the crises. According to *Bloomberg* site, dated 1st December, 2011, the Swiss Government was thinking of capital control and negative interest rates as possible tools for deployment. In recent times, the sovereign debt crises in Europe and the US debt burden have prompted investors to move to safe assets such as the Swiss- Franc, the Japanese Yen and gold. This is not the first time negative interest rates are surfacing as part of an instrument of monetary policy. In the 70s, the Swiss bank imposed negative interest rates on foreign accounts to deter inflows and in 2008, short-term Swiss market rates turned negative for a brief time. The same scenario prevailed in Japan in the late 90s. According to the *Wall*

---

[3]***Source:*** *World Socialist Website, 1998-2012.*

Street Journal, February, 2, 2012 investors are looking for havens where they can park their assets safely and are willing to pay a price for the same. Negative yields on short-term government debt have happened regularly because investors do not see alternate safe assets. In January, 2012, Germany sold Euro 3.9 bn of 5 months bill with a negative yield of .0122%.

KGN INDUSTRIES

On Tuesday, 20th May, 2008, a circular announced the re-listing of KGN industries and the exchange circular had initiated a *caveat* '***cautioning trading members not to enter orders at unrealistic prices***'. KGN industries are engaged in the business of trading in agro commodities like castor seeds, edible oils like soyabean oil, palm oil, non edible oils like petroleum products, lubricants, used oil.

On Wednesday, 21st May, 2008, morning, when the markets opened the KGN scrip sky rocketed from ₹ 72 to ₹ 55,000 (a 76,288% increase) breaking the previous record of MMTC which was the most expensive scrip on the bourses at ₹ 27,050. To plug further aberrations the authorities suspended the trading in the scrip at 12.20 pm as a "***pro-active surveillance measure***". KGN industries were known as Royal Finance, till it was delisted in February, 2001, when the last traded price was ₹ 11. However, on Wednesday, 21st May, 2008 morning, Memon, a businessman who is the main promoter of KGN industries was worth around ₹ 12 crores. When the stock prices rose to ₹ 66,000, he was worth ₹ 5,600 crores (a 466% increase in wealth).

HARSHAD MEHTA

Harshad Mehta who came to be known as a big bull was the prime mover of the ACC share which rose from ₹ 200 to ₹ 9,000 (approx.) on the Bombay Stock Exchange - a 4,400% rise in price (early 1992). The ACC share was expected to reach ₹ 10,000. Mr. Mehta used the replacement cost theory, as a ploy, to explain the reason for the high level bidding. His contention was that older companies should be valued on the basis of the opportunity cost principle that is to say the amount of money that would be needed to establish a similar company. Of course, Mehta's illicit methods of manipulating the stock market were exposed on 23rd April, 1992 by Ms Sucheta Dalal.

DEVAS MULTIMEDIA SHARE

Devas Multimedia Share of ₹ 10 rose to ₹ 1 Lakh in 2008: It is said that a controversial lucrative contract with ISRO led to such a staggering valuation. The said contract came under the scanner for review and was cancelled. However, because of the controversial contract Devas was able to get ₹ 1.14 lakh premium on its share worth ₹ 10 when it divested stake to Deutsche Telekom in 2008.

OTHER ACADEMIC ADVANCEMENTS IN FINANCE

There are other academic advancements in the field of finance which have greatly improved decision making processes by bringing objectivity and neutrality to decision making. However, there is at least one flaw in the diamond. Track records of investors have shown that the efficient market hypothesis does not always work and once men, supposedly rational animals, become bulls or bears, irrationality holds the fort and subjectivity, alongwith herd mentality, rules the waves. For example: the stock market crashes such as the great 1929, (black Thursday) crash, that triggered the great depression (1930), the October, 1987 crash (black Monday) which saw the Dow Jones industrial average fall by more than 22% and the Harshad Mehta Scam (1992) when P/E ratios catapulted to astronomical levels, all defy reason. Even today, P/E ratios of shares of Indian Cos. are higher than their counterparts in other continents. According to a *Business Standard* study, the average Price-to-Earnings (P/E) ratio of the 30-scrip Bombay Stock Exchange benchmark is currently just above the historical average of 15. However, this is on the higher side as compared to key world indices. Currently, (March, 2012) the Sensex P/E is 14.81 against the current 15.62., "***The European and US markets are comparatively cheap, trading at a P/E of 12-13 times earnings for calendar year 2011 and eight to 13 times for CY 11.***"[4]

Again, the recent September, 2008 crash of stock markets due to the failure of big financial institutions in the US and other parts of the World led to the closure of the stock markets World over. All these aforesaid episodes, events and experiences remind mankind again and again of irrational exuberance. In the words of John Maynard Keynes, who had said many years ago, "***the heart knows reasons that reason cannot know***"[5].

EXHIBIT 1(G)

GLOBAL MELTDOWN – 15TH SEPTEMBER, 2008

- *15th September was one of the worst days in the financial history of the world when the U.S. stock markets plunge was the worst since 2001.*
- *Dow Jones closed below 11,000 for the first time.*
- *Markets in Europe, Asia and Russia collapsed or were on the brink of a total breakdown.*
- *The Mumbai Sensex was down from a high of 20,301 on 1st January, 2008 to 13,531 on 15th September 2008. The lowest was 7697 on 27th October, 2008.*

The Financial Tsunami struck the world rather badly and the major investment banks, viz., Lehman Brothers, Merrill Lynch, Bear Sterns and Fannie Mae and Freddie Mac vanished. Lehman Brothers, a 158-year-old bank filed for federal bankruptcy protection lost 94% of its market value by 15th September 2008, after record losses from investments tide to mortgages. Bank of America snapped Merrill Lynch for 50 billion USD in an all stock transaction.

IMMEDIATE IMPACT:

- *Global stock market capitalization had declined by 41% during 2008, from USD 55.2 trillion to USD 32.6 trillion.*
- *The International Labour Organization (ILO) has predicted loss of 50 million jobs on worldwide basis.*

"The social object of skilled investment should be to defeat the dark forces of time and ignorance which envelope our future" *– John Maynard Keynes (1883-1946).*

FINANCE AS AN ART

To the extent that sentiments, emotions, intangibles and imponderables are brought into the decision making process, finance can be viewed as an art. When the proportion of domination of irrationality changes and irrational exuberance prevails, no formulae, however sound, can really help. Hence, the emergence of a new discipline called behavioural finance.

---

[4]"Sensex remains expensive against world market." *Business Standard* 9th March, 2012.

[5]Dillard, Dudley. *The Economics of John Maynard Keynes: The Theory of a Monetary Economy*. Kessinger Publishing, 1st March, 2005: p. 152.

John Maynard Keynes had further said in his general theory of employment, "Speculators may do no harm as bubbles on a steady stream of enterprise. But the position is serious when enterprise becomes the bubble on a whirlpool of speculation. When the capital development of a country becomes a by-product of the activities of a casino, the job is likely to be ill-done." – *The General Theory of Employment, Interest and Money,* Atlantic Publishers & Dist, 1st Jan., 2006: p. 142.

Exhibit 1(H)

BEHAVIOURAL FINANCE

A field of finance which uses psychology-based theories to explain irrationality in the stock market. It is assumed that the information structure and the characteristics of players in the market systematically influence individual investment decision making as well as market outcomes. Behavioural finance is a missing link between the assumption of the rational economic man in economics (efficient market hypothesis included) and the actual behaviour of man which is based inter alia on irrationality too. The perfect rational investor or consumer is an El Dorado par excellence.

Behavioural finance is an attempt to fill the gap.

WARREN BUFFET

Even within this debate on whether finance is an art or a science there is at least one person in the world who has developed the right balance between skills sets to manage finance both in a scientific manner and also the artistic way. Warren Buffet has been able to consistently outperform stock markets for long periods of time and is identified as one of the richest American whose wealth owes its origin primarily to long-term equity investments. Of course, the fact that only a few investors can beat the market does not offer much credibility to the efficient market hypothesis. Nevertheless, managing the finances on the stock market and being a successful equity investor requires an understanding of the science behind the farrago of numbers and the art behind cherry picking in the stock market - being confident as a rational contrarian rather than part of irrational herd behaviour. Of course, much has been written on Warren Buffet's mode of operation, *viz.*, how does he do it? What is Warren Buffet's investing style? The debate as to whether the field of finance is an art or a science will continue. However, for the purpose of this book we consider it to be an admixture or hybrid or both, the proportionality of art *vis-à-vis* science or *vice versa* being a question of judgement and also constrained and conditioned by style – eventually style is the man. Whether it's a financial analysts or a line manager posit in the role of a decision maker using the outcome of financial analysis or a person wanting to maximise their wealth in the markets (real estate, stock, commodity, metals *et al.*) – wherever one goes or whatever one does, the art and science of financial management or the science and art of financial management should be a part of the knowledge base of any individual. Thus, managing money or finances are not meant for enterprises or entrepreneurs only. Even if money making is an art, one can be an efficient and effective money maker provided they are well aware of the subject matter of analysis and interpretation of financial statements. However, so long as human beings are at the helm of affairs of business, the human element shall continue to be a part and parcel of decision making.

The users of the contents of the book are therefore forewarned not to be carried away by numbers and numbers alone. They are also advised to read the epilogue before entering the jungle of numbers.

Dr. Guruprasad Murthy

1

GLOSSARY

FINANCIAL STATEMENTS:

(a) Statements prepared in prescribed proforma dictated by law and or Generally Accepted Accounting Principle (GAAP).

(b) The principal financial statements include, income and other statements for the period ending, Balance Sheet as on a particular date and cash flow statement for the period ending '......'

(c) The income and other statements are also known as the Profit and Loss account for an accounting period ending '......' and show the results of business operations for any accounting period in terms of profit or loss for that accounting period.

(d) The final result of any business is captured as net profit or net loss.

BALANCE SHEET is a snapshot of the financial view of business as on a particular date and indicates the economic resources owned and owed by a business.

CASH FLOW STATEMENT indicates the sources of cash (from where money has come) and the uses of cash (where the money has gone).

PROFIT: Excess of revenue over expense.

LOSS: Excess of expense over revenue.

CASH SURPLUS: Excess of cash inflows (receipts) over cash outflows disbursements/payouts.

CASH DEFICIT: Excess of cash outflows, disbursements/payouts over cash inflows (receipts).

ASSETS: The economic resources owned by a company.

GROSS FIXED ASSETS: Total of all fixed assets without deducting depreciation.

NET FIXED ASSETS: Gross fixed assets minus accumulated depreciation.

DEPRECIATION PER ANNUM:

$$\frac{\text{Cost of the asset or cost adjusted for residual value}}{\text{Economic life or useful life of the asset}}$$

CURRENT DEPRECIATION: Depreciation charged to income statement of a particular accounting period.

ACCUMULATED DEPRECIATION: Sum of the current depreciation charged year after year up to date of balance sheet.

LIABILITIES: The economic resources owed by a company as on date.

CURRENT ASSETS: Also known as Gross Working Capital. Represents those assets which are to be converted into cash within a short period of time, usually a year. The three main items of current assets include cash, sundry debtors (accounts or trade receivables) and stock in a trading company or inventories in a manufacturing company.

CASH: Includes cash in hand, cash at bank and cash in transit.

SUNDRY DEBTORS (accounts or trade receivables): Parties from whom money has to be recovered, within a short period of time (usually a year), for goods sold or services rendered by the business.

STOCK: In a trading company refers to saleable (unsold) finished goods and unused consumables (if any) i.e., inventory as on the date of the balance sheet.

INVENTORY: In a manufacturing company means unused raw materials, unfinished production (work-in process), unsold finished goods and unused consumables as on the date of the balance sheet.

CURRENT LIABILITIES: Obligations which mature within a short period of time usually, a year. The principal items of current liabilities include, sundry creditors (account payable), short-term loans from individuals or institutions (banks), bank overdraft, provisions for income-tax and dividends, bills payable and non-funded liabilities, *viz.*, retirement benefits to employees.

SUNDRY CREDITORS: Parties to whom money has to be paid, within a short period of time (usually a year), for goods (accounts payable) purchased or services enjoyed by the business.

LONG-TERM LIABILITIES: Obligations to be discharged over a long period of time usually greater than a year. Maturing portion of long-term liabilities due within a year, are shown as part of current liabilities. Debenture bonds, term loans or any other long-term loans specially contracted.

NET WORKING CAPITAL: Current Assets *minus* Current Liabilities.

QUICK ASSETS: Current Assets *minus* Inventory.

CAPITAL EMPLOYED:

Net fixed assets + investments + net working capital

OR

Owners funds + long-term liabilities

NET WORTH: Excess of assets over all outside liabilities, *viz.*, current liabilities and long-term liabilities (loan capital) (**Exhibit 1**).

EXHIBIT 1

NET WORTH

"Is that part of the company which belongs to the shareholders. It is the total assets of the company less its current liabilities, long-term debt and miscellaneous expenses. Net worth is also known as shareholder's equity or shareholders funds or common stockholders funds. Net worth includes equity share capital and all reserves (including revaluation reserve) less expenses not written off. Net worth does not include preference share capital."

— *Equitymaster.com*

"Net worth means the aggregate of the paid-up share capital, share premium account and reserves and surplus (excluding revaluation reserve) as reduced by the aggregate of miscellaneous expenditure (to the extent not adjusted or written off) and the debit balance of the Profit and Loss Account."

— *Malegam Committee, SEBI*

N.B.: Some sources define Net Worth as inclusive of preference shares too. Yet other sources distinguish between Common stockholders' equity and Total equity. The former is net worth as defined above and the latter is inclusive of preference shares.

CURRENT ASSETS: Assets, which are to be converted into cash soon usually within a year or the phase of the accounting cycle. They consist of cash and bank balances, investments in marketable securities, inventories, accounts receivable or sundry debtors, loans and advances.

QUICK ASSETS: Assets, which are to be converted into cash very soon.

OUTSTANDING EXPENSES: Amounts owed to parties who have already provided benefits or services as on date of the balance sheet. Pending the actual payment of the outstanding amount, outstanding expenses are shown as a current liability on the liabilities side of the balance sheet.

PRE-PAID EXPENSES: Amounts paid in advance for the benefits or services to be received at a future point of time beyond the date of the balance sheet. Pending the actual receipt of benefits or services, prepaid expenses are shown as a current asset on the assets side of the balance sheet.

INCOME RECEIVED IN ADVANCE: Amounts received from customers/other parties for services or benefits to be provided at a future point of time beyond the date of the balance sheet. Pending the actual provision of services/benefits, income received in advance is shown as a current liability on the liabilities side of the balance sheet.

ACCRUED INCOME: Amounts to be recovered from parties to whom services or benefits have already been provided as on the date of the balance sheet. Pending the actual receipt of cash, accrued income is shown as a current asset on the assets side of the balance sheet.

ACCOUNTING PERIOD: Segment of time in respect of which the accounts are prepared-usually a year may be less or more depending on the circumstances or business exigencies.

DEPRECIATION: Fall in value of tangible assets (buildings, furniture and fixtures) for any reason whatsoever over a period of time.

DEPLETION: Fall in value of tangible wasting assets (oil wells, mineral mines).

AMORTISATION: Portion of intangible assets goodwill, patents, copyrights and trademarks or one time expenditure charged to income statement or amortised over a period of time.

BAD DEBTS: A customer who will not pay or an amount foregone as not recoverable from customer. An operating expenses which arises as and when customers fail to pay for the goods or services which they have received on credit.

DOUBTFUL DEBTS: An amount a customer may or may not pay. The accounting practice is to provide for the contingency of anticipated non–payment by the customer. Such a provision is known as provision for doubtful debts and is charged as an expense against the profit of a particular accounting period. The said amount is set aside as a provision for doubtful debts and is deducted from the debtors (accounts receivables) in the balance sheet (current asset section).

CURRENT LIABILITIES: Obligations for value received to be discharged within a short period of time usually a year or within the accounting cycle.

BONUS SHARES: The issue of shares, *gratis,* to the shareholders of a company, by capitalizing a part of the company's reserves. Bonus shares cause conversion of free reserves into equity capital.

OWNED CAPITAL: The amount of capital belonging to the owner, i.e., sum of equity share capital *plus* reserves (undistributed profits).

CAPITAL RESERVES: The reserves created on account of extraordinary transactions, *viz.,* sale of fixed assets at a profit, revalution of assets, profits arising out of exchange rate variation, issue of shares at a premium. These amounts are not available for distribution of dividends, except in accordance with the laws for the time being in force.

DIVIDEND: The payment made by a company to its shareholders – may be on equity shares or preference shares. Dividends are profits distributed to shareholders.

ECONOMIC VALUE ADDED (EVA): A tool for evaluating and selecting stocks for investment and also used as a measure of managerial performance. EVA = After tax operating profit – Total cost of capital employed.

EMPLOYEE STOCK OPTION PLAN (ESOP): Under this plan the company grants its employees, usually senior managers, the privilege to buy a certain number of shares at a fixed price irrespective of the actual price of the stock. The option becomes valuable when the market price of the stock rises above the exercise prices.

FACE VALUE: The nominal value of a security. The face value helps to know the denomination of the shares issued by a company.

FORFEITURE OF SHARES: It means the deprivation of shares held by an investor, usually as a consequence of default in paying money, called upon allotment, to the company. The investor ceases to be a shareholder and forfeits the amount paid till the time of forfeiture.

HOLDING COMPANY: The company which controls a majority shareholding of another company or controls the composition of the board of directors or exercises control through a subsidiary.

LIQUIDITY: The speed with which an asset can be converted into cash without suffering a loss as far as possible.

PAR VALUE: The nominal value of a security also termed as face value.

SHARE CAPITAL: The amount raised by a company by issuing equity or preference shares.

AUTHORISED CAPITAL: The limit up to which shares can be issued. This is a ceiling and cannot be exceeded without going through due legal processes.

ISSUED CAPITAL: The amount sought to be raised by the issue of shares and cannot exceed the authorised capital.

SUBSCRIBED CAPITAL: The extent to which investors subscribe.

PAID-UP CAPITAL: The amount actually paid by shareholders and also credited as paid-up amount to the share capital account.

WORKING CAPITAL: The funds deployed by a company in the form of cash, inventories, accounts receivable and other current assets as per business practices and the laws for the time being in force (e.g., Schedule VI of Companies Act as duly amended, *w.e.f.*, 1st April, 2011 – The Ministry of Corporate Affairs, General Circular No. 62/2011 states that ... "***the companies would ensure that it will prepare and file the Annual Accounts for the Financial Year 2011-12 as per revised Schedule VI of the Companies Act, 1956.***"

TOTAL ASSETS: Sum of current assets, net fixed assets and other assets (such as investments in shares, debentures, marketable securities *et al.*).

⊙⊙⊙

2

LEGAL DIMENSIONS OF FINANCIAL ACCOUNTING

EXHIBIT 2

AN INTRODUCTION TO CORPORATE ACCOUNTING STANDARDS AMERICAN ACCOUNTING ASSOCIATION, 1940

"A statement of Accounting Standard should avoid any appearance of encouraging violations of the existing law, but it need not accept as good accounting all definitions, policies and practices which legislators and the courts have added to the accounting structure."

— Paton, W. A., and Littleton, A. C.

Section 211 of the Companies Act provides the mandate for disclosure of financial statements in a prescribed format along with the relevant notes/instructions/requirements as the case may be. Section 211 is titled as '***Form and content of Balance Sheet and Profit and Loss Account***'. The gist of Section 211 of the Companies Act is as follows:

- Every balance sheet of a company shall give a true and fair picture of the state of affairs of the company at the end of the financial year.
- Every balance sheet shall be in the form set out in Part I of Schedule VI or as near thereto.
- In preparing the balance sheet, due regard shall be had, as far as may be, to the general instructions for preparation of balance sheet, under the heading 'Notes' at the end of that part.
- Every balance sheet shall comply with the accounting standards (Section 211-3A).
- Deviation from accounting standards, reasons for deviation and the financial effect of such deviation shall be disclosed.
- Section 211 is guided by Schedule VI, which contains the prescribed mandatory formats for the balance sheet and other requirements and directives regarding the preparation and presentation of financial statements.

EXHIBIT 3

SECTION 211 OF THE COMPANIES ACT, 1956

*Form and contents of balance sheet and profit and loss account – Every balance sheet of a company shall give a true and fair view of the state of affairs of the company as at the end of the financial year and shall be subject to the provisions of this section, be in the form set out in Part I of Schedule VI, or as near thereto as circumstances admit or in such other form as may be approved by the Central Government either generally or in any particular case and in preparing the balance sheet due regard shall be had, as far as may be, to the general instructions for preparation of balance sheet under the heading '**Notes**' at the end of that part:*

Every Profit and Loss account of a company shall give a true and fair view of the profit or loss of the company for the financial year and shall subject as aforesaid, comply with the requirements of Part II Schedule VI, so far as they are applicable thereto.

EXHIBIT 4

AN OVERVIEW OF THE REQUIREMENTS OF THE COMPANIES ACT (1956)

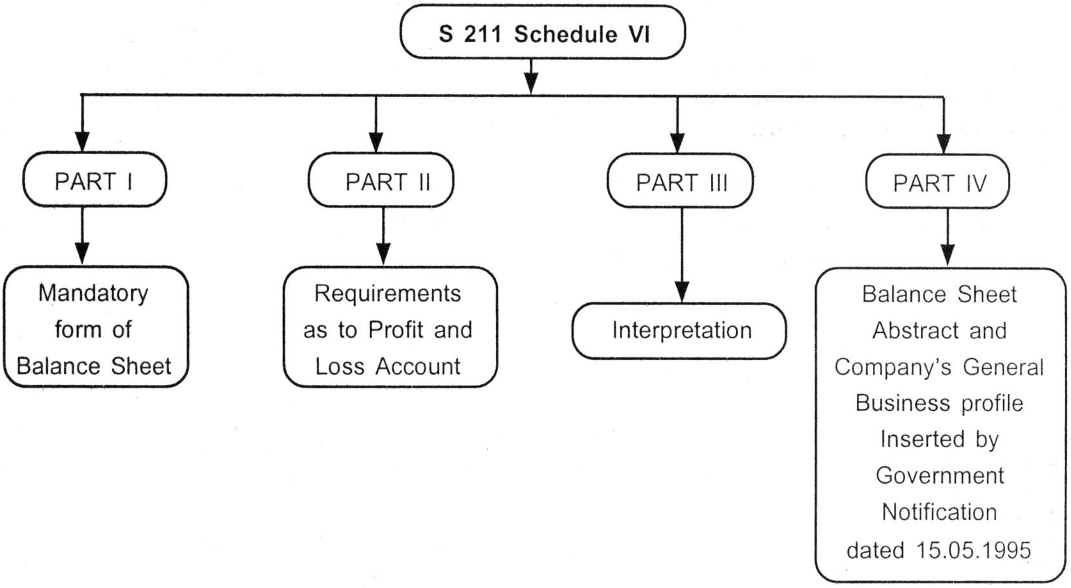

In addition to the requirements of Section 211 Schedule VI (Parts I to IV), as shown in Exhibit 4 there are a few other disclosures:

SECTION 219 (1) COMPANIES ACT, 1956*:** A company is required to lay before, in general meeting, a copy of every balance sheet (including the profit and loss account, the auditors' report and every other document required by law to be annexed or attached, as the case may be, to the balance sheet) ...... The said financial statements have to be prepared in a prescribed proforma presented in Form no. 23 AB and is titled as Statement containing salient features of Balance Sheet and Profit and Loss Account, etc., as per Section 219 (1) (b) (iv). The data to be presented is in an abridged form and is known as 'Form of Abridged Balance Sheet followed by Abridged Profit and Loss Account.***' Further, the said two forms are to be accompanied by notes to the abridged balance sheet and abridged profit and loss account. Again, there is an annexure titled as "***Salient features of Additional Information on the Profit and Loss Account for the year ended .....***" which has to be disclosed. This section has been inserted by (Third Amendment) Rules, 1992 *vide* GSR 484 (E), dated 11-5-1992.

CASH FLOW STATEMENT: According to SEBI requirements, as part of the listing agreement, listed companies shall present a cash flow statement in accordance with the accounting standard on Cash Flow Statement (AS-3) issued by the Institute of Chartered Accountants of India and the Cash Flow Statement shall be presented only under the Indirect Method as given in AS-3. The disclosure of the Cash Flow Statement by listed companies came into effect with effect from 26th June, 1995 which was further amended by SEBI on 25th January, 2000.

PREPARATION AND SUBMISSION OF FINANCIAL RESULT IN ACCORDANCE WITH CLAUSE 41 OF SEBI LISTING REQUIREMENTS: Listing companies are required to prepare and submit the financial results on the basis of accrual accounting policy and in accordance with uniform accounting practices adopted for all the periods. Such financial information has to be submitted for the prescribed periods of time, *viz.*, quarterly, half-yearly and annual. In order to encourage transparency, the said financial results shall be published in at least one English daily newspaper circulating in the whole or substantially the whole of India and in one daily newspaper published in the languages of the region, where the registered office of the company is situated. The financial information referred to in Clause 41 shall be presented in a prescribed proforma. However, according to Clause 41 "***Disclosure of Balance Sheet items as per items (ea) shall be in the format specified in Annexure IX drawn from Schedule VI of the Companies Act, or its equivalent formats in other statutes, as applicable.***"

PART I – MANDATORY FORM OF BALANCE SHEET

Companies Act (1956) [as amended by Cos. Amendment Act (2001)

Section 211: Schedule VI Part I – Form of Balance Sheet

HORIZONTAL FORMAT

BALANCE SHEET OF (name of the company)

AS AT (date at which the balance sheet is made out)

Table – 1

	ASSETS	**₹	*₹		*LIABILITIES*	**₹	*₹
1	Fixed Assets			6	Share Capital		
2	Investments			7	Reserves and Surplus		
3	Current Assets, Loans and Advances			8	Secured Loans		
4	Miscellaneous (not written off) Expenditure			9	Unsecured Loans		
5	Profit and Loss (if loss) Account			10	Current liabilities and Provisions		
	TOTAL				**TOTAL**		

*Figures for the previous year in rupees; **Figures for the current year in rupees.

PART – I – MANDATORY FORM OF BALANCE SHEET
VERTICAL FORMAT

In the alternative, a Company may use a vertical format to set out the balance sheet BALANCE SHEET OF (name of the company) AS AT (date at which the balance sheet is made out)

Table – 2

	Particulars *(*current Financial year)* *(**previous Financial year)*	*Sch. No.*	*Figures as at the end (*CFY)* (₹)	*Figures as at the end (**PFY)* (₹)
I.	**SOURCES OF FUNDS**			
	Shareholders' funds:? ◆ Capital? ◆ Reserves and surplus			
	Loan funds: ◆ Secured loans? ◆ Unsecured loans			
	TOTAL			
II.	**APPLICATION OF FUNDS**			
	Fixed assets: ◆ Gross block ◆ *Less:* depreciation ◆ Net block ◆ Capital work-in-progress			
	Investments			
	Current assets, Loans and advances ◆ Inventories ◆ Sundry debtors ◆ Cash and bank balances ◆ Other current assets ◆ Loans and advances			
	***LESS:* Current liabilities and provisions** ◆ Liabilities ◆ Provisions			
	Net current assets ◆ Miscellaneous expenditure (to the extent not written off or adjusted) ◆ Profit and Loss account less carried forward (Debit balance) (Less carried forward)			
	TOTAL			

***N.B.**: Total (₹) of I = Total (₹) of II*

FIXED ASSETS

Fixed assets must be distinguished as far as possible between the items presented in the format. The items forming part of fixed assets are to be presented in terms of:

- Original cost of the asset.
- Additions thereto during the year.
- Deductions therefrom during the year.
- Total depreciation written off or provided up to the end of the year.

Fixed assets acquired out of foreign currency, may encounter exchange rate variations after such purchase. There is thus an increase or reduction in the liability of the Company in terms of rupees, for making payment towards the money borrowed in foreign currency. The amount by which the liability has increased or decreased is adjusted against the cost of the asset to arrive at the relevant revised cost of the asset. Where the original cost of the asset cannot be ascertained without unreasonable expense or delay, the valuation shown by the books must be given. Such valuation shall be the amount at which the asset stood in the books of the Company at the commencement of the Companies Act, 1956, after deduction for depreciation with adjustment for sale proceeds of assets sold.

N.B.: Depreciation charged to profit and loss account should be allocated under the different heads of assets as shown above. Such depreciation as is charged to the profit and loss account is deducted to arrive at the value of the fixed assets which is known as net block or written down value or book value or net fixed assets.

Where any sum has been written off on a reduction of capital or upon revaluation of assets, every balance sheet shall subsequent to such reduction or revaluation show the reduced figures and the date of the reduction. For a period of five years, the amount of reduction made shall be shown.

Similarly, where sums have been added by writing up the asset, each subsequent balance sheet, should show the increased figures with the date of the increase. Each balance sheet shall show the increased amount for a period of five years subsequent to the date of writing up.

CAPITAL WORK-IN-PROGRESS (CWIP)

Funds already invested in fixed assets under construction. No depreciation is charged on CWIP.

INVESTMENTS

The Company shall show the aggregate amount of quoted investment and also the market value. The aggregate amount of the company's unquoted investment shall also be shown. Further, the company shall disclose the nature of investments and mode of valuation (for example cost or market value) distinguishing between:

- Investments in government or trust securities.
- Investments in shares, debentures or bonds (showing separately shares, fully paid up and partly paid up and also distinguishing the different classes of shares, debentures or bonds of subsidiary companies).
- Immovable properties.
- Investments in the capital of partnership firms.
- In case there are unutilized monies out of any issue, the same shall be separately disclosed along with the manner of utilization of the excess monies.

CURRENT ASSETS LOANS AND ADVANCES

Mode of valuation of works in progress shall be stated. In regard to sundry debtors, particulars to be given separately of:

- Debts considered good and in respect of which the Company is fully secured.
- Debts considered good for which the Company holds no security other than the debtor's personal security.
- Debts considered doubtful or bad.
- Debts due by directors or other officers of the Company.
- Debts due from other Companies under the same management.
- The maximum amount due by directors or other officers of the Company at any time during the year to be shown by way of note.
- The provision to be shown under this head should not exceed the amount of debts stated to be considered doubtful or bad and any surplus of such provision if already created should be shown at every closing under '***Reserves and Surplus***' (on the liability side) under a separate subhead '***Reserve for Doubtful or Bad Debts***'.

CASH AND BANK BALANCES

In regard to cash and bank balances, the following should be disclosed separately:

- The balances lying with Scheduled Banks on current accounts, call accounts and deposit accounts.
- The nature of the interest, if any, of any director or his relative or the managing agent in each of the bankers (other than scheduled banks).
- All unutilized monies out of the issue must be separately disclosed in the balance sheet.

MISCELLANEOUS EXPENDITURE

It is a fictitious asset and is shown to the extent not written off or adjusted.

PROFIT AND LOSS ACCOUNT (DEBIT BALANCE)

The accumulated losses of profit and loss account carried forward after deductions of the uncommitted reserves, if any, shall be shown here.

SHARE CAPITAL

Share capital shall distinguish between various classes of capital, *viz.*, preference and equity share capital. The following expressions need to be understood:

- ***AUTHORIZED SHARE CAPITAL:*** The maximum amount of capital that can be raised by a Company. The authorized capital which represents the ceiling on the amount of capital, which can be raised, can be altered after going through the prescribed secretarial procedure stipulated in Section 94 of the Companies Act, 1956.
- ***ISSUED SHARE CAPITAL:*** Is the portion of authorized share capital which is offered to for subscription.
- ***SUBSCRIBED SHARE CAPITAL:*** Is the response received from investors who wish to be shareholders in the Company.
- ***CALLED UP SHARE CAPITAL:*** Is the portion of issued capital which is expected to be paid for, by the investors aspiring to be shareholders.
- ***PAID-UP SHARE CAPITAL:*** The actual consideration received in cash or otherwise from the investors and credited to share capital account.

The difference between the called up capital and paid-up capital is known as Calls-in-Arrears – monies due from shareholders not yet received by the Company. The relevant item for the balance sheet total is the '***paid up capital***', which is matched by either cash at bank or other assets on the asset side of the balance sheet.

CONTINGENT LIABILITIES

- Claims against the company not acknowledged as debts.
- Uncalled liability on shares partly paid (on those held as investment).
- Arrears of fixed cumulative dividends on preference shares.
- Estimated amount of contracts remaining to be executed on capital account and not provided.
- Other money for which the company is contingently liable.

RESERVES AND SURPLUS

Reserves and Surplus refers to the combined total of reserves on capital account (capital reserves) and revenue account (revenue reserves).

The items listed for including under this head is shown in Part I of Schedule VI under Section 211 of the Company's Act 1956.

The instructions in accordance with which the reserves and surplus should be made out include:

- Additions and deductions in the reserves since last balance sheet must be shown under the specified heads.
- The word fund should be used only when such reserves are specifically represented by earmarked investments.

The expression Share Premium account requires special mention. Share Premium is the excess amount over and above the face (par) value of shares paid-in by the shareholders at the time of subscribing to the share capital of a Company. Share Premium is also referred to as paid-in surplus. The ways and means of dealing with share premium is spelt out in Section 78 of the Companies Act, 1956 as shown in **Exhibit 5**.

EXHIBIT 5

S 78 OF THE COMPANIES ACT, 1956

SHARE PREMIUM ACCOUNT

As per the said section, the premium account may be applied by the Company – in paying up unissued shares of the Company to be issued to members of the Company as fully paid bonus shares;

— *in writing off the preliminary expenses of the Company.*

— *in writing off the expenses of, or the commission paid or discount allowed on, any issue of shares or debentures of the Company.*

— *in providing for the premium payable on the redemption of any redeemable preference shares or of any debentures of the Company.*

N.B.: *Share Premium account is now referred to as Securities Premium Account following the Companies (Amendment) Act 1999, w.e.f., 31.10.1998.*

(1) In case of '***Other Reserves***', the nature and the amount of each reserve must be specified; e.g., General reserves, Dividend Equalization Reserves, etc.
(2) The balance in the profit and loss appropriation account, should be the balance after providing for all proposed allocations namely for dividends, bonus or reserves.
(3) The debit balance in the profit and loss account should be shown as a deduction from the uncommitted reserves, if any.

PROVISIONS vs. RESERVES

Reserves are the accumulated and undistributed profits of a business. Provisions are the amounts set aside out of profits as estimates of future costs.

RESERVES vs. SURPLUS

Reserves are resources garnered from the accumulated and undistributed profits of a business and earmarked to meet specific intentions of management with respect to plough back.

Surplus represents the unfettered resources parked as Profit and Loss account (credit balance) readily available for distribution.

SECURED LOANS

- Loans from directors and managers must be shown separately under each head.
- Interest accrued and due on secured loans should be included under the appropriate sub-heads under the head '***Secured Loans***'.
- Nature of security must be mentioned in each case.
- Where loans have been guaranteed by managers and/or directors, a mention thereof shall also be made and also the aggregate amount of such loans under each head.
- In case of debentures, the terms of redemption or conversion, if any, of debentures issued must be stated together with earliest date of redemption or conversion.
- Particulars of redeemed debentures which the Company has power to reissue should be given.
- Where any of the Company's debentures are held by a nominee or a trustee for the Company, the nominal amount of the debentures and the amount at which they are stated in the Company's books shall be stated.

UNSECURED LOANS

- Loans from Directors or Managers should be separately shown.
- Interest accrued and due on unsecured loans must be included under the appropriate subheads under the head '***Unsecured Loan***'.
- Where loans have been guaranteed by the managers and/or directors a mention thereof should be made and also the aggregate amount of such loans under each head.
- Short-term loans are defined to include those loans which are due for not more than 1 year as on the date of the balance sheet.
- Maximum amount raised through '***Commercial Paper***' and outstanding balance at year-end to be disclosed as per RBI stipulations. This item is a current liability.

CURRENT LIABILITIES AND PROVISIONS

- Advance receipts/unexpired discounts: These current liabilities represent that portion for which value has still to be given, e.g., in case of following companies, *viz.*, Newspaper, Fire insurance, Theatres, Clubs, Banking Companies, Steamship companies, etc.

- Current account balances with directors, and managers shall be shown separately.
- The name(s) of the small-scale undertaking(s) to which the Company owes a sum exceeding ₹ 11 lakh and which is outstanding for more than 30 days are to be disclosed.

OTHER GENERAL INSTRUCTIONS

- If the required information cannot be given conveniently in the given form in the balance sheet itself, it may be furnished in separate schedules annexed and forming part of the balance sheet.
- Except in the case of the first balance sheet, the corresponding amounts for the immediately preceding financial year for all items shall also be shown.
- Paise can also be given in addition to rupees, if desired.
- Dividends declared by subsidiary companies after the date of the balance sheet should not be included unless they are in respect of the period, which closed on or before the date of the balance sheet.
- Any reference to benefits expected from contracts to be executed shall not be made in the balance sheet but shall be made in the Board's Report.

3

Pro Forma Financial Statement and Instructions (Schedule VI)

PART I – MANDATORY FORM OF BALANCE SHEET

A. HORIZONTAL FORMAT

Balance Sheet of .... (Name of the company) ....

As at ....(date as at which it is made out)

Table – 3

Figures for the Previous Year (₹)	*LIABILITIES*	*Figures for the Current Year (₹)*	*Figures for the Previous Year (₹)*	*ASSETS*	*Figures for the Current Year (₹)*
	SHARE CAPITAL ◆ Authorised ...Shares of ₹...each. ◆ Issued ...Shares of ₹...each. ◆ Subscribed..Shares of ₹...each. ◆ Paid-up ₹.... per share called up. *LESS:* Unpaid calls and designs *ADD:* Forfeited shares (if they are re-issued).			**FIXED ASSETS** ◆ Goodwill ◆ Land ◆ Buildings ◆ Leaseholds ◆ Railway Sidings ◆ Plant and Machinery ◆ Furniture and Fittings ◆ Development of Property Patents, Trademarks and Designs	

RESERVES AND SURPLUSES

- Capital Reserves.
- Capital Redemption Reserve.
- Share Premium Account.
- Other Reserves.

LESS: Debit balance in profit and loss account, if any:

- Balance in the profit and loss.
- Appropriation account.
- Proposed addition to Reserves.
- Sinking Funds.

SECURED LOANS

- Debentures.
- Loans and Advances from Banks.
- Loans and Advances from Subsidiaries.
- Other Loans and Advances.

UNSECURED LOANS

- Fixed Deposits.
- Loans and Advances from Subsidiaries.
- Short-term Loans and Advances.

(a) From Banks

(b) From Others

Other Loans and Advances:

(a) From Banks.

(b) From Others.

- Livestock
- Vehicles etc.

INVESTMENTS

- Investments in Govt. or Trust Securities.
- Investments in shares, debentures or bonds.
- Immovable properties.
- Investments in the capital of partnership firms.
- Balance of unutilized monies.
- Raised by Issue.

CURRENT ASSETS, LOANS AND ADVANCES

A. Current Assets

- Interest accrued on Investments
- Stores and spare parts.
- Loose tools.
- Stock-in-trade Works-in-progress.
- Sundry debtors.
- Debts outstanding for a period exceeding 6 months.

	CURRENT LIABILITIES AND PROVISIONS **A. Current Liabilities** (1) Acceptances. (2) Sundry Creditors. ◆ Total outstanding dues of small-scale industrial undertaking(s). ◆ Total outstanding dues of creditor. ◆ Other than small-scale industrial undertaking(s). (3) Subsidiary Companies. (4) Advance payments and unexpired discounts. (5) Unclaimed Dividends. (6) Other Liabilities (if any). (7) Interest accrued but not due on loans. **B. Provisions** (8) Provision for Taxation. (9) Proposed Dividends. (10) For Contingencies For Insurance, pension and similar staff benefit scheme. (11) Other Provisions.			Other debts. *LESS*: Provision Cash Balance. ◆ On hand. ◆ Bank balances: (i) With Scheduled Banks. (ii) With others **B. Loans and Advances** ◆ Advances and Loans *(a)* To subsidiaries *(b)* To partnership firms in which the co. or its subsidiary is a partner. ◆ Bills of Exchange (Bills Receivables). ◆ Advances recoverable in cash or in kind or for value to be received; e.g., Rates, Taxes, Insurance, etc. ◆ Balances with Customs, Port, Trust, etc. (where payable on demand).	

				MISCELLANEOUS EXPENDITURE (to the extent not written off or adjusted)? ◆ Preliminary Expenses. ◆ Expenses including commission/ brokerage on underwriting of subscription for shares or debentures. ◆ Discount allowed on issue of shares or debentures ◆ Interest paid out of capital during construction. ◆ Development expenditure not adjusted. ◆ Other Items (Specifying nature). **PROFIT AND LOSS ACCOUNT** (Debit Balance)	
	TOTAL			**TOTAL**	

PART – I : MANDATORY FORM OF BALANCE SHEET VERTICAL FORMAT

Table – 4

Name of Company Balance Sheet as on	*Schedule No*	*Figures as at the end of the Current Financial Year (₹)*	*Figures as at the end of the Previous Financial Year (₹)*
I. Sources of funds. II. Application of Funds.			

NOTES:

Details under each of the above items shall be given in separate Schedules. The Schedules shall incorporate all the information required to be given under a Horizontal Form read with notes containing general instructions for preparation of balances sheet. The Schedules, referred to above, accounting policies and explanatory notes that may be attached shall form an integral part of the balance sheet.

- The figures in the balance sheet may be rounded off to the nearest '***000***' or '***00***' as may be convenient in terms of decimals of thousands.
- A footnote to the balance sheet may be added to show separately contingent liabilities.

PART – II : REQUIREMENTS AS TO PROFIT AND LOSS ACCOUNT

Items to be disclosed separately in profit and loss account as required by Part II of Schedule VI.

The Profit and Loss Account shall disclose every material feature, including credits or receipts and debits or expenses in respect of non-recurring or exceptional transactions.

(1) **A. ITEMS OF INCOME**

(a) **Turnover**: Aggregate amount of sales, amount and quantity of sales of each class of goods separately. (In case of service companies gross income derived from services).

(b) Income from investments distinguishing between Trade investments and Other investments. Other income by way of interest specifying nature of income. TDS should be shown separately if deducted.

(c) Profits or Losses on investments (showing distinctly the profits or losses from a partnership firm). Profits or Losses in respect of transaction of a kind, not usually undertaken by the company, if material. Amount, if material by which any items shown in Profit and Loss Account are affected by any change in basis of accounting.

(d) Miscellaneous Income.

(e) Dividend from subsidiary companies.

B. EXPENSES

(a) Commission paid to sole selling agents and other selling agents. Brokerage and Discount on sales other than trade discount.

(b) In case of manufacturing companies, item wise break-up of value and quantity of all important basic raw materials consumed. (Items valuing 10% or more of the total value of the raw materials consumed shall be shown as a separate item) Value and quantity of opening and closing stocks of each class of goods produced. Work-in-progress at the commencement and at the end of the accounting period. In case of

trading companies, value and quantity of purchases, opening and closing stocks of each class of goods.

(c) Consumption of stores and spare parts, power, fuel, rent, repairs to building and machinery, salaries, wages and bonus, contribution to other funds, workmen and staff welfare expenses, insurance and miscellaneous expenses.

(d) Depreciation, renewals or diminution in the value of fixed assets.

(e) Interest on debentures and other fixed loans, showing separately amount paid/ payable to the Managing Director, Manager.

(f) Donations to political parties, giving name of party/person.

(g) Income Tax.

(h) Dividends paid and proposed stating that it is subject to deduction of tax.

(i) Provision for losses of Subsidiary Companies.

(j) Amounts reserved for repayment of share capital/loans.

(k) Amount set aside to reserves and any amounts withdrawn from such reserves.

(2) Payment to Directors including Managing Directors, Manager, if any by the company, subsidiary of the company and any other person.

(3) Computation of net profit u/s 349 with details of the commission payable as percentage of profits to the directors including Managing Directors, Managers (if any).

(4) Payments to the Auditors (whether as fees, expenses or otherwise for services rendered).

(5) In case of manufacturing companies, in respect of each class of goods manufactured, detailed quantitative information in regards to the licensed capacity, installed capacity and actual production.

(6) Following information to be included by way of note:

(a) Value of imports on C.I.F. basis in respect of raw materials, components and spare parts and capital goods.

(b) Expenditures in foreign currency for royalty, know-how, professional and consultation fees, interest and other matters.

(c) Value of imported raw materials, spare parts and components consumed, value of indigenous raw materials, spare parts and components consumed and percentage of each to total consumption.

(d) Dividend remitted in foreign currencies, number of non- resident shareholders, number of shares held by them on which dividends are due and the year to which dividends relate.

(e) Earnings in foreign exchange namely exports, royalty, know-how, professional and consultation fees, interest and dividend, other income.

(7) Except in the case of the first Profit and Loss Account, the corresponding amounts for the immediately preceding financial year for all items shall also be shown.

PART III – INTERPRETATION

(8) *(a)* For the purpose of Parts I and II of this Schedule, unless the context otherwise requires:

(i) The expression "***provision***" shall subject to subclause (b) of this clause, mean any amount written off or retained by way of providing for depreciation, renewals or diminution in value of assets, or retained by way of providing for any known liability of which the amount cannot be determined with substantial accuracy.

(ii) The expression "***reserve***" shall not, subject as aforesaid, include any amount written off or retained by way of providing for depreciation, renewals or diminution in value of assets or retained by way of providing for any known liability.

(iii) The expression "***capital reserve***" shall not include any amount regarded as free for distribution through the profit and loss account, and the expression "***revenue reserve***" shall mean any reserve other than a capital reserve and in this sub-clause the expression "***liability***" shall include all liabilities in respect of expenditure contracted for and all disputed or contingent liabilities.

(b) Where:

(i) any amount written off or retained by way of providing for depreciation, renewals or diminution in value of assets, not being an amount written off in relation to fixed assets before the commencement of this act; or

(ii) any amount retained by way of providing for any known liability, is in excess of the amount which in the opinion of the director is reasonably necessary for the purposes of this schedule as be shown as a reserve and not as a provision.

(9) For the purposes aforesaid, the expression "***quoted investment***" means an investment in respects of which there has been granted a quotation or permission to deal on a recognized stock exchange, and the expression "***unquoted investment***" shall be constructed accordingly.

*PART – IV : BALANCE SHEET ABSTRACT AND CO.'S GENERAL BUSINESS PROFILE

(1) COMPANY'S REGISTRATION DETAILS:

- Registration No.
- State Code
- Balance Sheet Date

(2) CAPITAL RAISED DURING THE YEAR:

- Public Issue
- Right Issue
- Bonus Issue
- Private Placement

(3) DETAILS OF MOBILISATION AND DEPLOYMENT OF FUNDS (AMOUNT ₹ IN THOUSANDS):

- Total Liabilities
- Total Assets

SOURCE OF FUNDS:

- Paid up Capital
- Reserves and Surplus
- Secured Loans
- Unsecured Loans

APPLICATION OF FUNDS:

- Net Fixed Assets
- Investments
- Net Current Assets
- Miscellaneous Expenditure
- Accumulated Losses

(4) PERFORMANCE OF COMPANY (AMOUNT ₹ IN THOUSANDS):

- Turnover

**Inserted by Government notification dated 15th May, 1995*

- Total Expenditure (Profit/Loss before and after tax, earnings per share in ₹ and dividend rate %)

(5) GENERIC NAMES OF THREE PRINCIPAL PRODUCTS/SERVICES OF COMPANY (AS PER MONETARY TERMS):

- Item code no. (ITC Code)
- Product Description

(6) PARTICULARS OF EMPLOYEES u/s 217 (2A) of COMPANIES ACT (1956): Particulars regarding company's employees to be attached to and forming part of Directors report u/s 217 (2A) read with Companies (Particulars of Employees) Rules, 1975, is to be given in case of employees having remuneration of ₹ 12 lakhs or more than per annum, and in case of employees employed for a part of the year having remuneration above ₹ 1,00,000 per month

(7) DIRECTORS RESPONSIBILITY STATEMENT u/s 217 (2AA) OF COMPANIES ACT (1956):

The Directors report shall also include a Director' responsibility statement which contains specified matters.

4

ACCOUNTING PRINCIPLES

Accounting Principles are general decision rules derived from the accounting concepts. According to the American Institute of Certified Public Accountants (AICPA), US, a principle means a "***general law or rule adopted or professed as a guide to action, a settled ground or basis of conduct or practice***".

EXHIBIT 6

ACCOUNTING PRINCIPLES

"Accounting Principles are man-made. Unlike the principles of physics, chemistry and other natural sciences, accounting principles were not deducted from basic axioms, nor can they be verified by observation and experiment. Instead, they have evolved. This evolutionary process is going on constantly; accounting principles are not eternal truths."

— Anthony, Robert N., and Reece, James S.

Generally Accepted Accounting Principles (GAAP) is the standard framework of guidelines for financial accounting.

EXHIBIT 7

GENERALLY ACCEPTED ACCOUNTING PRINCIPLES (GAAP)

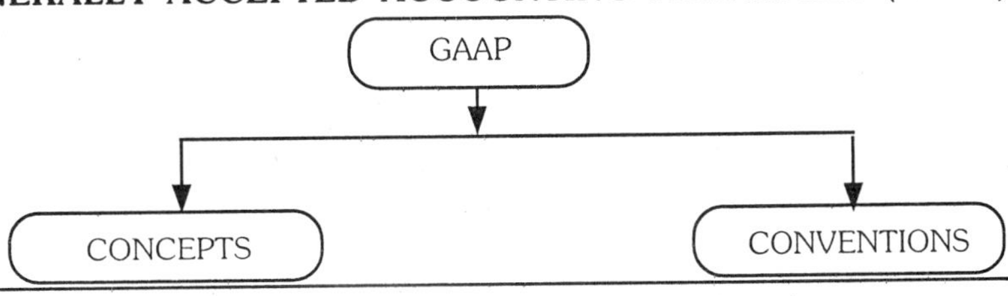

Concepts are the assumptions on which the accounts are based.

Conventions are the customs and traditions that have been followed since years.

ENTITY CONCEPT

Business is a separate, exclusive and separate legal person. Hence the owners and the business are two different entities. Thus, capital brought in by the owners is recorded on the liabilities side. Capital on the liabilities side of the balance sheet indicates the amount owed by the business to the owner. Profit is a liability and loss is an asset. Profit as a liability implies that the obligation of the business to the owner has increased to that extent. Loss as an asset signifies an opposite situation; business has to claim the amount of loss from the owner. Thus, a Company is a distinct legal *persona* existing independent of its members. The Company is thus vested with a corporate personality separate and distinct from its members.

GOING CONCERN CONCEPT

The going concern concept is an important assumption. Accounting policies hover around this assumption. The implication is that enterprise has an indefinite life and enjoys perpetual succession. If not perpetual it is expected that enterprise will continue to be in business at least till the foreseeable future. For instance, depreciation is charged to the income statement periodically, to provide resources for replacement. It therefore assumes that enterprise will still be in operation at that point of time.

DUALITY CONCEPT

Every transaction has a two-fold impact – once on the debit side and once on the credit side. Thus every debit has a corresponding credit of equal amount. All debits and all credits therefore get equated. This gives rise to the two equations as shown below:

Total Debits = Total Credits

Assets + Expenses = Liabilities + Capital + Income

Thus, Profits = Income – Expenses (Income statement equation)

Assets = Liabilities + Capital (Balance Sheet equation)

The excess of income over expenses (profit) gets added to the capital. Further, if the expenses exceed income, the resultant loss is deducted from the capital or added to assets. Profit is a liability and loss is an asset to reiterate.

HISTORIC CONCEPT

Chartered Institute of Management Accountants (CIMA), UK Terminology defines historic cost concept as '***a system of accounting in which all values are based on the historical costs incurred***'. Items put on the financial statements are valued at the costs at the time of inception of the transactions. Of course, adjustments are made for change in values of items due to appreciation or depreciation, as the case may be. However, more often than not values of items on the financial statements encounter depreciation.

ACCRUAL CONCEPT

Incomes and expenses accrue with respect to the time period to which they pertain. The receipts or payments of cash are not relevant for measuring income or expenses for a particular period. Thus relevant incomes and relevant expenses are matched ignoring the flow of cash. The four items, which need to be addressed, include:

Accrued expense; prepaid expense; accrued income; income received in advance.

(1) Accrued expenses: An expense is incurred whether cash is paid now or later.

(2) Prepaid expenses: An expense is not incurred merely because cash is paid.

(3) Accrued income: An income is earned whether cash is received or not.

(4) Income received in advance: An income is not earned merely because cash is received.

MATCHING CONCEPT*

The matching concept facilitates the application of the accrual concept. They are like two sides of a coin, and are interlinked. "***Matching concept is used when identifying costs and revenues with products or with equipment used to make products***".

"***Accrual concept deals with expenses and incomes which are time related***". Thus, relevant incomes and expenses pertaining to like segments products, equipment and time (usually accounting period) are matched and brought together.

PERIODICITY CONCEPT

Since enterprise is a going concern and has a long life, it is necessary to determine its financial health periodically. Hence, there is a need to determine profit by measuring incomes and expenses. Further the value of the assets and liabilities are also to be determined along with the value of the owner's funds. Periodicity is determined by the needs of the users as well as dictates of law. The usual time period for financial reporting to shareholders is 12 months ending 31st March of any year. For some reason if the accounting period gets extended, necessary permission of the competent authorities has to be sought. Similarly interim reporting takes place.

EXHIBIT 7 (A)

PREPARATION OF BALANCE SHEET - SECTION 210 OF THE COMPANIES ACT, 1956

Every company shall prepare a balance sheet at the end of a financial year and profit and loss account for the period ending of the said financial year. Further, the annual accounts should be presented at the Annual General Meeting of the members as prescribed in Section 210 (1) of the Companies Act within six months from close of the financial year. The Registrar of Companies may extend the said period of six months by a further period of three months, i.e., to say the annual accounts shall be presented within nine months from the close of the financial year. A financial year of a company can be less or more than twelve months but cannot be more than fifteen months. However, the financial year can be extended to eighteen months by obtaining special permission from the Registrar of Companies (Section 210 of the Companies Act, 1956). The extension of time referred to in the Companies Act, 1956 shall however not affect the obligations of such companies under the provision of the Income Tax Act, 1961, which requires that all companies must submit their income tax returns on the basis of uniform financial year, i.e., to say closing on 31st March every year. Thus, all companies need to prepare their accounts for income tax purposes on 31st March every year.

It should be noted that closing dates of financial year can and does vary in the case of companies vis-à-vis the Companies Act (1956). Thus, subsidiaries or associates of foreign companies close their accounts on 31st March and some German companies close their accounts on 30th June. Again, American companies close their accounts on 31st December and sugar companies in India usually close their accounts on 30th September for company law purposes.

CONVENTION - PRUDENCE (CONSERVATISM)

Prudence demands conservative approach to determine incomes or measure costs. Thus, anticipated profits are to be ignored as against anticipated losses which are to be charged as soon as they are identified or known. For instance:

***Source:** Wilks, C., and M. Weave. *Financial Accounting Fundamentals Stage 1 Knowledge, p. 114*

- Assets are presented in the balance sheet at cost adjusted for accumulated depreciation. However, if there is a fall in the market value of assets, the assets are valued at cost price or market price whichever is lower.
- The above valuation rule is applicable to other assets too, *viz.*, inventory and debtors
  - If sundry debtors contain bad debts or doubtful debts they are to be written off immediately.
  - If inventory loses value due to obsolescence or fall in the market value, the prudence principle applies and inventory is invariably valued at cost price or market price whichever is lower.

Prudence prevents overstatement of assets and incomes and understatement of costs and liabilities too. Prudence builds in abundant caution into the process of preparing financial statements.

CONVENTION – MATERIALITY

Materiality refers to significance of a particular item in the overall context of the business. An item may be rather trivial and hence it may not be material enough to justify a separate disclosure. What is trivial is a matter of judgement and usually left to the discretion of the auditors, along with the opinions of those at the helm of affairs, will prevail. Materiality also makes sure that the users are not flooded with superfluous information. In the UK, it is believed that a relatively small (5 per cent) monetary value is not significant unless they change a profit into loss or *vice versa* or affect sensitive issues. However the balances on director's current accounts must be exactly correct, notwithstanding the amount of the balance. The cardinal feature concerning materiality is the need for separate disclosure of items, which are significant enough and are relevant to keep the end-users duly informed.

OBJECTIVITY CONCEPT

Objectivity refers to disclosure that is unbiased and presents a true and fair picture of the financial position of the business. Objectivity is free from bias when valuation of items in the financial statements is based on actual cost, which can be verified with the voucher and related documents concerning the transaction. From time to time objectivity is hemmed in by subjective inputs when items are to be presented using current cost, realizable value or present value. In such situations, the subjective inputs attempt to provide as objective an estimate as possible.

Objectivity is a key input in facilitating the presentation of a true and fair picture of the financial position of business. The Generally Accepted Accounting Principles are intended to facilitate objectivity and consistency in accounting policies and practices at the enterprise level. As a result the financial statements, which emerge, are supposed to meet the rigours of '***truth and fairness***' of the accounts of the business. In the process the financial statements stand the test of reliability, verifiability and other standard acid tests of probity of accounting concepts, principles and policy.

5

ACCOUNTING STANDARDS

Having studied, the procedure to prepare the Income Statements and Balance Sheets, it is also important to know the rules that govern these statements. In order, that the methods and principles adopted by various reporting enterprises are transparent and can be compared across domains, there is a need for standardization.

WHAT ARE ACCOUNTING STANDARDS?

Accounting Standards are written documents, policy documents issued by expert accounting body or Government or other regulatory bodies covering the aspects of recognition, measurement, treatment, presentation and disclosure of accounting transactions in the financial statements. Accounting Standards in India are issued by the Institute of Chartered Accountants of India (ICAI). Accounting Standards aim to provide comparability and uniformity as far as possible coupled with transparency to these Financial Statements.

OBJECTIVES OF ACCOUNTING STANDARDS

The objective of Accounting Standards is to standardize the diverse accounting policies and practices with a view to eliminate to the extent possible the non-comparability of financial statements and add to the reliability to the financial statements. The Institute of Chartered Accountants of India, recognizing the need to harmonize the diverse accounting policies and practices, constituted an Accounting Standard Board (ASB) on 21st April, 1977.

COMPLIANCE WITH ACCOUNTING STANDARDS ISSUED BY ICAI

SECTION 211(3A) and (3B) requires that:

Every Balance Sheet and Profit and Loss Account of the Company shall comply with the Accounting Standards.

(a) In case it does not comply with Accounting standards it must disclose:

(i) Deviations from Accounting Standards.

(ii) Reasons for such deviations.
(iii) Financial implications if any, due to such deviations.

SECTION 211(3C): Accounting Standards to mean standards of accounting recommended by ICAI, as may be prescribed by Central Government in consultation with National Advisory Committee on Accounting Standard (NACAS) set up u/s 210A. Until such time NACAS is established, standards prescribed by ICAI as mandatory will be the Accounting Standards.

ADVANTAGES AND DISADVANTAGES OF ACCOUNTING STANDARDS

The setting of Accounting Standards has the following advantages:

- Standards reduce to a reasonable extent or eliminate altogether confusing variation in the accounting treatments used to prepare the financial statements.
- There are certain areas where important information is not required by law to be disclosed, standards may call for disclosure beyond that required by law.
- It facilitates comparison of financial statements of different companies situated at different places.

The disadvantages of setting Accounting Standards are:

- There may be a trend towards rigidity and away from flexibility in applying accounting standards.
- Differences in accounting standards are bound to be because of differences in the traditions and legal system from one country to another.
- Accounting standards cannot override the law. The standards are required to be framed within the ambit of prevailing statute even though it is not an acceptable standard.

ACCOUNTING STANDARDS AND THE AUDITORS

Auditors are duty bound while discharging their attest function to ensure that the Accounting Standards issued and made mandatory by ICAI are implemented. Section 227(3) of Companies Act, 1956, requires the auditors to report whether in his opinion the Profit/Loss account and Balance Sheet comply with the Accounting Standards referred to in Sec 211 (3C) of the Companies Act, 1956.

ACCOUNTING STANDARDS AND BOARDS' REPORT

Section 217 (2AA)(1) of the Companies Act, 1956, states that Directors' Responsibility Statement should indicate that in the preparation of the annual accounts the applicable Accounting Standards had been followed along with proper explanation relating to material departure.

PROCEDURE FOR ISSUING ACCOUNTING STANDARDS BY THE INSTITUTE OF CHARTERED ACCOUNTANTS OF INDIA (ICAI)

Broadly the following procedure is adopted for formulating the Accounting Standards:

- Accounting Standards Board (ASB) shall determine the broad areas in which Accounting Standards need to be formulated and the priority in regard to the selection thereof.
- In the preparation of Accounting Standards, ASB will be assisted by Study Groups constituted to consider specific subjects. In the formation of Study Groups, the members of the Institute and others will make provision for wide participation.
- ASB will also hold a dialogue with the representatives of the Government, Public Sector Undertakings, Industry and other organizations for ascertaining their views.

- On the basis of the work of the Study Groups and the dialogue with the organizations referred to above, an exposure draft of the proposed standard will be prepared and issued for comments by members of the Institute and the public at large.
- The draft of the proposed standard will include the following basic points:
  - A statement of concepts and fundamental accounting principles relating to the standard.
  - Definitions of the terms used in the standard.
  - The manner in which the accounting principles have been applied for formulating the standard.
  - The presentation and disclosure requirements in complying with the standard.
  - Class of enterprise to which the standard apply.
  - Date from which the standard will be effective.
- After taking into consideration the comments received, the draft of the proposed standard will be finalised by ASB and submitted to the Council of the Institute.
- The Council of the Institute will consider the final draft of the proposed standard and if found necessary, modify the same in consultation with ASB. The Accounting Standard on the relevant subject will then be issued under the Authority of the Council.

OTHER REGULATIONS AND ACCOUNTING STANDARDS

In respect of banks, financial institutions and finance companies the Reserve Bank of India (RBI) pronounces policies *inter alia* on revenue recognition, provisioning and assets classifications. Similarly the Foreign Exchange Dealers Association of India (FEDAI) provides guidelines regarding accounting for foreign exchange transactions. Since the Securities and Exchange Board of India (SEBI) is an important regulatory body it would also like to have its own accounting standards and in fact, it has started the process by notifying cash flow reporting format. It is also in the process of issuing a standard on the accounting policies for mutual funds. It appears as if several authorities in our country are keen to have a say in the matter of framing accounting rules of measurement and reporting.

INDIAN ACCOUNTING STANDARDS

- AS 1 Disclosure of Accounting Policies
- AS 2 Valuation of Inventories
- AS 3 Cash Flow Statements (CFS)
- AS 4 Contingencies and Events Occurring after the Balance Sheet Date
- AS 5 Net Profit or Loss for the period, Prior Period Items and Changes in Accounting Policies
- AS 6 Depreciation Accounting
- AS 7 Construction Contracts (Revised 2002)
- AS 8 Accounting for Research and Development
- AS 9 Revenue Recognition
- AS 10 Accounting for Fixed Assets
- AS 11 The Effects of Changes in Foreign Exchange Rates (Revised 2003)
- AS 12 Accounting for Government Grants
- AS 13 Accounting for Investments
- AS 14 Accounting for Amalgamations
- AS 15 (Revised 2005) Employee Benefits
- AS 15 (Issued 1995) Accounting for Retirement Benefits in the Financial Statement of Employers
- AS 16 Borrowing Costs

- AS 17 Segment Reporting
- AS 18 Related Party Disclosures
- AS 19 Leases
- AS 20 Earnings Per Share (EPS)
- AS 21 Consolidated Financial Statements
- AS 22 Accounting for Taxes on Income
- AS 23 Accounting for Investments in Associates in Consolidated Financial Statements
- AS 24 Discontinuing Operations
- AS 25 Interim Financial Reporting (IFR)
- AS 26 Intangible Assets
- AS 27 Financial Reporting of Interests in Joint Ventures
- AS 28 Impairment of Assets
- AS 29 Provisions, Contingent Liabilities and Contingent Assets
- AS 30 Financial Instruments: Recognition and Measurement and Limited Revisions to AS 2, AS 11 (Revised 2003), AS 21, AS 23, AS 26, AS 27, AS 28 and AS 29
- AS 31 Financial Instruments: Presentation

AS 1: DISCLOSURE OF ACCOUNTING POLICIES

- All accounting policies followed in preparation of accounts should be disclosed at one place along with the financial statements.
- Any change in the accounting policies, which have a material effect in the current period or future periods, should be disclosed.
- If fundamental assumptions (going concern, consistency and accrual) are not followed, it should be separately disclosed.
- Major considerations governing selection and application of accounting policies are Prudence, Substance over form and Materiality.
- Policies adopted by the business should represent '***true and fair***' view of the state of affairs of the enterprise as disclosed in the financial statements.

AS 2: VALUATION OF INVENTORIES

- AS 2 is applicable for all inventories other than work in progress arising under construction contracts, work in progress of service providers, shares, debentures and securities held as stock in trade, producers' inventories of livestock, agricultural and forest products and mineral oils, ores and gases to the extent measured at net realisable value in accordance with well established practices in those industries.
- Inventories are assets
  (a) held for sale in ordinary course of business.
  (b) in the process of production for such sale.
  (c) in form of materials to be consumed in production process or rendering of services.
- Inventories are to be valued at **lowest cost** or net realizable value.
- Inventories do not include machinery spares which can be used with an item of fixed asset and whose use is irregular.
- Cost of inventories comprise of all costs incurred for bringing the inventories to their present location and condition, i.e., cost of purchase, cost of conversion, storage/distribution costs, transit insurance, etc.
- Net realisable value is the estimated selling price less estimated cost of completion and estimated cost necessary to make the sale.

- Generally, weighted average cost or FIFO method is used in cases where goods are ordinarily interchangeable. Specific Identification Method to be used when goods are not ordinarily interchangeable or have been segregated for specific projects. The method of valuing the inventories should be reviewed annually. There should be a proper disclosure of the inventory valuation policy and the changes, if any, from previous years' policy.

AS 3: CASH FLOW STATEMENTS (CFS)

- CFS should be prepared and presented for the period in question along with other financial statements.
- CFS can be divided into three segments: Operating Activities; Investing Activities and Financing Activities.
- There are two ways of presenting the Operating Activities:
- Direct Method = Gross basis.
- Indirect Method = Net profit is adjusted for non-cash items, etc.
- Net basis reporting has to be followed when cash flows are from: items of large amounts; Fixed deposits from public and advances from customers.
- Treatment of select important items:
  - *(a)* Foreign Currency Cash Flows disclose separately.
  - *(b)* Interest/Dividends received and paid – disclose separately.
  - *(c)* Extraordinary items – disclose separately under individual activity head.
  - *(d)* Cash flows arising out of acquisitions/disposals of subsidiaries or other business units – disclose separately.
  - *(e)* Hedging or derivative contracts – disclose separately under individual activity head.
  - *(f)* Unavailable cash or cash equivalents for use – disclose separately along with comments.

AS 4: CONTINGENCIES AND EVENTS OCCURRING AFTER BALANCE SHEET DATE

- Contingency refers to a situation or condition, on balance sheet date, the ultimate outcome of which will be known or determined only on the occurrence or non-occurrence of uncertain events.
- There can be contingent gains as well as contingent losses.
- As per conservative principle, we do not recognize contingent gains. But contingent losses are to be provided for as per prudence policy.
- Events occurring after balance sheet date can be of two types Adjusting events, Non-adjusting events.
- When the amount involved can be reasonably estimated or when the going concern assumption is rendered invalid, it becomes an "***Adjusting Event***".
- Examples of adjusting events: Dividends received, Changes in tax rates.
- When the event does not affect reported figures, we do not need to adjust it and thus, it is called **Non-adjusting Event**.
- Examples of non-adjusting events: Purchase or sale of fixed assets; Changes in exchange rates and Capital (loan) repayments.
- Material changes in respect of adjusting events have to be disclosed separately.

AS 5: NET PROFIT/LOSS FOR THE PERIOD, PRIOR PERIOD ITEMS AND CHANGES IN ACCOUNTING POLICIES

- All items of income and expense, which are recognised in a period, should be included in determination of net profit or loss for the period.
- Profit from ordinary and extraordinary activities should be disclosed separately.
- Prior period items arise as a result of errors or omission in the preparation of financial statements.
- Prior period items should be disclosed separately and the nature and amount of such items should be specified.
- Effect of a change in the accounting estimate should be included in the determination of profit or loss of the period of change and also future periods if it is expected to affect future periods.
- Accounting policies should not be changed unless it is required by statute/standard or leads to better presentation.
- Change in accounting policy, which has a material effect, should be disclosed separately. If the change does not have a material impact in the current period but is expected to have a material effect in future periods then the fact should be disclosed.

AS 6: DEPRECIATION ACCOUNTING

- It is applicable to all assets except: Wasting assets, Natural assets, R&D expenditure, Goodwill and Livestock.
- Allocate depreciable amount of the asset on a systematic basis over useful life of asset.
- Useful life of asset is determined on the basis of
  (a) physical wear and tear.
  (b) obsolescence.
  (c) legal or other limits on the use of the asset.
- The method of charging depreciation should be consistent.
- A change in method of depreciation is made only if required by statute, for compliance with an accounting standard or for appropriate presentation of the financial statements.
- Where the historical cost undergoes a change due to fluctuation in exchange rate, price adjustment, etc., depreciation on the revised amount should be provided over the balance useful life of the asset.
- Sale or purchase of an asset should be disclosed separately.
- Deficiency or surplus in case of disposal, destruction, etc., should be disclosed separately.

AS 7: CONSTRUCTION CONTRACTS (REVISED 2002)

- Construction contract may be for construction of a single/combination of interrelated or interdependent assets.
- Contract may be fixed price or cost plus contract.
- When a contract covers a number of assets, the construction of each asset should be treated as a separate construction contract when
  (a) separate proposals have been submitted for each asset.
  (b) each asset has been subject to separate negotiation and the contractor and customer have been able to accept or reject that part of the contract relating to each asset.
  (c) the costs and revenues of each asset can be identified.
- Contract revenue and expenses to be recognised when outcome can be estimated reliably up to stage of completion on reporting date.

- A contract may provide for the construction of an additional asset at the option of the customer or may be amended to include the construction of an additional asset. The construction of the additional asset should be treated as a separate construction contract when
  (a) the asset differs significantly in design, technology or function from the asset or assets covered by the original contract.
  (b) the price of the asset is negotiated without regard to the original contract price.
- An enterprise should disclose
  (a) the amount of contract revenue recognised as revenue in the period.
  (b) the methods used to determine the contract revenue recognised in the period.
  (c) the methods used to determine the stage of completion of contracts in progress.

AS 8: ACCOUNTING FOR RESEARCH AND DEVELOPMENT

- Salaries, wages, personnel costs, depreciation, cost of materials and services, etc., related to research and development, payment to outside institution, reasonable allocation of overhead costs and amortisation of patents and licences be included in research and development cost to be disclosed in profit and loss account.
- Such cost to be charged as an expense unless the product or process is separately identifiable. It may then be deferred for allocation in future years on systematic basis and to be separately disclosed in Balance Sheet and reviewed at end of each accounting year.

NOTE: In view of operation of AS 26, this standard stands withdrawn.

AS 9: REVENUE RECOGNITION

- Revenue is inflow of cash, receivables or other considerations.
- Revenue can be generated by sale of goods, services or use of enterprise resources by others, i.e., interest, royalty and dividend.
- Recognition criteria.
- Revenue from sales of goods – at the time of sale if collection is reasonably certain; i.e., when risks and rewards of ownership are transferred to the buyer.
- Rendering of services – either on completed service method or proportionate completion method.
- Interest – time proportion basis – for banks – different standards.
- Royalty – accrual basis.
- Dividends – when right to receive is established.
- If revenue recognition is postponed, reasons should be disclosed.

AS 10: ACCOUNTING FOR FIXED ASSETS

- It applies to all fixed assets except – forest, plantations, mines and similar non-regenerative resources.
- Fixed asset is an asset held with the intention of being used for producing or providing goods and/or services and is not held for sale in the normal course of the business.
- Cost of fixed asset equals purchase price plus incidental expenses incurred to bring the asset to its working condition.
- Gross fixed assets are at historical cost unless revalued.
- When fixed assets are sold, deduct the value from gross fixed assets.
- Disclosure:
  (a) Opening and closing gross and net book value.
  (b) Expenditure incurred in acquisition/construction.

(c) Details of revaluation.
(d) Additions, disposals, acquisitions of fixed assets.

AS 11: THE EFFECTS OF CHANGES IN FOREIGN EXCHANGE RATES (REVISED 2003)

- Initial recognition of a foreign currency transaction shall be by applying the foreign currency exchange rate as on the date of transaction.
- In order to include foreign currency transactions and foreign operations in the financial statements of an enterprise, transactions must be expressed in the enterprise's reporting currency and the financial statements of foreign operations must be translated into the enterprise's reporting currency.
- At each balance sheet date:
  (a) Foreign currency monetary items should be reported using the closing rate.
  (b) Non-monetary items which are carried in terms of historical cost denominated in a foreign currency should be reported using the exchange rate at the date of the transaction.
  (c) Non-monetary items which are carried at fair value or other similar valuation denominated in a foreign currency should be reported using the exchange rates that existed when the values were determined.
- Forward exchange contract may be entered to establish the amount of the reporting currency required or available at the settlement date.
- An enterprise should disclose
  (a) the amount of exchange differences included in the net profit or loss for the period.
  (b) net exchange differences accumulated in foreign currency translation reserve as a separate component of shareholders' funds and a reconciliation of the amount of such exchange differences at the beginning and end of the period.

AS 12: ACCOUNTING FOR GOVERNMENT GRANTS

- Grants can be in cash or in kind and may carry certain conditions to be complied.
  (i) Government grants should not be recognised until there is reasonable assurance that the enterprise will comply with the conditions attached to them.
  (ii) The grants will be received.
- Government grants related to specific fixed assets should be deducted from the gross value of the assets.
- Government grants related to revenue should be recognised on a systematic basis in the profit and loss statement over the periods necessary to match them with the related costs which they are intended to compensate.
- Government grants in the form of non-monetary assets, given at a concessional rate, should be accounted for on the basis of their acquisition cost.
- Grants when it become refundable, be shown as extraordinary item.
- The following should be disclosed:
  (i) The accounting policy adopted for government grants, including the methods of presentation in the financial statements.
  (ii) The nature and extent of government grants recognised in the financial statements, including grants of non-monetary assets given at a concessional rate or free of cost.

AS 13: ACCOUNTING FOR INVESTMENTS

- Investments are assets held to earn interest, dividend, rentals, capital appreciation or other benefits. However, assets held as stock-in-trade are not classified as investments.
- It is applicable to all investments except
  (i) Operating and finance leases.
  (ii) Investments in mutual funds or banks.
  (iii) Investments may be current (1 year or less) or long-term (more than a year) investments.
- Classification of Investments:
  - Government or Trust Securities.
  - Shares, debentures or bonds.
  - Investment in "properties".
  - Others – specifying nature.
- Cost of investments should include incidental charges, i.e., brokerage, fees, etc.
- Current investments are valued at lowest cost or fair value as on the balance sheet date, whereas long-term investments are valued at cost. Disclosure of
  - classification or reclassification.
  - carrying amount of investments.
  - loss or gain on disposal of investments.
  - other restrictive covenants.

AS 14: ACCOUNTING FOR AMALGAMATIONS

- Amalgamation in nature of merger be accounted for under pooling of interest method.
- Amalgamation in nature of purchase be accounted for under purchase method.
- In case on conflicting accounting policies existing in transferor and transferee Company, a uniform policy is adopted on amalgamation.
- Effect on financial statement of any change in policy be reported as per AS 5.
- Any non-cash item included in the consideration on amalgamation should be accounted at fair value, e.g., Goodwill or Capital Reserve.
- Specified disclosures be made appropriately in financial statements after amalgamation.

AS 15: (REVISED 2005) EMPLOYEE BENEFITS*

AS 15: (Issued 1995) Accounting for Retirement Benefits in the Financial Statement of Employers

- For retirement benefits of provident fund and other defined contribution schemes, contribution payable by employer and any shortfall on collection from employees is charged to profit and loss account.
- For gratuity and other defined benefit schemes, accounting treatment will depend on the type of arrangements which the employer has made.
- If retirement benefits are paid out of employers funds, appropriate charge to profit and loss account is to be made through a provision for accruing liability.
- If liability for retirement benefit is funded through a scheme administered by an insurer, an actuarial certificate or confirmation from insurer is obtained.
- Any alteration in the retirement benefit cost should be charged or credited to profit and loss account and change in actuarial method should be disclosed.

**'Not relevant for the subject matter of this book.'*

- Financial statements should disclose method by which retirement benefit cost have been determined.

AS 16: BORROWING COSTS

- Borrowing costs refer to interest and other costs incurred by an enterprise in relation to borrowed funds.
- A qualifying asset is an asset that takes substantially long time, to be ready for intended use or sale.
- Borrowing costs that are directly attributable to the acquisition, construction or production of any qualifying asset they should be capitalized.
- The capitalization commences when the activity (i.e., acquisition, construction or production) is in progress and borrowing cost is being incurred.
- When the activity is suspended for avoidable reasons, then suspend the capitalization of borrowing costs. However, when activity is suspended for unavoidable reasons, continue the capitalization.
- The capitalization stops when substantially all the activities are completed.
- Disclosure: The accounting policy followed for treatment of borrowing costs and the amount of cost capitalized during the period.

AS 17: SEGMENT REPORTING

- Requires reporting of financial information about different products and services an enterprise provides and different geographical areas in which it operates.
- A business segment is a distinguishing component of an enterprise providing a product or service or group of products or services that is subject to risks and returns that are different from other business segments.
- Internal financial reporting system is normally the basis for identifying the segments.
- The dominant source and nature of risk and returns of an enterprise should govern whether its primary reporting format will be business segments or geographical segments.
- If total external revenue is attributable to reportable segment constitutes less than 75% of total revenues then additional segments should be identified.
- Reconciliation between Information about reportable segments and Information in financial statements of the enterprise is also to be provided.
- Intra segment transfers and composition of the segment should be disclosed.

AS 18: RELATED PARTY DISCLOSURES

- Parties are considered related, if, one party has the ability to control or exercise significant influence over the other party during the reporting period.
- AS 18 deals with the following related party relations:
  - *(a)* Enterprises that directly or indirectly control or are controlled by or are under common control with reporting enterprise.
  - *(b)* Associates, Joint Ventures of the reporting entity; Investing party or venture in respect of which reporting enterprise is an associate or a joint venture.
  - *(c)* Individuals owning voting power giving control or significant influence.
  - *(d)* Key management personnel and their relatives.
  - *(e)* Enterprises over which any of the persons in (c) or (d) are able to exercise significant influence.
- The AS also gives definitions of control, significant influence, related party transactions, associate, joint venture, etc.

- The basic disclosure requirements are
  - *(a)* names of the related party and nature of relationship.
  - *(b)* full details of the material transactions.

AS 19: LEASES

- Lease is classified as financial lease or operating lease.
- This AS applies in accounting for all leases other than leases to explore for or use natural resources, licensing agreements for items such as motion pictures films, video-recording plays, etc., and lease for use of lands.
- In case of finance lease in the books of lessee,
  - *(a)* Lease to be recognised as an asset and liability at lower of fair value of the leased asset.
  - *(b)* Payment should be appropriated between Finance charge and the Reduction of outstanding liability.
  - *(c)* Depreciation policy should be consistent.
- In case of finance lease in the books of lessor,
  - *(a)* Recognize the asset as a receivable equal to net investment in lease.
  - *(b)* Finance income should be based on pattern reflecting a constant periodic return on net investment in lease.
- In case of operating lease in the books of lessee,
  - *(a)* Lease payment should be recognised as an expense on straight-line basis or other systematic basis.
  - *(b)* Relevant disclosures should be made.
- In case of operating lease in the books of lessor,
  - *(a)* Lessors should present an asset given on lease under fixed assets and lease income should be recognized on a straight-line basis.
  - *(b)* Relevant disclosures should be made.

AS 20: EARNINGS PER SHARE (EPS)

- The standard deals with two kinds of EPS: Basic EPS; Diluted EPS.
- Basic EPS is calculated by dividing net profit or loss for the period attributable to equity shareholders by weighted average of equity shares outstanding during the period.
- For calculating diluted EPS, net profit or loss attributable to equity shareholders and the weighted average number of shares are adjusted for the effects of dilutive potential equity shares.
- Dilutive potential equity shares mean certain events, which may take place in the near future that may increase the equity shares in the company.

AS 21: CONSOLIDATED FINANCIAL STATEMENTS

- To be applied in the preparation and presentation of consolidated financial statements for a group of enterprises under the control of a parent.
- Consolidated financial statements to be presented in addition to separate financial statements.
- All subsidiaries, domestic and foreign to be consolidated except where control is intended to be temporary or the subsidiary operates under severe long-term restrictions impairing transfer of funds to the parent.
- Financial statements used in consolidation should be drawn up to the same reporting date.

- Consolidation should be prepared using the same accounting policies.
- Disclosure is to be of all subsidiaries giving name, country of incorporation, residence, proportion of ownership and voting power if different, nature of relationship between Parent and Subsidiary, effect of the acquisition and disposal of subsidiaries on the financial position, names of subsidiaries whose reporting dates are different than that of the parent.

AS 22: ACCOUNTING FOR TAXES ON INCOME*

AS 23: ACCOUNTING FOR INVESTMENTS IN ASSOCIATES IN CONSOLIDATED FINANCIAL STATEMENTS*

AS 24: DISCONTINUING OPERATIONS

- The standard requires an enterprise to segregate information about discontinuing operations from continuing one and establishes principles for reporting information about discontinuing operations.
- A discontinuing operation is a part of an enterprise
  - which is being disposed of or abandoned pursuant to a single coordinated plan.
  - it represents separate line of business or geographical area of operations.
  - can be distinguished operationally and for financial reporting.
- For an enterprise to be discontinuing, the above three conditions need to be satisfied simultaneously.
- When an enterprise decides to discontinue any of its operations, it should make an initial disclosure of the same to the stakeholders through a public announcement.
- Once all the details are finalized and agreed upon, a proper presentation and disclosure should be done as per the AS.
- The disclosures should be narrative as well as quantitative.
- The basic disclosure requirements are:
  - Description of the discontinuing operation.
  - Date and nature of initial disclosure event.
  - Date when it would be completed.
  - The gain/loss on the sale of assets.

AS 25: INTERIM FINANCIAL REPORTING (IFR)

- Interim financial reports are financial statements (complete or condensed) for an interim period that is shorter than a full financial year.
- IFR should include at a minimum a condensed balance sheet, condensed profit and loss statement, cash flow and selected explanatory notes.
- The selected explanatory notes will include: aspects on accounting policies, changes in estimates, dividends, issues and buy-back, any other major event or activity during that reporting period.
- The EPS if disclosed is to be calculated and presented as per AS 20.
- Interim reports to include:
  - *(a)* Balance Sheet of current interim period and a comparative balance sheet of the preceding financial year.
  - *(b)* Statements of Profit and Loss for current interim period and cumulative for current financial year to date and comparative statements of the previous year (current and year to date).

**'Not relevant for the subject matter of this book.'*

(c) Cash Flow statement cumulatively for the current financial year to date with a comparative statement of previous year (year to date).

AS 26: INTANGIBLE ASSETS

- An intangible asset is an identifiable non-monetary asset, without physical substance, held for use in the production or supply of goods or services, for rental to others or for administrative purposes. An asset is a resource
  - controlled by an enterprise as a result of past events; and from which future economic benefits are expected to flow to the enterprise.
  - internally generated goodwill, brands, mastheads, publishing titles, etc. should not be recognised as an asset.
- Recognise intangible assets at cost only if the definition and recognition conditions are met.
- An intangible asset is to be amortised over its useful life in the pattern in which the assets' economic benefits are consumed or on a straight-line method.
- The disclosure requirements are
  (a) amortisation of intangible asset during the year.
  (b) accounting policy adopted.
  (c) gain/loss on disposal or retirement of the intangible asset.

NOTES:

- Accounting Standards 1, 2, 4 to 16 and 18 are mandatory.
- AS 3 Cash Flow statements and AS 17 Segment Reporting apply only to enterprises whose equity or debt securities are listed or enterprises that are in process of issuing such equity or debts securities which are to be listed or enterprises whose turnover exceeds ₹ 50 crores.
- AS 20 Earnings per Share applies to the enterprise whose equity shares are listed on a recognised stock exchange. If the enterprise is not so covered but chooses to present EPS, then it should calculate EPS in accordance with the standard.
- AS 21 Consolidated Financial Statements is recommendatory. However if consolidated financial statements are presented, these should be prepared in accordance with the standard.
- The Central Government has in exercise of its power under section 211 (3C) of the Companies Act, 1956, read with Section 210A (1) and Section 642 (1) (a) of the Act, notified the Companies (Accounting Standards) Rules, 2006 on 7-12-2006. In terms of the Rules, the existing Accounting Standards 1 to 7 and 9 to 29 issued by the ICAI shall be the Accounting Standards (Notified AS) under the aforesaid provisions.
- Existing AS 11 has become the notified AS.
- AS 18 is now made applicable to all Companies including SMCs.

The Accounting Standards Board of the Institute of Chartered Accountant of India, which sets the standard for the country, has formulated two new Standards on Financial Instruments — AS 30 (Financial Instruments: Recognition and Measurement) and AS 31 (Financial Instruments: Presentation). These standards were placed in public domain as exposure drafts for comments up to March 31, 2007 and are now being finalised. While AS 30 is the equivalent of International Accounting Standard IAS 39, AS 31 corresponds to IAS 32.

AS 27: FINANCIAL REPORTING OF INTERESTS IN JOINT VENTURES*

AS 28: IMPAIRMENT OF ASSETS*

AS 29: PROVISIONS, CONTINGENT LIABILITIES AND CONTINGENT ASSETS*

AS 30: FINANCIAL INSTRUMENTS: RECOGNITION AND MEASUREMENT

- AS 30 is a complex standard. The purpose is to identify principles for recognising and measuring financial instruments which come within the fold of the expressions financial assets and financial liabilities in an entity's balance sheet.
- AS 30 deals with recognition (or otherwise) and measurement of financial instruments. It also deals with derivatives and hedge accounting.
- AS 30 is a mixed measurement model which captures the values of assets and liabilities using both the fair value principle and cost-based valuation.
- "***The concept of fair value is central to the standard as also the concept of symmetry. Fair value is the amount for which an asset could be exchanged or a liability settled between knowledgeable willing parties in an arm's length transaction***" (Ravimohan, P. R., Migrating to New Accounting Standards, *The Economic Times,* Mumbai, 27th June, 2007, pg. 17).
- The standard specifies valuation of assets and liabilities at fair value. However, there may be exceptions to the rules. The purpose of using fair value is to identify the realisable value in the event of disposal which is key to decision making.
- The ongoing measurement of financial assets is driven by the classification at the initial stages of identification into specific categories viz. Financial assets at fair value through profit and loss account (held for trading), held to maturity investments, loans and receivables and available for sale financial assets.
- The ongoing measurement of financial liabilities is also classified under fair value through profit and loss account. The measurement is at fair value and the resulting profits or losses are adjusted against the profit and loss account. All other financial liabilities are values at '***amortised cost using the effective interest method***'.
- AS 30 also specifies '***the criteria to qualify for hedge accounting and the recognition and measurement of gains and losses for different types of hedging relationships such as fair value hedges, cash flow hedges and hedge of a net investment in a non-integral foreign operation***' (Ravimohan, P. R., Migrating to New Accounting Standards, *The Economic Times,* Mumbai, 27th June, 2007, p. 17).
- Derivatives shall be recorded in the balance sheet at fair values. Any changes thereof will be shown in the profit and loss account unless stringent hedge accounting criteria are satisfied.

---

*'*Not relevant for the subject matter of this book.*'

AS 31: FINANCIAL INSTRUMENTS PRESENTATION

- Accounting Standard (AS) 31, Financial Instruments: Presentation, issued by the Council of the Institute of Chartered Accountants of India will come into effect in respect of accounting periods commencing on or after 1-4-2009.
- It will be recommendatory in nature for an initial period of two years.
- This Accounting Standard will become mandatory in respect of accounting periods commencing on or after 1-4-2011 for all commercial, industrial and business entities except to a small and medium sized entity.
- The objective of this Standard is to establish principles for presenting financial instruments as liabilities or equity and for offsetting financial assets and financial liabilities.
- It applies to the classification of financial instruments, from the perspective of the issuer, into financial assets, financial liabilities and equity instruments; the classification of related interest, dividends, losses and gains and the circumstances in which financial assets and financial liabilities should be offset.

EXHIBIT 8

NEW ACCOUNTING STANDARDS CHALLENGED IN SUPREME COURT

A few corporates have moved the Supreme Court challenging the new accounting standards issued by the Institute of Chartered Accountants of India on deferred tax liability of listed companies. AS-22 has brought in a new concept called ***deferred taxation****. Under this, a company became liable to provide for deferred tax liability on the first day the company accounted for its income in accordance with the AS-22 even when there was no certainty. The petitioners pleaded that deferred tax liability is a notional liability that can be charged to the Profit and Loss Account (PLA). Deferred tax liability arises when a firm underpays its taxes due to a difference between how it accounts for an asset on its book versus how it accounts for it on tax basis. The Calcutta High Court while upholding the accounting standards had observed that deferred tax liability was not a notional tax liability but a real liability because it would result in future cash outflow in the form of tax payment to the tax recovering authority. The deferred tax liability, therefore, was a real liability which existed on the balance sheet date for the financial year in which it originated and the question of liability being contingent in nature did not arise, it had held.*

SOURCE: *The Economic Times, 29th July, 2007.*

ESTABLISHMENT OF NATIONAL ADVISORY COMMITTEE ON ACCOUNTING STANDARDS (NACAS)

Section 210A discusses about the establishment of the NACAS. The Central Government is empowered by virtue of the provisions of section 210A (1) to establish NACAS which would advise the Central Government on the formulation and laying down of accounting policies and accounting standards for adoption by companies or class of companies under the Act. The NACAS shall give its recommendations to the Central Government on such matters of accounting policies, standards and auditing as may be referred to it for advice from time-to-time. The ICAI is free to set accounting standards as it has been doing since 1977. For the purpose of the Companies Act, the Central Government enjoys the authority to prescribe such accounting standards which are recommended by the ICAI. While prescribing any accounting standard, the Central Government may consult the NACAS.

EXHIBIT 9

BODIES CONCERNED WITH ACCOUNTING STANDARDS

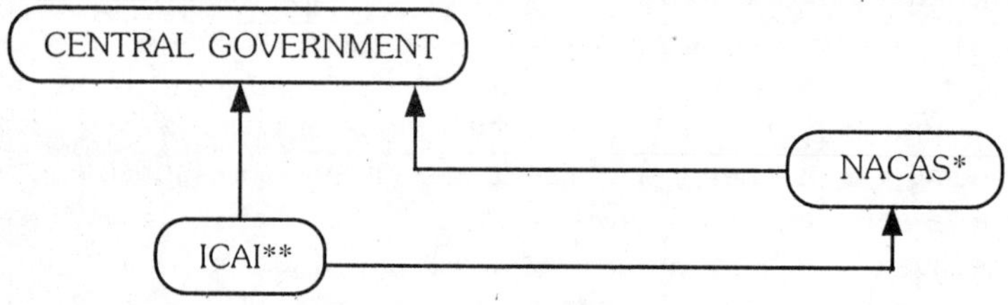

**NACAS: National Advisory Committee on Accounting Standards*

***ICAI: The Institute of Chartered Accountants of India*

SOURCE: Ghosh, T.P., *Accounting Standards and Corporate Accounting Practices with International Accounting Standards and US GAAP*. 4th ed. New Delhi: Taxmann Allied Services (P) Ltd., August, 2001.

EXHIBIT 10

GAAP IN ACCOUNTING SYSTEM

*Generally Accepted Accounting Principles (GAAP) is a perceived mantra for clean balance sheets. However, doubts are raised on Indian Accounting Standards and the financial statement based on the same. Further, it is also perceived that if an Indian company is drawing its financial statements in accordance with the American Accounting Standards the resultant financial statements are clean ab initio because the standards are flawless and holier than thou, ex hypothesi. In 2002, when Infosys prepared its balance sheet according to the GAAP, the business world in India were quite excited. Further, the profits of Infosys post-tax were reduced under the GAAP. This added further credibility to GAAP. As a result of this initiative of Infosys other companies like ICICI, Silverline and other companies followed suit. Listing on NASDAQ and NYSE became a '**fetish**' benchmark for India Inc. However, it shows Indian mentality towards anything which comes from the West. In fact Enron says it all. According to a news item in the Business Standard (22nd January, 2002) "**With Enron, two holy icons of the US can be set to rest. One is Arthur Anderson – or Accenture as it is now called - and the other is GAAP. Kenneth Lay, the Chairman of Enron, knew all that was happening and quite possibly encouraged it.**" Similarly, in the case of Sun Bean Corporation when Al Dunlap had '**falsified accounts, inflated profits, suppressed bad debts and exaggerated income**' to inflate share prices he was sacked ignominiously when the truth came to light and yet in this case all the principles of GAAP were supposedly adhered to. In fact, Warren Buffet had warned about GAAP and the '**blatant hypocrisy or fairy tales**' attributed to GAAP. Thus, GAAP is like any other set of accounting standards. Followed judiciously and correctly, the resultant financial statements will present a true and fair picture. However, if the people behind the standards are delinquents or perverts, with intent to fudge accounts, no standards can pre-empt or prevent frauds. It then does not matter where the standards originate from – USA, India, Germany, Japan or UK. Yet, every country looks upon the standard of some other country with suspect. The Americans distrust the German standards, the Germans view the American accounts under GAAP as American fables, the Japanese reveal very little under their accounting standards and the Indians believe all these to be gospels. The Indian accounting standards, over the last few years, have been held by Indians with disdain in comparison with GAAP. We forget that we have many firsts to our credit. As the Business Standard news item puts it, Ardeshir Godrej started manufacturing vegetable oil-based soap for the first time in India. Again, Jamshedji Tata introduced the '**pension systems**' in the Tata organisation when the West were not even aware about this expression in business. Instead of being a forerunner in establishing and pursuing benchmarks of*

contd. ...

contd. ...

excellence, in accounting standards, we tend to mechanically transplant and indiscriminately adopt anything which comes from the west or is a product of foreign soil. In fact, anything which is Indian is looked upon with scorn and contempt. We need to shun this approach "**Let Enron be the symbol. Enron is what GAAP leads to. GAAP means Enron. When you think of GAAP, think Enron. We are well rid of both.**" (Sharma, Saurabh. "GAAPs in the accounting system." The Business Standard [New Delhi] 22nd January, 2002.)

EXHIBIT 11

MIGRATION TO INTERNATIONAL FINANCIAL REPORTING STANDARDS (IFRS) SCENARIO: INDIA AND THE GLOBE POSITION AS ON 31/03/2012

The IFRS has been formulated by UK-based International Accounting Standards Board (IASB). It will replace the Generally Accepted Accounting Practices (GAAP) in the US. According to informed sources nearly 150 countries of the world would change over to the IFRS. Many other countries may also follow suit. An official spokesperson of the Institute of Chartered Accountants of India (ICAI), President Ved Jain said in 2008 that "**A common accounting standard is in the interest of the investors who are exploring investment opportunities in other geographical areas as well**". Of course, there is a delay in the migration towards IFRS for various reasons. In the US, the Securities and Exchange Commission (SEC) has issued a road map of transition to IFRS by US domestic companies from 2014. The issues hovering around the road map is now under active debate and set out for public commentary. The migration towards IFRS is perceived as a "**significant move towards the emergence of IFRS as a global accounting language.**" (PricewaterhouseCooper, National Leader of the IFRS practice, 27th December, 2008).

India was supposed to migrate to IFRS from 2011. In fact, the Prime Minister Manmohan Singh had committed to implement the first phase of IFRS by April, 2011 at a group of 20 (G20 Conference) in London in 2009. It was then reported that aligning with IFRS norms will help Indian companies "**raise cheaper capital overseas, besides making foreign listings and setting up subsidiaries and joint ventures abroad less cumbersome.**" (Mint, 12th February, 2012). However, this initiative stands postponed. According to a Business Standard report from New Delhi (6th February, 2012), India has deferred its plans to implement the new set of accounting rules consistent and compatible with the IFRS. Earlier, the plan was to converge towards IFRS in phases – 1st April, 2012, 2013 and 2013 respectively. The new ICAI deadline, in this behalf, is 1st April, 2013.

In the meantime, it is necessary to note that there are many changes in the offing in the Indian financial environment in terms of new legislation, viz., pending Companies Bill (2011), pending implementation of '**Direct Taxes Code**' (DTC) and of course the voices of competent authorities prescribed by legislation or otherwise, viz., the ICAI and Ministry of Corporate Affairs apart from Securities and Exchange Board of India (SEBI), Bombay Stock Exchange (BSE), National Stock Exchange (NSE) and other regulatory authorities. Considering that the US will implement the IFRS in 2014 and Japan in 2015, the ICAI IFRS implementation committee (Mr. Amarjit Chopra) had gone on record to say that India should "**takes a categorically stand that our implementation will be aligned with these countries.**" (Business Standard [New Delhi], 6th February, 2012,). Experts feel that India is still preparing for the convergence towards IFRS and the work is in progress in terms of issuance of tax accounting standards and new accounting standards consistent with the planned amendments to the Companies Act (1956), presently in the form of a Companies Bill (2011).

Further, it may be observed that the European Commission (EC) has allowed Indian companies that have listed their Global Depository Receipts (GDRs) on European exchanges, time till December 2014, to migrate to the IFRS. However, the extension in time, for migration to IFRS, provides breathing

contd. ...

contd. ...

space to many companies and it is believed that Indian companies with GDRs listed on the regulated EU markets will not have to maintain two sets of books of accounts to comply with IFRS. The general mood in the accounting world, however, is to migrate to IFRS and prove to the world at large that Indian companies are not in any way lagging behind in terms of readiness to disclosures that can sustain global benchmarks relating to financial reporting standards.

*An offshoot of US corporates migrating to IFRS is the huge business opportunities for BPO and KPO organisations in India. It is believed that the US does not have enough resources to manage the shift over to IFRS on its own. A substantial portion of the work will come to India as part of the outsourcing decision of US companies. This will mean a lot of bookkeeping work and India can become an "**accounting hub**" of the world. Thus, India will be seen as an important contributor, through value additions, to the efforts of US companies migrating to IFRS.*

WHAT IS IFRS?

International Financial Reporting Standards (IFRS) are standards and interpretations adopted by the International Accounting Standards Board (IASB). IFRSs are considered a "***principles-based***" set of standards in that they establish broad rules as well as dictate specific treatments. International Financial Reporting Standards comprise:

- International Financial Reporting Standards (IFRS) — standards issued after 2001.
- International Accounting Standards (IAS) — standards issued before 2001.
- Interpretations originated from the International Financial Reporting Interpretations Committee (IFRIC) — issued after 2001.
- Standing Interpretations Committee (SIC) — issued before 2001.

ICAI has already set 29 accounting standards as per IFRS, issued the guidance note for another one and is preparing eight more standards. When this process is consummated, India's accounting standards for listed companies will be in complete harmony with IFRS. The convergence to IFRS will greatly enhance Indian entities' ability to raise and attract foreign capital at low cost. It will also mean escape from multiple reports for huge Indian multinational companies that have to prepare their financial statements under multiple GAAPs.

US GAAP

WHAT IS US GAAP?

In the U.S., generally accepted accounting principles, commonly abbreviated as US GAAP or simply GAAP, are accounting rules used to prepare, present and report financial statements for a wide variety of entities, including publicly-traded and privately-held companies, non-profit organizations and governments. Generally, GAAP includes local applicable accounting framework, related accounting law, rules and accounting standard.

Similar to many other countries practicing under the common law system, the United States government does not directly set accounting standards, in the belief that the private sector has better knowledge and resources. US GAAP is not written in law, although the U.S. Securities and Exchange Commission (SEC) requires that it be followed in financial reporting by publicly-traded companies. Currently, **the Financial Accounting Standards Board (FASB) is the highest authority** in establishing generally accepted accounting principles for public and private companies, as well as non-profit entities. For local and state governments, GAAP is determined by the Governmental Accounting Standards Board (GASB), which operates under a set of assumptions, principles and constraints, different from those of standard private-sector GAAP. Financial reporting in federal government entities is regulated by the Federal Accounting Standards Advisory Board (FASAB).

The SEC has the statutory authority to establish GAAP for filings made with it. While allowing most of the standard setting to be done in the private sector, the SEC is still very active in both its overnight responsibility as well as establishing guidance and interpretations, as it believes appropriate. US GAAP has the reputation around the world of being more prescriptive and detailed than accounting standards in other countries.

US GAAP COMPRISES OF

- Statements of the Financial Accounting Standards Board (FASB)
- FASB Interpretations
- Statement of Financial Accounting Concepts
- FASB Technical Bulletins
- Opinions of the Accounting Principles Board
- American Institute of Certified Public Accountants (AICPA), Accounting Research Bulletins, Consensus of the Emerging Issues Task Force and Discussion Topics
- AICPA Industry Audit and Accounting Guides
- AICPA Statement of Positions
- AsSec Practice Bulletins
- AICPA Accounting Interpretations
- SEC Rules Accounting Series Releases
- Financial Reporting Releases
- Staff Accounting Bulletins
- Accounting and Auditing Enforcement Releases
- Regulation S-X
- Other Commission Forms and Releases
- Informal Staff Communications

HOUSE OF GAAP

The term "***House of GAAP concept***" derives from an article by Steven Rubin in the *Journal of Accountancy,* June 1984, issue and is commonly used to illustrate the hierarchy of pronouncements, standards and similar literature which establish US GAAP.

Table 5

HOUSE OF GAAP

Category (A) (Most authoritative)	FASB Standards and Interpretations	Accounting Principles Board (APB) Opinions	AICPA Accounting Research Bulletins (ARBs)
Category (B)	FASB Technical Bulletins	AICPA Industry Audit and Accounting Guides	AICPA Statements Of Position (SOPs)
Category (C)	FASB Emerging Issues Task Force (EITF)	AICPA AcSEC Practice Bulletins	
Category (D) (Least authoritative)	AICPA Accounting Interpretations	FASB Implementation Guides (Q and A)	Widely recognized and prevalent industry practices

Category **A** and **B** are considered authoritative. Category **C** and **D** are considered marginally authoritative, thoughts on interesting and unique issues, but could be invalid given a large level of materialism. Category **C** and **D** are considered a talking and reasoning phase of bringing issues to an authoritative level of GAAP.

Globalisation and access to Global Capital and Securities Market has enhanced the need to assimilate the principles of US GAAP into national Accounting Standards. To get listed on NYSE or NASDAQ and float GDR, an Indian company either needs to publish accounts under US GAAP or expressly publish the reconciliation of its Financial Results with US GAAP. Further many foreign companies whose shares are listed on US Stock Exchanges, require that their Indian Subsidiaries or Associates, should prepare separate sets of Accounts under US GAAP for ease of consolidation.

Some Indian Companies which have launched GDR/ADR are Bajaj Auto, Dr Reddy's Lab, HDFC Bank, Hindalco, ICICI Bank, Infosys, ITC, L&T, MTNL, Ranbaxy Labs, Reliance, Satyam Computers, SBI, VSNL and WIPRO and required to follow US GAAP Accounting/Reconciliation.

SOURCE

(1) Murthy, Guruprasad. *Financial Accounting.*

(2) Rawat, D.S., *Student's Guide to Accounting Standards.* 7th ed. New Delhi: Taxmann Allied Services (P) Ltd., June, 2006.

(3) *Bombay Chartered Accountants Referencer,* 2007-2008. Mumbai: 45th year of Publication.

6

INDIAN ACCOUNTING STANDARDS VS. US GAAP

There are significant differences between Indian GAAP and US GAAP. US GAAP stipulates stringent accounting treatment as well as disclosure norms, whereas their Indian GAAP in many cases has relaxed requirements (AS 18, 17, AS 3). Similarly, there are several areas where no Accounting Standards have been issued by ICAI. These differences lead to wide variations when Financial Results of Indian Companies are computed under US GAAP and it is found that profits computed under US GAAP are generally lower.

Some of these major differences between US GAAP and Indian GAAP which give rise to differences in profit are highlighted hereunder:

UNDERLYING ASSUMPTIONS

Under Indian GAAP, Financial statements are prepared in accordance with the principle of conservatism which basically means "***Anticipate no profits and provide for all possible losses***". Under US GAAP conservatism is not considered, if it leads to deliberate and consistent understatements.

PRUDENCE vs. RULES

The Institute of Chartered Accountants of India (ICAI) has been structuring Accounting Standards based on the International Accounting Standards (IAS), which employ concepts and '***prudence***' as the principle in contrast to the US GAAP, which are "***rule-oriented***", detailed and complex. It is quite easy for the US accountants to handle issues that fall within the rules, while the International Accounting Standards provide a general framework of accounting standards, which emphasise "***substance over form***" for accounting. These rules are less descriptive and their application is based on prudence. US GAAP has thus issued several Industry specific GAAP, like SFAS 51 (Cable TV), SFAS 50 (Record and Music Industry), SFAS 53 (Motion Picture Industry), etc.

FORMAT/PRESENTATION OF FINANCIAL STATEMENTS

Under Indian GAAP, financial statements are prepared in accordance with the presentation requirements of Schedule VI to the Companies Act, 1956. On the other hand financial statements prepared as per US GAAP are not required to be prepared under any specific format as long as they comply with the disclosure requirements of US GAAP. Financial statements to be filed with SEC included.

CONSOLIDATION OF SUBSIDIARY COMPANIES

Under Indian GAAP (AS 21), consolidation of accounts of subsidiary companies is not mandatory. AS 21 is mandatory, if an enterprise presents consolidated financial statements. In other words, the accounting standard does not mandate an enterprise to present consolidated financial statements but, if the enterprise presents consolidated financial statements for complying with the requirements of any statute or otherwise, it should prepare and present consolidated financial statements in accordance with AS 21. Thus, the financial income of any company taken in isolation neither reveals the quantum of business between the group companies nor does it reveal the true picture of the Group. Savvy promoters hive off their loss making divisions into separate subsidiaries, so that financial statement of their Flagship Company looks attractive. Under US GAAP (SFAS 94), Consolidation of results of subsidiary companies is mandatory, hence eliminating material, intercompany transaction and giving a true picture of the operations and profitability of the various majority owned business of the group.

CASH FLOW STATEMENT

Under Indian GAAP (AS 3), inclusion of Cash Flow statement in financial statements is mandatory only for companies whose shares are listed on recognized stock exchanges and certain enterprises whose turnover for the accounting period exceeds ₹ 50 crores. Thus, unlisted companies escape the burden of providing cash flow statements as part of their financial statements. On the other hand, US GAAP (SFAS 95) mandates furnishing of cash flow statements for 3 years – current year and immediate two preceding years irrespective of whether the company is listed or not.

INVESTMENTS

Under Indian GAAP (AS 13), investments are classified as current and long-term. These are to be further classified Government or Trust securities, shares, debentures or bonds, investment properties in others – specifying nature. Investments classified as current investments are to be carried in the financial statements at the lowest cost and fair value determined either on an individual investment basis or by category of investment, but not on an overall (or global) basis. Investments classified as long-term investments are carried in the financial statements at cost. However, provision for diminution is to be made to recognise a decline, other than temporary, in the value of the investments, such reduction being determined and made for each investment individually. Under US GAAP (SFAS 115), Investments are required to be segregated in three categories, i.e., held to Maturity Security (Primarily Debt Security), Trading Security and available for sales Security and should be further segregated as Current or Noncurrent on Individual basis. Debt securities that the enterprise has the positive intent and ability to hold to maturity are classified as held-to-maturity securities and reported at amortized cost. Debt and equity securities that are bought and held principally for the purpose of selling them in the near term are classified as trading securities and reported at fair value, with unrealised gains and losses included in earnings. All other securities are classified as available-for-sale securities and reported at fair value, with unrealised gains and losses excluded from earnings and reported in a separate component of shareholders' equity.

DEPRECIATION

Under the Indian GAAP, depreciation is provided based on rates prescribed by the Companies Act, 1956. Higher depreciation provision based on estimated useful life of the assets is permitted, but must be disclosed in Notes to Accounts. (Guidance Note no. 49). Depreciation cannot be provided at a rate lower than prescribed in any circumstances. Similarly, there is no compulsion to provide depreciation at a higher rate, even if the actual wear and tear of the equipment is higher than the rates provided in Companies Act. Thus, an Indian Company can get away with providing with lessor depreciation, if the same is in compliance to Companies Act, 1956. Contrary to this, under the US GAAP, depreciation has to be provided over the estimated useful life of the asset, thus making the accounting more realistic and providing sufficient funds for replacement when the asset becomes obsolete and fully worn out.

FOREIGN CURRENCY TRANSACTIONS

Under Indian GAAP (AS11) Forex transactions (Monetary items) are recorded at the rate prevalent on the transaction date. Year end foreign currency assets and liabilities (Non Monetary Items) are re-stated at the closing exchange rates. Exchange rate differences arising on payments or realizations and restatements at closing exchange rates are treated as profit/loss in the income statement. Exchange fluctuations on liabilities incurred for fixed assets can be capitalized. Under US GAAP (SFAS 52), Gains and losses on foreign currency transactions are generally included in determining net income for the period in which exchange rates change unless the transaction hedges a foreign currency commitment or a net investment in a foreign entity. Capitalization of exchange fluctuation arising from foreign liabilities incurred for acquiring fixed assets does not exist. Translation adjustments are not included in determining net income for the period but are disclosed and accumulated in a separate component of consolidated equity until sale or complete or substantially complete liquidation of the net investment in the foreign entity takes place. US GAAP also permits use of average monthly exchange rate for translation of revenue, expenses and cash flow items, whereas under Indian GAAP, the closing exchange rate for the tansaction date is to be taken for translation purposes.

EXPENDITURE DURING CONSTRUCTION PERIOD

As per the Indian GAAP (Guidance note on '***Treatment of expenditure during construction period***'), all incidental expenditure on construction of assets during project stage are accumulated and allocated to the cost of asset on completion of the project. Contrary to this, under the US GAAP (SFAS 7), such expenditures are divided into two heads – direct and indirect. While, direct expenditure is accumulated and allocated to the cost of asset, indirect expenditures are charged to revenue.

RESEARCH AND DEVELOPMENT EXPENDITURE

Indian GAAP (AS 8) requires research and development expenditure to be charged to profit and loss account, except equipment and machinery which are capitalized and depreciated. Under US GAAP (SFAS 2), all R&D costs are expenses except intangible assets purchased from others and tangible assets that have alternative future uses which are capitalised and depreciated or amortised as R&D expense. Under US GAAP, R&D expenditure incurred on software developments are expenses until technical feasibility is established (SOP 81.1). R&D cost and software development cost incurred under contractual arrangement are treated as cost of revenue.

REVALUATION RESERVE

Under Indian GAAP, if an enterprise needs to revalue its asset due to increase in cost of replacement and provide higher charge to provide for such increased cost of replacement, then the asset can be revalued upward and the unrealised gain on such revaluation can be credited to Revaluation Reserve (Guidance Note no. 57). The incremental depreciation arising out of higher book value may be adjusted against the Revaluation Reserve by transfer to P&L Account. However for window dressing some promoters misutilise this facility to hoodwink the shareholders on many occasions. US GAAP does not allow revaluing upward property, plant and equipment or investment.

LONG-TERM DEBTS

Under US GAAP, the current portion of long-term debt is classified as current liability, whereas under the Indian GAAP, there is no such requirement and hence, the interest accrued on such long-term debt in not taken as current liability.

EXTRAORDINARY ITEMS, PRIOR PERIOD ITEMS AND CHANGES IN ACCOUNTING POLICIES

Under Indian GAAP (AS 5), extraordinary items, prior period items and changes in accounting policies are disclosed without netting off for tax effects. Under US GAAP (SFAS 16) adjustments for tax effects are required to be made while reporting the prior period items.

GOODWILL

Under the Indian GAAP goodwill is capitalized and charged to earnings over 5 to 10 years period. Under US GAAP (SFAS 142), Goodwill and intangible assets that have indefinite useful lives are not amortized, but they are tested at least annually for impairment using a two-step process that begins with an estimation of the fair value of a reporting unit. The first step is a screen for potential impairment and the second step measures the amount of impairment, if any. However, if certain criteria are met, the requirement to test goodwill for impairment annually can be satisfied without a remeasurement of the fair value of a reporting unit.

CAPITAL ISSUE EXPENSES

Under the US GAAP, capital issue expenses are required to be written off when incurred against proceeds of capitals, whereas under Indian GAAP, capital issue expense can be amortized or written off against reserves.

PROPOSED DIVIDEND

Under Indian GAAP, dividends declared are accounted for in the year to which they relate. For example, if dividend for the FY 1999-2000 is declared in September, 2000, then the corresponding charge is made in 2000-2001 as below the line item. Contrary to this, under US GAAP dividends are reduced from the reserves in the year they are declared by the Board. Hence, in this case under US GAAP, it will be charged to profit and loss account of 2000-2001 above the line item.

INVESTMENTS IN ASSOCIATED COMPANIES

Under the Indian GAAP (AS 23), investment in associate companies is initially recorded at cost using the Equity method whereby the investment is initially recorded at cost, identifying any goodwill/capital reserve arising at the time of acquisition. The carrying amount of the investment is adjusted thereafter for the post acquisition change in the investor's share of net assets of the investee. The consolidated statement of profit and loss reflects the investor's share of the results of operations of the investors carried at cost. Under US GAAP (SFAS 115) Investments in Associates are accounted under equity method in Group accounts but would be held at cost in the Investor's own account.

PREOPERATIVE EXPENSES

Under Indian GAAP, (Guidance Note 34 - Treatment of Expenditure during Construction Period), direct revenue expenditure during construction period like preliminary expenses, project related expenditure are allowed to be capitalised. Further, indirect revenue expenditure incidental and related to construction are also permitted to be capitalised. Other indirect revenue expenditure not related to construction, but since they are incurred during construction period are treated as deferred revenue expenditure and classified as Miscellaneous Expenditure in Balance Sheet and written off over a period of 3 to 5 years. Under US GAAP (SFAS 7), the concept of preoperative expenses itself doesn't exist. SOP 98.5 also mandates that all Start-up Costs should be expensed. The enterprise has to prepare its Balance Sheet and Profit and Loss Account as if it was a normal running organization. Expenses have to be charged to revenue and assets are capitalised as a normal organization. The additional disclosures include reporting of cash flow, cumulative revenues and expenses since inception. Upon commencement of normal operations, notes to Statement should disclose that the company was but is no longer is a development stage enterprise. Thus, due to above accounting anomaly, Accounts prepared under Indian GAAP, contain higher charges to depreciation which are to be adjusted suitably under US GAAP adjustments for indirect preoperative expenses and foreign currencies.

EMPLOYEE BENEFITS

Under Indian GAAP, provision for leave encashment is accounted based on actuarial valuation. Compensation to employees who opt for voluntary retirement scheme can be amortized over 60 months. Under US GAAP, provision for leave encashment is accounted on actual basis. Compensation towards voluntary retirement scheme is to be charged in the year in which the employees accept the offer.

LOSS ON EXTINGUISHMENT OF DEBT

Under Indian GAAP, debt extinguishment premiums are adjusted against Securities Premium Account. Under US GAAP, premiums for early extinguishment of debt are expensed as incurred.

Table 6

US GAAP vs. INDIAN GAAP

Sr. No.	*US GAAP*	*Indian GAAP*
(1)	In case of mergers and amalgamation consolidated position is reckoned from date of deal.	In India it is done from date of legal effect, e.g., Reliance Industries.
(2)	Profit or loss on sale of shares (as investment) is adjusted directly to net worth and not taken to profit and loss account.	This is included in profit and loss account and can influence profit or loss for the year substantially.
(3)	Material effect is considered more important than technical effect.	Presentation is driven by British practises.
(4)	Research and development expenses are charged to year when incurred.	Research and development expenses are amortised over beneficial years.
(5)	Indirect expenses in acquisition of assets, e.g., interest on borrowed funds, are not capitalized with assets, but charged to accounts, in the year when incurred.	Interest capitalisation is allowed and depreciation is allowed on it, when added to the asset profit implication of this is different for current and future years. An overstatement of assets also take place.
(6)	Liability for leave encashment for employees is valued on actual expense basis.	Actuarial value is taken for consideration of provision for liability of future leave encashment.
(7)	Compensation offered on Voluntary Retirement Scheme (VRS) is charged in the year of acceptance by employees.	VRS is allowed to be amortised over 4 – 5 years subsequent to year of VRS.
(8)	Compensation cost of employees stock options is amortised over the vesting period and accounted for.	Difference in market price and price at which stock option offered to employees does not require separate accounting.
(9)	Investment in securities is classified separately as tradable (at fair price to market) and long-term (as cost of purchase).	Demarcation of securities as current or permanent is not very clear except for banks.
(10)	Expenses on issue of debt instruments are amortised over debt period.	Expenses on debt issue can be adjusted against share premium account or is amortised over certain number of years.

SOURCE: *The Economic Times,* July 2003. Compiled by Mr. K. K. Nijasure.

7

SCHEDULE VI REVISED

INTRODUCTION

Section 211 and Schedule VI of the Companies Act, 1956, became applicable and effective legislation in 1960, for all companies so defined under Sections 2 (10) and 3* of the said Act.

Indian companies since then were required to prepare and present their annual accounts in the formats prescribed by Schedule VI which had three parts, with effect from 1960, *viz.*, Parts I, II and III. Part IV was introduced in 1995 (15th May, 1995). Thus, the said legislation of Section 211, alongwith Schedule VI, has been in force for nearly five decades. Over the years, corporate experience has revealed that a lot of financial and other information are presented through annual accounts (annual reports) to shareholders (in particular) and different stakeholders in general. Annual reports of some companies run into hundreds of pages and provide very valuable information to the readers from various perspectives (**See Table 12**).

The main objective of '***Annual Accounts***' reporting in the format as prescribed by Schedule VI was to present a '***true and fair***' picture of the company's financial position to shareholders within six months from the close of the financial year (Section 166 of the Companies Act, 1956, as amended from time to time). The financial statements thus were prepared in accordance with the dictates of law and in prescribed format in the case of a Balance Sheet as on date and as per requirements prescribed by law in the case of Profit and Loss account, for the period ending with that date, These were based on the generally accepted accounting principles which in turn followed the accounting assumptions, concepts and conventions. In India in the past, while the law prescribed a *pro forma* for the balance sheet (Part I), there was no such prescribed *pro forma* as such for the profit and loss account. In preparation of the balance sheet and profit and loss account, Part III of schedule VI provided for interpretation and Part IV that was introduced in 1993, provided for the

---

**S3 of Companies Act defines a company as follows: existing company, private company and public company. However, S3 (2) provided for exclusion of companies on account of location of registered office and territorial jurisdiction. Companies registered in Burma, Aden or Pakistan were deemed to be formed and registered outside India.*

format of a cash flow statement. Though the annual reports of the company had voluminous information it was not always easy to sift the relevant from the irrelevant and the fine print from the bold print. Yet many improvements and changes took place over a period of time as presented below:

CHANGES IN COMPANIES ACT (1973)

(1) On 30th October, 1973, one more item was introduced as part of Section 211 and Schedule VI. Part II, then required that quantitative details, with respect to sales, purchase, production, opening and closing balances of stock, shall be presented.

(2) Turnover details in respect of each class of good dealt with by the company, had to be indicated alongwith quantity sold.

(3) In the case of manufacturing companies, similar details of raw materials, WIP and finished goods had to be given alongwith opening and closing balances of stocks.

(4) Similar information, about purchases in case of trading companies, was required to be given and also details about important expenses heads were to be given.

(5) Along with this change, another provision required that if any item shown in the profit and loss account is affected by any change in the basis of accounting, the same should be reported. This provision was there since 1961. A change brought about in 1973 required that: *"any item of the expenses exceeding 1% of the total revenue of the company or ₹ 5,000 whichever is higher, shall be shown as a separate and distinct item against an appropriate account head in the profit and loss account and shall not be combined with miscellaneous expenses."*

(6) One more item related to membership of partnership firm. With effect from 30th October, 1973, it was necessary for companies to show distinctly *"profit or losses earned or incurred on account of membership of a partnership firm"*. This provision introduced in 1973, was a progressive change at that point of time. Now in 2011, it acquires greater import because of the introduction of the concept of Limited Liability Partnership in India since 2008.

(7) October 1998: Accounting Standards had to be followed in preparation of profit and loss account and Balance Sheet. This was made obligatory by an amendment to Section 211 with insertion of new subsections, *viz.*, (3A), (3B) and (3C) with effect from 31st October, 1998. Section 211, Subsection 3B stipulated that as and when there is deviation from the said accounting standards, such deviations should be disclosed alongwith reasons and financial implications thereof. As a result of these subsections, companies started giving separately and in one place the accounting policies of the company to enable the users to understand the accounting themes governing or underlying the financial statements. Prior to this amendment, references to policies adopted concerning individual items in the financial statements, were presented in a rather disjointed manner. Thus, the spirit underlying the accounting policies, followed in the preparation of financial statements, could not be gauged, as the subject matter of accounting policy was geographically spread throughout the Annual Report. Auditors' report also made gross references to such notes, whenever and wherever there was a disagreement by way of disapproval, stricture or qualification regarding final accounts or any part thereof.

The expert committee on Company Law (2005), admitted to the right of shareholders to be informed through simple disclosures bereft of excessive technicalities in its format. Further, the committee also pointed out that small enterprises need not be subjected to the same treatment as large companies with respect to accounting and financial disclosures.

(8) The above changes introduced from time to time, though incremental, rather than quantum jumps, brought to surface information which added value to the shareholders knowledge. It provided a built-in-transparency to transactions which prior to the respective amendments was opaque. Keeping in mind the needs of the emerging environment in the post-liberalisation era of privatisation and globalisation, changes have been introduced in Schedule VI disclosure requirements. In a way, this was long overdue because while continuing with any practice for nearly five decades without change speaks for continuity, it also speaks of obsolescence to the extent of the radical changes that have taken place in the world of finance and accounting.

Large companies with a strong resource base and wide network of stakeholders can afford the cost of an elaborate information system. Small companies can ill afford to expend their exiguous resources on installing elaborate information systems suited to meet technicalities and legalities of disclosures whose nuances and subtleties govern the disciplines of accounting, finance and law.

Accordingly, the Ministry of Corporate Affairs had given the mandate to review Schedule VI to the Institute of Chartered Accountants of India. The mandate, included, *inter alia*, the following:

(a) Simplification of information reporting under Schedule VI.

(b) Prescription of SARAL for Schedule VI for small and medium sized companies

EXHIBIT 12

ICAI STUDY GROUP

The specific objectives of the study group were:

(1) *Simplification of presentation.*

(2) *Examining the existing format with respect to superfluous and obsolete disclosures.*

(3) *Bringing about a synthesis and convergence of accounting and financial disclosures in India with global disclosure requirements and practices.*

(4) *Minimization of disclosure requirements for small and micro companies for reasons mentioned above.*

In addition to the above the study group also expressed the need to induct state-of-the-art inputs by considering ***International Financial Reporting Standards*** (**IFRS**) and other reporting practices.

CHANGES IN SCHEDULE VI

(A) ***Rounding off in Financial Statements: Schedule VI Part II (1960-2002)***: Rounding off of figures presented in the financial statements was permitted. Notes to Balance Sheet, i.e., Schedule VI Part I (Point 3) as "**the figures in the balance sheet may be rounded off to the nearest '000' or '00', as may be convenient or may be expressed in terms of decimals of thousands**." By an amendment with effect from 1st August, 2002, companies were classified on the basis of amount of turnover in any financial year. Three categories were established, based on turnover, *viz.*, less than ₹ 100 crores, ₹ 100 crores to ₹ 500 crores and more than ₹ 500 crores.

Earlier paise could also be given in addition to rupees, if desired. The said expression means that disclosure could be made either only in rupees after being rounded-off to the nearest rupee or paise could also be given. With the change that has been made, financial statements may be rounded off as shown below:

Table 7

REVISED SCHEDULE VI: TURNOVER vs. ROUNDING OFF

TURNOVER	*ROUNDING OFF*
(i) Less than one hundred crore rupees	(i) To the nearest hundreds, thousands, lakhs or millions or decimals thereof.
(ii) One hundred crore rupees or more	(ii) To the nearest, lakhs, millions or crores or decimals thereof.

This change facilitates uniformity to the extent that the unit of measurement is kept consistent over a period of time. However, globally, reporting in millions is a fairly standard and uniform practice. The options to report to the nearest lakhs, million or crores is still an issue in India in financial reporting. Actually, reporting has to be consistent with the global reporting unit of measurement. It would have been a good idea to recommend uniformity in reporting, by all companies, in millions of rupees without ascribing or imputing too much value to choice of reporting as part of consumer sovereignty. In India, understanding and reporting numbers take place through a three tier classification: thousands (three zeros), lakhs (five zeros) and crores (seven zeros). However, in western countries a four tier classification is followed, *viz.*, in thousands (three zeros), millions (six zeros), billions (nine zeros) and trillions (twelve zeros). An inconsistent unit of measurement, with global practice renders the job of inter-country financial reporting a rather difficult and sometimes a hazardous proposition. Without conversions to a standard unit of measurement, comparisons become difficult or can lead to dangerous, wrong information, interpretation and decision making.

(B) ***Change in nomenclature of reporting period:*** The current with respect to the reporting period required that every company presented information for two years, *viz.*, current year and that of previous year for the purpose of comparison of financial results and position as on Balance Sheet date. The exception naturally was for reporting information relating to first year of operation. The expression used in the Companies Act was "**year**" though data for the two accounting periods could be for two different units of time, *viz.*, any combination of nine months, twelve months, fifteen months or eighteen months taken two at a time. This was an anomaly in the present law. It was preposterous but true. This anomaly has been rectified and the expression used now is "**reporting period**" instead of '***year***' earlier. Thus, reporting for any combination of two units of measurement makes sense whatever be the duration of financial accounts for a particular period of operation.

(C) ***Changes on the liability side of the Balance Sheet:*** The broad heads of reporting under the old and new order, for the liabilities side, are presented in **Table 11**.

In the proposed new grouping the following changes can be seen:

ITEM NO.1: SHAREHOLDERS' FUNDS: The nomenclature has changed and is a substitute for the previous title Share Capital. The expression '***Shareholders' Funds***' is broader than the previous expression "**Share Capital**" to include, as shown in **Table 11**, share capital, (1a) reserves and surplus (1b) and money received against share warrants (1c). It is well known that shareholders' funds are also known in accounting parlance as "**Owners' Funds**" or "**Net Worth**".

The new item to be reckoned with is '***Money received against share warrants***'. Warrants, were introduced in the year 2003 (*vide* SEBI Circular dated 14th August, 2003), as part of the Unlisted Public Companies (Preferential Allotment) Rules, 2003.

Section 81 (1A) of Companies Act, 2006 as Amendment in 2004, deals with issuance of "**share warrants**" which is a financial instrument convertible at an agreed exchange ratio into equity shares at a later date and at a predetermined price on a private placement basis. This applies to listed companies whose equity shares are listed on any stock exchange.

Thus, share warrants represent a transaction which results into an increase in the cash at bank on the Asset side and pending the allocation of equity capital to the warrant holders it stands as a "**liability**" to be discharged and shown under the caption '***money received***'.

In the context of changes taking place in methods of mobilizing funds and with a wide array of financial instruments for stakeholders in the market place, this new item helps to capture a situation which normally escaped the attention of existing shareholders. The status of these holders of warrants was innocuous in as much as they were not entitled to receive any dividends and had no voting rights until such time as their contributions got converted into equity share capital and their status altered from a potential to an "**actual stakeholder**". Another reason for the explicit inclusion of "**monies received against share warrants**" is that the "**conversion into equity capital**" by the warrant holders is a certainty. In fact, it is a ***"fait accompli"***. There is no choice in the matter. For some reason if the warrant holders fail to accept the impending status of a shareholder, the monies contributed so far can be forfeited under the terms of issue and the cash received by the company shall be added to reserves account.

This mode of accounting of money raising operations over a period of time has to be contrasted with the item to follow, *viz.*, Share Application Money Pending Allotment, that is to say in case of public issue of shares.

EXHIBIT 13

S 69 – THE COMPANIES ACT, 1956

Section 69 of the Companies Act which relates to prohibition of allotment unless minimum subscription is received, reads as follows: "No allotment shall be made of any share capital of a company offered to the public for subscription, unless the amount stated in the prospectus as the minimum amount which, in the opinion of the Board of Directors, must be raised by the issue of share capital in order to provide for the matters specified in clause 5 of Schedule II has been subscribed and the sum payable on application for the amount so stated has been paid to and received by the company, whether in cash or by a cheque or other instrument which has been paid.

If the conditions aforesaid have not been complied with on the expiry of one hundred and twenty days after the first issue of the prospectus, all moneys received from applicants for shares shall be forthwith repaid to them without interest; and if any such money is not so repaid within one hundred and thirty days after the issue of the prospectus, the directors of the company shall be jointly and severally liable to repay that money with interest at the rate of six per cent per annum from the expiry of the one hundred and thirtieth day.

ITEM NO. 2: SHARE APPLICATION MONEY PENDING ALLOTMENT: If any issue is oversubscribed the excess monies in the hands of the company shall be refunded to the shareholders after adjusting amount towards allotment of shares. In fact, under the provisions of Section 69, the monies accepted towards issue of shares shall be refunded to the applicants within stipulated period if the minimum subscription amount is not received.

This is true for monies received from the general public that is to say parties other than those who are in receipt of preferential offer. However, even under the provisions of section 81 (1A) of Companies Act, relating to private placement bases to any select group of persons in the case of money accepted from investors who are promoters, which is not a public offer, monies can be held under the heading "***Share application money - pending allotment***" indefinitely without any time limit. In the event of the investor (promoter) wanting to divest himself of the status of the shareholder, there is a choice and when so exercised the company shall refund the monies. As mentioned above, such refund facility option is not available for holders of share warrants. Thus, share application money, pending allotment is a stand-alone item which is not to be taken into account as part of net worth and is also not to be taken into account as a base for equity, while computing Debt-Equity ratio. In fact this is not even quasi-equity. Money received against Share Warrants is included as para of item 1 (C) and for all practical purposes it's a part of shareholders funds and is a definite part of either equity share capital or reserves, in the event of forfeiture.

ITEM 1 AGAIN: SHAREHOLDERS FUNDS: (a): **SHARE CAPITAL**: The new schedule VI format and details require that the item Share Capital shall be presented with certain details attached to it. In the present scenario, there are many changes that have taken place with respect to ways and means of financing an enterprise. Thus, today an array of new financial instruments and approaches are in place, *viz.*,

- GDR/ADR, Share Warrants, Employee Stock Options (ESOP) that are convertible into equity.
- Buy-back of shares permitted by Section 77 (A), 77 (AA) and 77 (B) of Companies Act, (with effect from 31st October, 1998) causing a reduction in share capital.
- Share split allowed under the provisions of Section 94 (1(d)) Companies Act increases the number of shares outstanding as on the date of the split.

Most of theses changes are a product of post-liberalisation era. Hence, the new disclosure norms require that all the above financial transactions shall be separately presented through a reconciliation statement regarding numbers of shares outstanding as on Balance Sheet date. In the past, changes to share capital were rather limited and restricted in particular to subsequent issue of share capital (rights issue or public issue); bonus shares, issued out of capitalization of reserves and surplus; shares issued for consideration other than cash; redemption of preference shares and numbers of shares held by majority shareholder/holding company.

Since additions/reduction/changes in any accounting period were not complex, a separate reconciliation statement, as such, was not required particularly for disclosure. However, now, in the revised Schedule VI, a separate reconciliation statement shall be given on the face of the balance sheet to establish a link between Opening and Closing balances of outstanding equity shares at the beginning or closing of the financial year respectively. The events linking the reconciliation could be various episodes described above. Prior to the new disclosure, shares held by promoter/majority shareholder/holding company had to be disclosed separately only if such holding exceeded 50% of the total holding. In other words, disclosure was restricted to promoters having controlling interest. However, now it is necessary that if any entity holds more than 5% of the outstanding shares in the company, the same shall be disclosed completely. This is an offshoot of International Accounting Standard 1 which deals with fair presentation of shareholding pattern.

ITEM 1 (B): RESERVES AND SURPLUS: Section 2 (29 (A)) defines "***net worth***" as "***the sum total of the paid-up capital and free reserves after deducting the provisions or expenses as may be prescribed.***" (*w.e.f.*, 1st April, 2003).

Explanation: For the purposes of this clause, "***free reserves***" means all reserves created out of the profits and share premium account but does not include reserves created out of revaluation of assets, write back of depreciation provisions and amalgamation.

Thus, reserves represent undistributed profits.

There is a change in disclosure with respect to an item called "***Debit balance of Profit and Loss account***". Prior to the recent change the said item was disclosed on the assets side of the Balance Sheet after the caption "***Miscellaneous Expenditure (to the extent not written off or adjusted)***". In the amended disclosure it is necessary that Profit and Loss account (Debit Balance) shall be shown as a deduction from the item called "***Reserves and Surplus***". Thus, disclosure of accumulated profits shall be on a net basis only and that too only on one side of the Balance Sheet that is to say the Liabilities side. In the event of losses in successive years and complete erosion of reserves and surplus, a negative balance i.e. "***Debit balance of Profit and Loss account***" resulting in a negative balance of reserves and surplus shall be presented. Thus, the algebraic sum of share capital and negative reserves and surplus will result in a reduced Net Worth or Shareholder's Funds to that extent.

This is a major departure in disclosure and professionally more realistic as is also the practice adopted by corporates in the US. The changes described above with respect to reconciliation between opening and closing balances of outstanding shares and the disclosure of profit and loss account debit balance as deduction from reserves and surplus are important tools in analysis of financial statements. The former item (outstanding shares) provides ready data for computation and comparison of the diluted earnings per share on a year on year basis and also the price earnings multiple which has its own implication for valuation purposes. The latter item (profit and loss account) plays an important role in the computation of Book Value. Given the new disclosure practice, '***Book Value***' of corporates can be made more comparable year on year basis to assess the financial health of companies. Effective analysis and meaningful interpretation of financial statements is better facilitated through the new disclosure practice.

ITEMS 3 AND 4: NON-CURRENT AND CURRENT LIABILITIES: The present disclosure of sources of borrowed funds under three main headings did not facilitate effective financial analysis and interpretation. It required many assumptions to be made regarding the tenure of the liability. The disclosure of "***Loans***" was with respect to security available, i.e., morgages, hypothecation, lien as the case may be. Very rarely companies disclosed under '***secured or unsecured loans***' the tenure of the loan, in terms of '***short-term***' or '***long-term***' since it was not required as such. In the case of long-term loans, the maturing portion of the principal and the interest accrued but not due within a year was segregated and reclassified to be shown separately as a current liability. Even then '***short-term or long-term***' could not be easily ascertained from the items shown under the caption '***secured***' and/or '***unsecured***'. The focus at that time, to reiterate, was on the nature of the transaction with respect to '***security or otherwise***'. The risk of unsecured liabilities also had implications for assets and whether they were encumbered or not.

This reflected on the fund raising ability of companies in the near future. If security protection is near exhaustion then fund raising capacity also got diluted and was so reflected in the Balance Sheet. Some companies did show the classification of loans under the provisions of Schedule VI and also disclosed the tenure of the loan. Hoechst Pharmaceuticals in the mid 70s is a good example in this behalf. Perhaps there were other companies too. However, there was no uniformity with respect to the definition of short-term and long-term items captured under the caption '***Secured/ Unsecured Loans***'. This defied comparisons between companies and made analysis and interpretation of financial statements a difficult and even hazardous proposition. In many companies, the present disclosure scheme does not disclose the tenure of the loan which is classified as secured loans or unsecured loans. Further, the disclosures are equivocal and do not throw light on the background in which a liability has arisen (See Essar Oil Ltd., 16th Annual Report 2005-06, Schedule III – explanation about Non-convertible Debentures). The amended disclosure required by the new Schedule VI would compel companies to disclose details regarding the tenure of the loans. Similarly,

Gammon India Ltd. in its annual report 2005-06, pg, 62 has given information relating to stock split and other transactions. However, transactions of these types have to be disclosed in a simplified and unequivocal manner, in the future.

AMENDED DISCLOSURE

The amended disclosure requirement with respect to these items in Balance Sheet stipulates that sources of funds be presented under two headings: '***Non-current Liabilities***' and '***Current Liabilities***'. Non-current liabilities include: long-term borrowings, deferred tax liabilities (net), other long-term liabilities and long-term provisions (provisions for retirement benefits).

An excellent example of proactive disclosure of the break-up of Net Deferred Tax Liability is that of Blue Star Ltd. (Annual Report 2005-06) which is presented below:

Table 8

BLUE STAR LTD.

ANNUAL REPORT 2005-06

Net Deferred Tax Liability

Statement showing the break-up of Net Deferred Tax Liability		
	As at March 31, 2006	
	Deferred Tax Asset	*Deferred Tax Liability*
Timing differences on account of: Difference in Book and Income-Tax Depreciation under IT Act, 1961		3126.09
Provision of Doubtful Debts, Advances and Inventories	276.33	
Leave Encashment Provision	160.16	
TOTAL	**436.49**	**3126.09**
Net Deferred Tax Liability	2689.6	
Tax on Net Deferred Tax Liability	905.31	

In the above Table the company has presented the computations of deferred tax assets and liabilities.

Current liabilities include short-term borrowings, trade payables, other current liabilities and short-term provisions. These changes include a migration from three tier classification of sources of funds to a two tier classification. This is a simplification to be commended. Further, in the earlier disclosure norms "***provisions***" were a '***potpourri***' of short and long-term items. This has been done away with and '***provisions***' find a place in both the sections depending upon the tenure of the obligation. This is again a pragmatic amendment and better alignment of individual items to the caption under which they are disclosed. However, certain items have a different position. The earlier disclosure used the expression "***Acceptances***" to disclose "***Bills Payable***". In the amended format it is not clear as to where "***Bills Payable***" shall be included, under "***trade payable***" or "***other current liabilities***". Again certain items like amounts due to subsidiary companies, i.e., (advances from subsidiaries), advance payments from customers/deposits from customers and unexpired portion of subscription/fees for which value is still to be given as may happen in different types of businesses, *viz.*, newspaper companies, insurance companies, clubs, associations, etc. Further certain important items are to be shown separately, *viz.*, investor education and protection fund, unpaid dividend, unpaid application money due for refund, unpaid matured deposits, unpaid matured debentures and interest accrued on the said listed items.

ASSET SIDE OF SCHEDULE VI

The asset side of Schedule VI, in the prevailing sequence, started with assets of the longest tenure i.e. Fixed Assets followed by Investments and Current Assets, Loans and Advances. The last two items that do not fit into above were: Miscellaneous Expenditure (to the extent not written off or adjusted) and Profit and Loss Account (Debit Balance).

In the amended order, the assets side (present in **Table 11**) is classified in terms of tenure in the main (non-current and current assets in that order) and tangibility or otherwise. The classification earlier in the fixed assets category was in terms of movable or immovable fixed assets. Of course, it did include intangible assets, *viz.*, goodwill, patents, trademarks and copyrights *et al.* The immovable assets included "***Land and Buildings and Leaseholds***". "All other tangible and movable were also included under Fixed Assets, *viz.*, plant and machinery, furniture and fittings, livestock, vehicles and railways sidings.

In the amended Schedule VI "***Fixed Assets***" included under the caption non-current assets are classified as "***Tangible Assets***" and "***Intangible Assets***".

The tangible assets include all the items which were present earlier with scope for special items if any, to be included under the caption '***others***' after specifying the nature, keeping it open to include, amongst other things, items like railway siding, livestock and biological assets like plants, standing trees and development of property. The note to para 1 says "***assets under lease shall be separately specified under each class of asset***". For example in Siemens Ltd., the note to fixed assets discloses the plant and machinery which includes equipment given on lease. (Annual Report 2008, pg. 69).

Para 3 says that a reconciliation of the gross and net carrying amounts of each class of asset shall be presented after taking into account the opening and closing balances and also accounting for "***additions, disposals and acquisition through business combinations***" and "***other adjustment including the related depreciation and impairment losses/reversals shall be disclosed separately.***" There is yet another instruction which has to be followed while drawing the Balance Sheet of the company, i.e., changes in the value of asset that are caused "***due to reduction of capital or revaluation of assets***". In such cases, every balance sheet subsequent to date of such decrease or increase shall show the relevant new values as applicable. Such information shall be presented for the first five years subsequent to the date of such change (decrease or increase) occurs.

INTANGIBLE ASSETS

Intangible assets include a long list and starts with goodwill, brands/trademarks, computer software, mastheads and publishing titles, mining rights, copyrights and patents and other intellectual property rights, services and operating rights, recipes, formulae, models, designs and prototypes, licenses and franchise, other (specify nature). The last category, *viz.*, "***others***" would include items like toll collection rights, (unexpired periods) development rights or transferable development rights purchased). The rules of reconciling opening and closing and also disclosures regarding changes in values due to reduction/re-valuation applicable to tangible assets shall apply to intangible assets too.

The new items in the revised Schedule VI are computer software and mining rights. Items like paintings, works of art, antiques, old stamps and coins, philately and numismatics, were already on the list. However, the expression, intellectual property rights, finds a place in the list of intangible assets which include *inter alia* slogans, catch-lines, music, lyric dimension and other creative aspects, connected with advertising, particularly commercials. Again, recipes formulae, models, designs and prototypes, licenses and franchise, other (specify nature) which find a place, now in intangible asset, is augmented by the first three items, *viz.*, mast heads and publishing titles, mining rights and computer software.

'***Non-current Investments***' refers to a new title to the extent of prefix '***non-current***'. The expression investment was an independent, standalone caption in the former Schedule VI list of assets. In the amended Schedule VI, '***non-current investment***' shall be classified, again like the erstwhile requirements into '***Trade Investments***' and '***Other Investments***'. There is no change on that count. However, the list of Non-current Investments include '***investments in property***' and '***investments in financial assets***' like equity instruments, preference shares, Government or Trust securities, debentures or bonds, mutual funds. Of course '***investments in partnership firms***' and apparently '***investments in limited liability partnerships***' also find a place. There is no specific mention of '***Limited Liability Partnership***' in this category, as understood by a separate legislation in this behalf, *viz.*, the Limited Liability Partnership Act (LLP) (2008). Again, there is no separate inclusion of LLP in any other category. In the earlier Schedule VI only '***investments in partnership***' had to be recorded and disclosed. However, in the amended Schedule VI additional information has to be provided, *viz.*, names of the firms, names of all their partners, total capital and the share of each partner. It is useful to note, that the item '***investment in partnership firms***' was first introduced on and from 9th November, 1973. It was to highlight investment in land, by manufacturing and other companies in the garb of investment in Partnership Firm.

There is one more change which is reflected in the revised Schedule VI *vis-à-vis* the former classification of investments. In the earlier classification "***Balance of unutilized monies raised by issue of Share Capital or Debentures/Bonds***". (Inserted by notification no. GSR 423(E), dated 13th September, 1996). In the revised Schedule VI, this item finds a place in the list of Current Assets, because of its nature in terms of its tenure. The amount held by a company against this account has to be refunded if the company does not make allotment or allots only partially.

Any item in the "***Non-current Investment***" category which does not find a specific designated position in the above list, is to be shown as "***other non-current investments***". There is a detailed note as to the information to be given regarding the destination of these investments and the form of organisation, alongwith the amount of investment in which such non-current investments are made. Further, investments carried at any value other than cost should be separately disclosed and the basis of valuation has to be specified. Disclosure regarding the investments (quoted and unquoted), market valuation and diminution thereof shall be separately disclosed as was required earlier too.

LONG-TERM LOANS AND ADVANCES

The security aspect is also to be brought into the classification by identifying a three-tier security, *viz.*, secured, considered good, unsecured, considered good and unsecured doubtful. Depending upon the integrity of debtors, '***allowance for bad and doubtful loans and advances***' shall be disclosed under the relevant heads separately. This applies to loans and advances due by Directors or other officers or by firms or private companies in which any Director is a partner or a Director or member. There is no specific change in the contents of the items for inclusion under this caption except in the nomenclature and inclusion and exclusion of certain items under each subheading. Thus,

(1) Capital advances will now include '***advances to suppliers of goods, services and capital goods***'.

(2) Security deposits will include balances with customs, port trust, municipality, electricity companies *et al.* (where they were payable on demand).

(3) Loans and advances to related parties will include "***advances and loans to subsidiaries***" or "***partnership firms in which the company or its subsidiary is a partner***". This will also include "***associate companies/parties***".

(4) "***Other loans and advances (specify nature)***" will include bills of exchange, prepaid expenses and advances recoverable in cash or in kind or for value to be received (e.g., rates and taxes, insurance, subscriptions, etc.). With respect to classification on account of security, assessment of integrity of debtors and disclosure, regarding loans and advances due by principal officers, there is no change with respect to "***disclosures***". Earlier, such details were shown as part of instructions defined as '***instructions in accordance with which assets should be made out***'.

The next item is "***Other Non-current Assets***" which is again long-term in nature and will include long-term trade receivables and shall follow all the rules of disclosure, concerning security and integrity of receivables and amounts due from principal officers of the company. It is useful to note that long-term trade receivables include '***trade receivables on deferred credit terms***'. However, the revised Schedule VI does not mention anything about items such as '***Leased Rentals Receivable***' (against leased assets that are leased out to third parties). However, assets taken on lease are separately covered in the category of "***non-current assets***" for disclosure of leased assets.

The last item in the '***other non-current assets***' reads as '***Others (specify nature)***'. Apparently, this is a residual subtitle to capture items which do not fit into any of the earlier categories.

CURRENT ASSETS: CURRENT INVESTMENTS

Items are classified on similar lines as "***non-current investments***" and the rules of disclosure are similar, except for the item "***investment in property***" which finds a first place in "***non-current investments***".

The next item is inventory. The list of items to be included in inventories is identical to the earlier list presented in the old Schedule VI which uses the expression "***stock-in-trade***" alongwith the condition that mode of valuation of stock shall be stated and the amount in respect of raw materials shall also be stated separately. Further it also mentions that for "***work-in-progress***" mode of valuation should be stated. However, the new Schedule VI requires that for all elements of inventory listed, the mode of valuation shall be stated. The new Schedule VI mentions specifically the inclusion of "***goods-in-transit***" under the relevant subhead of inventories. This was not so in the old Schedule VI, though the accounting convention about disclosure practices did mention about "***goods-in-transit***". The exigencies posted by "***branch accounting***" necessitated the same. Post-liberalisation the import profile of India Inc., has undergone a radical change in a number of items and volume too. Hence, the disclosure practices with respect to "***goods-in-transit***" has perhaps found specific mention.

It is recommended that investments held by business as stock-in-trade should be shown accordingly with clear and specific mention about the same with respect to type of security, opening and closing balances alongwith the physical and financial value of the investments in order to present a true and fair picture of the assets held by a company in the category of current investments. A good example again of such a forward looking disclosure can be seen in the annual report of Blue Star Ltd. of 2005-06 (pp. 78) which shows the investment held as stock-in-trade separately.

It may be noted that inventories which form a part of the current assets are disclosed at cost price or market price whichever is lower based on the conservatism principle. Further, if the market price is lower than cost price there is no specific reserve required to be created to account for the depreciation in the value of stock. However, investment was and continues to be disclosed at cost when shown under the caption '***investment***'. Even though the market price of the investment may be lower than the investment cost, investments are disclosed at cost. However, a specific reserve is created to account for the different between the Market price and the Cost price. In the revised Schedule VI wherever the company has investments held as stock-in-trade, the disclosure has to be on a '***mark to market***' basis. In other words, investments will be disclosed at market price in case the market price is lower than cost price. Thus, putting the conservatism principle automatically into action. The difference between Cost price and Market price automatically gets charged to profit and loss account for the said accounting period. To that extent the disclosures present a true and fair picture of the reported profits and the value of the concerned assets (investment) held as stock-in-trade. In the context of the global meltdown and the consequent debacle in the stock market when the BSE sensex was at its lowest on 6th March, 2009 at 8104. The extent of loss on account of investments was almost 50% of purchase price. In the case of real estate company the fall was of the order of 80% of their peak value of 8th January, 2008 when the BSE Sensex was at 20,873. Yet the fall in value of assets (investment) remained unaccounted for leaving the bottomline bolstered to that extent. This was contrary to the principle of conservatism.

Table 9

BLUE STAR LTD.

ANNUAL REPORT 2005-06

Investment held as Stock-in-trade

Statement showing investment held as stock-in-trade					
Investment	*Type of Security*	*Opening Balance*		*Closing Balance*	
		Nos.	*Value (₹ in lakhs)*	*Nos.*	*Value (₹ in lakhs)*
Master Gain 92	Mutual Fund units	3600	0.35	3600	0.35
Master Plus	Mutual Fund units	38200	4.68	38200	4.68
TOTAL		**41800**	**5.03**	**41800**	**5.03**

TRADE RECEIVABLES: There is no change in the disclosure contents of this item which was previously called "***Sundry Debtors***".

CASH AND CASH EQUIVALENT: There are a few changes in this category. It is necessary to disclose separately: "***cheques and drafts on hand***". Earmarked balances with banks (eg., unpaid dividend) shall be separately stated. "***Balances with banks to the extent held as margin money or security against the borrowings, guarantees, other commitments, etc.,***" shall be disclosed separately. Thus, maturity of bank deposits has to be separately disclosed. If the bank deposits have a maturity periods exceeding 12 months they will still be classified as current investment because they are readily convertible into cash on demand, even before maturity, albeit after suffering penalty charge/loss of interest. "***Repatriation restrictions***", if any, in respect of cash and bank balances shall be separately stated. Bank deposits with more than 12 months maturity shall be disclosed separately. Now the destination of cash is ascertained in a specific manner and the information presented is made more meaningful and intelligible to the reader rather than a generic picture of "***cash and cash equivalent***" which aggregates all and sundry items. Such a detailed classification helps to know the extent to which liquid cash is blocked in assets which cannot be easily converted into cash. This provides financial analysts with a new vista for establishing relevant liquidity indicators in the "***current ratio and acid test ratio*** *" and the* "***ratio of cash and cash equivalent to total current assets***". Decisions have to be taken for inclusion and exclusion of relevant items prior to the computation of these ratios, e.g., software companies holding large cash balances for the purpose of acquisitions in "***All Cash Deals***" and do not consider the same as "***idle cash***" with them.

SHORT-TERM LOANS AND ADVANCES*:** The earlier Schedule VI used the expression "loans and advances***". However, now the prefix "***short-term***" has been provided because classification of items is driven by the "***tenure of loan/advance***". Earlier loans and advances to subsidiary associate companies were held so for a long period of time as a means of financing their business operations. However, they were not disclosed as such. Hopefully, this will become clear when classified in terms of tenure *viz.* short-term or long-term.

OTHER CURRENT ASSETS*:** The revised Schedule VI itself mentions that this heading is residual in nature and 'is an all-inclusive heading***' which incorporates current assets that do not fit into any other asset categories. For example, the earlier Schedule VI had an item called '***interest accrued on investments***'. Since this item does not find a specific place in the revised Schedule VI apparently it will be included in '***other current assets***'. The last item above the line in old order was "***Miscellaneous Expenditure (to the extent not written off or adjusted)***". There are three other items which find a place above the line, *viz.*,

(a) "***Dividends proposed to be distributed to shareholders***" (equity and preference) alongwith the arrears of fixed cumulative dividends.
(b) If funds raised through issue of securities, made for specific purpose and as on the date of Balance Sheet the whole amount has not been used, unutilised amount has to be shown separately along with an explanation as to how they have been deployed. This has a cross reference to the item "***earmarked balances under cash and cash equivalents***".

If in the opinion of the Board, any of the assets other than fixed assets and non-current investments do not have a value on realization in the ordinary course of business at least equal to the amount at which they are stated, the fact that the Board is of that opinion, shall be stated. This item is an explanatory note to be observed while preparing the balance sheet for specific disclosure. It is not an item "***per se***". None of the above inputs are items *per se*.

PROFIT AND LOSS ACCOUNT

Part II of Schedule VI provided for "***Item to be disclosed separately in Profit and Loss A/c.***" The first instruction provided for a general guidelines on disclosure and reads as follows: '***The Profit and Loss Account shall disclose every material feature, including credits or receipts and debits or expenses in respect of non-recurring or exceptional transactions***'. This general guideline is followed by specific disclosure requirements listed with respect to items of income and expenses. In the revised Schedule VI, Part II for the first time in the history of corporate accounting, the Act specifies the form of profit and loss account now which is reworded as statement of profit and loss. The said *pro forma* is followed by general instructions to be followed for its preparation.

The first conspicuous change is the title of the statement from profit and loss account to statement of profit and loss. Now, there is compatibility between the title and the contents of the statement. Earlier, a statement used to be called as profit and loss account because the law stipulated so. The law stipulates that the erstwhile profit and loss account shall be called as '***statement of profit and loss***'. Thus, companies which were till recently following the '***T***' shaped ledger format to present the profit and loss account have to compulsorily change over to what is known in business parlance as '***vertical format***'.

The key features of the new statement of profit and loss are as follows:

On the income side rather than using the expression '***income***' followed by specific expressions like '***sales income, other income, profit/loss on investments, profit/loss on sale of assets***' Part II uses the expression '***revenue from operations***' and includes '***sale of products, sale of services and other operating revenues***'. Further, adjustment (deductions) for excise duty has to be shown. The second item is '***other income***' which includes, *inter alia*, '***interest income, dividend income, net gain or loss on sale of investment***', '***other non-operating income***' (net of expenses directly attributably to such income). The above classification of earnings of a company into two distinct categories revenues from operations and other income, provide for a natural classification of items of income which facilitates analysis of the earnings profile of a company in terms of the originating source of earnings. The disclosure is clear and important sources of earnings do not get merged into an omnibus title called miscellaneous. Even though a particular item was material enough to be shown separately yet rules of classification put such item by default in miscellaneous income. Its not untrue to say that in quite a few places, the miscellaneous income used to exceed the net profit shown by the company thus helping enterprise to make up for the losses from operations.

The next item is category of expenses which includes raw materials consumed, purchases of stock-in-trade, changes in inventory, employee benefits expense, finance cost and other expenses. This is a standard classification of individual elements of manufacturing cost with respect to materials and adjustment of inventories. Finance cost shown separately includes interest expense, other borrowing cost and applicable net gain/loss on foreign currency transaction and translation. Earlier, a manufacturing company used to classify its expenses as manufacturing and other expenses, depreciation and interest (net). In some companies, '***interest charges***' are captured under the heading '***finance charges***'. Further, invariably non-cash charges were presented under the heading '***depreciation***'. With the emergence of the knowledge society and currency of intellectual property rights, the disclosure requirements have kept pace with changing times and the new expression '***in lieu of depreciation***' is '***depreciation and amortisation***'. However, it may be noted that the expenses mentioned above have to be presented in a particular manner: employee benefit expenses shall show separately salaries and wages, contribution to provident and other funds, expense on Employee Stock Option Scheme (ESOS) and Employee Stock Purchase Plan (ESPP), staff welfare expenses.

There is one more item to be reckoned with which in the earlier Schedule VI part II read as follows: Miscellaneous expenses (Expense totaling 1% of total revenue of the Company or ₹ 5,000 whichever is higher shall be shown as a separate item). In the revised Schedule VI para 5 (c) says "***any item of income or expenditure which exceeds one per cent of the revenue from operations or ₹ 1,00,000 whichever is higher***". Keeping in mind the nature of business, inflation and other changes in the environment, the limit has been raised to ₹ 1,00,000. This change applies to both income and expenditure.

Given the total revenue and total expenses the difference is the profit before exceptional and extraordinary items and tax against which exceptional items are adjusted.

Yet another item, *viz.*, other expenses which includes any recurring debit on expense account which is not captured under any one of the items listed as expenses. A special feature of the notes to profit and loss account shows two items which need to be specially mentioned, *viz.*, (g) and (h), i.e., to say net gain/loss on sale of investments and adjustments to the carrying amount of investments. Since, there are many companies which are cash rich and carry huge amounts of cash and other financial assets under the heading investment, companies are required to make special mention about the impact of holding such investments. Two aspects need to be disclosed in the body of the statement of profit and loss account as just mentioned. Presently, companies do disclose in the Schedules, for e.g., in Hero Honda Motors Ltd., for the financial year ended 31st March, 2010, there is a provision for diminution in value of investment which is presented as follows:

PROVISION FOR DIMINUTION IN VALUE OF INVESTMENT	₹ CRORES
Current non-trade investment	2.27
Long-term non-trade investment	0.38

Incidentally, Hero Honda Motors which is in the business of manufacturing bikes has investment equivalent to ₹ 3926 crores which exceeds the gross block of the company in the said year by ₹ 1175 crores. There are quite a few companies which have staggering amounts of investments and therefore interest/dividend income. Hence, the disclosure of information relating to the provision for diminution in the value of investment is of utmost importance. Hence, this provision helps to present a true and fair picture in the case of non-banking, financial companies and banks too. In view of the stringent capital adequacy norms and other checks and balances on the risk exposure of banks, disclosure regarding fall in value of investments becomes very important. Cash rich companies like TCS, Wipro, Infosys, Maruti Udyog, Glaxo, Hindustan Unilever, Colgate *et al.*, will find this provision very important to disclose the rise and fall in the value of their investment portfolio.

Another item net gain or loss on foreign currency transaction and translation (other than considered as finance cost) assumes significance in the context of derivatives trading (currency futures). Companies which have a large import obligations like oil and fertilizer companies) will be affected by this item. Further, companies whose earnings are mainly in foreign exchange, *viz.*, shipping, airlines, export-oriented companies particularly IT companies (Infosys, TCS, Wipro), jewellery exports *et al.*, will also be affected. The impact of exposure to export earnings and import expenses was seen during the global meltdown when the rupee depreciated from 1 USD = ₹ 44 to 1 \$ = ₹ 52. Such as massive depreciation had a whopping impact on the bottom-line of the company and hence accounting for the same immediately along with appropriate disclosure is a must for presenting a true and fair picture of the financial position of a company. The volatility of the foreign exchange rate position had its own toll on companies. Software companies gained because of the deprecation in rupee and oil companies gained because of the fall in the crude oil prices by more than 50% around that time. In the same vein, companies which had a huge import and minimal or no exports, specially chemical companies, suffered because the devaluation of the rupee increased the obligation to the foreign exporter and there was no accompanying benefits for lack of export sales. Thus, this disclosure regarding gain or loss on foreign currency transaction and translation is extremely important because of the impact on exposures to risk of vagaries and volatility of the foreign exchange market in the context of liberalisation, privatization and globalization. In the earlier disclosure, such transactions and translations did not find specific mention. Hence, the new requirement in this behalf represents an improved and extended disclosure of business transactions along with its impact on the bottom-line of the company. Further, such a disclosure leaves the financial statements impeccable from the point of view of conservatism.

In this context, the disclosure by Siemens Ltd., merits special mention as shown below:

EXHIBIT 14

SIEMENS LTD.
DERIVATIVE INSTRUMENTS

The Company's exposure to foreign currency fluctuations relates to foreign currency assets, liabilities and forecasted cash flows. The Company limits the effects of foreign exchange rate fluctuations by following established risk management policies including the use of derivatives. The Company enters into forward exchange contracts, where the counterparty is a bank.

*As per Accounting Standard ('AS') 11 - "**The effects of changes in foreign exchange rates the premium or the discount on forward exchange contracts not relating to firm commitments or highly probable forecast transactions and not intended for trading or speculation purpose is amortized as expense or income over the life of the contract. Forward contracts, which are not covered by AS 11, are measured using the mark-to-market principle with the resulting gains/losses thereon being recorded in the profit and loss account**".*

Again Siemens in its profit and loss account for the year ended 30th September, 2008 (**Table 10**) is a good example of disclosure of profit before tax and profit after tax as shown, given the break-up of profit from discontinued operations, as well as continuing operations:

Table 10

SIEMENS Ltd.

Profit and loss account for the year ended 30 September 2008
(CURRENCY: INR Thousands)

		2008
Profit before tax before exceptional income		
Exceptional income:		
— Profit on sale of Information and Communication division		—
— Profit on sale of Building Technologies division		10,635
— Profit on sale of Automotive division		1,235,151
— Profit on sale of long-term investment		0
		8,917,686
Profit before tax		
Consists of:		
— Discontinued operations	4	8,232
— Continuing operations		8,909,454
		8,917,686

contd. ...

contd. ...

Provision for tax		
Current tax		–3,493,161
Fringe benefit tax		–120,296
Deferred tax credit/(charge)		629,037
		5,933,266
Profit after tax		
Consists of:		
— Discontinued operations	4	5,434
— Continuing operations		5,927,832
Amount available for appropriation		**5,933,266**

EXHIBIT 15

REVISED SCHEDULE VI (SECTION 211)

PRELUDE

Six General Instructions Plus one note

PART I

(1) *Revised Form of Balance Sheet*

(2) *General Instructions for preparation of Balance Sheet (Twenty Three Main Instructions)*

And

PART II

(1) *Form of Statement of Profit and Loss (Sixteen Items) (Prescribed form introduced for the first time)*

(2) *General Instructions for preparation of Statement of Profit and Loss (Five Main Instructions)*

Table 11

REVISED SCHEDULE VI — AMENDED BALANCE SHEET PRO FORMA

I. EQUITY AND LIABILITIES	II. ASSETS
(1) Shareholders' funds	**(1) Non-current assets**
(a) Share capital	*(a)* Fixed assets
(b) Reserves and surplus	(i) Tangible assets
(c) Money received against share warrants	(ii) Intangible assets
	(iii) Capital work-in-progress
	(iv) Intangible assets under development
(2) Share application money pending allotment	*(b)* Non-current investments
	(c) Deferred tax assets (net)
	(d) Long-term loans and advances
	(e) Other non-current assets
(3) Non-current liabilities	**(2) Current assets**
(a) Long-term borrowings	*(a)* Current investments
(b) Deferred tax liabilities (Net)	*(b)* Inventories
(c) Other long-term liabilities	*(c)* Trade receivables
(d) Long-term provisions	*(d)* Cash and cash equivalents
	(e) Short-term loans and advances
	(f) Other current assets
(4) Current liabilities	
(a) Short-term borrowings	
(b) Trade payables	
(c) Other current liabilities	
TOTAL	**TOTAL**

Table 12

TATA STEEL LTD.

CONTENTS OF ANNUAL REPORT 2009-10

8

CASH FLOW DEFINITIONS

In the normal course, financial statements usually meant a profit and loss account (income statement) and balance sheet. However, in the late 1980s to **improve transparency and disclosure** it was thought necessary to augment the quantum and content of information supplied to users of accounting information. Since then, cash flow statements have come to stay as part of the package of financial statements prepared and presented to disclose the financial affairs of the business. This helps users or stakeholders to be better informed and guided for decision making.

A typical profit and loss account is drawn using the accrual system which recognizes income and expenses regardless of whether cash has come in (income) or whether cash has gone out (expenses). The four accrual rules – two concerning income and two concerning expenses need to be recapitulated.* I when cash flows are to be captured, a new look at the profit and loss account is necessary. Presented below are a few inputs concerning the definitions and computations concerning cash flows.

(1) NET WORTH:

Equity Share Capital + Reserves and Surplus

Net Worth is also known as Owners Funds or Shareholder's Equity.

N.B.: Some sources define Net Worth as inclusive of preference shares too. Yet other sources distinguish between Common stockholders' equity and Total equity. The former is net worth as defined above and the latter is inclusive of preference shares.

(2) CAPITAL EMPLOYED:

Net Worth + Long-term Liabilities OR Net Fixed Assets + Net Working Capital where

Net Working Capital = Current Assets *minus* Current Liabilities

**An income is not earned merely because cash is earned; an income is earned whether cash is received now or later; an expense is not incurred merely because cash is paid and an expense is incurred whether cash is paid now or later.*

(3) **ACCOUNTING PROFIT also known as BOOK PROFIT:**
Net Income **OR** Profit after Interest and Taxes **OR** Earnings after Interest and Taxes.

(4) **NET CASH FLOW (Cash Profit):**
Profit after Interest and Tax + Non Cash Charges, *viz.*, Depreciation, Amortization and Notional Losses, *viz.*, losses on exchange rate variation, gains on account of revaluation. Cash Profits differ from accounting profit because some of the revenues and expenses reflected in accounting profits may not have been received or paid out in cash during the year.

(5) **CASH FLOW STATEMENT:**
- Net Cash Flow.
- Changes in Net Working Capital include: Increase in Inventories (Use of Cash), Decrease in Inventories (Source of Cash), Increase in Sundry Debtors (Use of Cash), Decrease in Sundry Debtors (Source of Cash), Increase in Loans and Advances, Decrease in Loans and Advances, Increase in any other current assets and Decrease in any other current assets.
- Changes in Cash are handled separately.
- Other Current Assets.

(6) Cash Profit as defined, in 4 above, adjusted for changes in current assets (other than cash) and current liabilities (non-interest bearing current liabilities, *viz.*, accrued expenses and accounts payable, gives "***Cash Flows from Operating Activities***". Adjustments with respect to current liabilities are to be identified as increase in sundry creditors (source of cash) and decrease in sundry creditors (use of cash). The same rule applies to increase or decrease in accrued expenses.

(7) Thus a **statement of 'Cash Flows' captures** three dimensions, *viz.*, operating activities, investing activities and financing activities.
The sum of the above three types of cash flows reflects Net (Increase or Decrease) of Cash and Cash Equivalents.

(8) **CASH FLOW FROM OPERATIONS:**
Net Income + Depreciation/Amortization (+ or –) Adjustments due to: Current Assets (Inventories and Sundry Debtors) and Current Liabilities (Sundry Creditors and Accrued Expenses)

(9) **Cash Flow from Long-term Investing Activities:**
- Increase in Fixed Assets due to acquisitions (Use of Cash).
- Decrease in Fixed Assets due to disposal of (sale) of fixed assets (Sources of cash).

The algebraic sum of the above two items is the cash flow from '***Long-term Investing Activities.***'

(10) **Cash Flow from Financing Activities:**
- Increase in Bills Payable
- Increase in Bonds/Debentures
- Increase in Borrowings

→ **Sources of Cash**

- Issue of Shares.
- Special Cases (e.g.: Bonus Debentures – HLL (HUL) – where no cash came in or went out. However, a portion of reserves was converted into redeemable loan liability which created a claim on future cash flows by way of payment of interest and re-payment of loans).

CASH FLOW STATEMENT

A company runs its day to day business with cash and not the profits. The bank account of a company records and runs on the basis of cash receipts and cash payments. A cheque is issued not out of the profits, but out of the cash lying in the bank account. Of course, the profits earned or losses incurred influence the cash position strongly. A company reporting losses might still be generating cash, since there are many non-cash charges that enter into the determination of profit/loss. One such non-cash charge is depreciation. For example, a company reporting a loss of ₹ 11.5 crore after charging depreciation of ₹ 22.50 crore still generates a cash profit of ₹ 11 crore, assuming there were no other non-cash charges. It is therefore crucial to understand the cash flows generated by a company.

EXHIBIT 15 (A)

CASH FLOWS

- *"An accounting presentation showing how much of cash generated by the business remains after loan amortisation obligations (interest payment + loan instalment repayment).*
- *A projected cash flow statement indicates whether the business will have cash to pay its expenses, loans and make a profit.*
- *Cash flows can be calculated for any given period of time, normally done on a monthly basis.*
- *Cash flow is also, one of the "Cs" evaluated in determining a loan applicant's creditworthiness. The four other Cs are Character, Collateral, Creditworthiness and Capital."*

SOURCE: *www.investordictionary.com*

INCOME STATEMENT

The income statement is a summary of the revenues, costs and expenses based on the accrual system. Most companies use accrual basis for accounting. In accrual basis accounting income is recognised when the sale is completed and expenses are recognized when they are incurred. Many operating cash movements do not appear in the income statement. However, *the cash flow statement represents monies*, that is to say *cash actually moving in and out of a business*. This method gives emphasis to cash basis accounting rather than accrual basis. In cash basis accounting, revenue is not counted until the cash is received and expenses are recognized only when the cash is paid out.

EXHIBIT 16

CASH FLOW OF A BUSINESS – DEFINITION

Cash Flow of a business for a particular accounting period is defined as

Profit after Interest and Taxes	+	Non cash charges, *viz.*, Depreciation and Amortization	=	Cash Flow
₹ 4061		₹ 577		₹ 4638*

****SOURCE:*** *Annual Report 2010-11, Larsen & Toubro, p. 125*

The cash flow arrived at using the above formula **shows the liquidity profile of business in terms of quantum of cash generated from operations for a particular accounting period.** It is an important measure of business performance using cash as the criteria and excludes capital expenditure or working capital requirements. The cash flow from operations should be positive to absorb the burden of future needs of cash outlays on fixed and current assets. Negative cash flow is indicative of a cash crunch and the inability of cash inflows to cover the cash outflows.

Many schools of thought vow by cash as the key criteria of successful business management rather than book profits, though statutes demand that the financial statements namely the profit and loss account and balance sheet be drawn using the accrual system. Yet today, even statutes have recognized the role and importance of cash as one of the key variables to be taken into account in presenting a true and fair picture of the financial position of business. Hence, corporates today prepare amongst other statements, a cash flow statement using professional guidelines. Invariably, a cash flow statement captures cash implications arising out of operations, investment and financing activities.

METHODS FOR PRESENTING CASH FLOWS

"A cash flow statement is a statement produced for management showing, by broad category, cash receipts and payments in a period or forecasts for future periods."

–The Chartered Institute of Management Accountants (CIMA)

It is prepared either by the receipts and payments method or the balance sheet method.

Table 13

CASH FLOW STATEMENT – RECEIPTS AND PAYMENTS METHOD

	₹	₹	₹
Bank overdraft at beginning			**(1000)**
Receipts			
Payment by debtors	300		
Investment income (net)	200		
		500	
Payments			
Materials	100		
Wages and salaries – net	60		
Capital expenditure	70		
Interest charges	15		
Advance tax	10		
Dividend payments	45		
		(300)	
OVERDRAFT AT END			**(1200)**

Table 14

CASH FLOW STATEMENT – BALANCE SHEET METHOD

	₹	₹	₹	₹
Bank overdraft at beginning				**(1000)**
Inflows				
Profit after tax	80			
Depreciation	20			
Cash from operations		100		
Investment income		130		
Reduction in debtors		20		
Increase in creditors		5	**255**	
Outflows				
Increase in stocks		20		
Capital expenditure		40		
Interest chargeable		20		
Corporate tax		40		
Dividends		20	**(140)**	**115**
OVERDRAFT AT END				**(385)**

The cash flow statement can be reported in two methods:

(a) Direct Method.

(b) Indirect Method.

The **direct method** reports the sources of operating cash and the uses of operating cash. The major source of operating cash is cash received from customers. The major uses of operating cash include cash paid to suppliers for merchandise and services and cash paid to employees for wages. The difference between Operating cash receipts and Cash payments is the net cash flow from operating activities. The primary advantage of the direct method is that it reports the sources and uses of cash in the statement of cash flows. Its primary disadvantage is that the necessary data may not always be readily available.

The **indirect method** reports the operating cash flows by beginning with net income and adjusting it for revenues and expenses that do not involve the receipt or payment of cash. In other words, accrual net income is adjusted to determine the net amount of cash flows from operating activities. The major disadvantage of indirect method is that it focuses on the differences between Net income and Cash flows from operations. In this sense, it shows relationship between Income statement, the balance sheet and the Statement of cash flows. The data are readily available to use the indirect method.

CASH BUDGET

Budgets or cash flow projections are very specific month-by-month or week-by-week or may be day by day where cash deficits or surpluses are intense even on a day to day basis.

REPORTING CASH FLOW STATEMENT

The ICAI had issued Accounting Standard (AS-3), '***Changes in Financial Position***' in June 1981, which was superseded by revised standard with the new title '***Cash Flow Statements***'. This was later made mandatory for all listed companies, in respect of their financial statements prepared for periods commencing on or after 1st April, 2001. The revised standard sets out the significance of cash flow statement, specifies its scope and coverage and prescribes the principles and norms of standard accounting treatment for various aspects of accounting for cash flow statement, i.e., cash and cash equivalents and accounting policy on their composition, basis for and classification of activities into operating activities, investing activities and financing activities, methods of reporting cash flows, issues requiring special considerations, additional information and disclosures.

FACTORS AFFECTING CASH POSITION

Indeed, the company's cash position as reported on the balance sheet is affected by many factors, including the following:

(1) ***CASH FLOW***: Other things held constant, a positive net cash flow will lead to more cash in the bank. However, other things are generally not held constant.

(2) ***CHANGES IN WORKING CAPITAL***: Net working capital, is defined as current assets minus current liabilities. Increases in current assets other than cash, such as inventories and accounts receivable, decrease cash, whereas decreases in these accounts increase cash. For example, if inventories are to increase, the firm must use some of its cash to buy the additional inventory, whereas if inventories decrease, this generally means the firm is selling off inventories and not replacing them, hence generating cash. Increases in current liabilities such as accounts payable increase cash, whereas decreases in these accounts decrease cash. For example, if payables increase, the firm has received additional credit from its suppliers, which saves cash, but if payables decrease, this means the firm has used cash to pay off its suppliers.

Table 14(A)

CHANGES IN WORKING CAPITAL – AN OVERVIEW

Nature of Change	*Impact*
Increase in accounts payable	Improves cash position by causing reduction in outflow of cash for the time being due to the availability of credit
Decrease in accounts payable	Reduces cash because of payment made and cash outflows causing extinguishment of current liabilities (accounts payable)
Increase in accounts receivable	Reduces cash due to credit facilities extended to customers
Decrease in accounts receivable	Improves cash position because cash inflow increases and current asset (accounts receivable) is liquidated

(3) ***FIXED ASSETS***: If a company invests in fixed assets, this will reduce its cash position. Contrarily sale of fixed assets will increase cash.

(4) ***SECURITIES OR CAPITAL TRANSACTIONS***: If a company issues stock or bonds during the year, the funds raised will enhance its cash position. However, if it uses cash to buy-back outstanding debt or equity, or pays dividends to its shareholders, this will reduce cash.

Exhibit 17

FINANCIAL FITNESS - BETTER GET IN SHAPE

Starting a new business requires a good product or service and a sound marketing plan. But many entrepreneurs don't pay enough attention to the financial aspects of their business, according to Bradley Feld, the managing director of a company that provides capital to start up firms. And what is the first item on Feld's financial fitness checklist? You guessed it – ***CASH***

Cash is king: No matter what, don't run out of money. Nothing else in this article matters if you run out of money. This means know your burn rate (the net cash that is flowing out of your business each month) and be aware that your low cash point for any given month may not be at the end of the month. In other words, don't get caught making plans based on full-month figures only to find that you don't have enough money to pay your most important vendor on the 15th because customers won't be paying until the 30th.

"Entrepreneurs spend years nurturing and building their businesses. Those that stay in business know how to control cash."

SOURCE: Feld, Bradley. "The Entrepreneur's Financial Fitness Checklist." *Business Week Online.* 24th March, 2004. <*http://www.businessweek.com/smallbiz/content/mar2004/sb20040324_1277.htm*>

IMPORTANCE OF CASH FLOW STATEMENT

The cash flow statement helps in understanding:

- Amount of cash generated and the extent of surfeit or deficit cash.
- Surfeit cash provides advance warning signals to management regarding the need for cash deployment into profitable and productive ventures, that is to say identification of reinvestment opportunities.
- Deficit cash provides advance warning signals to the management regarding procurement of cash and also evolving ways and means of tackling deficit reduced cash outflows, embargo on superfluous operating expenses and postponement of capital expenditures.
- Changes in net assets of an enterprise, its financial structure, including its liquidity and solvency.
- Comparability of the reporting of operating performance by different enterprises because it eliminates the effects of using different accounting treatments for the same transactions.

DISCLOSURES IN CASH FLOW STATEMENT

The standard does not specify the disclosure requirements separately. However, various disclosures have been mentioned in the text of the standard. They are listed as follows:

- Cash flow statement should be presented for each period for which the financial statements are presented.
- The cash flow statement should report cash flows during the period classified by operating, investing and financing activities.
- Disclosure of cash flows from operating activities using either the direct method or indirect method.
- Separate disclosure of major classes of gross cash receipts and gross cash payments arising from investing and financing activities, except as permissible on a net basis. (e.g., special disclosures).
- Disclosure of the components of cash and cash equivalents and a reconciliation of the amounts in cash flow statement with the equivalent items reported in the balance sheet.
- Separate disclosures relating to special issues (if any).
- Disclosures regarding non cash investing and financing transactions, restricted cash and cash equivalents and additional information.

9

MEASURING, OPERATING, FINANCING AND INVESTING CASH FLOWS

EXHIBIT 18

CASH FLOW STATEMENT ACTIVITIES

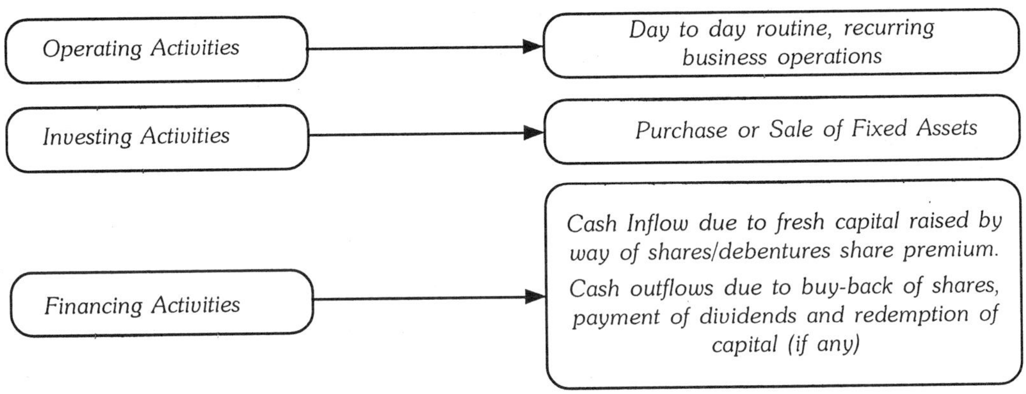

The sum total of the above three segments reflects the cash flow profile of any business.

CASH FLOWS FROM OPERATING ACTIVITIES

Cash flows from operating activities measure the cash inflows and outflows caused by core business operations. The operations component of cash flow reflects how much cash is generated from a company's products or services. Generally, changes made in cash, accounts receivable, depreciation, inventory and accounts payable are reflected in cash from operations.

Cash flow is calculated by making certain adjustments to net income by adding or subtracting differences in revenue, expenses and credit transactions (appearing on the balance sheet and income statement) resulting from transactions that occur from one period to the next. These adjustments are made because non-cash items are calculated into net income (income statement) and total assets and liabilities (balance sheet). Many items have to be accounted when calculating cash flows from operations because there are many transactions which does not involve actual cash.

For example, depreciation is not really a cash expense; it is an amount that is deducted from the total value of an asset that has previously been accounted for. That is why it is added back into net sales for calculating cash flow. The only time income from an asset is accounted for in cash flow calculations is when the asset is sold.

Changes in accounts receivables on the balance sheet from one accounting period to the next must also be reflected in cash flow. If accounts receivable decreases, this implies that more cash has entered the company from customers paying off their credit accounts - the amount by which accounts receivable has decreased is then added to cash sales. If accounts receivable increases this implies that more customers have entered into the current assets and the amount must be deducted from gross sales because revenue has increased and cash has not.

An increase in inventory, on the other hand, signals that a company has spent more money to purchase more raw materials. If the inventory was paid for in cash, the increase in the value of inventory is deducted from cash sales. A decrease in inventory would be added to cash sales. If inventory was purchased on credit, an increase in accounts payable would occur on the balance sheet and the amount of the increase from one year to the other would be added to net sales. It would not affect cash.

The same logic holds true for taxes payable, salaries payable and prepaid insurance. If something has been paid off, then the difference in the value owed from one year to the next has to be subtracted from receipts. If there is an amount that is still owed, then any differences will have to be added to cash earnings.

CASH FLOWS FROM INVESTING ACTIVITIES

Cash inflows from investing activities normally arise from selling fixed assets, investments and intangible assets. Cash outflows normally include payments to acquire fixed assets, investments and intangible assets. Changes in equipment, assets or investments relate to cash from investing. Usually cash changes from investing are a "***cash out***" item, because cash is used to buy new equipment, buildings or short-term assets such as marketable securities. However, when a company divests itself of an asset, the transaction is considered "***cash in***" for calculating cash from investment.

CASH FLOWS FROM FINANCING ACTIVITIES

Cash inflows from financing activities normally arise from issuing debt or equity securities. It includes cash raised during the year by issuing short-term debt, long-term debt or stock. Cash outflows from financing activities include paying cash dividends, repaying debt, and acquiring treasury stock. Also, since dividends paid or cash used to buy back outstanding stock or bonds reduces the company's cash, such transactions are included here. Accounting texts explain how to prepare the statement of cash flows, but the statement is used to help answer questions such as these:

Is the firm generating enough cash to purchase the additional assets required for growth? Is the firm generating any extra cash that can be used to repay debt or to invest in new products?

Inadequate cash flows calls for response action from management which may include, *inter alia,* additional borrowings, issuance of capital, postponement of capital expenditures and postponement of future outflows including stretching accounts payables. Such information is useful both for managers and investors. Hence, the statement of cash flows is an important part of the annual report. Financial managers generally use this statement, along with the cash budget, when forecasting their companies' cash positions.

OPERATING CAPITAL

A firm captures its series of cash flows for a particular period through realisations from existing and new (reinvestment) assets.

EXHIBIT 19

ELEMENTS OF OPERATING CAPITAL

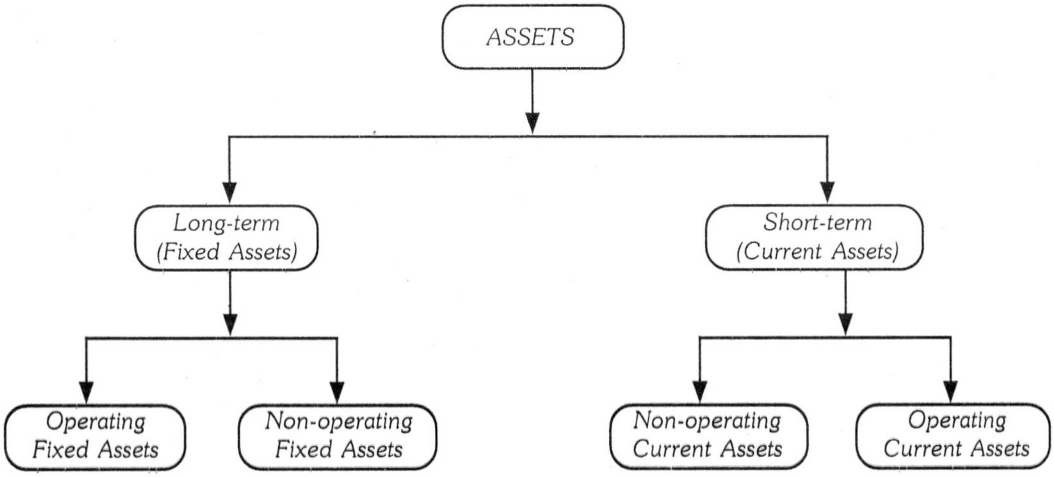

***N.B.**: The word operation refers to the act of actually keeping the assets under active utilisation. Idleness of any asset renders it non-operative.*

The assets used by managers at the helm of their respective operations are known as operating assets. Operating capital can be defined on a gross or net basis and includes short and long-term assets (capital). Working capital that is the resources required for the day to day functioning of any business can be understood as either Gross Working Capital which equals current assets, i.e., cash plus accounts receivables plus inventories used in operations **OR** net working capital which equals all current assets minus all current liabilities that do not entail a financial charge (interest). However operating capital includes working capital as well as long-term assets, that is to say, short and long-term uses of funds.

A *caveat* is in order. Management confronting huge amounts of cash, cannot saddle their segment heads or Strategic Business Units (SBUs) with the same as part of their operations. A business may want to park such cash and use the surplus for profitable deployment in the future. Hence, assumptions need to be made regarding the levels of cash and the intentions of holding to the same. Another dimension of performance is the profits generated by business. The usual measure is profit defined as output (profit) minus input (expenses). However, the expression profit cannot be used in an unfettered manner. In the current context, the relevant metric is net operating profit/loss after taxes i.e. **NOPLAT**

NOPLAT is defined as:

$$\text{EBIT}\ (1 - t)$$

Where: **EBIT** = earnings before interest and tax; ***t*** = applicable income tax rate (%)

Given NOPLAT as the starting point, we go back to fundamentals to arrive at cash flows. NOPLAT indicates the profit strength (on a book basis) of operations enunciated as the operating excellence using accounting nuances as spelt out by the accrual system. The end result is net operating profit after taxes as defined above.

EXHIBIT 20

ANALYSTS ARE INCREASINGLY RELYING ON CASH FLOW TO VALUE STOCKS

*A few years ago, Tokyo-based Softbank acquired several Internet-related businesses, including Ziff-Davis Inc., which publishes more than 80 magazines including PC Week and PC Magazine. Ziff-Davis also provides training courses in computer technology, and it distributes information through the Internet and computer trade shows. In an article on Softbank, Barron's indicated that Ziff-Davis has been "**losing money**", and a quick look at the company's income statements confirms that it had losses in 1998 and the first quarter of 1999. Despite the company's negative reported earnings, the company's chief financial officer, Timothy O'Brien, took exception with the notion that Ziff-Davis was "losing money". So he sent Barron's the following response:*

We are a diversified media company. Analysts measure our strength and stability relative to our ability to generate EBITDA (Earnings Before Interest, Taxes, Depreciation and Amortization). Analysts' project that we will generate EBITDA of approximately $220 million in 1999 and that takes into account our substantial investment in ZDTV, the company's 24 hour cable network devoted to computing and the Internet. Ziff-Davis did report a net loss for 1998 and for the first quarter of 1999. However, this loss was due to non cash expenses, primarily the amortization of approximately $120 million in goodwill per year. Even with continuing investments on our key businesses, Ziff-Davis has the financial flexibility to continue to repay indebtedness with free cash flow.

Timothy C. O'Brien,

Chief Financial Officer, Ziff-Davis

Cash flow measures such as EBITDA have long been popular with bankers and other short-term lenders, who focus more on borrowers' ability to generate cash to pay off loans than on accounting earnings. In the past, these measures were less popular with stock analysts, who focused on reported earnings and price-earnings ratio. However, today more and more Wall Street analysts are siding with Tim O'Brien, arguing that cash flow measures such as EBITDA often provide a better indication of true value than do earnings per share.

These analysts note that the DA part of EBITDA reduces reported profits but not cash, so EBITDA reflects the cash available to a firm better than accounting profits. *It is logical that credit analysts interested in a company's ability to repay its loans focus heavily on EBITDA, but what about equity analysts, who are seeking to find a firms' value to its stockholders? First, most analysts agree that firms' value depends on its ability to generate cash flows over the long run. If Depreciation and Amortization (DA) charges truly reflect a decline in the assets used to produce cash flows, then the DA will have to be reinvested in the business if cash flows are to continue. The DA may reflect the available cash in the short run, but it is not truly available to investors because it will have to be reinvested if the business is to continue to operate.*

So analysts must consider the nature of the **D** *and* **A** *charges. If these charges are related to essential assets then they should be deducted to get an idea of the firm's long run cash generating potential. The key question then becomes, "**Will the company be required to reinvest the cash flow reflected in the DA part of EBITDA if it is to continue to generate cash flow on into the future?**" If the answer is yes, then the* **DA** *component is not "**free cash flow**" that is available to investors and it should be deducted when determining the firms' long run earning power. If the answer is no, then* **DA** *does represent free cash flow and is available to investors.*

contd. .....

contd. .....

As it turns out, Ziff- Davis' performance has been much weaker than expected. In 2000, Softbank split up the company and sold the magazine portion to Willis Stein & Partners, where it now operates under the name Ziff-Davis Media. More recently, Ziff-Davis Media has struggled to meet its large debt obligations in the face of a declining economy and its struggling technology sector. So, it may be the case that original Barron's article was correct and that the company's net loss was an early indicator of troubles to come.

***SOURCE**: Barron's, July 19, 1999, 54.*

***Legend: D** = Depreciation; A = Amortisation*

Table 15

TYPICAL CASH FLOW STATEMENT:

Bajaj Electricals Limited

Cash flow statement for the year ended 31st March 2005.

₹ in Lakhs

Particulars	*Amount Yr. 2004*	*Amount Yr. 2005*
A. Cash flow from operating activities		
Profit / loss before tax	1672.33	2179.26
Less: Liability written back	– 86.88	– 38.33
Add: Amounts written off	243.20	266.43
Add: Loss/(profit on sale of asset)	1191.78	46.73
Net profit/loss before tax provision and extraordinary items	636.87	2370.63
Adjustments for:		
Amortisation of deferred revenue expenditure	296.04	65.08
Depreciation	602.32	598.75
Adjustment in fixed assets on account of discontinued operations	—	221.42
Interest on loans	2119.49	1833.43
Interest received	(254.36)	(195.84)
Dividend received	(0.04)	(1.65)
Compensation under voluntary retirement scheme	98.97	15.03
Operating profit before working capital changes	3301.35	4876.79
Adjustments for increase/decrease in:		
Trade and other receivables(Gross before written offs and making provision for doubtful recoveries)	(1191.30)	(3278.75)
Inventories	+ 360.51	(3219.97)
Increase/decrease in trade payable before written back	(1694.31)	1326.99
Cash generated from operations	776.25	(–294.94)
Direct taxes paid	(31.37)	(282.70)
Prior period items	(105.29)	(18.49)
(A) Cash flow from operating activities	639.59	(–596.13)
Cash flow from investing activities		
Purchase of fixed assets	(348.60)	(736.33)
Sale of fixed assets	1476.17	639.66

contd. .....

contd. .....

TYPICAL CASH FLOW STATEMENT:

Assets written off	34.07	24.33
Redemption/Diminution (purchase) of investments	(0.54)	10000.77
Loan given to the company	—	694.13
Interest received	246.67	243.46
Dividend received	.04	1.65
(B) Net cash flow from investing activities	1340.75	182.53
Cash flow from financing activities:		
Proceeds from issue of share capital		
Equity share capital	432.15	
Securities premium account	648.22	
Less: Share issue expenses	18.17	
Interest paid	2171.55	1810.44
Proceeds from/(repayments) of borrowings	862.96	2811.63
Dividends paid	112.00	187.10
(C) Net cash flow from financing activities	2084.31	814.09
Net Increase/(Decrease) in cash and cash equivalents	103.97	35.43
Cash and cash equivalents (at the beginning of the year)	1739.33	1635.36
Cash and cash equivalents (at the end of the year)	1635.36	1670.79

SOURCE: *Annual Report 2004-2005, Bajaj Electricals Limited .*

Table 16*

Bajaj Electricals Limited

Cash Flow Statement – A Summary

₹ *in Lakhs*

	Particulars	*2004*	*2005*
A	Cash generated from operating activities	639.59	596.13
B	Cash generated from investing activities	1340.75	(182.53)
C	Cash flow from financing activities	(2084.31)	814.09
D	Cash and cash equivalents as at 01.04.2004	1739.33	1635.36
E	Cash and cash equivalents as at 31.03.2005	1635.36	1670.79
F	Net increase or decrease in cash or cash equivalents	103.97	35.43

N.B.: (A+ B + C + D) = E

Net increase or decrease in cash or cash equivalents = **F = D-E**

***Table 17** does not exist

NET CASH FLOWS

On studying income statements in accounting, the emphasis is on the firm's net income. In finance, however, the focus is on **net cash flow.** The value of an asset (or a whole firm) is determined by the cash flow it generates. The firm's net income is important, but cash flow is even more important because dividends must be paid in cash and cash is necessary to purchase the assets required to continue operations. A firm's goal should be to maximize its stock price. Since the value of any asset, including a share of stock, depends on the cash flow produced by the asset, managers should strive to maximize the cash flow available to investors over the long-run. Net cash flow of any enterprise generally differs from its **accounting profit** because some of the revenues and expenses listed on the income statement were not paid in cash during the year. The relationship between Net cash flow and Net income can be expressed as follows:

> Net cash flow = Net income — Non cash revenues
> + Non cash charges

The primary examples of non cash charges are current depreciation and amortization. These items reduce net income but are not paid out in cash. Hence, they are to be added back to net income when calculating net cash flow. Another example of a non cash charge is deferred taxes. In some instances, companies are allowed to defer tax payments to a later date even though the tax payment is reported as an expense on the income statement. Therefore, deferred tax payments would be added to net income when calculating net cash flow. At the same time, some revenues may not be collected in cash during the year and these items must be subtracted from net income when calculating net cash flow.

Such items of revenue are accrued incomes, which may be collected in the ensuing financial year. However, for the current period they are non cash revenues.

Usually, depreciation and amortization are the largest noncash items and in many cases the other non cash items do not form a significant portion. For this reason, it is assumed that net cash flow equals net income plus depreciation and amortization *(circa)*:

> Net cash flow = Net income + Depreciation
> and amortization

Depreciation is a non cash charge and must be added back to net income to obtain the net cash flow. If all other non cash items (including amortization) are assumed to sum to zero, then net cash flow is simply equal to net income plus depreciation. Net cash flow represents the amount of cash a business generates for its shareholders in a given year. However, the fact that a company generates high cash flow does not necessarily mean that the amount of cash reported on its balance sheet will also be high. The cash flow may be put to use in a variety of ways. For example, a firm may use its cash flow to pay dividends to increase inventories, to finance accounts receivable, to invest in fixed assets, to reduce debt or to buy-back common stock and a wide variety of legitimate cash deployment strategies limited only by the genius of financial wizardry available to an enterprise.

FREE CASH FLOWS

It must be noted, though, that cash flows cannot be maintained over time unless depreciating fixed assets are replaced and new products are developed. Thus management is not completely free to use cash flows indiscriminately. Hence, the concept of Free Cash Flows to the Firm (FCFF) which is the cash flow actually available for distribution to all investors (stockholders and debt holders) after the company has made all the investments in fixed assets, new products and working capital necessary to sustain ongoing operations. On studying income statements in accounting, the emphasis probably was on the firm's net income, which is its accounting profit. However, the value of a company's operations is determined, not by the profits but by the stream of cash flows that the operations will generate now and in the future preferably on a sustained basis.

WHY FREE CASH FLOWS?

In the normal course net cash flow of any business for a particular accounting period is defined as: - Profit after interest and taxes plus depreciation/amortization for the said accounting period. However, there is a difference between Net cash flows and Free cash flows as shown below:

Table 18

NET CASH FLOWS vs. FREE CASH FLOWS TO FIRM

NET CASH FLOWS	*FREE CASH FLOWS TO FIRM*
◆ Profit after interest and taxes plus depreciation and amortization	◆ NOPAT minus Net investment.
◆ Funds available to equity shareholders	◆ Funds available to all investors
◆ Planned capital expenditures and increases in working capital required to sustain ongoing operations are not deducted	◆ Planned capital expenditures and increases in working capital required to sustain ongoing operations are deducted.

EXHIBIT 21

FREE CASH – WE ALL WANT SOME

*According to The Motley Fool, **Free Cash Flow** is the lifeblood of a company, so it's surprising that analysts don't talk about it much more often. "**Free cash flow**" – that has the ring of something everyone should want. Break it down into its parts. Free: Who can argue with free? Cash: Ah, crisp new cash – a printed ticket to opportunity. Flow: A consistent happening. Put it all together and what do you have? A flow of free cash!*

We celebrate Free Cash Flow (FCF) all across The Motley Fool because it is the most important thing that a public company can accomplish. Lacking free cash flow, it's difficult for a business to pursue new opportunities, acquire other businesses or pay dividends. When achieving free cash flow, a company is much more capable of those things plus paying down debt, saving cash for a rainy year and building shareholder's equity.

There are a number of ways that analysts define free cash flows. The most common is the definition we studied – Free cash flow = Net cash from operating activities – Cash dividends – Capital expenditures. Analysts and investors don't give the statement of cash flows the attention it deserves, according to The Motley Fool. By scrutinizing the elements of net cash from operations, a knowledgeable investor may be able to make adjustments that can make the calculation of free cash flow even more useful, like removing unusual or nonrecurring amounts. When you get ready to invest, don't forget free cash flow. After all who doesn't love cash?

SOURCE: Fischer, Jeff. "Joy of Free Cash Flow." *The Motley Fool.* 28th February, 2002. *<http://www.fool.com/dripport/2002/dripport020228.htm>*

CASE STUDY 18: INFOSYS LTD.

The financial statements of Infosys Ltd., for the four years ending 31.03.2009 are presented as follows:

(1) Balance Sheet as on 31.03.2009 of the respective years.
(2) Profit and Loss Account for the period ending 31.03.2009 of the respective years.
(3) Abridged cash flow statement for the period ending 31.03.2009 of the respective years.

(4) With the help of the above financial statements of INFOSYS LTD. identify the following:
   (a) Gross Working Capital (GWC)
   (b) Net Working Capital (NWC)
   (c) Net Fixed Assets (NFA)
   (d) Gross Investment (GI)
   (e) Net Investment (NI)
   (f) Net Operating Profit or Loss After Taxes (NOPLAT)
   (g) Operating Cash Flows (OCF)
   (h) Cash Flow from Operations (CFO)
   (i) Free Cash Flow to Firm (FCFF)
   (j) Free Cash Flow to Equity (FCFE)

Table 18A

INFOSYS LTD.

Balance Sheet As at March, 31

₹ *in crore*

	Sched.	*2006**	*2007**	*2008**	*2009**
SOURCES OF FUNDS					
SHAREHOLDERS' FUNDS					
Share Capital	1*	138	286	286	286
Reserves and Surplus	2*	6759	10876	13204	17523
		6897	11162	13490	17809
APPLICATION OF FUNDS					
FIXED ASSETS	3*				
Original Cost		2837	3889	4508	5986
Less: Accumulated depreciation		1275	1739	1837	2187
Net book value		1562	2150	2671	3799
Add: Capital work-in-progress		571	957	1260	615
		2133	3107	3931	4414
INVESTMENTS	4*	876	839	964	1005
DEFERRED TAX ASSETS, NET	5*	56	79	99	102
CURRENT ASSETS, LOANS AND ADVANCES					—
Sundry debtors	6*	1518	2292	3093	3390
Cash and bank balances	7*	3279	5507	6429	9039
Loans and advances	8*	1252	1162	2705	3164
		6049	8961	12227	15593
Less: CURRENT LIABILITIES AND PROVISIONS					
Current liabilities	9*	808	1162	1483	1507
Provisions	10*	1409	662	2248	1798
NET CURRENT ASSETS		3832	7137	8496	12288
		6897	**11162**	**13490**	**17809**

N.B.: *Figures for the year 2006 and 2007 are taken from the Annual Report for the year ending 31.03.2007, p. 29*
Figures for the year 2008 are taken from the Annual Report for the year ending 31.03.2008, p. 66
Figures for the year 2009 are taken from the Annual Report for the year ending 31.03.2009, p. 64

Table 18B
INFOSYS LTD.
Profit and Loss account
For the year ended March 31

₹ in crore, except per share data

	Sched.	2006*	2007*	2008*	2009*
Income from software services and products		9028	13149	15648	20264
Software development expenses	11*	4887	7278	8876	11154
GROSS PROFIT		4141	5871	6772	9119
Selling and marketing expenses	12*	499	719	730	933
General and administration expenses	13*	653	927	1079	1280
		1152	1646	1809	2213
OPERATING PROFIT BEFORE INTEREST AND DEPRECIATION		2989	4225	4963	6906
Interest		—	—	—	—
Depreciation		409	469	546	694
OPERATING PROFIT BEFORE TAX AND EXCEPTIONAL ITEMS		2580	3756	4417	6212
Other income, net	14*	144	375	683	502
Provision for investments		—	2	—	
NET PROFIT BEFORE TAX		2724	4129	5100	6714
Provision for taxation	15*	303	352	630	895
NET PROFIT AFTER TAX			8.5%	12.3%	13.3%
(BEFORE EXCEPTIONAL ITEMS)		2421	3777	4470	5819
Income on sale of investments, net of taxes		—	6	—	
NET PROFIT AFTER TAX AND EXCEPTIONAL ITEMS		2421	3783	4470	5819
Balance brought forward		1428	2195	4844	6642
Less : Residual dividend paid		—	4	—	1
Dividend tax on the above		—	1	—	—
		1428	2190	4844	6641
AMOUNT AVAILABLE FOR APPROPRIATION		3849	5973	9314	12460
Dividend					—
Interim		177	278	343	572
Final		234	371	415	773
Dividend (Silver Jubilee – 2006)					
Dividend (Special – 2008)		827	—	1144	—
Total dividend		1238	649	1902	1345
Dividend tax		174	102	323	228
Amount transferred to general reserve		242	378	447	582

contd. .....

contd. .....

Balance in profit and loss account		2195 3849	4844 5973	6642 9314	10305 12460
EARNINGS PER SHARE*					—
Equity shares of par value ₹ 5/- each					—
Before exceptional items					—
Basic		44.34	67.82	78.24	101.65
Diluted		43.1	66.33	77.98	101.48
After exceptional items					—
Basic		44.34	67.93	78.24	—
Diluted		43.1	66.44	77.98	
Number of shares used in computing earning per share					
Basic		5459890 22	5568523 39	5713983 40	5724902 11
Diluted		5616566 20	5693426 94	5733068 87	5734631 81

N.B.: **Figures for the year 2006 and 2007 are taken from the Annual Report for the year ending 31.03.2007, p. 30*
Figures for the year 2008 are taken from the Annual Report for the year ending 31.03.2008, p. 67
Figures for the year 2009 are taken from the Annual Report for the year ending 31.03.2009, p. 65

Table 18C
INFOSYS LTD.
Cash flow statement
For the year ended March 31

₹ in crores

	Sched.	*2006**	*2007**	*2008***	*2009****
NET CASH GENERATED BY OPERATING ACTIVITIES		2309	3256	3816	5152
Cash flow from investing activities before exceptional items		–392	–1065	-978	–195
NET CASH USED IN FINANCING ACTIVITIES		172	–316	–777	–2430
Effect of exchange differences on translation of foreign currency cash and cash equivalents		7	–4	18	73
NET INCREASE/(DECREASE) IN CASH AND CASH EQUIVALENTS		2096	1871	2079	2600
CASH AND CASH EQUIVALENTS AT THE BEGINNING OF THE PERIOD		1683	3779	5610	7689
CASH AND CASH EQUIVALENTS AT THE END OF THE PERIOD		3779	5650	7689	10289

N.B.: **Figures for the year 2006 and 2007 are taken from the Annual Report for the year ending 31.03.2007 p. 64*
***Figures for the year 2008 are taken from the Annual Report for the year ending 31.03.2008 p. 68*
****Figures for the year 2009 are taken from the Annual Report for the year ending 31.03.2009, p. 66*

*CASE STUDY 19: INFOSYS is part of Chapter 9 - Measuring, Operating, Financing and Investing Cash Flows. For the year 2007 solution is built into the Chapter itself. However, for the years 2008 and 2009 the case poses problems for readers to address. Solutions are accessible through softcopy.

CASE STUDY 18D: (SOLUTION)
INFOSYS

MEASUREMENT OF CASH FLOWS

A	Earnings Before Interest and Tax (EBIT)
	MINUS
B	Income Tax (t)
	EQUALS
C = A - B	Net Operating Profit or Loss After Tax (NOPLAT) **1**
	PLUS
D	Current Depreciation and Amortisation (CDA)
	EQUALS
E = C + D	Operating Cash Flows (OCF) **2**
	MINUS
F	Incremental investment in Net Current Assets (NCA) during the year (Closing Balance – Opening Balance)
G = E - F	Cash Flow from operations (available for capital expenditure) **3**
	MINUS
H	Incremental Investment in Net Fixed Assets (NFA) during the year (Closing Balance – Opening Balance)
	EQUALS
I = G-H-D **OR I = E-F-H-D**	Free Cash Flow to Flow (FCFF) **4**
	OR
J = C- (F + H)	Free Cash Flow to Firm (FCFF) **5**
K	Free Cash Flow to Equity (FCFE) I or J plus new debt raised minus debt repaid, plus preference shares raised minus preference shares redeemed **6**

RELATIONSHIP BETWEEN FACTORS AFFECTING DIFFERENT CASH FLOWS

(1)	NOPLAT	=	EBIT (1-t)
(2)	FCFF	=	NOPLAT - NI
		=	EBIT (1-t) - NI
(3)	EBIT (1-t)	=	FCFF + NI
(4)	NI	=	NOPLAT - FCFF
(5)	ΔNCA	=	Closing balance of NCA of Nth year MINUS Opening balance of NCA of Nth year
(6)	ΔNFA	=	Closing balance of NFA of Nth year MINUS Opening balance of NFA of Nth year
(7)	Net Investment	=	ΔNCA + ΔNFA
(8)	Gross Investment	=	ΔNCA + ΔNFA + CDA
(9)	FCFF	=	OCF – Gross Investment in Operating Capital
		=	NOPLAT + CDA – ΔNCA – ΔNFA – CDA
		=	NOPLAT – ΔNCA – ΔNFA
		=	NOPLAT – (ΔNCA + ΔNFA)
		=	NOPLAT – Net Investment in Capital Assets
(10)	OCF	=	NOPLAT + CDA
(11)	NOPLAT	=	OCF – CDA
(12)	CDA	=	OCF – NOPLAT
(13)	FCFF	=	OCF – (Net investment in operating capital plus non cash charges)
		=	(OCF – non cash charges) – (net investment in operating capital)
		=	NOPLAT – net investment in operating capital
(14)	CFO (Available for CAPEX)	=	OCF minus ΔNCA
(15)	FCFE	=	FCFF plus new debt raised minus debt repaid, PLUS preference shares raised minus preference shares redeemed.

N.B: *Operating capital refers to short-term (working capital) and long-term (capital expenditures) uses of funds.*

Table 18E

INFOSYS LTD.

DATA REQUIRED FOR COMPUTATION OF CASH FLOWS

₹ in Crores				
	2006	*2007*	*2008*	*2009*
Gross Operating Working Capital (Current Assets)	6049	8961		
Current Liabilities	2217	1824		
Net Working Capital (NWC) OR Net Current Assets (NCA)	3832	7137		
Net Fixed Assets (Including capital work in progress) (NFA)	2133	3107		
Total Operating Capital (Net Basis) (NCA + NFA)	5965	10244		
Current Depreciation and Amortisation (CDA)	409	469		
Gross Investment in Capital Assets(NCA + NFA + CD)	6374	10713		

N.B.:

(1) The relevant closing balances as on 31.03.2005 of key items necessary for computation, are as follows Rupees in Crores: Current Assets ₹ 3730, Current Liabilities ₹ 1346 and Net Fixed Assets ₹ 1495.

(2) Changes in Investment and Deferred Tax Assets/Liabilities are excluded from the above computations.

INCOME TAX RATES OF RESPECTIVE FINANCIAL YEARS

2006	*2007*	*2008*	*2009*
$= \frac{303}{2724} \times 100$ $= 11\%$	$= \frac{352}{4129} \times 100$ $= 8.5\%$		

Income Tax Rates (%) for the respective years have been computed using the formula:

$$\left(\frac{\text{Provision for Income Tax (₹)}}{\text{Profit Before Tax (₹)}} \times 100 \right)$$

Table 18F

INFOSYS LTD.

Changes in Net Current Assets (ΔNCA) and Net Fixed Assets (ΔNFA)

₹ in Crores				
NCA AND NFA (Opening and Closing Balance)	*2006*	*2007*	*2008*	*2009*
NCA (Opening Balance)	2384	3832		
NCA (Closing Balance)	3832	7137		
Changes in NCA (ΔNCA)	**+ 1448**	**+ 3305**		
NFA (Opening Balance)	1495	2133		
NFA (Closing Balance)	2133	3107		
Changes in NFA	**+ 638**	**+ 974**		
Net Changes in Current Assets and Fixed Assets (ΔNCA + ΔNFA)	**2086**	**4279**		

N.B.:

(1) Opening balance of any year is the closing balance of the previous year.

(2) NCA is defined as the difference between Current Assets and Liabilities of any financial year.

(3) For computation of cash flows Δ NCA and Δ NFA are required. Hence if cash flows are to be computed for the nth financial year relevant data for the $(n-1)^{th}$ financial year is required.

(4) Change in NCA (Δ NCA) is defined as the difference between the Closing and Opening balances of any financial year.

(5) **STEPS:**

(a) Assemble Relevant data:

(i) KEY ELEMENTS concerning working capital (NCA) Capital Expenditures (NFA) and current Depreciation and Amortisation.

(ii) Identify tax rates relevant for each financial year.

(b) Compute key indicators, *viz.*, NOPLAT, OCF, Net Investment, FCFF (Alternate formulas) and FCFE

(c) Present an overview of the computations.

(6) The closing balances of NCA as on 31.03.2005 and 31.03.2006, are ₹ 3730 and ₹ 1346 crores respectively. Thus the NCA as on 31.03.2006 is ₹ 2384 crores. The NFA as on 31.03.2006 is ₹ 1495 crores.

Table 18G

INFOSYS LTD.

KEY INDICATORS — CASH FLOWS' COMPUTATIONS

Net Operating Profit/Loss After Tax (NOPLAT)	₹ in Crores			
Year	*2006*	*2007*	*2008*	*2009*
EBIT (after Depreciation)	2580	3756		
(-) Income Tax on EBIT (Per Table __)	284	319		
NOPLAT = EBIT (1-t)	2296	3437		

OPERATING CASH FLOWS (OCF)	₹ in Crores			
Year	*2006*	*2007*	*2008*	*2009*
NOPLAT	2296	3437		
+ Current Depreciation and Amortisation	409	469		
= OCF	2705	3906		

NET INVESTMENT (NI)	₹ in Crores			
Year	*2006*	*2007*	*2008*	*2009*
(ΔNCA + ΔNFA)	2086	4279		

Year	*2006*	*2007*	*2008*	*2009*
FCFF (NOPLAT – NI) (Per Table __)	+210	–842		
FCFF (OCF – ΔNCA – ΔNFA – CDA) (Per Table __)	+210	–842		

Year	*2006*	*2007*	*2008*	*2009*
FCFE (Per Table __)		–496		

***N.B.:** If NOPLAT is greater than NI the balance is positive, (2006) and vice versa (2007)*

Table 18G (Contd ......)

INFOSYS LTD.

KEY INDICATORS – CASH FLOWS' COMPUTATIONS

	₹ in Crores			
	2006	*2007*	*2008*	*2009*
Profit After Tax	2421	3783		
(–) [Change in Net Fixed Assets]	–638	–974		
(–) Changes in Working Capital	–102	–3305		
(+) New debt issue		—		
(+) New preference shares issue		—		
(–) Change in investment in marketable securities		—		
FCFE		–496		

Table 18H

ELEMENTS OF FCFF — AN OVERVIEW

₹ in Crores

FCFF	=	Net Operating Profit Profit / Loss After Tax NOPLAT	— (MINUS)	Net Investment ΔNCA	— (MINUS)	ΔNFA	=	
2006	=	2296	—	1448	—	638	=	210
2007	=	3437	—	3305	—	974	=	- 842
2008	=		—		—		=	1691
2009	=		—		—		=	1111

₹ in Crores

FCFF		Operating Cash Flows OCF		ΔNCA	—	Gross Investment ΔNFA	—	CDA		
2006	=	2705	—	1448	—	638	—	409	=	210
2007	=	3906	—	3305	—	974	—	469	=	–842
2008	=		—		—		—		=	1691
2009	=		—		—		—		=	911

N.B.:

(1) FCFF can be alternatively presented as FCFF = OCF - (ΔNCA + ΔNFA + CDA).

(2) Cash flow from operations is defined as (OCF - ΔNCA) and equals ₹ 1257, ₹ 601 crores respectively for the year ended 2007.

Table 18 I

MEASUREMENT OF CASH FLOWS

₹ Crores									
		2006		*2007*		*2008*		*2009*	
A	EBIT	2580		3756					
B	Income Tax on EBIT (Per Table __)	(284)		(319)					
C = A-B	NOPLAT		2296		3437				
D	Current Depreciation and Amortisation (CDA)		409		469				
E = C+D	Operating Cash Flow (OCF)		2705		3906				
F	Changes in Net Current Asset (ΔNCA)	3832 2384	1448	7137 -3832	3305				
G = E-F	Cash Flow From Operations (CFFO)		1257		601				
H	Changes in Net Fixed Asset ΔNFA	2133 1495	638	3107 2133	974				
I = G-H-DOR	Free Cash Flow to Firm	210			–842				
J = C-(F+H)	Free Cash Flow to Firm	210			–842				

N.B.: I = G – H – D or I = E – F – H – D or I = E – (F + H + D)

Table 18J
DIFFERENT CASH FLOWS

Sr. No.	Cash Flow	Definition	Purpose
(1)	Cash Flow from Financing Activities	Cash flow from issue/ repayment of debt, equity securities, stock.	Deployment of cash surplus towards productive capital expenditures or reduction of borrowings or both.
(2)	Cash Flow from Investment Activities	Cash flow from sale/ purchase of fixed asset, investment and intangible assets.	Assess the profits or gains from investments made in the assets of a business
(3)	Net Cash Flows (NCF)	Cash flow from operating activities + Cash flow from investing activities + Cash flow from financing activities	◆ Assess dividend paying capacity ◆ Justify increases in working capital ◆ Assets-inventories / receivables ◆ Increased capital expenditures ◆ Reduce borrowings ◆ Buy-back equity shares ◆ Productive deployment of cash surplus
(4)	Operating Cash Flow (OCF)	NOPAT + Depreciation + Amortization	Assess the operating excellence of business through the gross margin of operations
(5)	Cash Flow from Operations (CFO)	Operating Cash Flows – Incremental Net Current Assets	Cash flows available for capital expenditures
(6)	Free Cash Flows to Firm (FCFF)	NOPAT – Net Investment in Capital Assets OR Operating Cash Flows – Gross Investment in Capital Assets	◆ Cash without encumbrance with respect to capital expenditures, new product launches and incremental working capital requirements.
(7)	Free Cash Flows to Equity (FCFE)	FCFF plus new debt raised minus debt repaid, plus preference shares raised minus preference shares redeemed.	Cash available to Equity Share holders.

A NOTE ON CASH FLOWS:

APPENDIX TO CHAPTER 19

CASH SURPLUS vs. CASH DEFICIT

Cash management in a corporate environment is an exciting and challenging issue. The technique usually used to understand cash flows is a cash budget, which maps out the periodic –

daily, weekly or monthly cash inflows and cash outflows. If the cash inflows are greater than cash outflows, it is referred as to excess cash and *vice versa*. Cash flows are also presented in terms of points of origination and end use, individual items in the respective segments, *viz.*, operations, investment and financing. The respective categories are evaluated for their contribution on the cash flows.

Surfeit or Deficit cash compels management to identify options to tackle the situation. Deficit cash is easier to handle than surplus cash. Deficit cash requires prudent deployment of payments and alertness to recoveries. It usually attracts an embargo on superfluous and unaffordable luxuries. Further, management are motivated to identify ways and means of procurement of funds – right time, right amount, right lender, right rate, right country and currency, right covenants regarding amortization – interest and loan instalments.

However surfeit cash is a big problem. If not handled in time with skill and dexterity, it can lead to idle cash or liquid assets earning returns comparable to gilt-edged returns or even lower, thus depressing the overall return on capital or assets employed in the business. If the assets employed in the core business are earning an overall return of 15 % and the gilt-edged returns on liquid assets is 8%, the overall return on assets (core business plus liquid assets) is depressed to the extent of the gap between efficiency of capital in core assets *vis-a-vis* liquid assets.

If a large chunk of reserves are blocked in liquid assets, as is the case with cash rich companies in lieu of plant and machinery (core business assets) the issue of taxes come into picture. This is particularly true in case of companies in the financial services sector viz. banks and other financial companies. This is also true in the case of service companies in the IT industry and companies which are doing extremely well and flushed with cash, from time to time, if not always. The liquidity ratios of such companies indicate that the companies enjoy (in fact suffer from) surfeit cash. The question before such companies whichever industry or business it may be, is - how to find ways and means of deploying surplus cash into productive assets both in the short and medium-term and in the long-term?

In the short and medium-term, such companies look for avenues which can absorb funds at competitive rates of interest comparable to the best available through gilt-edged financial assets or instruments. Thus, in the financial markets, companies with surplus cash are always on the look for good corporate borrowers, well rated for their creditworthiness, to deploy or park their surplus cash at rates of interest higher than gilt-edged financial assets. In the long-term such companies need to look for reinvestment opportunities which can absorb funds in ventures whose rates of return on the capital employed exceed the cost of capital. To what extent the rates of return on new investment proposals will surpass the standards of financial performance laid down for new projects will depend upon so many factors like entrepreneurial initiative, pipeline investments proposals, quick decision making and eternal vigil on the key parameters affecting financial performance, *viz.*, revenue management (price per unit and volume of business), cost management and of course managing the denominator of the immortal ROI, i.e., to say the investment by whatever name called, *viz.*, total assets or capital employed or net worth as the case may be. Insofar as taxation is concerned the provisions of Income Tax Act, 1961, provide substantial amounts of depreciation and possibly other incentives, from time-to-time, which provide tax shelter to protect the bottom line of the business. However, cash rich companies can always look for cash deals in lieu of borrowings. There is a double edged advantage. One, upfront cash discounts can be expected. Second, the absence of borrowings reduces the stress on the business and also saves interest cost (reduction in outflow of cash). For example, Infosys sitting on huge amounts of cash from time to time is well placed to handle takeovers and acquisitions than companies which need to mobilise financial resources to complete the deal. In fact, tax management plays a key role in facilitating the transmission of operating excellence to the shareholders. However, this exercise is rendered defunct if there are liquid funds blocked in assets of non-core businesses. Thus, in these cases, the rate at which cash flows come into the business is far greater than the rate at which new opportunities can absorb cash to create assets in core businesses or even in new diversified business ventures providing returns higher than liquid assets. Hence, surfeit cash is a serious problem – at best a blessing in disguise and at worst a value destroyer, if not laid to rest in time through right investment opportunities and aliged business decisions.

Of course there is another side to the deployment of surplus cash. In the anxiety to get rid of the surfeit cash, leasing companies got into trouble because of high investment in leased capital assets. The recovery was very weak. Hence, leasing companies landed with huge amounts of non-performing assets. A *caveat* is in order. In case of finance companies like banks and services companies like Fed-express, capital investment in tangible physical assets are rather limited. Liquid assets dominate the balance sheet. Managing working capital is thus the key factor to success. There was some interesting development in the behaviour of corporates with respect to their approaches to business. In the pre-liberalisation days, manufacturing companies like Colgate, Pfizer and other companies in similar sectors wanted to grow but could not. Monopolies Restrictive Trade Practices Act, Foreign Exchange Regulation Act and a panoply of other controls and farrago of laws demotivated enterprise. In the post-liberalisation for such companies growth was possible. However they were not interested due to the cold competition that emerged *vis-à-vis* their likes namely multinational foreign corporations. Instead of the possible growth path such companies chose by design the route of divestment to become lean and mean. They used their surplus cash and healthy financial position to distribute high dividends because of liberal tax laws governing dividends in terms of reduced corporate tax rates and tax free statutes governing Government dividend distribution. Further, unlike in the past Foreign Exchange Regulation Act was replaced by Foreign Exchange Management Act. This provided opportunities for better and liberal repatriation.

There is one more dimension, to the behaviour of corporates in the post-liberalisation period. Cash rich companies in the IT sector like Infosys, Wipro, TCS deployed surplus cash to grow inorganically. The motivation was deployment of surplus cash into ventures which were profitable (export earnings) which enjoyed tax advantages. Mergers, acquisitions and takeovers were the order of the day.

CASH FLOWS AND LIFE CYCLE STAGE OF A COMPANY

Cash is financial power and an analysis of a stock is not complete without evaluating a company's cash flow. Companies and industries go through a predictable and often repeated blueprint of development, growth, cash consumption and cash generation that can be attributed to its stage in the life cycle. A firm's position within its life cycle helps to identify its risks, needs, and growth potential.

During the business life cycle, companies and industries typically go through a pattern of formation, accelerated growth, growth, maturity and possibly decline.

- In the first stage of formation, a firm is started to produce and sell a product or service. Usually money from the founders or a venture capital group provides fuel for the development and expansion during this formation stage. Promising companies often go through a few rounds of venture capital infusion during the development stage as the company begins to implement its business plan. Sales growth may be strong during this stage, but earnings may be low or non-existent as the company experiences high start-up costs.

- Generally, most start-up companies fail and never get far beyond the formation stage. Some firms have growth and profit potential and move on to the accelerated growth stage. As in the formation stage, the company's demand for expansion capital is great, but with a positive sales track record and the promise of even stronger sales and earnings, an Initial Public Offering ("IPO") is common. The IPO proceeds are used to raise capital for the firm and reward venture capital investors for their seed money. IPO proceeds, business cash flow, and cash borrowing fuel expansion at this aggressive growth stage.
- Once a firm's growth rate reduces but remains strong, it enters the growth stage. In this stage, most companies are able to finance expansion from internal cash generation and also by issuing long-term debt. Usually in this stage, a firm is expanding at a supportable rate that is still normally greater than and largely independent of the rate of overall economic expansion. A token cash dividend may be paid, but most of the generated cash flow will be reinvested in the firm until the late stages of growth, when cash flow is still strong but the number of profitable capital expenditure opportunities decreases.
- If new products are not created and markets are not expanded, the company enters a mature stage in which it grows at roughly the same growth rate as the overall economy. Dividend payouts are typically high during this stage. If the market for a company's goods and services diminish and no new prospects exist, the company enters a period of decline.

Another indicator of a company's position in the life cycle can be the P/E ratio. In the business cycle of companies, P/E ratios are higher when expected growth rates are high for newer companies. Conversely, P/Es decline as a company approaches maturity.

Cash rich companies may adopt different paths. Companies desirous of re-investing surfeit cash may enjoy high reception by shareholders because of optimistic expectations. Monies reinvested are expected to multiply at high speed using historic rates of growth. For such companies, if re-investment succeeds shareholders will continue to vow by their investment and would like to stay invested, examples, Colgate, Glaxo Pharma, Nestle, Wyeth Laboratories. If such companies distribute high dividends, shareholders may not be very happy because monies multiply faster in companies' hands rather than the investors hands. However, shareholders stay invested and prefer to enjoy the benefits of loyal investors in terms of bonanza gains on all accounts – payout and plough back through cash dividends and continuous appreciation in the bank value of shares and consequently the market price. Thus, the P/E ratio is always high.

OPERATING CASH FLOWS (OCF)

OCF is indicative of the cash throw off of business. If OCF is greater than the investments made in net fixed assets and net current assets, it means that the OCF is able to fund the investment needs of business for the accounting period in question. However, OCF need not always be greater than the net investments made - working capital or fixed assets. In fact during high growth phases when the rate of investment tends to exceed the rate of cash accruals from operations, OCF, though positive, will be less than the net investments made. It is also possible that whatever the status of OCF, the net investments made in working capital or fixed assets may be negative. Thus, net investments in these situations represent a cash inflow indicating that cash inflows from sale of assets is greater than the cash outflows on account of purchase of fixed assets or commitments made in favour of working capital. In some situations, high OCF plus negative net investments may augment cash flows. There is then a need to identify ways and means of deploying the emerging excesses of liquidity - particularly cash and bank balances positive or negative. If cash throw off is negative, it signals inadequacy of cash generated from business operation. Cash is thus not enough to pay for the operating costs of business.

CASH FLOW FROM OPERATIONS (CFO)

CFO intercepts OCF and FCFF. OCF adjusted for investments in the incremental working capital[1] on a net basis, results in CFO. A positive CFO indicates the ability of a business to absorb impending outlays on capital expenditures. A negative CFO, which is also a possibility, presents a situation of inadequate OCF and continued increases in incremental working capital requirements-rate and volume of increase in current assets is greater than the rate and volume of increase in current liabilities.

FREE CASH FLOW TO THE FIRM (FCFF)

FCFF is a measure of financial performance and indicates the profitability of a business from the cash perspective. FCFF is an useful benchmark to compare and analyse the financial health of a business on an intra firm and inter firm basis from time to time. Companies with a higher FCFF are prone to make acquisitions. However, it is empirically proved that "firms with high free cash flows are more likely to make bad acquisitions than firms with low free in terms of cash flows."[2] "In a 1986 paper in the *American Economic Review*, Michael Jensen noted that free cash flows allowed firms' managers to finance projects earning low returns which therefore might not be funded by the equity or bond markets. Examining the US oil industry, which had earned substantial free cash flows in the 1970s and the early 1980s, he wrote that "[the] 1984 cash flows of the ten largest oil companies were $48.5 billion, 28 per cent of the total cash flows of the top 200 firms in Dun's Business Month survey. Consistent with the agency costs of free cash flow, management did not pay out the excess resources to shareholders. Instead, the industry continued to spend heavily on [exploration and development] activity even though average returns were below the cost of capital." *(Source: Wikipedia)*"

Thus, FCFF provides business with an opportunity to venture into capital expenditures. New investment proposals are explored to enable the business to sustain its profit maximisation goal. So long as the present value, of outflow of new investments, is less than the present value of inflows, the Net Present Value (NPV) is positive. Value is created to the extent of the positive NPV. However, in the urge to go in for massive expansion if there is an over investment and even proposals, as mentioned earlier, with negative NPV are taken on board. There is an immediate and future crisis. The strategy is to induce managers to deploy funds only in favour of investment proposals with a positive NPV. Available FCFF should not be gorged in favour of all kinds of proposals including those with negative NPV at the prevailing minimum acceptable rate of return is always greater than or equal to the cost of capital. Otherwise there is an overwhelming burden on the available cash flows and levered capital structures emerge. Once borrowings are present in the capital structure the bankers appear on the scene to keep a tab on the cash flow profile of a business and its ability to honour the amortisation schedule. However, such monitoring by the banker protects the interests of other stakeholders too – particularly shareholders, if the strategy is to protect shareholders, interest and maximise value creation (in any case pre-empt value destruction). Accordingly, the free cash flow hypothesis says that dividends are beneficial to shareholders inasmuch as they reduce the

---

(1) *Incremental net working capital for the nth year is defined as the difference between the Net Current Assets of the nth and (n-1)th years.*

(2) *L. Lang and R. Stulz and R. Walking "Managerial Performance, Tobin's Q and Gains in Tender Offers, "Journal of Financial Economics", 1989.*

opportunities afforded to managers to take decisions which may encourage wasteful and counter productive financing/investment decisions. As mentioned above debt circumvents management freedom to the extent of the presence of bankers or other individual/institutional creditors alongwith their covenants. Thus, debt also monitors the productivity towards wasteful and unproductive financing decisions. FCFF is the amount of cash which a business can pay out to investors after encumbrances with respect to all investments are met. The residual cash flow is free and accessible to equity shareholders if and only if the firm is fully financed through equity. In case the business is levered debt also finds a place in the structure. The value of the firm then represents a valuation given the capital structure which is a mix of debt and equity. To ascertain the value of the firm, from the equity shareholders perspective, debt implications of repayment and new debt raised, alongwith preference share capital raised and redeemed, have to be taken into account.

FREE CASH FLOW TO EQUITY (FCFE)

FCFE starts with FCFF and adjusts the same for net debt flows (new debt raised minus debt repaid). Thus, FCFE may be defined as (FCFF minus all non equity payments). Equity shareholders do not have access to the cash balances of the firm per se. However they do own a share of the aggregate FCFF. Nevertheless, dividends are a tangible access to cash flows on a periodic basis. In any case debt holders enjoy a prior claim to fixed cash flows per covenants. Since all encumbrances are adjusted for, FCFE is regarded as a measure of a company's value, from the equity shareholders perspective.

Free cash flow to equity (FCFE) is indicative of the financial performance which expresses the cash generated, on a net basis, after all non equity payments. FCFE computation starts with profit after interest and tax or net income. FCFE refers to the cash after all debt services and expenses have been met and reinvestment needs are taken care of. FCFE is computed as follows:

FCFE = Profit after interest and tax minus changes in net working capital minus investments plus new debt raised minus amortisation of debt (debt repayment). Another way of looking at FCFE is to define it as:

FCFE = Cash flow from operations PLUS Sources MINUS Uses

where: **Cash flow from operations** = Profit after Interest and Taxes plus non cash charges (depreciation and amortisation).

Sources = increased in debt and other liabilities in favour of working capital and liquidation of investments (if any).

Uses = Amortisation of debt plus increases in assets in favour of working capital + new investments.

FCFE is considered as an improved holistic measure of valuation in relation to the dividend valuation model which does not adequately portray the value of a firm from the shareholders perspective. The dividend valuation model suffers from serious problems. If reinvestment of profits is the order of the day and it is in many businesses, the cash surplus belonging to equity shareholders exceeds dividend by leaps and bounds.

Of course the inherent assumption in the computation of FCFE is that the inputs required for computation are readily available. Dividends are only a part of the total quid pro quo to equity. As Prof. Damodaran puts it, "***Clearly, free cash flows to equity models cannot be used when***

the inputs needed to compare free cash flows to equity - capital expenditures, depreciation, working capital and net cash flows - are difficult or impossible to estimate."[3] FCFE, also known as 'mad money' is the cash a business has generated for its shareholders after meeting all relevant expenses and also investing in the net requirements of capital for day to day needs (working capital) and capital expenditures (fixed assets). Thus, FCF is the earnings before interest and taxes adjusted for taxes and also the non cash charges (depreciation and amortisation) alongwith adjustments for outlays on working capital and capital expenditures. FCFE is a good barometer of the financial health of a business as it is bereft of all accounting assumption affecting the bottom line of business involved in the computation of book profit. A business may report high book profit. However, this is no guarantee that money exists in business ultimately alongwith the shareholders in general are interested in cash. Cash is truth, real, tangible and actual unlike book profits which are 'fictional' and the result of several accounting assumptions and contrivances.

---

(3) Damodaran, Aswath. Damodaran on Valuation: Security Analysis for Investment and Corporate Finance. Wiley Finance. Second Edition. P. 186.

10

RATIOS — INTRODUCTION

WHAT IS A RATIO?

The dictionary meaning of the word "***RATIO***" is the relation of one thing to another of which the quotient is the measure. A ratio is nothing more than a simple division of two numbers. It is a mathematical yardstick that measures the relationship between two figures, which are related to each other and mutually interdependent.

Ratio is thus a relationship between one amount, '***x***' to another, '***y***', expressed as "***a ratio of x to y***". The relationship between two figures 10 and 5 expressed as a ratio can be presented as:

(1) 10:5, i.e., 10 is to 5 (numerator is to denominator).
(2) 10/5, i.e., numerator (dividend)/denominator (divisor).
(3) 2, i.e., quotient of 10 (dividend) divided by 5 (divisor), i.e., 2 times.
(4) 2:1 dividend (10):divisor (5).
(5) 200, i.e., quotient (2) multiplied by 100.

Thus, a ratio has a numerator and denominator and a ratio can be expressed as a simple fraction, integer, decimal fraction or percentage.

The final expression of a ratio can be in the form of:

(1) $x : y$ or 2 : 1 which is known as a "***PURE RATIO.***"
(2) $(x)/(y) \times 100$ or $2/1 \times 100$ i.e., 200 % which is known as "***PER CENT***" or "***PERCENTAGE***" ratios.
(3) 2 : 1 expressed as twice or two times which is known as '***times ratio.***'

DIFFERENT MODES OF EXPRESSING RATIOS

Ratio can be expressed in different ways as follows:

(a) ***SIMPLE OR PURE RATIO***: Simple ratio is merely a quotient arrived by division of one number by the other, e.g., Current Assets = (CA) ₹ 80,000, Current Liabilities (CL) = ₹ 20,000. The ratio of CA/CL is expressed as 80,000/20,000 = 4: 1

(b) ***PERCENTAGES***: Ratios are expressed in percentage form when simple or pure ratios are multiplied by 100. The resulting ratios are known as percentage ratios. Thus, current assets divided by current liabilities can also be expressed as 80,000/20,000 × 100 = 400%.

(c) ***RATES***: Ratios are expressed as rates which refers to ratios for a period in terms of '***number of times***', **e.g.,** in the ratio sales (₹ 10) divided by capital (₹ 5), it can be seen that the ratio is (10 ÷ 5), i.e., 2 times or twice. In other words, capital has turned over twice or the velocity of capital is '**2**'.

WHAT IS RATIO ANALYSIS?

Ratio Analysis is

- a method or process by which the relationship of items or groups of items in the financial statements are determined, computed, and presented for analysis and interpretation.
- an attempt to derive quantitative measures or guides concerning the financial health of a business enterprise in terms of profitability, liquidity, activity (utilisation), valuation and stability (capital structure).
- used both for trend analysis and also establishing and performing other statistical analysis, *viz.*, forecasting which is an input for financial planning and control.

NATURE OF RATIO ANALYSIS

An individual ratio may not be capable of providing answers required for various problems facing business. An individual ratio may provide valuable information only when it is studied and compared

(*a*) with several other complementary ratios.

(*b*) for an entity over a period of time.

(*c*) for similar entities, over a period of time, along with other complementary ratios.

Ratio analysis will be more meaningful when certain standards and norms or benchmarks are laid down so that the resultant ratios can be compared and continuously assayed with the said standards. This provides a base for decision making and assists in taking measures to rectify any drawback or inefficiency. In the alternative if the ratios signal good health, the '***status quo***' may be recommended.

Thus, it is better to understand the nature of ratios so that they can be employed judiciously under appropriate conditions, after understanding that ratios are a means to an end rather than an end in themselves.

WHY RATIOS?

Business ratios are the guiding stars for the management of enterprises and provide targets and standards for review and control. Further, ratios help managers in the following ways: assessing the financial health of the business enterprise from various angles; providing a true and fair view of the financial condition of a business to all stakeholders of a business enterprise; directing managers towards the most beneficial long-term strategies as well as effective short-term decision making; informing management about the most important issues requiring their immediate attention; enabling managers of different functions to work more easily towards overall business objectives; highlighting the important relationships and the need for proper balance between different segments of business and benchmarking for evaluating physical and financial performance.

The common language of business is finance or money. Universally, money measurement is the key to financial reporting. Therefore, ratios that are financially based are important. The manager will of course understand that financial numbers are only a reflection of what is actually happening and that it is the reality, not the ratios that must be managed. Physical planning always precedes financial planning. Physical activities well planned and controlled result in good results on the productivity front. This is finally reflected in operating excellence measured in financial terms. Thus, ratios can and are expressed in physical as well as financial terms.

USES

Ratio analysis can be particularly useful as an indicator of the performance of a business in relation to: the organization's own past performance and projected future performance; the recent performance of other, similar, concerns – intra industry and inter industry performance and the expectations of investors/other stakeholders, *viz.*, customers, staff, vendors, lenders, government, social activists, *et al.*, Companies can also be made with the performance.

DIFFERENCE BETWEEN ANALYSIS AND INTERPRETATION

Analysis of financial statements is a systematic and specialized treatment of the information presented in financial statements. The said information helps to arrive at useful conclusions about the economic performance of a business with respect to profitability, liquidity, solvency, activity, valuation, *et al.*, '***Financial Statement Analysis***' is largely a study of the interrelationships between various financial factors in an enterprise as disclosed by a single set of statements and study of the trends of these factors as shown in the series of statements.

To quote the Stock Exchange Official Directory, analysis means reorganisation of "***the data in ... financial statements and make it more intelligible and meaningful by simplification, re-grouping and rearrangement.***" Given, the re-arrangement of the financial data, further analysis is possible and necessary. The *pro forma* analytical statement of a particular accounting period does not by itself serve the intended purpose. If the end objective is to measure the economic performance of an enterprise, it is necessary to know the progress of an enterprise, which can be evaluated, if the analysed data (re-arranged information) is converted into meaningful yardsticks by using different tools of financial analysis. Thus, according to the stock exchange official directory "***a method, a technique of understanding and interpreting financial statements is indispensable.***"

According to the Dictionary (Microsoft Works) – Interpretation means: (1) establishment of meaning: an explanation or establishment of the meaning or significance of something, (2) ascribing particular meaning or significance to something and (3) performance of something: the way in which any work is presented in order to convey a specific understanding of the work.

Thus, interpretation is the mental process or conception of a person, with respect to the understanding of the elements of information presented in complicated and compounded financial statements. Such an interpretation helps to arrive at opinions or draw inferences or conclusions about different dimensions of business as indicated above. Further, interpretation also helps to explain the meaning and significance of the data re-arranged in an intelligible manner through further analysis. Thus, analysis and interpretation are mutually inclusive, continuous and complementary to each other.

CLASSIFICATION OF RATIOS

Ratios can be classified in different ways. Classification refers to grouping of ratios into homogeneous subsets to meet certain objectives. The objectives of any classification are driven by the end purposes to be achieved. The end purposes in turn could be driven by many factors. **Hence, the theme, different classification for different purposes as shown in Exhibit 22.**

EXHIBIT 22

CLASSIFICATION OF RATIOS

Different Classification for Different Purposes

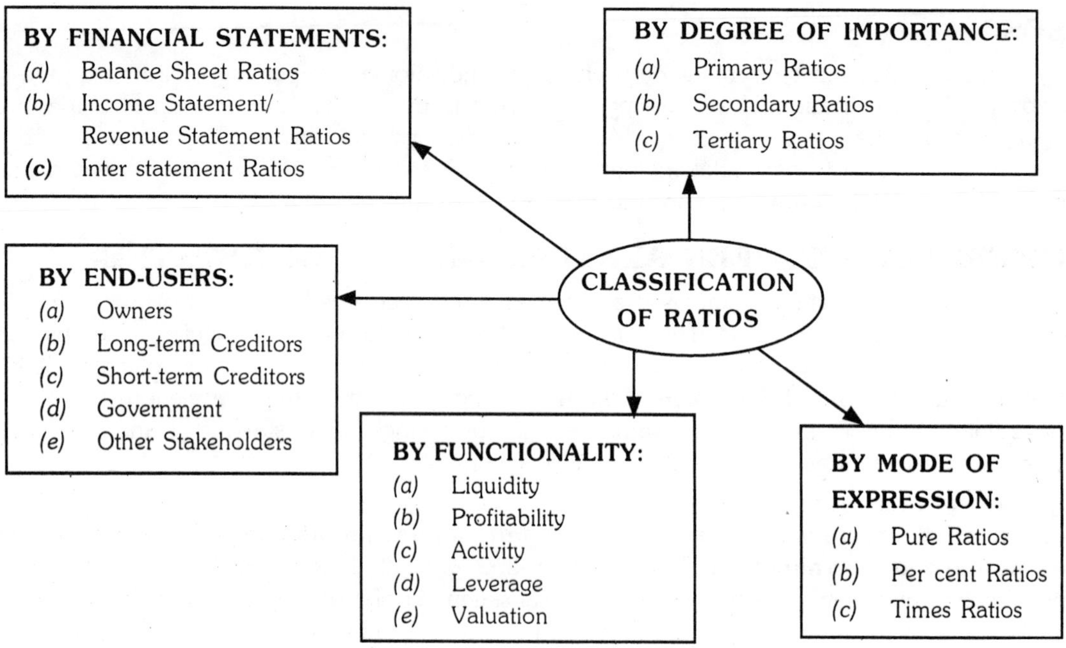

***N.B.**: The above classification is illustrative rather than exhaustive.*

CLASSIFICATION OF RATIOS

Ratios can be classified, as shown in **Exhibit 23**, in accordance with the financial statements from which they can be derived, *viz.*,

- income statement/profit and loss account / revenue statement ratios.
- balance sheet ratios/position statement ratios.
- combined statements/inter statement ratios.
- cash flow statement ratio (wherever cash flow statements are available).

The income statement ratios refer to the ratios which can be calculated from an income statement. In other words, both the numerator and the denominator can be ascertained from the income statement itself. Examples include the '***expenses: sales***' ratios or '***inventory: sales***' ratios. It is also possible to say that the income statement ratios relate to the '***results of operations***'. These ratios are known as operating ratios and are a measure of operating excellence (or otherwise).

The balance sheet ratios relate to those ratios whose numerator and denominator can be identified in the balance sheet. The balance sheet is an index of the financial performance of an enterprise, as on a given date. Examples of the balance sheet ratios include '***current assets: current liabilities***'; '***assets: proprietor's funds***'; '***debt: equity***' and so on.

The combined statement/inter statement ratios, refer to those ratios, which rely, on the income statement and balance sheet, simultaneously, for their computation. The numerator can be ascertained

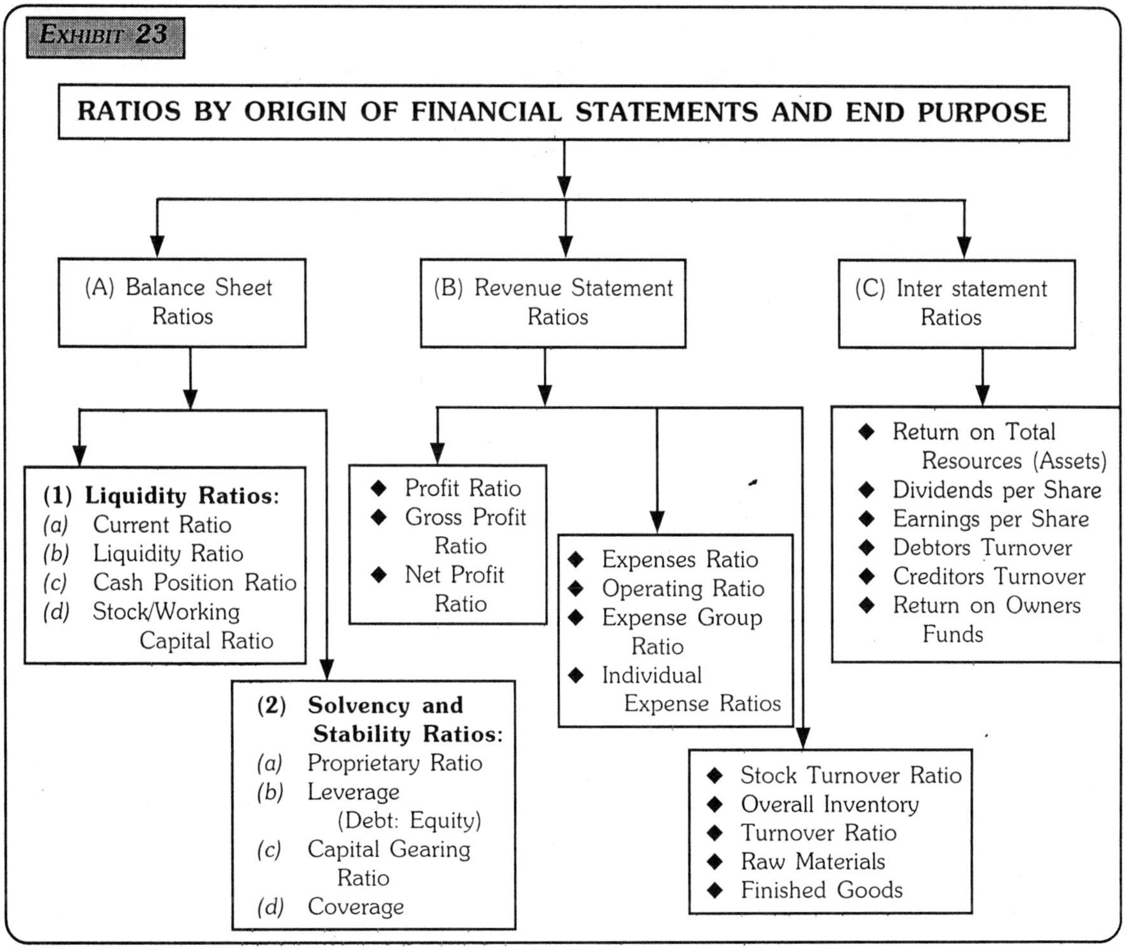

from the balance sheet and the information for the denominator comes from the income statement. In the alternative the reverse is also possible. The denominator can be obtained from the balance sheet and the numerator comes from the income statement. Thus, examples of the inter statement ratios include '***profit: assets***'; '***sundry debtors: sales***' and so on.

PROFIT: ASSETS	Profit	→	Income Statement
	Assets	→	Balance Sheet
SUNDRY DEBTORS: SALES	Sundry Debtors	→	Balance Sheet
	Sales	→	Income Statement

Prof. L. C. Gupta's* Recommendations:

- Profit & Loss account ratios are far superior than Balance Sheet ratios.
- Profit to sales ratio is more reliable than profit to assets ratio.
- Ratios calculated on cash profit basis give fairer picture than ratios calculated on book profit basis.

*Gupta, L. C., *Controlling Corporate Sickness.*, Oxford University Press, 1988, pg. 42

EXHIBIT 24

PROFIT RATIOS ARRANGED IN A FLOW CHART

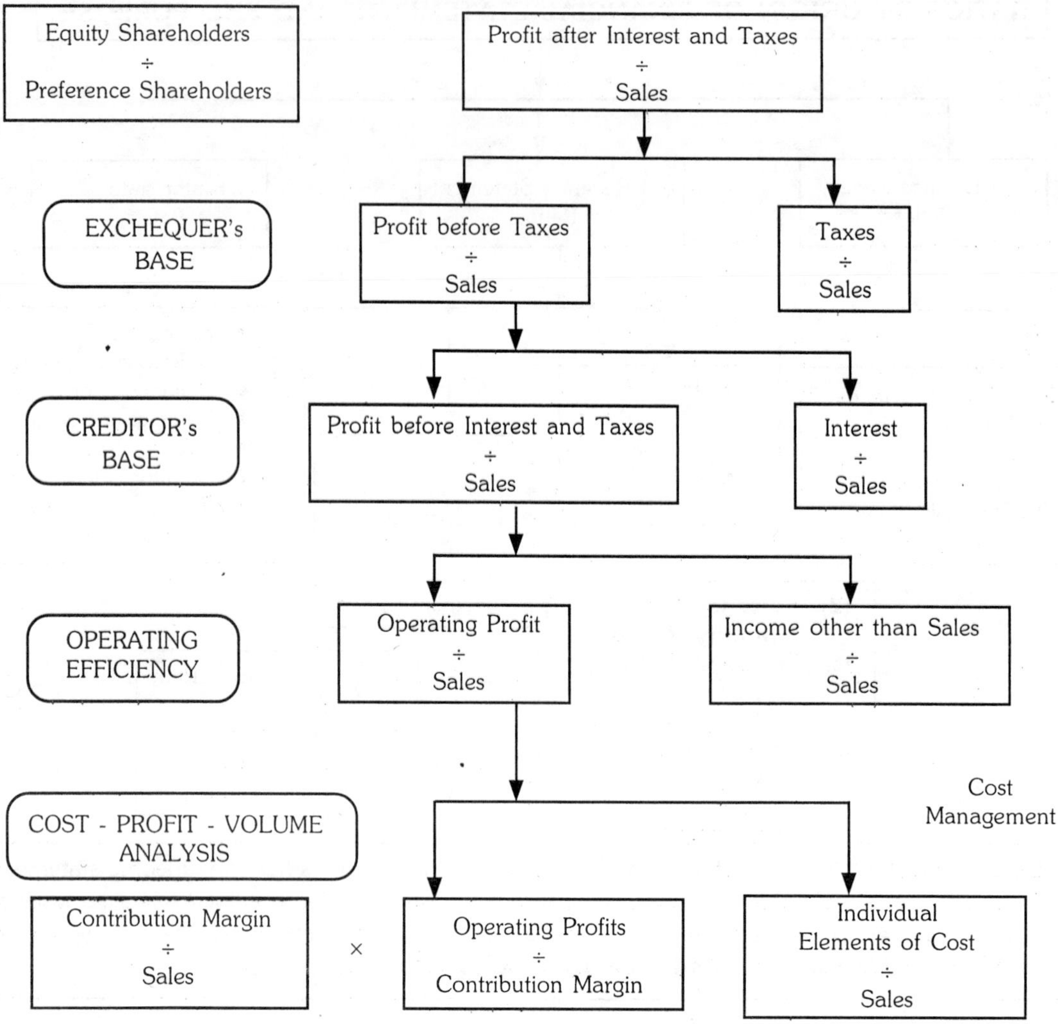

***N.B.**: The profit ratios have been arranged using sales, in the main, as a denomitor.*

FUNCTIONAL CLASSIFICATION OF RATIOS

- ***LIQUIDITY RATIOS***: These ratios measure the short-term and immediate financial position of a business and indicate its ability to meet short-term commitments out of short-term resources. Liquidity ratios measure the ability of a business to meet its current obligations (liabilities). Liquidity ratios relate to the liquid strength or cash ability of an enterprise.
- ***LEVERAGE RATIOS (CAPITAL STRUCTURE OR STABILITY RATIOS)***: These ratios measure the relationship between Proprietor's funds and Borrowed funds. Leverage ratios show the proportion of debt and equity in financing the firm's assets. They indicate the mix of funds provided by owners and lenders. The stability of an enterprise is also

measured with the help of cover ratios which indicate the adequacy of cash flows to sustain amortization obligations.

- ***ACTIVITY RATIOS (UTILISATION RATIOS)***: Activity or Turnover or Velocity ratios relate to the quality of the management of the resources employed in an enterprise. Activity relates to the total resources, i.e., assets employed and the effective use made of the same. It also relates to the effectiveness of the utilization of the available resources. Activity, therefore, is an important indicator of the performance of an enterprise.

PROFITABILITY RATIOS

Profitability ratios relate to the results of business operations. It includes ratios relating to sales, expenses and various concepts of profit margins. Profit is an important indicator of the performance of an enterprise. **In fact, it is a fairly reliable yardstick of effectiveness and efficiency.**

These ratios are intended to reflect the overall efficiency of the organization, its ability to earn a reasonable return on capital employed or on shares issued and the effectiveness of investment policies.

Profits measure effectiveness and efficiency. Hence, it is regarded as a dynamic measure of performance.

EXAMPLE

A salesperson given a target of selling 10 units at a price of ₹ 10/unit and a cost of ₹ 6/unit has to achieve (say) *(a)* volume of sales of 10 unit (effectiveness), *(b)* margin of ₹ 4/unit (efficiency) and *(c)* a sales of ₹ 100 and a profit of ₹ 40 (combined effort of effectiveness and efficiency). **Table 19** presents various outcomes.

Table 19

EFFECTIVENESS AND EFFICIENCY – OUTCOMES

I	Sell 11 units Price ₹ 11 per unit Profit ₹ 55	◆ Very effective and very efficient
II	Sell 9 units Price ₹ 12 per unit Profit 54	◆ Ineffective with respect to physical measure of performance but efficient. Overall effective and efficient
III	Sell 1 unit Price ₹ 20 Profit ₹ 14	◆ Very ineffective. However and very efficient. Ineffective though efficient
IV	Sell 1 unit Price ₹ 101 Profit ₹ 95	◆ Very ineffective, with respect to volume of sales. Extraordinarily efficient and overall effective and efficient. The outcome can also be labelled as ineffective but very efficient.

11

GROUPS OF RATIOS—LIQUIDITY RATIOS

VARIOUS GROUPS OF RATIOS

- *LIQUIDITY RATIOS*: There are three liquidity ratios to be understood as shown below:

Table 20

LIQUIDITY RATIOS

Name of Ratios	*Formulae*
◆ Current Ratio	$\frac{\text{Current Assets}}{\text{Current Liabilities}}$
◆ Quick Ratio or Acid Ratio	$\frac{\text{Quick Assets}}{\text{Current Liabilities}}$
◆ Cash Position Ratio	$\frac{\text{Cash Near Cash Assets}}{\text{Current Liabilities}}$

Prudent management requires that there should be an appropriate balance between different items comprising current assets. Excessive build-up of any of the items, *viz.*, cash, sundry debtors or inventories is uncalled for. The seasonal and other peculiar characteristics of certain industries need to be kept in mind. Seasonality of business results in fluctuation in sales and related factors. The current and related ratios may be prone to fluctuations. Hence, interpretation of the liquidity ratios should always take into account adjunct ratios like proportion of individual items, comprising current assets to the total current assets.

Table 21

ADJUNCT LIQUIDITY RATIOS

Per Cent Ratios	*Times Ratios*
$\left\{\dfrac{\text{Inventory}}{\text{Current Liabilities}} \times 100\right\}$	$\left\{\dfrac{\text{Sales}}{\text{Gross Working Capital}}\right\}$
$\left\{\dfrac{\text{Account Receivables}}{\text{Current Liabilities}} \times 100\right\}$	$\left\{\dfrac{\text{Sales}}{\text{Net Working Capital}}\right\}$
The above ratios throw light on the composition of the current assets section of the balance sheet. The skewed nature, or otherwise of the balance sheet can be identified.	The above ratios indicate the relationship between results (sales) and resources (gross working capital, i.e., current assets) or between sales and net working capital. Higher the ratios better the results for any given resource or better the utilisation of resource for any given results.

◆ ***CURRENT RATIO***: This ratio is also known as working capital ratio and is a favourite of lenders (individuals or institutions).

FORMULA

$$\frac{\text{Current Assets}}{\text{Current Liabilities}}$$

The current ratio is defined as current assets: current liabilities and can be expressed as a pure number or a percentage ratio. Generally, it is expressed as a pure ratio.

Current Assets are those assets which are converted into cash within an accounting period, usually a year. It includes items like cash in hand, cash at bank, account receivables, temporary investments like marketable securities and short-term securities, inventories of raw materials, work-in-process, finished goods, stores, spares, packing materials, accrued income, advance tax, prepaid expenses.

Current Liabilities are those liabilities which have to be paid within an accounting period. It gives an indication of impending cash requirements. Current liabilities include sundry creditors, bills payable, outstanding expenses, short-term loans from individuals, institutions, taxes payable, income received in advance, proposed dividends, unclaimed dividend and provision for taxation.

ILLUSTRATION

Calculate current ratio:

Current Assets = ₹ 5,00,000; Current Liabilities = ₹ 2,00,000

Current Ratio = Current Assets ÷ Current Liabilities = 2.5:1

A ratio of 2.5:1 means that for every rupee of current liability there are ₹ 2.50 worth of current assets. Thus, this ratio indicates the short-term solvency of a business and its ability to meet its current liabilities as and when they become due.

SALIENT FEATURES OF CURRENT RATIO

- A barometer of the short-term solvency of an enterprise.
- An index of the adequacy of working capital in an enterprise.
- An obligation of a business to honor its soon maturing obligations promptly.
- An indicator of
  - economic health of an enterprise because liquidity is one of the underlying factors contributing to economic health.
  - the extent to which the creditors' claims are protected by assets which are convertible into cash, within the maturity period of the creditors' obligations.
  - possible tendencies of the business to over trade or under capitalise or over invest in stocks or receivables.

DEMERITS OF CURRENT RATIO

- Any concept of a standard current ratio is rather vague and subjective. Hence, comparison with scientifically predetermined norms is difficult if not impossible.
- The current ratio does not communicate the inherent quality of liquidity *vis-à-vis* the composition of current assets.
- The current ratio is susceptible to window dressing.
- The current ratio, computed from any balance sheet, is subject to the principle of '***realization***'. Thus, the current ratio is suggestive of the cash power of an enterprise in the event of liquidation. However, the questions of working capital needs are based on the assumption that the enterprise will continue. The going concern assumption is implied in the very nature of accounting measurements and the resultant financial statements. Hence, a ratio with an assumption of liquidation, which is ruled out by definition, is of questionable conceptual integrity and theoretical soundness.
- Current ratio is regarded by many as a very crude test of liquidity as it does not take into account the liquidity or quality of each individual current asset.

Thus, it is dangerous to consider current ratio as a sole index of short-term solvency. It should always be supported with a study of other ratios and additional complementary analysis.

EXHIBIT 25

WINDOW DRESSING

"Window Dressing" means the practice of bolstering and improving the current ratio through manipulation to make it appear colourful. It is the practice of colouring the current ratio artificially.

Window Dressing may be done in the following ways:

(1) *Manipulation of inventory values.*
(2) *Recording in advance in the current year, any cash receipts of the following year.*
(3) *Deliberate deferring of purchases of fixed assets till the balance sheet date.*
(4) *Liquidation of current liabilities.*
(5) *Permitting stock to fall below normal levels.*
(6) *Postponing certain pressing payments.*
(7) *Postponing purchase of inventories till balance sheet date pressurizing customers to pay their dues.*
(8) *Considering short-term obligations as long-term debts.*
(9) *Organizing special sales and reducing inventory.*

DEFINITION

*An attempt to present a position, which is not really present. Crudely put, it is an attempt at manipulating the financial position of an enterprise. "**Window dressing**" refers to boosting of the current ratio to make it appear stronger than it really is. Since the current ratio is supposed to indicate the liquidity strength, an attempt is made to improve the current ratio on the date the balance sheet is drawn.*

ILLUSTRATION:

Current Assets = ₹ 50,000; Current Liabilities = ₹ 20,000

Current Ratio = Current Assets ÷ Current Liabilities = 2.5 times

When creditors are paid to the extent of ₹ 10,000/- out of cash balance, the current ratio is manipulated as follows:

$$\frac{50{,}000-10{,}000}{20{,}000-10{,}000}=\frac{40{,}000}{10{,}000}=4 \text{ times}$$

The current ratio earlier was merely 2.5 times.

Thus, an equal increase in the both numerator and denominator, i.e., current assets and a current liabilities, would decrease the current ratio. Similarly, an equal decrease in both the figures would improve the ratio.

Window Dressing is something which the analyst must continuously guard against, the existence of which itself is very difficult to detect in live business situations.

EXHIBIT 26

ICT SECTOR – LEAD COMPANIES
CURRENT RATIO (TIMES)

	2002	2003	2004	2005	2006
Infosys	3.7	3.9	2.35	2.19	2.77
Satyam*	5.3	6.15	6.42	7.12	6.50
Wipro	3.26	2.97	1.60	1.32	1.46

SOURCE: *CAPITAL MARKET: 2006 Compendium of Top 500 Companies in India Published. pp. 43, 63, 46 and 44 respectively and 2011 pp 42 and 51.*

Infosys and WIPRO had very high current ratio by default rather than design. Excellent business and timely collections unsupported by effective and efficient cash deployment policies into successive productive reinvestment opportunities. Even after 2006, for the five year period 2007-11, the average current ratio of Infosys and WIPRO 4.15 and 2.25 times.

**Post-Satyam scam, it is known that the current ratio, nay the financial statement of Satyam were fudged. Yet in the meantime the interpretation of Satyam's balance sheet was universally praised for its extraordinary financial performance including the extraordinary liquidity.*

EXHIBIT 27

SATYAM'S BALANCE SHEET

On 7 January 2009, company Chairman Ramalinga Raju resigned after notifying board members and the Securities and Exchange Board of India (SEBI) that Satyam's accounts had been falsified.

Raju confessed that Satyam's balance sheet of 30 September 2008 contained:

- *Inflated figures for cash and bank balances of ₹5,040 crores (US$1.09 billion) as against 5,361 crores (US$1.16 billion) reflected in the books.*
- *An accrued interest of 376 crores (US$81.59 million) which was non-existent.*
- *An understated liability of 1,230 crores (US$266.91 million) on account of funds was arranged by himself.*
- *An understated debtors' position of 490 crores (US$106.33 million) (as against 2,651 crores (US$575.27 million) in the books).*

SOURCE: *www.wikipedia.org.*

Table 22

CUREENT RATIO vs. QUICK RATIO

	Current Ratio	Quick Ratio
Approach I	$\frac{\text{Current Assets}}{\text{Current Liabilities}}$	$\frac{\text{Current Assets} - \text{Stock}}{\text{Current Liabilities}}$
Approach II	$\frac{\text{Current Assets}}{\text{Current Liabilities}}$	$\frac{\text{Current Assets} - \text{Stock}}{\text{Current Liabilities}}$ Bank Overdraft – Income Received in Advance

Quick Ratio is also known as ***'liquid ratio'*** or ***'quick assets ratio'*** or ***'acid test ratio'.***

This ratio is designed to indicate the liquid financial position of an enterprise. Thus, the ratio indicates the firm's ability to meet its immediately maturing obligations promptly. It measures the relationship between Quick assets and Quick liabilities.

CALCULATION

The quick ratio is calculated by dividing quick assets by quick liabilities. This is expressed as a pure or per cent ratio.

FORMULA

$$\frac{\text{Quick Assets}}{\text{Quick Liabilities}}$$

Quick assets are those current assets which can be realized immediately, at short notice without much difficulty or undue losses. These assets are also known as '***near cash***' assets. Quick assets include cash and other assets that are converted quickly into cash. Quick assets are current assets less inventories and prepaid expenses.

Quick liabilities are those current liabilities which mature within a very short period of time. They are fluctuating and fall due for payment at any time during the year.

All current liabilities with the exception of bank overdraft and incomes received in advance are regarded as quick liabilities.

EXHIBIT 28

CURRENT ASSETS (CA) vs. QUICK ASSETS (QA)

CA are assets which are to be converted into cash soon (usually a year).

QA are assets which are to be converted into cash very soon (less than a year).

***N.B:** The same analogy is applicable to Current vs. Quick Liabilities.*

PURPOSE

The purpose of quick ratio is to measure the immediate solvency position of the business and indicate the availability (or otherwise) of ready cash to meet its immediate commitments.

SIGNIFICANCE OF QUICK RATIO

- Indicates the immediate solvency position of business. Short-term creditors study quick ratio along with the current ratio of a firm to understand its overall solvency position.
- This ratio is a true test of business solvency and will indicate the role of inventory in disfiguring the solvency of any business.

EXAMPLE:

If two firms have same current ratio but different quick ratios, it clearly indicates an over investment in inventories by the firm having a relatively low quick ratio. The quick ratio eliminates inventory and is a therefore rigorous test of liquidity. Again, this ratio is more important for lenders.

REASON FOR EXCLUDING INVENTORY

The reason why items like inventory are omitted is to ascertain the intrinsic ability to generate cash. Inventories are regarded the least liquid of current assets. Moreover, it is not untrue to say that inventories are assets on which the largest losses will occur in the event of liquidation. There may be exceptional situations when accumulated inventory suddenly assumes importance due to shortages.

Analysts recognize that current assets include inventory, which is sometimes slow moving and not as readily realizable into cash as is implied by the current ratio. The reason for excluding inventory figure is that its liquidity can be a problem. It may be re-called that "***liquidity***" is used to express how quickly, and what portion of its book value, an asset can be converted into cash, if need arises. Situations may arise where a business has a constant current but a falling quick ratio. This would be a most dangerous sign. It tells us that inventory is building up at the expense of progressively and relatively more liquid assets like receivables and cash.

The acid test helps in identifying the ability to command cash without disposing inventory, because it is assumed that inventory will not supply cash as readily as debtors or cash. The acid test is, therefore, supposed to be an improved, stringent, version of the current ratio in measuring the liquidity of an enterprise.

CURRENT RATIO vs. QUICK RATIO

If the quick ratio indicates a rather substantial decline in the liquidity index, compared to the current ratio, the quick ratio reveals an unfavourable situation. However, it is implied that an unfavourable quick ratio is associated with a favourable current ratio in view of inventory which bolsters the current ratio.

The lesser the quick ratio, higher the incidence of inventory in inflating the current ratio. Inventory accumulation and quick ratio bear an inverse relation with each other. The higher the quick ratio, lower the incidence of inventory in inflating the current ratio. However, a high quick ratio need not necessarily signal a favourable liquidity position. It is quite possible that resources are blocked in accounts receivables instead of the prior stage input, *viz.*, finished goods/other elements of invenroty.

IS QUICK RATIO A BETTER MEASURE OF LIQUIDITY?

Generally, a quick ratio of (1:1) is considered as a satisfactory current financial condition. Although quick ratio is a more penetrating test of liquidity than the current ratio, yet it should be used cautiously. A quick ratio of (1:1) or more does not necessarily, as mentioned above, imply sound liquidity position. It should be remembered again, that all debtors may not be liquid and cash may be immediately needed to pay operating expenses. It should also be noted that inventories are not absolutely non-liquid. To a measurable extent, inventories are available to meet current obligations. Thus, a company with a high value of quick ratio can suffer from shortage of funds if it has slow paying, doubtful and long-duration outstanding debtors. On the other hand, a company with a low value of quick ratio maybe really prospering and paying its current obligation in time if it has been turning over its inventories efficiently. Nevertheless, the quick ratio is an important, maybe an improved and acid, index of the firm's liquidity.

EXHIBIT 29

WHAT IS ACID TEST? - A TAILPIECE

*An acid test ratio is supposed to provide, beyond any doubt, an answer to a question which may otherwise be unsettled. There was an enigma "**of the two great Indian batsmen Sir Sunil Gavaskar and Mr. G. Vishwanath who is the taller.**" In a function in Bangalore, which both the batsmen attended, they were seated on a chair of equal height. Mr. Gavaskar's feet could comfortably touch the ground unlike that of Mr. Vishwanath. This is an acid test to ascertain who is the taller or who is the shorter of the two.*

CASH POSITION RATIO

The cash position ratio is defined as:

FORMULA

$$\frac{\text{Cash on Hand and Bank}}{\text{Current Liabilities}}$$

The cash position ratio and quick ratio bear between themselves an inverse relationship. Higher the cash position ratio less is the role of receivables in quick ratio and *vice versa*.

While creditors may feel increasingly comfortable with the increasing value of this ratio, enterprise has to reconcile itself with the idea of declining profitability.

Both the current ratio and quick ratio are most widely used measures of short-term liquidity but a problem with these two ratios is that they are static. They reflect values at a point in time only, as of the balance sheet date. It is possible to window dress a company's account so that it looks good on this one day only, *a la* Satyam.

EXHIBIT 30

LIQUIDITY vs. SOLVENCY

"Insolvent banks survive. Liquid banks die"

In finance or business, solvency is the ability of an entity or individual to pay debts. Solvency can also be described as the ability of a corporation to meet its long-term fixed expenses and to accomplish long-term expansion and growth. The better a company's solvency, the better it is financially. When a company is insolvent, it means that it can no longer operate and is facing bankruptcy, or in fact it is bankrupt.

In accounting, liquidity is a measure of the ability of debtors to pay their debts as and when they fall due. It is usually expressed as a ratio or a percentage of relevant assets to current liabilities.

Solvency is essentially the ability to repay debts. Liquidity is the ability to easily convert assets into cash.

They both describe two different cash flow-related characteristics of a business.

Solvency means that a business can pay its bills.

Liquidity is a measure of a business's ability to have cash ready (as opposed to cash tied up in investments, inventory or receivables).

A liquid business is more likely to be solvent than a non-liquid business. However, not all businesses with liquid assets are solvent and not all solvent businesses have strong liquidity.

SOURCE: www.wikipedia.org

STOCK WORKING CAPITAL RATIO

The Stock Working Capital ratio brings out the relationship between Stock and Working Capital. It is alternatively known as '***Inventory-working capital ratio***' or '***inventory-current assets ratio***' and is expressed as per cent ratio. The stock-working capital ratio is defined as:

FORMULA

$$\frac{\text{Stock or Inventory}}{\text{Working Capital}}$$

Stock or inventory is defined as the rupee value of raw materials, work-in-progress, finished goods, stores and packing materials. It may be noted that stock is valued at cost price or market price whichever is lower. Stock can mean either rupee value of the closing stock as on the date of the balance sheet or the average rupee value of the stock, defined as:

$$\left\{\frac{\text{Opening Stock plus Closing Stock}}{2}\right\}$$

Working capital means either gross working capital (current assets) or net working capital (current assets minus current liabilities).

The Stock-Working Capital ratio can be expressed as: closing stock/gross working capital; closing stock/net working capital; average stock/gross working capital and average stock/net working capital.

Inventory, as mentioned earlier, is the least liquid of the three principal items viz. inventory, sundry debtors and cash comprising current assets. Its realisation value is rather low. Hence, this ratio measures the extent to which a business has committed the gross or net working capital funds in the least liquid item of inventory. In other words, it indicates the degree of importance of inventory in the working capital of a business.

PURPOSE

This ratio is related to, and used in conjunction with current and quick ratio. The purpose of this ratio, to reiterate, is to show the extent to which the working capital is locked in inventories.

SIGNIFICANCE

- This ratio highlights the predominance of stocks in the current financial position of the company.
- A higher ratio indicates weak working capital and doubtful immediate-liquidity and solvency position. High ratios for temporary periods may indicate liquidity problems only. However, continued high ratios may result in solvency issues too.
- This ratio is an indicator of the adequacy (or otherwise) of working capital.

STOCK: NETWORKING CAPITAL

This ratio, as can be seen by definition, uses the difference between Current assets and Current liabilities as the denominator. The denominator, in rupees, shrinks to the extent of current liabilities. The ratio in integer form or percentage gets inflated automatically. Lower the ratio, greater the extent to which inventory in particular, current assets in general, are financed out of current liabilities. Higher the ratio greater the role of current liabilities in funding current assets. A high ratio indicates short-term funding of long-term uses and a low ratio indicates long-term funding of short-term uses.

SIGNIFICANCE

- This ratio is suggestive of the role of non-current liabilities in supporting current assets.
- This ratio indicates financial policy in proportioning its networking capital in favour of stock.

STOCK: GROSS WORKING CAPITAL

This ratio indicates the percentage of current assets committed in the form of inventory or stock and measures the liquidity of an enterprise, given the premise that higher the proportion of stock to gross working capital, lower the liquidity of the working capital. Thus, at first sight we may say that this ratio and the liquidity of the enterprise bear an inverse relationship. However, the extent to which inventory tends to immobilise the cash strength of an enterprise, depends on the quality rather than the quantity of inventory which can be put to some use-resale or utility value. In many enterprises, a low level of obsolete inventory may be more serious than an excess stock of actively usable material – which has utility and or resale value.

STANDARD RATIO

It is very difficult to lay down a standard stock-working capital ratio as the level of stock to be maintained differs from business to business and within a business from time to time or season to season.

The difficulty in fixing a standard for the ratio is due to the fact that it is necessary to build up stock in the initial stages in case of newly started business. Further, the idea of stock-working capital ratio will not work particularly when judgmental considerations are involved, the intangible factors have to be assessed and the imponderables have to be evaluated and mindsets governing decision making vary from industry to industry, person to person and one business group to the other.

Exhibit 31

ZERO LEVEL INVENTORY - A NORM

In the context of change in the state of the art in terms of mindset and technology the concept of a standard, in this context, has undergone a radical change with just-in-time as a strategy and logistics having improved speed of delivery and massive outsourcing of inventory management processes. The question of levels of inventory is becoming redundant. While companies like Fedex and DHL and several other BPOs have played an important role in this revolution, companies like Toyoto and Dell have established new landmarks in inventory levels. The norm is zero or near zero levels of inventory.

12

GROUPS OF RATIOS—PROFITABILITY RATIOS

PROFITABILITY RATIOS

GROSS PROFIT RATIO

It is also known as "***Margin***" or "***Gross Margin Ratio***" or "***Trading Margin Ratio***" or "***Manufacturing Margin Ratio***". It brings out the relationship between Gross Profit and Net sales. It is expressed as a percentage of Net Sales. This ratio is very important in evaluating results of trading operations.

$$\frac{\text{Gross Profit}}{\text{Net Sales}}$$

NUMERATOR: "***Gross Profit***" defined in the trading business as the difference between the credits to the trading account minus the debits to the trading account. In a manufacturing business, gross profit refers to '***gross manufacturing profit***' and is the difference between the Credits and Debits to the manufacturing account, *viz.*, (sales minus factory cost of goods sold).

FUNCTIONS OF GROSS PROFIT RATIO

- Measures the results of trading or manufacturing operations.
- Shows the gap between Revenues and Expense at a point after which the enterprise has to meet expenses related to non-manufacturing or non-trading activities like marketing, administration, finance and also taxes and other appropriations.
- Gross profit is a sensitive barometer reflecting the quality of two important functions of business, namely, production and marketing.
- It reveals the extent to which sales promotion and cost control are successful in an enterprise.

Table 23

GROSS PROFIT RATIO – REASONS FOR CHANGE

	SP / UNIT	C.P / UNIT	COMMENT
(a)	↑	*k*	Good marketing performance
(b)	*k*	↓	Good cost management
(c)	↑	↓	Good marketing performance and good cost management
(d)	↑	↓	Not so good marketing performance offset by very good cost performance **provided rate of ↓ CP/unit is more than rate of ↓ SP/unit**
(e)	↑	↑	Excellent marketing performance sustains rise in CP per unit **provided rate of ↑ SP/unit is more than rate of ↑ CP/unit**

SP = Selling Price, CP = Cost Price, ↑ = Increase, ↓ = Decrease

The reasons for decline in gross profit ratio can be easily identified given the above framework of analysis. With the help of useful software packages, sensitivity / simulation analysis can be carried out to guide management decision making.

STANDARD GROSS PROFIT RATIO

The process of setting a standard gross profit ratio is dependent upon many factors viz. the typicality of business, inter-firm data, philosophy of the enterprise in respect of the standard – attitude towards excellence and the extent to which prices and cost lend themselves to the idea of standards.

Thus, in the ultimate analysis, a balance has to be struck between the various factors listed and a policy decision relating to the standard gross profit ratio has to be taken.

OPERATING RATIO

Operating ratio is defined as Cost of Goods Sold plus other operating expenses divided by Net Sales.

Cost of Goods Sold could be either trading cost of goods sold or factory cost of goods sold.

Operating ratio is the relationship between cost of activities, trading or manufacturing and net sales. This ratio brings out the relationship between Total costs of goods sold and Net sales.

In other words, operating ratio indicates what percentage the operating expenses bear to net sales.

EXHIBIT 32

OPERATING RATIO: FORMULAE

The operating ratio may, therefore, be written as follows:

$$\frac{\textit{Total Cost of Sales}}{\textit{Sales}}$$

↓

Where: ***total cost of sales*** *is the sum of factory cost of sales and non-manufacturing expenses like administration, marketing and interest and* ***sales*** *are the sales adjusted for sales returns and sales discounts.*

OR

$$\left[1-\frac{\textit{Net Profit}}{\textit{Sales}}\right]$$

↓

Where: ***Net Profit*** *= Net Sales minus Factory Cost of Sales minus non-manufacturing expenses like administration, marketing and interest and* ***sales*** *is the sales adjusted for sales returns and sales discounts.*

OR

$$\left[1-\frac{\textit{Gross Profit}}{\textit{Sales}}\right]+\frac{\textit{Non-manufacturing expenses}}{\textit{Sales}}$$

↓

Where: ***Gross Profit*** *is net sales minus factory cost of sales; and non-manufacturing expenses which include administration, marketing and interest expenses and sales are sales adjusted for sales returns and sales discounts.*

The operating ratio as defined above indicates the extent to which the costs or debits to the profit and loss account absorb the sales.

ILLUSTRATION

$$\text{OPERATING RATIO} = \frac{\text{Cost of goods sold plus other operating expenses*}}{\text{Net Sales}} \times 100$$

**Other operating expenses include marketing, administration and finance inputs.*

FUNCTIONS

The operating ratio indicates the efficiency with which the enterprise has managed the factory operations and the non-manufacturing segments, *viz.*, marketing, administration and financing. It provides management with vital clues as to which segments of business require attention for improvement and also indicates those segments which are performing very well.

RELATIONSHIP OF OPERATING RATIO WITH NET PROFIT RATIO AND GROSS PROFIT RATIO

The operating ratio tells us about the burden which sales have to bear before contributing to Net Profit. It can be seen that (1 minus Operating Ratio) gives (Net Profit/ Sales), *i.e.*, the Profit Margin Ratio. The operating ratio indicates the cost picture or the debit aspect of the profit margin ratio. Higher the operating ratio, given a level of sales, lowers the profit margin ratio or the net profit ratio. The reverse is also true.

The operating ratio is also related to gross profit ratio. A high gross profit ratio has the potential of absorbing a high operating ratio (high incidence of operating expenses) and yet retains the net profit ratio at a satisfactory level. However a high gross profit ratio coupled with an unfavourable operating ratio, is indicative of abnormal non-manufacturing expenses. Again, a low gross profit ratio coupled with disciplined amount of non-manufacturing expenses can help the operating ratio to be within reasonable bounds. Simultaneously, the net profit ratio may be salvaged at least, to that extent.

EXHIBIT 33

GROSS PROFIT RATIO, OPERATING RATIO AND NET PROFIT RATIO – INTERRELATIONSHIP

(a) Gross Profit Ratio $= 1 - \frac{\text{Factory Cost of Sales}}{\text{Sales}}$

(b) 1 – Gross Profit Ratio $= \frac{\text{Factory Cost of Sales}}{\text{Sales}}$

(c) Operating Ratio $= 1 - \frac{\text{Factory Cost of Sales + Non Manufacturing Expenses}}{\text{Sales}}$

(d) 1 – Operating Ratio $= \frac{\text{Net Profit}}{\text{Sales}}$

Table 24

GROSS PROFIT RATIO, OPERATING RATIO AND NET PROFIT RATIO – INTERRELATIONSHIP AGAIN

GROSS PROFIT RATIO	OPERATING RATIO	NET PROFIT RATIO	COMMENTS
HIGH	HIGH £	LOW £	The favourable gross profit is offset by the unfavourable non-manufacturing expenses.
HIGH	LOW $	HIGH $	The favourable gross profit is complemented by a net profit ratio because of the control over expenses.
LOW	LOW ($)	HIGH $	The unfavourable gross profit ratio is offset by the control over non-manufacturing expenses with a result that the net profit ratio is sustained.
LOW	HIGH (£)	LOW £	The unfavourable gross profit ratio is worsened by the increase in non-manufacturing expenses and the net profit ratio is adversely affected to that extent.

NOTE:

- £ Unfavourable tendencies of non-manufacturing expenses.
- $ The increase in factory cost of sales is at least offset by the decrease in the non-manufacturing expenses.

STANDARD RATIO

Though a standard operating ratio cannot be precisely laid down, the ratio in case of manufacturing concerns is normally high, while in case of other firms, the ratio may be low.

EXPENSE RATIO

The expense ratios give an indication of the extent to which the credit effects of the revenue are neutralised by the debit impact of the expenses. The expense ratios can therefore, be said to have an inverse relationship with the profit ratios. The following generalizations can be made:

- Higher the expense ratio, lower the profit ratio and *vice versa*.
- Higher the factory cost of sales ratio, lower the gross profit ratio and vice versa.
- Higher the (manufacturing/non-manufacturing) expenses lower the net profit ratio and *vice versa*.

NET PROFIT RATIO

The definition of this ratio is related to the end use proposed. The theme is "***Different Profits for Different Purposes***". The end purposes include:

(a) Evaluating operating efficiency in respect of two concepts of profit-margin ratios viz. operating profit/sales and net operating profit/sales.

(b) Assessing creditor's position by the ratio of profit before interest and taxes / interest) which shows the protection enjoyed by creditors in terms of their periodic claims.

(c) Measuring exchequer's base, which is given by the profits before taxes.

(d) Identifying the position of preference shareholders which is given by the profit after interest and taxes.

(e) Identifying the position of equity shareholders, which is given by the profits after interest, taxes and preference dividends.

We may consider the following ratios for our study:

- OPERATING PROFIT/SALES
- NET OPERATING PROFIT/SALES
- PROFIT BEFORE INTEREST AND TAXES/SALES
- PROFIT AFTER INTEREST AND TAXES/SALES

OPERATING PROFIT/SALES

NUMERATOR: Operating profit is defined as sales minus factory costs of sales minus marketing and administrative expenses.

Operating profit/sales is a yardstick to measure the profitability of the operations of the enterprise and shows the surplus which exists after meeting the marketing and administrative expenses.

This ratio is functionally related to sales price per unit and costs per unit. Improvements in '***unit cost***' can take place if there is a favourable movement of the unit price (?) and/or costs (?). (Operating profit/sales) accounts simultaneously for the performance of the production and marketing segments of an enterprise and is indicative of the internal efficiencies (or otherwise) of an enterprise. The ability of an enterprise to attain, maintain and sustain in the competitive edge is dependent upon effective management of price and cost per unit.

NET OPERATING PROFIT/SALES

In this ratio it is assumed that interest is an operating expense and should be deducted before arriving at the profit figure. This ratio measures the profitability of the business by indicating the surplus which exists after meeting factory cost of sales and all non-manufacturing expenses, namely, marketing, administration and finance (interest). The idea of including interest as part of the non-manufacturing expenses may not necessarily meet with a favourable consideration from within the enterprise. The decision to include/exclude interest depends upon the view management takes on how much pressure to bring on the employees to show results with respect to input management including finance costs. Thus, tough standards justify using interest costs as a valid input. Low standards may exclude interest charges.

PROFIT BEFORE INTEREST AND TAXES/SALES

Profit before interest and taxes/ sales ratio shows the amount of pre-interest and pre-tax profit generated for every ₹ 100 sales. Higher the ratio better the performance and *vice versa*. Incidentally, the numerator also forms the basis to know the amounts available to meet the dues to lenders on account of interest.

PROFIT AFTER INTEREST AND TAXES/SALES

(Profit after interest and taxes/sales), shows the efficiency of operating management and also the efficiency with respect to '***interest management***' and '***tax management***'.

The ratio reveals the surplus that is to accrue to shareholders (preference shares and equity shares) that is to say the owners.

However, the first claim shall be that of preference shareholders. They are entitled to a fixed consideration which like interest is a periodic, but post-tax, obligation. Again while interest is a charge to profit and loss account, dividend is an appropriation and chargeable to profit and loss appropriation account. The preference shareholders will view their safety by the (profit after interest and taxes/sales) and the size of the numerator in rupees.

Once the dividends on preference shares are met, the profits which exist belong to the equity shareholders. The relevant profit is then profit after interest, taxes and preference dividends.

SIGNIFICANCE

Net profit ratio is considered to be the most significant of all revenue ratios.

- It is a measure of overall profitability and it is very useful to entrepreneurs and investors in judging the prospects of return on their respective investments.
- It indicates as to what portion of net sales is finally available for appropriation in favour of entrepreneurs.
- It is a clear index of cost control, managerial efficiency and sales promotion. This ratio is often called ***'the index of operational efficiency.'***
- Read along with gross profit ratio and operating ratio, net profit ratio provides deeper insight into in terms of the effectiveness and efficiency of overall business operations.

Table 25

DIFFERENT RATIOS FOR DIFFERENT PURPOSES

END PURPOSES	*RATIO*
• Evaluating operating efficiency	• Operating profit/sales
• Assessing creditor's position	• Net operating profit/sales
• Measuring exchequer's tax base	• Profit before interest and taxes/sales
• Identifying preference shareholder's position	• Profit before taxes (This is not a ratio.)
	• Profit after interest and taxes/sales
• Identifying equity shareholder's position	• Profit after interest and taxes and preference dividends/sales

ACTIVITY RATIOS

Funds of creditors and owners are invested in various assets to generate sales and of course profits. The larger the amount of sales in monetary terms better the utilization of assets and returns in terms of sales per rupee of investment in total assets. The returns (sales) per rupee of investment are indicative of the utilisation of assets or the level of activity in business.

MEANING

Activity ratios are employed to evaluate the efficiency with which a business manages and utilises its assets. These ratios are also called **turnover ratios** because they indicate the speed with which assets are being turned over into sales. Activity ratios, thus, involve a relationship between Sales and Assets. A proper balance between sales and assets generally reflects that assets are managed well and of course that adequate output (sales) is generated per unit of input (investment). Several activity ratios can be calculated to judge the effectiveness of assets utilization.

Activity or **Turnover Ratios** include the following:

$$\frac{\text{Sales or Cost of Goods Sold}}{\text{Investment}}$$

Investment can mean any one or more of the following expressions, *viz.*, total gross assets, total net assets, total capital employed, gross working capital, networking capital, investment can also mean individual elements of gross working capital, *viz.*, inventory, receivables and cash. In the alternative, individual elements of inventory, *viz.*, finished goods, work-in-progress and raw materials.

The ratio of Sales/Total Assets indicates the following:

- Brisk business activity (or otherwise).
- How many times the assets have rolled over.
- Velocity or rolling of monies invested in the total assets.
- Marketing productivity of every rupee of asset.
- High ratio indicates hectic activity, brisk selling and a relatively lean asset portfolio.
- Very high ratio may lead to overtrading and increase the risk profile of business in terms of increased receivables and potential bad debts, assuming that the increased receivables are due to liberal credit policy, increased marketing expenses apart, further '***over trading***' may require dipping into reserves and/or additional borrowings to absorb the burden of brisk activity. Both these actions can contribute towards undercapitalisation – inadequate owners' funds and also a potentially speculative position with chances of supernormal profits or abnormal losses. Business is thus exposed to high risks.
- Low ratio indicates depressed activity, limited sales and redundant assets or under-utilisation of available assets.
- A very low ratio may lead to under trading and also increase the risk profile of business in terms of reduced sales and increased inventory. Inventory obsolescence is an imminent threat. Business may be rather dull. Again a high level of assets coupled with leverage may build-up creditors' pressure creating a new set of problems. This may cause over-capitalisation. However to plug the adverse effects of under trading and the associated imbalances in the capital structure (overcapitalisation), higher the ratio better the performance.
- A ratio of '***2***' times indicates that every rupee invested in the total assets is able to earn twice as much in terms of '***revenue***'.

The performance of the working capital section is measured through turnover ratios and are as follows:

OPERATING CYCLE

The operating cycle represents the flow of enterprise values through the firm.

The flow of enterprise values, in a dynamic setting with fast changing events, needs to be monitored on a moment to moment basis.

Working capital management is assessed through the efficiency with which the components of working capital, which include raw material, work-in-process, finished goods and accounts receivables are utilised. All these inputs relate to the current assets of an enterprise and are also known as gross working capital. Again, most of the listed inputs can be identified in the production operations. Hence, working capital management, in this context, is known as management of Operating Cycle (OC).

OC is the time lag between the purchases of inputs initiating the production activity to the receipt of cash from customers. Efficiency is measured through the time taken for the entire operating cycle to complete a given set of activities for a given production period. The operating cycle may be a few days or a few months. In some cases, like capital intensive units, *viz.*, manufacture of ships, aircrafts and the like, the cycle may extend beyond a year depending on the efficiency of the organization. Operating cycle is concerned in the main with the age of inventory (raw materials, work-in-process and finished goods) and the speed with which the inputs (customers or sundry debtors) get converted into cash. The measurement process of an operating cycle is presented with the help of an illustration.

EXHIBIT 34

TYPICAL OPERATING CYCLES

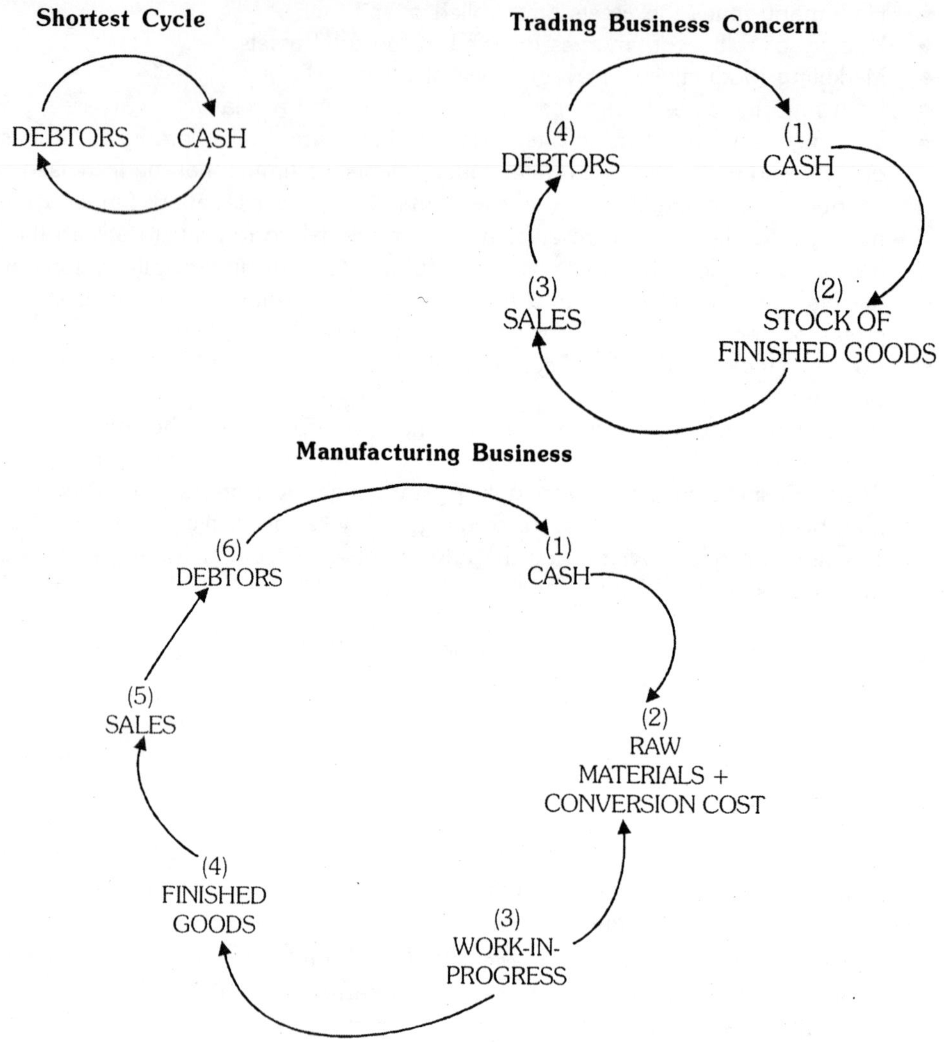

Table 26

WORKING CAPITAL CYCLE – ILLUSTRATION

Consider the following data:

PARTICULARS	₹
● Raw materials (Opening Stock)	2,501
● Raw materials (Closing Stock)	2,611
● Raw materials consumed	10,164
● Work-in-progress (Opening Stock)	489
● Work-in-progress (Closing Stock)	363
● Finished goods (Opening Stock)	3,862
● Finished goods (Closing Stock)	5,553
● Sundry debtors (Opening Stock)	9,123
● Sundry debtors (Closing Stock)	10,185
● Sales	59,852
● Cost of Goods Sold	50,693
● Purchases	10,274
● Sundry creditors (Opening Stock)	9,480
● Sundry creditors (Closing Stock)	11,697

REQUIRED

Given the above data, calculate the working capital cycles (in days) and estimate the working capital in monetary terms.

OPERATING CYCLE (in days)

RAW MATERIALS (R_m):

$$R_m = \frac{\text{Average Inventory of Raw Materials}}{\text{Raw Materials Consumed per Day}} = \frac{(2501 + 2611)/2}{10164/365} = 92 \text{ days}$$

WORK IN PROGRESS (W_m):

$$W_m = \frac{\text{Average Inventory of WIP}}{\text{Cost of Goods Sold per Day}} = \frac{(489 + 363)/2}{50693/365} = 3 \text{ days}$$

FINISHED GOODS (R_{Fg}):

$$R_{Fg} = \frac{\text{Average Inventory of Finished Goods}}{\text{Cost of Goods Sold per Day}} = \frac{(3862 + 5553)/2}{138.88} = 34 \text{ days}$$

SUNDRY DEBTORS (R_{DRS}):

$$R_{DRS} = \frac{\text{Average Sundry Debtors}}{\text{Sales per Day}} = \frac{(9123 + 10185)/2}{(59852/365)} = 59 \text{ days}$$

Gross Operating Cycle = 188 days

SUNDRY CREDITORS (R_{CRS}):

$$R_{CRS} = \frac{\text{Average Sundry Creditors}}{\text{Purchases per Day}} = \frac{(9480 + 11697)/2}{(10274/365)} = 376 \text{ days}$$

Net Operating Cycle = (188) days

According to the computations shown above, the gross operating cycle, expressed in days, is equal to 188 days. This means that the time lag between purchase of inputs and actual conversion of credit sales, as mentioned above, into cash takes a little more than six months. Thus, operating cycle refers to the gestation period between the purchase of raw materials and the actual receipt of cash from customers. It captures the journey of the initial input namely, raw material, along with the conversion cost (direct labor plus direct expenses plus factory overheads) into finished goods via the work-in-process. Subsequently, the finished goods inventory is sold either for cash, or against credit, at which point the operating cycle is complete. In the event of credit sales, the time lag between the sale and the actual receipt of cash is yet another input which will contribute to the extended duration of the operating cycle.

The above analysis does not take into account the credit availed of by a business. When the production process is on, the inputs required for production are funded through creditors who provide credit for a given period depending upon the contract or custom of trade. If the credit period availed of by a business is factored into the computation of the operating cycle, the arithmetic will change, usually in favour of the business. The operating cycle minus the duration of the credit availed of by the business, defined in days again, will be the net operating cycle. In the immediate context, in the illustration presented, the credit facility is availed of for 376 days. Thus, the net operating cycle is 188 days negative given a credit period of 376 days. Hence the net operating cycle is negative implying that the company is able to fully leverage it's goodwill in the market place (factor market, financial market and output market). Thus, the operating cycle *per se* is the sum of the inventory period and the collection time (both expressed in days). However, the cash cycle (net operating cycle) is defined as a operating cycle adjusted for the credit facility available (in days).

N.B.: If sundry creditors (opening balance) are ₹ 1,000 and closing balance is ₹ 1,500 the cycle with respect to sundry creditors will be 44 days as computed below:

$$\left\{\frac{\text{Average Sundry Creditor}}{\text{Purchases per Day}}\right\} = \frac{1000 + 1500/2}{10274/365} = \frac{1250}{28.14} = 44 \text{ days}$$

The net operating cycles will therefore be Gross Operating Cycle of 188 days less sundry creditors cycle of 44 days, i.e., 144 days.

Table 26 (A)

ALTERNATE PROJECTIONS

PROJECTING WORKING CAPITAL IN FINANCIAL TERMS

The operating cycle (in days) is useful to extrapolate the working capital requirements in financial terms. Thus, given the net operating cycle in days (D) as 144 days the projected working capital required for a given cycle can be arrived at using the following formulae:

FORMULA NO.	*FORMULA*	*QUANTIFYING WORKING CAPITAL REQUIRED*
1	$\left\{D\times\frac{\text{Sales (₹)}}{365}\right\}$ $\left(144\times\frac{59,852}{365}\right)$	144 × ₹ 163.97 = ₹ 23,613
2	$\left\{D\times\frac{\text{Cost of Goods Sold}}{365}\right\}$ $\left(144\times\frac{50,693}{365}\right)$	144 × ₹ 138.88 = ₹ 19,999
3	$\left\{D\times\frac{\text{Cost of Goods Produced}}{365}\right\}$ $\left(144\times\frac{52,384}{365}\right)$	144 × ₹ 143.51 = ₹ 20,667
4	$\left\{D*\frac{\text{Sales – Profit Margin – Depreciation}}{365}\right\}$ $387\times\left\{144\times\frac{59,852-9,159-3,650}{365}\right\}$	144 × ₹ 128.88 = ₹ 18,559

OTHER RELEVANT INFORMATION:

Sales = ₹ 59,852; Cost of Goods Sold = ₹ 50,693; Factory Cost of Goods Produced = ₹ 52,384*

Profit = ₹ 9,159; Profit Margin (%) = 15% Depreciation per annum = ₹ 3,650;

Factory Cost of Goods Produced	₹
= Cost of Goods Sold	50,693
– Finished Goods (Opening Balance)	(3,862)
+ Finished Goods (Closing Balance)	+ 5,553
Factory Cost of Goods Produced	52,384

WEIGHTED OPERATING CYCLE ANALYSIS

The detailed procedure of calculation of the weighted operating cycle, step by step is given hereunder:

STEP 1: Calculate the durations of the various stages of the operating cycle

The durations of the various stages, *viz.*:

D_{rm} (duration of the raw materials and stores etc., stage).

D_{wip} (duration of the work-in-progress stage).

D_{fg} (duration of the finished goods stage).

D_{ar} (duration of the sundry debtors stage).

D_{ap} (duration of the sundry creditors stage).

We arrive at the durations using the following formulae:

DURATION OF THE RAW MATERIALS (AND CONSUMABLE STORES AND SPARES) STAGE (D_{rm})

This reflects the number of days for which raw materials, consumable stores and spares etc., remain in the inventory before these are issued for production purposes. This is calculated as under:

$$D_{rm} = \frac{\text{Average Stocks of Raw Materials Stores, etc.}}{\text{Average Raw Materials Consumed per Day}}$$

DURATION OF THE WORK-IN-PROCESS STAGE (D_{wip})

This indicates the number of days that elapse in the work in progress stage and is computed as under:

$$D_{wip} = \frac{\text{Average Work-in-Process Inventory}}{\text{Average Work-in-Process Value of Raw Materials Committed per Day}}$$

DURATION OF THE FINISHED GOODS STAGE (D_{fg})

This represents the number of days for which the finished goods remain in the inventory, before these are sold out and is calculated as follows:

$$D_{fg} = \frac{\text{Average Stocks of Finished Goods}}{\text{Average Cost of Goods Sold per Day}}$$

DURATION OF SUNDRY DEBTORS (OR BILLS RECEIVABLE OR ACCOUNTS RECEIVABLE) (D_{ar})

This indicates the number of days required to collect the sundry debtors and is calculated as follows.

$$D_{ar} = \frac{\text{Average Sundry Debtors}}{\text{Average Credit Sales per Day}}$$

DURATION OF THE SUNDRY CREDITORS (OR ACCOUNTS PAYABLE OR BILLS PAYABLE) (D_{ap})

This denotes the number of days for which the suppliers' credit is available to the company and is calculated as follows:

$$D_{ap} = \frac{\text{Average Sundry Creditors}}{\text{Average Credit Purchases per Day}}$$

STEP 2: Determine the weights for the various stages of the operating cycle

The weights applicable to the various stages of the operating cycle should represent the proportions of the costs incurred up to that stage in relation to the selling price of the product. Hence, the weights, too have to be calculated as follows:

STAGE: RAW MATERIALS AND STORES STAGE

$$\text{WEIGHT: } W_{rm} = \frac{\text{Cost of Raw Materials Stores, etc., per Unit}}{\text{Selling Price per Unit}}$$

STAGE: WORK-IN-PROCESS STAGE (W_{WIP})

$$\text{WEIGHT: } W_{wip} = \frac{\text{Cost of Raw Materials Stores, etc., per Unit}}{\text{Selling Price per Unit}}$$

STAGE: FINISHED GOODS STAGE (W_{FG})

$$\text{WEIGHT: } W_{fg} = \frac{\text{Cost of Goods Sold per Unit}}{\text{Selling Price per Unit}}$$

STAGE: SUNDRY DEBTORS STAGE (W_{AR})

$$\text{WEIGHT: } W_{ar} = \frac{\text{Selling Price per Unit}}{\text{Selling Price per Unit}}$$

STAGE: SUNDRY CREDITORS STAGE (W_{AP})

$$\text{WEIGHT: } W_{ap} = \frac{\text{Cost of Raw Materials Stores etc. Per Unit}}{\text{Selling Price Per Unit}}$$

STEP 3: Calculate the weighted operating cycle (D_{woc})

The duration of the weighted operating cycle may be arrived at as under:

$$D_{woc} = W_{rm}\,(D_{rm}) + W_{wip}\,(D_{wip}) + W_{fg}\,(D_{fg}) + W_{ar}\,(D_{ar})$$

(A) $$\frac{\text{Sales}}{\text{Closing Stock}} \quad \text{OR} \quad \frac{\text{Cost of Sales}}{\text{Closing Stock}}$$

(B) Closing stock can be replaced by an alternate arithmetic, i.e.,

$$\left\{\frac{\text{Opening Stock} + \text{Closing Stock}}{2}\right\}$$

(C) Debtors Turnover Ratio:

$$\frac{\text{Net Sales}}{\text{Net Debtors or Net Receivables}}$$

(D) Sales/Inventory can also be split as follows:

$$\frac{\text{Sales}}{\text{Raw Materials}} \quad \text{OR} \quad \frac{\text{Cost of Goods Sold}}{\text{Raw Materials}}$$

$$\frac{\text{Sales}}{\text{Work-in-Process}} \quad \text{OR} \quad \frac{\text{Cost of Goods Sold}}{\text{Work-in-Process}}$$

$$\frac{\text{Sales}}{\text{Finished Goods}} \quad \text{OR} \quad \frac{\text{Cost of Goods Sold}}{\text{Finished Goods}}$$

13

GROUPS OF RATIOS – VALUATION RATIOS

VALUATION RATIOS

Valuation refers to the process of arriving at the value which a financial asset or liability will realise or fetch in the market on a given date. Thus, valuation refers to the market value of an asset or liability. Assets could refer to fixed assets, current assets or other assets, tangible or intangible. Valuations enable understanding of the financial worth of an asset or liability and is, usually, useful for investment appraisals and decisions, mergers, acquisitions and takeovers, budgeting, financial accounting and reporting, determination of tax liability to meet statutory requirements and litigation in business, property and personal matters. Valuation numbers expressed in absolute terms do not convey anything beyond the size of the valued item in monetary terms. Hence, valuation numbers need to be related to some unit expressed in physical or financial terms, *viz.*, returns on investment (profit/total assets) or earnings per share (profit after interest and taxes/nos. of equity shares) and so on. Thus, the need for valuation ratios. In the context of ratios, valuation is also required to assess the perceptions of different stakeholders – existing and potential investors, management, staff, Government, customers, *et al.*, Valuation ratios form an important component of tools of financial analysis available to analysts for deployment. The database for valuation ratios in particular and valuation in general, includes, *inter alia*, financial statements, *viz.*, income statement, balance sheet, cash flow statement, stock market data relating to prices of securities, *viz.*, shares, debentures, bonds and other related financial assets or instruments of finance. Thus, valuation ratios are useful to assess the performance of companies where the shares are traded on the stock market. The forces of demand and supply are in continuous operation, on an online basis, to determine the market price per share. Valuation ratios, thus, help to identify the relationship between the performance of the company and the market price. The performance of a company can be viewed from various angles, *viz.*, earning power, policies relating to plough back and payout, return on shareholder's equity (book and cash basis respectively), the book value per share and a host of other related indicators put together in the form of a numerator and denominator. The typical valuation ratios include the following:

EXHIBIT 35

TYPICAL VALUATION RATIOS

- Earnings per share (₹)
- Book Value per share (₹)
- Cash Flow per share (₹)
- Dividend per share (₹)
- Earnings-Price Ratio (%)
- Price-Earnings Ratio (Times)
- Price per Share to Cash Flow per Share (Times)

- Market Price per Share to Book Value per Share (Times)
- Market Capitalisation (₹)
- Pay out Ratio (%)
- Plough Back Ratio (%)
- Enterprise Value (EV) (₹)
- EV/EBITDA

The above ratios will be discussed in turn.

EARNINGS PER SHARE (₹)

Earnings per share is defined as:

$$\frac{\textit{Profit after Interest and Tax}}{\textit{Numbers of Equity Shares}}$$

If the share capital includes preference share capital too, the formula is modified as follows:

$$\frac{\textit{Profit after Interest and Tax and Dividends on Preference Share}}{\textit{Numbers of Equity Shares}}$$

The earnings per share is a very important valuation ratio and serves the following purposes:

- It is a powerful and practical tool to motivate investment decisions with respect to shares or with respect to the management of financial portfolios held by individuals or groups or businesses.
- It impacts the market price of shares and therefore enhances (or otherwise) the marketability of shares in the market.
- It plays a very important role in the financial management of an enterprise of an individual.
- It is a basis for setting specified corporate objectives and financial planning and control to subserve the objectives.
- It is useful as an index for inter period comparison of a company's performance and also inter firm comparison for any period/s of time. The trend of the earnings per share is indicative of the stability or otherwise of the earning power of the business and therefore, the shares.
- It indicates the productivity of every unit of money invested by the shareholders and guides them to take decisions which help them to either stay invested or shift portfolios.
- It is one of the inputs for determining the cost of equity capital and the valuation of equity shares.

- There are many methods of computing the cost of equity capital and in the same vein there are many purposes, which such a valuation serves. In the immediate context, when the earnings per share is used as an input to determine the cost of equity capital, it is the earnings per share divided by the market price per share that is expressed as the cost of equity capital usually denoted by an algebraic expression '***ke***'. Thus, *ke* is defined as the cost of equity capital and expressed as follows:

$$ke(\%) = \frac{e}{p} \times 100$$

where ke = cost of equity capital

e = earnings per share (₹)

p = market price per share

Maximising earnings per share is frequently used as a benchmark of financial performance to evaluate management's success in continuous maximisation of shareholders wealth.

BOOK VALUE PER SHARE (₹)

Book Value per share is defined as:

$$\frac{\textit{Net Worth or Owners' Funds}}{\textit{Numbers of Equity Shares}}$$

Net worth of a company is defined as:

Equity Share Capital + Reserves and Surplus

If there are any miscellaneous assets such as profit and loss account, debit balance, deferred revenue expenditure like advertising, training and development, research and development (R&D), then such items have to be deducted to arrive at, what is known as, '***tangible net worth***'. The book value per share shows the aggregate worth of every unit of investment in a business. It is indicative of the stake of equity shareholders. In accounting parlance, it is also known as break-up value of share, inasmuch as the net worth is a composite of share capital plus reserves and surplus (profits accumulated on year on year basis) and other adjustments (if any). While the earnings per share is driven by the income statement for an accounting period to reflect the results of operation of a business for a particular accounting period, the book value per share is driven by the balance sheet (net worth section) which is a cumulative of credits (addition) or debits (deductions) again on a year-on-year basis.

The characteristics of book value per share include the following:

- The book value per share refers to the owner's stake in the enterprise at any point of time.
- Higher the book value per share, greater the owners stake and *vice versa*. Further, a high book value per share indicates:
  - high retention and relatively low payout policy.
  - greater opportunities for reinvestment to take advantage of reinvestment opportunities.
- A high book value per share unsupported by subsequent, adequate, profits after interest and taxes, will depress the earnings per share.
- If the earnings do not eventually come up to expectations to sustain the amount of the resource base, there will be inclination towards overcapitalization.
- Volatility in earnings per share tend to impart instability to the market price of shares.

CASH FLOW PER SHARE (₹)

Cash Flow per Share is defined as:

$$\frac{\textit{Profit after Interest and Tax and Dividends on Preference Shares plus Non Cash Chargers Debited to the Income Statement for the Current Accounting Period}}{\textit{Number of Equity Shares}}$$

This is a modified version of earnings per share which captures the profit due to equity shareholders on a book basis, i.e., to say after all debits (cash and non cash) to the income statement. In the cash flow per share, the purpose is to ascertain the tangible cash that is generated per unit of investment by the equity shareholders. The non cash charges, usually include, depreciation (on tangible fixed assets) depletion (on wasting assets), amortisation (on intangible assets) and other debits like periodic charges on account of certain write-offs like deferred revenue expenditures (amortisation again). The cash flow per share is more closely related to the market price of share and is therefore regarded as a powerful tool like the earnings per share. All the advantages of the earnings per share are applicable, equally or with greater force, to this ratio.

Research studies have indicated that cash profit influences the financial health of an enterprise particularly in the case of sick companies and companies which are in the process of being turned around. Further, there is a better co-relation between the cash flow per share and the market prices of the shares. Again, according to a study conducted by Prof. L. C. Gupta* all ratios computes gross of depreciation provision were found to be more reliable than those computed net-of-depreciation provision.

DIVIDEND PER SHARE (₹):

$$\frac{\textit{Dividends paid to Equity Shareholders in a particular Accounting Period}}{\textit{Number of Equity Shares}}$$

This ratio indicates the results that are generated per unit of equity shareholders' investment. Shareholders are interested in periodic returns on their investment apart from other benefits. Corporate management policy plays an important role in influencing the dividend per share. Higher the amount of dividend distributed, greater the returns per unit of equity shareholder investment. Higher the dividend per share, lesser the plough back and *vice versa*. The dividend per equity share is an useful input in measuring the cost of equity capital.

Different companies have different approaches to the payment of dividend. Some companies articulate the dividend to be paid through the Director's report in the annual report and elaborate on the factors underlying the payment of dividend. For e.g., in the case of Reliance Industries Ltd. (Annual Report 2008-09), the company declared a dividend of ₹ 13 per equity share for the financial year ended 31st March, 2009. The company's annual report says "***the dividend payout and recommended bonus have been formulated keeping in view the Company's need for capital for its growth plans, the intent to finance such plans through internal accruals to the maximum and the ability to serve the enhanced capital.***"

Gupta, L. C., Controlling Corporate Sickness, Oxford University Press, 1988, pg. 42

Again, the annual report of Reliance Industries Ltd., for the year 2009-10 reads as follows:

"The dividend payout for the year under review has been formulated in accordance with the Company's policy to pay sustainable dividend linked to long-term performance, keeping in view the Company's need for capital for its growth plans and the intent to finance such plans through internal accruals to the maximum."

EARNINGS PRICE RATIO(%)

Earnings price ratio, also known as the earnings yield, is defined as:

$$\frac{\text{Earnings Per Share}}{\text{Market Price Per Share}} \times 100$$

- The earnings price ratio reflects the relationship between the earning power of the equity share investment and its market price.
- Higher the ratio greater the yield or the profitability/financial productivity of the portfolio *vis-à-vis* the market price.
- The numerator represents the results and the denominator the sacrifice, that is to say, the resources required to possess the equity share. In effect, the earnings price ratio is a '***result resource ratio***'.
- The earnings price ratio is used to measure the cost of equity capital, which is further used as an input in arriving at the hurdle rate to assay investment proposals. Cost of equity capital is always defined as a per cent.
- The earnings price ratio is a measure of the attitude of the existing and also potential shareholders.
- The earnings price ratio has a tendency to be stable. This is because, a rise in the earning power of the share will trigger off an increase in the market price thus, neutralizing the potential effects on the ratio. However, the changes in the market price per share need not necessarily be proportional to the changes in the earnings per share. Hence, there may be a marginal instability to the ratio. If the brand image of a company is very strong in the perception of the investors, the market price of shares may not be very sensitive to the changes in the earning per share though a broad correlation still remains. In companies, where the market price of the share is better correlated with dividend per share, rather than market price per share, so long as the dividend per share is stable the market prices will be stable in spite of a fall in earnings per share. Of course, in this case the dividend per share may be more than the earnings per share and the company would have clawed back into its reserves to compensate for the dips in earnings to sustain the dividend per share. So long as shareholders expectations are met, the market prices of equity share are well sustained, all other things being equal.
- The price earnings ratio which is the reciprocal of the Earnings Price Ratio is expressed in terms of times.
- The arithmetic movements of the Price Earnings Ratio will be in a direction opposite to that of the Earnings Price Ratio. Thus, higher the Earnings Price Ratio lowers the Price Earnings Ratio and *vice versa*. The relationship between P/E and E/P ratios are prescribed below:

$$\text{Price Earnings Ratio} = \frac{1}{\text{Earnings Price Ratio}}$$

$$\text{E/P Ratio} = \frac{1}{\text{P/E Ratio}}$$

The conceptual use and characteristics of the P/E ratio are discussed in the next ratio.

PRICE EARNINGS RATIO (Times)

The P/E ratio, as mentioned earlier, is a times ratio and is defined as:

$$\left\{ \frac{\text{Price per share}}{\text{Earnings per share}} \right\}$$

In the alternative P/E ratio (times) can also be computed as:

$$\frac{\text{Market capitalization of a company}}{\text{Total annual earnings}}$$

P/E ratio is also known as Price/Earnings multiple. The P/E ratio is a popular tool and, rightly or otherwise, used for evaluating the performance of a share.

P/E ratio can be viewed from several perspectives:

FIRST PERSPECTIVE: P/E ratios of various levels.

Interpretations of P/E Ratio

Various interpretations of a particular P/E ratio are possible and the table below is just indicative and suggestive:

Table 27

IMPLICATIONS OF DIFFERENT LEVELS OF P/E RATIO

Negative	A company with no earnings has an undefined P/E ratio. By convention, companies with losses (negative earnings) are usually treated as having an undefined P/E ratio, although a negative P/E ratio can be mathematically determined.
0-10	Either the stock is undervalued or the company's earnings are thought to be in decline. Alternatively, current earnings may be substantially above historic trends or the company may have profited from selling assets.
10-17	For many companies a P/E ratio in this range may be considered fair value.
17-25	Either the stock is overvalued or the company's earnings have increased since the last earnings figure was published. The stock may also be a growth stock with earnings expected to increase substantially in future.
25 +	A company whose shares have a very high P/E may have high expected future growth in earnings or the stock may be the subject of a speculative bubble.

SECOND PERSPECTIVE: Price per share refers to the sacrifice which the investor is willing to make for a unit of investment. Against the initial sacrifice of a given amount say ₹ 100, the earnings per share of ₹ 10 reveals the prospective annual returns. Thus, an outlay of ₹ 100 today in the hope of receiving annual benefits of ₹ 10 per share means, all other things being equal, it will take 10 years to recoup the initial outlay. In the financial year 2004, Infosys was trading around ₹ 2050 per share and the earnings per share were ₹ 46.50. The P/E ratio was 44 times. An investor desirous of buying an Infosys shares, at that point of time was mentally prepared to wait for 44 years to recover the initial sacrifice of ₹ 2050. The assumptions are many – earnings per share will be intact at least at the present level. However, dividends per share will facilitate steady recoupment of the initial investment and the performance of the company will motivate the investor to look forward for other benefits like bonus shares, hefty dividends, rights issue, advantageous buy-back and last but not the least capital appreciation resulting in quick recoupment of the initial high price investment. If the earnings per share goes up or down, the perceived payback period of 44 years will undergo due changes which may be favourable or unfavourable.

P/E ratio is an indicator of the payback period of an investment in shares. Payback refers to the time taken to recoup the initial investment.

THIRD PERSPECTIVE: A P/E ratio of 10 can also be looked at from a different angle. The ratio can be reversed and presented as follows:

$$\left\{ \frac{\text{Earnings per share}}{\text{Market Price per share}} \times 100 \right\}$$

$$\left\{ \frac{10}{100} \times 100 \right\} = 10\%$$

The above ratio can also be algebraically presented thus:

$$\{ 1 / \text{PE Ratio} \} \times 100$$

The inverse of the P/E ratio, presented in any format, indicates the yield from the investment. Such a yield expressed as a percentage lends itself for comparison with benchmark yields of competing investment options such as yields on gilt-edged instruments, debentures, preference shares and equity shares of other companies in the same or other industries. Investors can assay the performance of their investment to guide decision making – choosing from alternatives, *viz., status quo* (stay invested) or deployment of funds wholly or partially into alternate financial assets.

The inverse of the P/E ratio is expressed as a per cent. A 10 per cent yield on a share is a return to the investor. However, it is a cost to the company. Hence the yield on a share is the cost of equity capital to the company. It represents a convenient point of departure to decide as to what should be the minimum expectations from the use of equity capital in a business. In any case the minimum expectations cannot go below the yield derived from the reciprocal of the P/E ratio, that is to say the earnings price ratio. The minimum expected rate of return (say R) will always be greater than or equal to the cost of capital (say Ko). Hence, the equation $R \geq Ko$.

FOURTH PERSPECTIVE: The P/E ratio presents to the investor the market's assessment or valuation of the earnings. A high P/E ratio may indicate that the market is over reacting to the company's earnings and the shares are overvalued or over priced. However, in an efficient market, where market prices are a reliable arbiter of economic activity, high P/E ratio may signal optimistic expectations of the markets from the company in terms of future prospects. Thus, investor takes a fancy for such shares and are willing to buy even at a high price. A high price paid for a share is not always a bad investment. In addition, the owner's wealth is maximised, new funds can be raised at favourable price and successful hostile bids can be combated. On the contrary, high P/E ratio provides opportunities for making acquisition on favourable terms. All that a company has to do is to part with its fancily priced equity shares for cash.

P/E ratio in India: The more the investors are after a category of shares the higher the market price of such shares. The P/E ratio of such shares would be relatively higher than the shares of other companies. Historically, in the Indian stock market high P/E ratios were traditionally restricted to FERA companies because of the bonanza benefits, investors expected and actually realized, e.g.: Nestle, Colgate, HMM, Hindustan Lever. The P/E ratios of these companies were usually around

22-25 times compared to the average P/E ratios of 7 to 8 (times). Shares of a few companies touched 15. Since, liberlisation – 1990, onwards shares of all companies presented a bullish tendency.

In developing countries because of the high marginal efficiency of capital, not withstanding the high marginal cost of funds, there is a general overvaluation resulting in high P/E ratio.

In the 90s, developing economies like Indonesia, Malaysia and Thailand had higher P/E ratio in comparison with the US and Europe. According to the data of the International Finance Corporation, prior to the Gulf crises, P/E ratio of different countries was as follows:

Table 28

P/E RATIO – ASIAN COUNTRIES

COUNTRY	*P/E RATIO (Times)*
Indonesia	63
Taiwan	51
Thailand	23
Japan	52
Malaysia	31

Since the above economies were in boom condition, the bullish tendency of respective stock markets was reflected through the high P/E ratios shown above.

A low P/E ratio may convey an opposite meaning. First the share may be undervalued or underpriced. Second, markets may view the future of the company rather pessimistically. It is also possible that a low P/E ratio represent the dark horses likely to spring up with surprises. Such shares are known as '***value for money***'. Many investors look forward to shares in a bearish mood with low P/E ratios. These shares are the prospective fortune makers for the brave investors.

EXHIBIT 36

INVESTMENT COUNSEL

"A high P/E ratio need not detract investors. "If on the basis of projected EPS for the next 2 years and applying a most conservative PE ratio, you find that a share is likely to appreciate in the 2 year period by a proportion which covers your interest cost (actual or notional), then the share is good for investment and don't bother about the PE based on past/current earnings. Of course, take into consideration technical factors before you actually invest."

SOURCE: *Money Matter*, October, 1990 issue, pp. 27.

KGN REPORT

Relisting after 7 years, KGN stock rockets 76000%

The following points are pertinent to note:

(1) On 21st May 2008, KGN Industries wanted to be relisted and the exchange had cautioned against entering orders at unrealistic prices. The transaction opened on 21st May, 2008 and during the early hours of trading, orders were being placed at rather unrealistic prices. This was contrary to the caution notice. In order to prevent massive distortions with its own chain reaction, the trading of the scrip stood suspended at 12:20 hours as

a matter of abundant caution and proactive surveillance. By then the price of the scrip soared to a high of ₹ 55,000 that is to say by 76,288%. The intra-day low was ₹ 72.

(2) The scrip closed at the end of the day at ₹ 15,001.

(3) The price range of 76,288% was a meagre volume of 827 shares.

(4) The scrip was relisted on the exchange on May 21, 2008 after a gap of seven years.

(5) Individual shareholders had a stake of just 1.43% (or 3.18 lakh shares) at KGN. 49% is held by the promoter group with a similar per cent held by domestic corporate bodies.

(6) Apparently some group of persons initiated the manipulation process because on the day of relisting there is no price restriction.

(7) The incident brings to light the manipulation of shares that takes place at the listing date when "***intra-day circuit filters are relaxed to enable better price realisation***". Within the relaxed time frame manipulation was the order of the day.

(8) In the first few minutes of trading the scrip moved in a narrow band of ₹ 70-100. However in the next 90 minutes the bids touched ₹ 1,000 mark. By 12 noon suddenly the bid price started rising exponentially from ₹ 10,000 to ₹ 55,000 in 15 minutes. BSE suspended trading in the stock at around 12:20pm, when the scrip touched ₹ 15,000.

(9) Section 23(2) of the Securities Contracts (Regulation) Act "***Any person who enters into any contract in contravention of the provisions contained in section 15 62 [63s or who fails to comply with the provisions of section 21 64 [or section 21A] or with the orders of] or section 22 65 [or with the orders of the Securities Appellate Tribunal] 66 [shall, without prejudice to any award of penalty by the Adjudicating Officer under this Act, on conviction, be punishable with imprisonment for a term which may extend to ten years or with fine, which may extend to twenty-five crore rupees, or with both.]***"

In any case a high P/E ratio indicates that the shares enjoy the confidence (maybe overconfidence) of the investors. In fact the market reflects nothing but the sentiments of the investors. A low P/E ratio reflects the opposite, *viz.*, '***no confidence***' or undue diffidence. A high P/E ratio speaks for itself:

- Increase in the value of the shares of the investors (wealth accretion).
- Favourable investor mood which facilitates raising fresh capital from the market at competitive, may be rather fancy prices.
- Lower yield which makes the share relatively speaking an unattractive investment.
- Pre-empting a hostile takeover or friendly takeover. However if a takeover is imminent at favourable or at fancy prices, it occurs.
- Helps to negotiate with strength if the company is in a mood to acquire or takeover. The company can use shares in lieu of cash.

Contrarily, a low P/E ratio also speaks for itself. The situation will be diametrically opposite to the high P/E ratio scenario.

Among the 800 plus actively quoted shares in the stock markets in India in 1992*, 68 (9%) had P/E ratios of more than 75. Of these 68, 50 (73%) had P/E ratio of more than 100, 10 (1.5%) had P/E ratios of more than 500. Tata Honeywell was the most fancied scrip with a P/E ratio of 2000 for the week prior to 13th March, 1992. The average P/E ratio for the 30 shares, BSE Sensex was as high as 42 for the week compared with 21 about 12 months back. The spectrum of overpriced equities defied '***conventional financial wisdom***' and showed scant respect for fundamental strength (or weakness of company's performance). Extra fundamental factors have risen to the occasion to render the prevailing tenets of financial management as rather invalid and impracticable.

**1992 was the period during which the big bull, Mr. Harshad Mehta, was on a rampage.*

The investors now attach great value to Harshad and Shah's, of the markets than to the net profits of the company. Company's financial health is only a secondary consideration. However, the academics feel that market would once again take cognizance of financial parameters in deciding market rates although with a due allowance "***for the speculators***" (Puneet Jain; *The Economic Times,* Friday 13th March, 1992.)

P/E ratios on the eve of liberalisation Oct., 1990.

Multinationals, FERA Companies were the market darlings with very high price earnings ratios. Many companies diluted their foreign shareholdings as required by the then prescribed laws. There was a scramble for shares by the investing public. The demand for shares of such companies was very high because of attractive, increasing, earnings, liberal bonus shares and high, rather hefty payout ratios.

High Growth FERA companies like Nestle, Colgate, HMM, Hindustan Lever had P/E ratios of 20-25 times. For the Indian counterparts the range was 8-15 times. P/E ratio reflects the expectations of existing and potential investors in the growth prospects of the company in terms of increased earnings capability and the concomitant benefits to the shareholders.

Table 29

P/E RATIO – FERA COMPANIES

	1990-91 *Nestle*	*1990-91* *Colgate*	*1989-90* *HMM*
EPS (₹) (annualized)	4.68	9.5	12
Market price per share (₹)	165	350	400
P/E ratio (Times)	35	36	33

Table 30

HIGH vs. LOW P/E RATIOS

High P/E ratios reflect	*Low P/E ratios reflect*
◆ Positive corporate image	◆ Negative corporate image
◆ Low yield to investors who do not mind it	◆ High yield to investors who do not mind it
◆ Low cost of capital to the company-based P/E ratio	◆ High cost of capital to the company-based P/E ratio
◆ Capacity to sustain bids for hostile takeover	◆ No capacity to sustain bids for hostile takeover
◆ Capacity to benefit from friendly takeover	◆ No capacity to benefit from friendly takeover
◆ Improved capital raising capabilities on favourable terms.	◆ Unimproved capital raising capabilities on favourable terms

BENEFITS OF HOLDING ON TO EQUITY SHARES

- Periodic dividends
- Bonus issues
- Rights issues
- Buy-back facility
- Liquidating the investment when the market is very favourable in relation to the purchase price of the investor, the tenure of the holding and the tax implications.

CAVEAT

Merely because the P/E ratio of a share is high, it does not mean that a company is on a positive growth trial. There may be other factors that cause the prices to be high. Thus, a recent turnaround could catapult the prices from a prevailing low, to a very high level. There are extraneous factors that cause prices of shares to go up or down – may be big bulls or bears as the case may be. Market sentiments, as mentioned earlier, are driven by the Harshad Mehta's, Ketan Parekhs and Bhupen Dalals of this World. The fundamentals of the company, in terms of its prevailing and potential financial performance, are of little and sometimes of no consequences.*

P/E SCOREBOARD: 104 CO.S CRACK CENTURIES

When the bull market was in full action, rising valuations were the order of the day. In such situations, the P/E ratio is usually used as a guide. An analysis of the P/E ratio of more than 2,600 companies by the ET intelligence Group shows about 104 had a P/E of more than 100 as on May, 31, 2005. The P/E ratio, as mentioned earlier, is calculated by dividing the market price per share by the Earnings Per Share (EPS) of the company. However, there are several ways in which the P/E ratio can be calculated, depending on how the EPS is calculated. Here, the ratio is calculated by taking the earnings of the previous four rolling quarters into consideration. Many companies across sectors have a figure of over 1,000. The busy stretch of the P/E ratio is in the 201-300 range and lower. In the 201-300 range, a record 22 companies find place. These included Remsons, IQ Infotech, Supriya Phar, Essar Oil, Cosco (I), La Mere App and Rich Capital.

However, there is a word of caution. The 101 to 200 P/E ratio range includes the following:-

Table 31

VERY HIGH P/E RATIO – CERTAIN COMPANIES

P/E RATIO RANGE	*NAMES OF COMPANIES*
172	Mukta Arts
162	Shringar Cinema
162	Bhansali Engineering
162	Kale Consultants
162	Baffin Engineering
162	Bharat Imm
162	Hatsun Agro
162	HMT
162	Birla Erricsson

While P/E ratio may signal strong fundamentals, a very high P/E ratio does indicate over-valuation of companies' shares in a market.

**For a brilliant write-up on the above theme see Puneet Jain Investors Defy Financial Fundamentals, The Economic Times, Friday, 13th March, 1992.*

Table 32
BSE SENSEX AND P/E RATIO*

Date	*BSE Sensex*	*PE Ratio (times)*
01/01/2008	20301	27.67
08/01/2008	20873	28.51
21/01/2008	17605	22.44
29/02/2008	17579	21.99
26/06/2008	14422	17.68
08/07/2008	13350	16.57
22/07/2008	14104	17.63
14/08/2008	14724	18.3
05/09/2008	14484	17.99
15/09/2008	13531	16.77
17/09/2008	13263	16.53
06/10/2008	11802	14.87
26/11/2008	9027	11.56
08/12/2008	9163	11.73
31/12/2008	9647	12.36
07/01/2009	9587	12.18
29/01/2009	9236	12.71
16/02/2009	9305	12.93
09/03/2009	8160	11.62
18/05/2009	14284	19.43
08/07/2009	13769	18.12
26/11/2009	16855	21.41
31/12/2009	17464	22.36
21/09/2010	19860	23.69
03/01/2011	20561	23.59
10/02/2011	17463	19.02
05/04/2011	19687	21.43
22/06/2011	17551	18.63
05/08/2011	17306	18.03
22/08/2011	16341	18.19
23/08/2011	16498	18.32
26/08/2011	15848	17.59
29/08/2011	16416	18.14
30/08/2011	16676	18.36

EXHIBIT 37

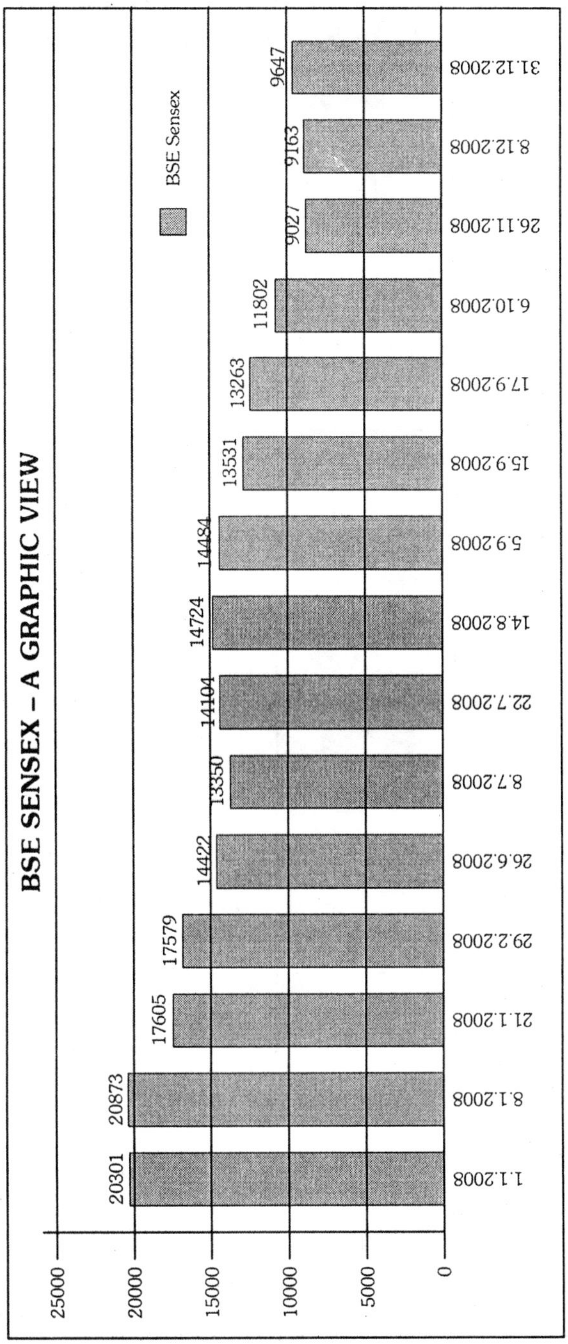

EXHIBIT 38

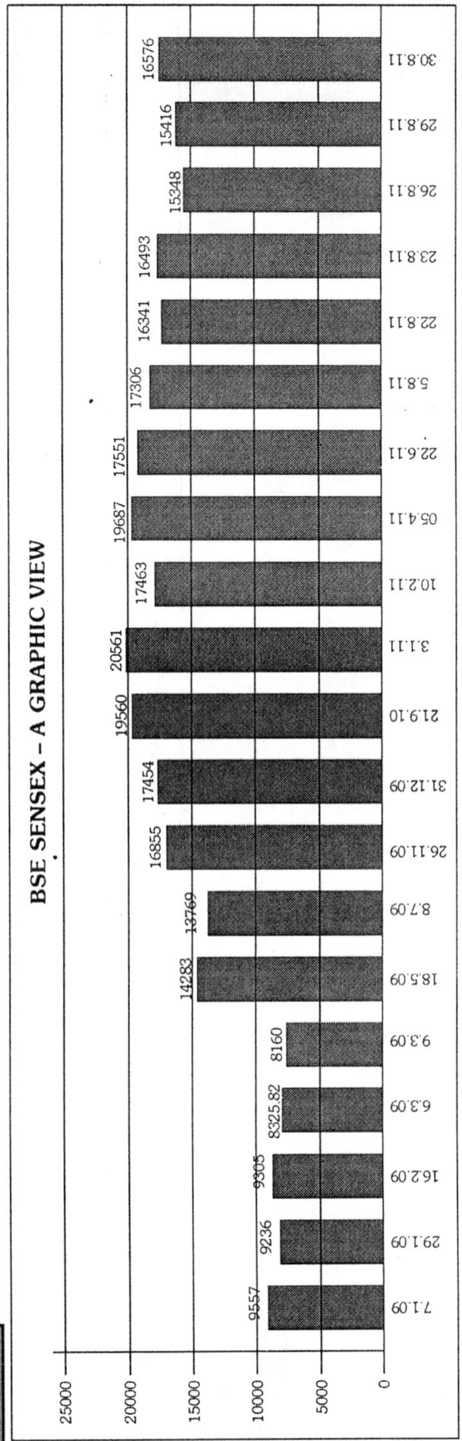

EXHIBIT 39

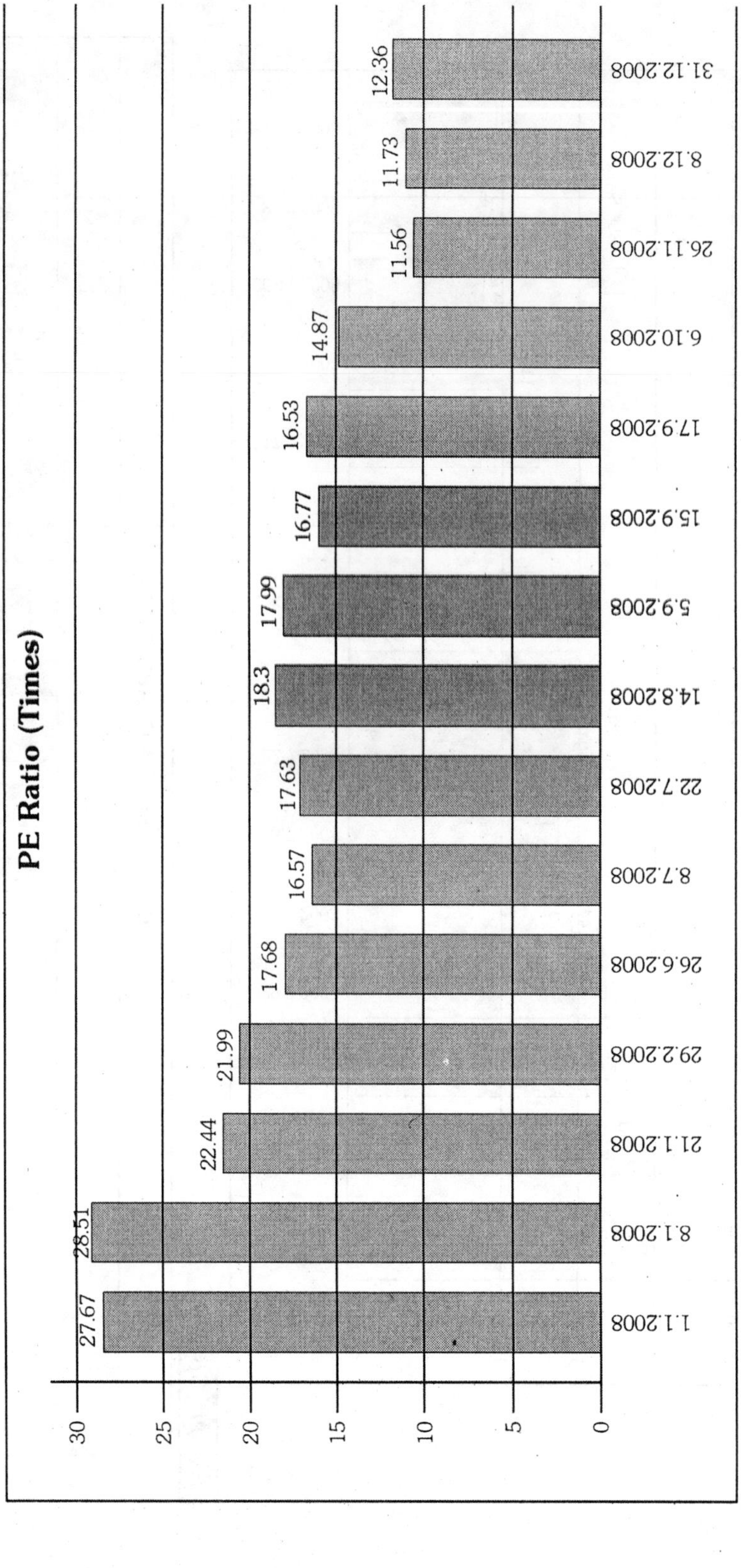
PE Ratio (Times)
0
5
10
15
20
25
30
1.1.2008
8.1.2008
21.1.2008
29.2.2008
26.6.2008
8.7.2008
22.7.2008
14.8.2008
5.9.2008
15.9.2008
17.9.2008
6.10.2008
26.11.2008
8.12.2008
31.12.2008
27.67
28.51
22.44
21.99
17.68
16.57
17.63
18.3
17.99
16.77
16.53
14.87
11.56
11.73
12.36

Exhibit 40

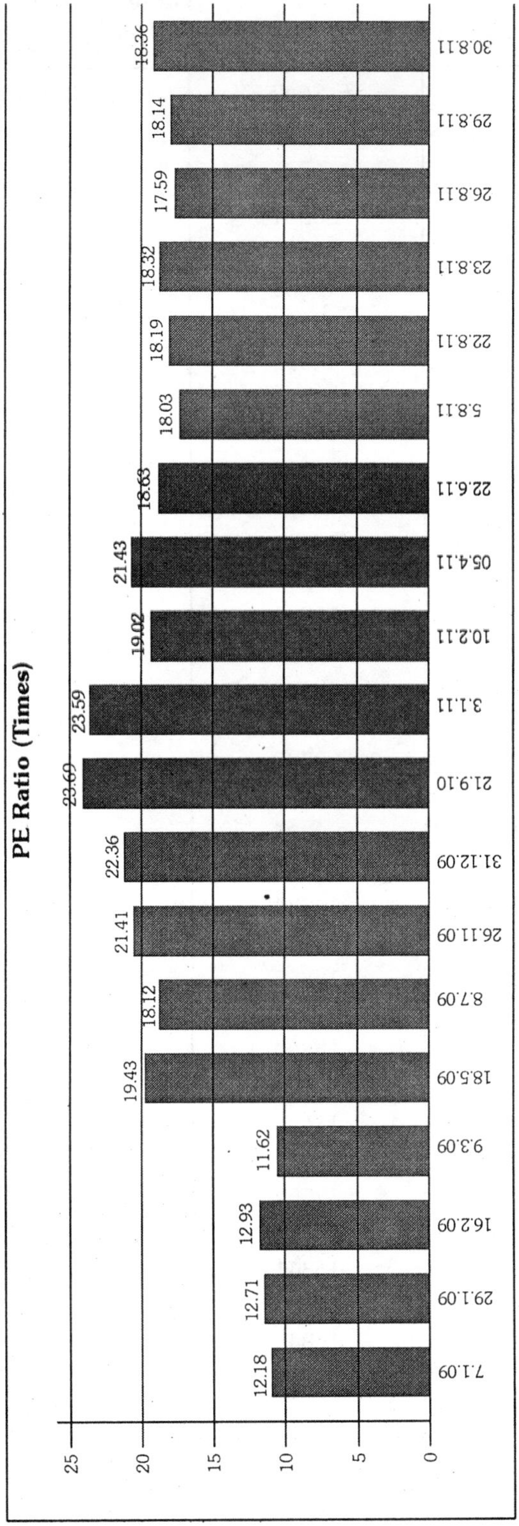
PE Ratio (Times)
0
5
10
15
20
25
7.1.09
29.1.09
16.2.09
9.3.09
18.5.09
8.7.09
26.11.09
31.12.09
21.9.10
3.1.11
10.2.11
05.4.11
22.6.11
5.8.11
22.8.11
23.8.11
26.8.11
29.8.11
30.8.11
12.18
12.71
12.93
11.62
19.43
18.12
21.41
22.36
23.69
23.59
19.02
21.43
18.63
18.03
18.19
18.32
17.59
18.14
18.36

Table 32 (A)

BSE SENSEX AND PE RATIO (TIMES) – CORRELATION (r)

DATE	*BSE SENSEX*	*PE RATIO (TIMES)*	*KARL PEARSONS' CORRELATION COEFFICIENT (R)**
01/01/2008	20301	27.67	0.9351
01/08/2008	20873	28.51	
21/01/2008	17605	22.44	Confidence Level at 95%
29/02/2008	17579	21.99	1.4941
26/06/2008	14422	17.68	Confidence Level at 99%
07/08/2008	13350	16.57	2.00725
22/07/2008	14104	17.63	*It may be noted that *r*
14/08/2008	14724	18.3	always lies between
09/05/2008	14484	17.99	'-1' and '+ 1'.
15/09/2008	13531	16.77	Thus: $-1 < r < +1$
17/09/2008	13263	16.53	
10/06/2008	11802	14.87	
26/11/2008	9027	11.56	
12/08/2008	9163	11.73	
31/12/2008	9647	12.36	
01/07/2009	9587	12.18	
29/01/2009	9236	12.71	
16/02/2009	9305	12.93	
03/09/2009	8160	11.62	
18/05/2009	14284	19.43	
07/08/2009	13769	18.12	
26/11/2009	16855	21.41	
31/12/2009	17464	22.36	
21/09/2010	19860	23.69	
01/03/2011	20561	23.59	
02/10/2011	17463	19.02	
04/05/2011	19687	21.43	
22/06/2011	17551	18.63	
08/05/2011	17306	18.03	
22/08/2011	16341	18.19	
23/08/2011	16498	18.32	
26/08/2011	15848	17.59	
29/08/2011	16416	18.14	
30/08/2011	16676	18.36	

BENJAMIN GRAHAM's APPROACH

Shareholders invest in stock market mainly to add value to their portfolio. Wise investors do not show panic reactions to a downward spiral in the market. On the contrary, its an opportunity to put Warren Buffet's axiom of contrarian view into action. The investors look for stocks which are quoted at a discount so that their margins, defined as a difference between the Anticipated and the Current market prices, are protected as per their expectations. One rule of thumb is to buy stock when they are quoted at 45 to 55 per cent discount to the intrinsic value. A higher discount would increase the comfort zone of the buyer. In this context there are several valuation ratios which are used to identify stocks which are worthy of buying because they meet the investors expectations with respect to the discount. The typical ratios are the Price Earnings Ratio (P/E Ratio) and Price-Book Value Ratio (P/B Ratio), dividend yield, enterprise value of shares, earnings per share, enterprise value to EBIT, return on equity and so on. All these ratios are useful albeit under different circumstances. This is particularly true of the two popular ratios used by the investors, *viz.*, the PE and PB ratios. The PE ratio is a good indicator for stocks which enjoy a relatively stable stream of cash inflows over a period of time so that the projection of the stream of cash inflows can be algebraically weighed against the outlay of cash in the purchase of the said share or stock. Again, the PB ratio is used when the company is not doing well and the earnings of cash flows are extremely volatile and unpredictable. In fact the company, may be incurring losses. Thus, a blind mechanical use of PE or PB or any ratio for all circumstances may be suicidal. A new thought which has come in the market place is known as a magic multiple which owes its origin to Benjamin Graham. He is considered to be the author of '***value investing***'. The magic multiple is a result of research done by Graham over several decades on thousands of company. The magic multiple is arrived as follows:

$$\frac{MPS}{EPS} \times \frac{MPS}{BVS}$$

***LEGEND:**

MPS = Market Price per Share; BVS = Book Value per Share; EPS = Earnings Per Share

Rather than identifying PE ratio and PB ratio in isolation a combination of the two would provide a better benchmark for purposes of choosing value stocks. Thus, if the PE ratio was 15 and the PB ratio was more than 2 the investors are advised to invest in stocks where the resultant multiple is less than $15 \times 2 = 30$. A recent study conducted by equity master on 200 stocks show that this magic multiple does work as a value investment proposition. The research shows that "***the stock with the lower multiple have significantly outperformed the stocks with a high multiple***". Thus, as an improvement over the immortal PE ratio which could be misleading as it was during the Harshad Mehta Scam or the price to the book value ratio which may also not be indicative of the intrinsic value of share, the magic multiple, indicated above, may provide the best of both the ratios.

PRICE PER SHARE TO CASH FLOW PER SHARE (Times)

This is the price earnings ratio on a cash flow basis. The PE ratio computed with book profit in the denominator is a standard measure of performance of an equity share as perceived by the market. However, the cash flow in the denominator shows how the market sentiments respond to the book profit adjusted for non-cash chargers. According to certain research studies, the cash flow per share is better correlated, than the book profit per share, with the market price. Hence, this ratio is a very useful tool to project how the market may value the equity share of a company.

MARKET PRICE PER SHARE TO BOOK VALUE PER SHARE (Times)

This ratio relates the market price per equity share to the aggregate stake of the equity shareholders.

The ratio is defined as follows:

$$\frac{\textit{Market Price per Share}}{\textit{Book Value per Share}} \quad OR \quad \frac{\textit{Market Capitalisation}}{\textit{Owners Funds}}$$

The ratio expresses the relationship between Market value and the Book value of the company. The numerical result of the ratio would be equal to, greater or less than unity. The index expresses the perception of investors regarding the overall economic performance of the company. An index of less than unity means that the market perceives the book value of their investments as relatively less worthy and *vice versa*. Further, an index of less than one indicates that the owners funds have been frittered away to that extent. The future performance of a company, as perceived by investors, is bleak given an index of less than unity. If the index of market value to book value is greater than unity, the owners' funds are being productively employed as perceived by the investor. However, a mere index of greater than unity (or less than unity) cannot seal the fate of the owners. The numerator (market price of shares) and denominator (book value of share) are susceptible to many factors. Thus, the market prices of shares may be high or low due to bullish or bearish tendencies in the market. Similarly, the book value of shares may be the result of accounting policies which have not adjusted for miscellaneous assets and other deferred revenue items on the assets side of the balance sheet. Thus, an index of unity or greater or less than unity has to be viewed in perspective.

For a given stake, higher the price better the worth of the investment. Companies which have a consistently high payout ratio, for a sustained level of earnings after tax, would have a relatively low plough back percentage and by implication the amount. Of course, the amount depends upon the size of the earnings to start with and the amount distributed. If the market responds proactively to the payout ratio because the shareholders are happy with it, the market price of the equity share will be relatively high. It is also possible that a company may adopt a low payout ratio and therefore show a relatively high plough back depending upon the quantum of earnings in a particular year. The response of the market price to this situation will depend upon the companies performance with respect to the amounts continuously ploughed back into business. If the reinvestment rates of return on new investments are high, the market sentiments would be in favour of the company's equity share. Hence, the price to book value ratio would be relatively high though the pay out may be low. Contrarily, if the reinvestment rates of return on investment are not adequate to motivate the shareholders to stay invested, the market may respond negatively and hence the price to book value per share may not be favourable. The key to this ratio lies in the performance of the company with reference to the reinvested amounts and the reinvested rates of return on the amounts reinvested.

Thus, so long as the incremental rate of return on the incremental capital invested is greater than the incremental cost of capital, the productivity of shareholders' incremental investment is sustained provided of course, prospective growth rates match the historical growth rates and the rates of units on an intra industry or inter industry basis. In a borderless World, returns on investment have to be comparable on an inter country and intercontinental basis. Hence, the marginal efficiency of capital has to be greater than the marginal cost of capital to justify use of incremental funds in successor projects postulated by management.

MARKET CAPITALISATION (₹)

Market capitalization is defined as the market value of shares (market price per share x the no.s of equity shares outstanding). It represents the total worth or value of business at any point of time. Since market capitalization is determined by the market price per shares it tends to be volatile. The market prices of shares, as revealed by the stock market, are liable to change every minute or second. However, market capitalisation is very useful in business for the following:

(1) To assess the size of the business or for that matter of fact the size of the corporate sector of a country in terms of its financial worth.

(2) To assess the value of shares on a per share basis and the company in totality.

(3) To know the perception of the investing public regarding the value of a particular share.

In general market capitalization in different countries are governed by the stock market indices such as Sensex, Nifty, S7P 900, Nikkei, Ibovespa and MSCI. Market capitalisation is driven on many occasions by speculation and on other occasions the rise and fall of market capitalization numbers is stimulated by vested groups bulls or bears, as the case may be. The intrinsic worth of assets may be totally different in such cases. If the market price of the shares are over valued then it is an indication of the worth of shares being stretched and pushed beyond the frontiers justified by the laws of economics. From time to time it is said that in India the prices of shares are over valued and to that extent the intrinsic worth of shares is less than the market price of the shares. Contrarily, if the prices of shares are undervalued, the intrinsic worth of the shares would be worth much more than the market price of the equity share. In view of this susceptibility of market capitalisation to speculation and a wide variety of external, logical or illogical and inexplicable forces, market capitalisation, at best, may be a rather rough and ready measure of the true worth of shares and size of a market. During the global meltdown, the stock market crashed from 20,301 on 01/01/2008 to 9027 on 26th November, 2008.

PAYOUT RATIO (%)

The payout ratio (%) is defined as:

$$\frac{\textit{Dividend Per Share}}{\textit{Earnings Per Share}} \times 100$$

OR

$$\frac{\textit{Dividends to equity shareholders}}{\textit{Profit after interest, taxes and dividends on preference shares}}$$

The payout ratio indicates dividend policy of management. It shows the portion of the earnings belonging to the shareholders, paid out to them in cash. In India, the dividend payment is governed, *inter alia*, by the provision of the Companies Act, 1956. Section 205 of the Companies Act says "***dividend shall be paid out of profits of the company***". Thus, the Companies Act allows payment of dividends. Further, the act allows dividends to be paid out of the following three sources:

(1) Profits of the company for the year for which dividends are to be paid.

(2) Undistributed profits of the previous financial years.

(3) Monies provided by the Central or State Government for the payment of dividends in pursuance of a guarantee by the Government concerned.

From the corporate financial management perspective, dividend per share is an important measure of performance. Shareholders who stay invested expect a reasonable return on the monies they have contributed to the business. Hence, there are expectations of a regular stream of earnings on the investments they have made. It's quite possible that the company has a stable pay out ratio, regardless of the earnings level in a particular accounting period. Hence, the dividends paid out in a particular period may exceed the earnings belonging to the shareholders. The expectations of the shareholders depend upon the income groups to which they belong to. If the shareholders belong to the low or medium income group they do expect a steady income from the investments they have made in the business. Hence, the market price of a share depends upon how the expectations of the shareholders are sustained. Any disappointment caused to the shareholder, due to decline in dividend per share, will adversely affect the market price of the share. On the other hand, if the shareholders of a company are predominantly from the high income category, the shareholders may be insensitive to the payout in a particular accounting period. Their expectations may be an overall appreciation of the market value of their portfolio over a medium/longer time horizon. In such cases, the expectations of the shareholders may be in favour of higher reinvestment or plough back so that reinvestments can enlarge the size of the reserves and consequently the book value of share. Through periodic bonus issues the shareholders are kept happy and the internally generated surpluses are productively redeployed in successor projects. The market prices of shares may move on a bullish trial if the proactive financial management is sustained through successive virtuous cycles. Thus, payout ratio is necessarily concerned with disposition of earnings and the periodic split of earnings into payout and plough back is under the scanner by concerned stakeholders, who may have a diverse set of mutually contradictory expectations. It is indeed a tight rope walking between Immediate consumption of surplus through dividend distribution and Sacrificing such consumption through reinvestment motivated by wealth accumulation on a medium/long-term basis.

PLOUGH BACK RATIO (%): The plough back ratio is defined as:

1 – Payout Ratio

This ratio is inversely related to the payout ratio. Higher the payout ratio lower the plough back and *vice versa*. The plough back ratio is governed by management policy regarding payout and of course its approach to financing new projects. Ezra Solomon in his book, *'The Theory of Financial Management'** presented a few thoughts which need to be noted. Approaches to manage the finances of an enterprise range from "***rules of thumb to fairly well crystallised theories***". One approach is to first decide the volume of capital expansion, based on the financial policy of the business and then allocate the said amount to competing end projects. There is a New England theory of capital expansion which "***limits the amounts of expansion in any period to the volume of profits being earned in that period***". Yet another approach for determining the volume of expenditure is to invest as much as may be required to maintain the relative competitive position of a business in a growing economy. One more alternative to the New England theory or other approaches is the banker's theory which reads as follows: "***This theory amounts to the proposition that expansion by borrowings should occur when, as and if the rate of earnings on the added capital is in excess of the rate paid by the corporation for that capital.***" Depending on the approach to deploy profits in favour of capital expenditures, the dividend policy gets formulated as a residual. There may be situations when dividend policy is a key factor and reinvestment is residual.

However, the payout ratio is undoubtedly guided by the triad financial management decisions of investment, financing and dividend. In addition to what is said above regarding the various approaches to managing the finances of an enterprise the payout ratio is influenced, inter alia, by legal requirements, restrictive covenants, liquidity, shareholders expectations, shareholders economic

**Solomon, Ezra. The Theory of Financial Management, Columbia University Press 1961, p. 33*

profile, cost of alternative sources of financing, control considerations, reinvestment opportunities, market considerations, corporate philosophy, beliefs, policy, tax considerations and access to capital markets. In India S205 (2A) of the Companies Act, 1956, duly amended from time to time, provides directions regarding dividend policy as presented in the table below. Section 205 (2A) in the Companies Act, 1956 reads as follows: "***[Notwithstanding anything contained in subsection (1), on and from the commencement of the Companies (Amendment) Act, 1974, (41 of 1974) no dividend shall be declared or paid by a company for any financial year out of the profits of the company for that year arrived at after providing for depreciation in accordance with the provisions of subsection (2), except after the transfer to the reserves of the company of such percentage of its profits for that year, not exceeding ten per cent, as may be prescribed: Provided that nothing in this subsection shall be deemed to prohibit the voluntary transfer by a company of a higher percentage of its profits to the reserves in accordance with such rules as may be made by the Central Government in this behalf.]***"

Table 33

DECLARATION OF DIVIDEND OUT OF RESERVES AND TRANSFER OF PROFITS TO RESERVES RULES

Rate of Dividend		*% of Current Profits*
Exceeding	*Up to*	
10.0%	12.5%	2.5%
12.5%	15.0%	5.0%
15.0%	20.0%	7.5%
20.0%		10.0%

The following points need to be noted:

(1) No amount need ti be transferred to reserves if the dividend declared does not exceed 10%.

(2) No dividend can be declared and paid in excess of 10% unless minimum amount prescribed as under is transferred to Reserves.

EV is the economic value of company and represents, for purposes of takeover decisions, the modicum amount which an acquirer will be required to pay in the event of a takeover. EV is the price to be paid for every single share of a company plus the cost of paying off a company's debt so that it does not owe anything to anyone else at that point of time. The elements which comprise the EV computation are found in the balance sheet of any business, e.g., cash and cash equivalents, debts, both short and long-term and of course the number of equity and preference shares outstanding. The only extra input required is the market price of shares which is available from the market. Market capitalisation, as defined above, can then be computed. Thus, enterprise value is what it would cost to buy out all the shares of a company or from the sellers point of view it is the price tag attached to an enterprise to identify the sale price of business. Ideally speaking debt, like equity has to be computed on a market value basis. However, this is not always possible. Hence, historic cost is used as a surrogate.

EXHIBIT 40 (A)

CORPORATE FINANCIAL DECISIONS AN EMPIRICAL STUDY

A study conducted by K. Krishnamurthy and D. U. Shastri had brought out certain interesting interrelationships between the triad decisions of investment, financing and dividends. The key findings of the study were as follows:

(1) *Profit is the key determinant of deployment of funds in favour of consumption (dividends)/saving (reinvestments). Infact dividends get a first claim and hence internal generation available for reinvestment is residual in character.*

(2) *Dividend decisions are autonomous of investment decisions and the availability of external financing.*

(3) *Given stable dividend policies there is an upper limit on internal funds and an implied ceiling on external finance, particularly debt, because of the constraints posit by debt-equity ratio.*

(4) *Funds available for capital formation are influenced, in the main, by profits.*

(5) *Fiscal policies aimed at encouraging investment, unsupported by incentives for profit motivation, are rendered sterile.*

(6) *Fixed asset investment is conditioned primarily by internal sources and secondarily by borrowings.*

(7) *Inventory investment is influenced by borrowings and since interest is tax deductible the speculative motive is dominant. This has also been empirically proved by studies conducted by late Professor Dr. P.R. Brahmananda*. According to Professor Dr. P.R. Brahmananda, "**We must deem the influence of the speculative motive as ubiquitous in the Indian economy ... from 1950-51 and 1971-72, the rate of gross profit in speculation would have been of the order of 13 per cent.**"*

(8) *The Krishnamurthy-Shastri study concluded that the triad decisions investment, dividends and external finance are not interdependent. However, taking two of the three parameters at a time viz. '**investment decisions and external financing**', they found, are interdependent in many industries.*

Ratios per se may facilitate understanding the health of an enterprise from particular viewpoint, viz., liquidity, profitability, valuation, capital structure or any other facet. However, the domain knowledge of corporate finance and the interrelationships between key parameters affecting the triad decisions, referred to above, need to be kept in mind to facilitate quality, informed decision making. Of course, there will also be some exceptions to the rule.

SOURCE: *Investment and Financing in the Corporate Sector in India* by K. Krishnamurthy and D. U. Sastry; Published by Tata McGraw-Hall Pulishing Co. Ltd. New Delhi; pp. 160.

*See Dr. Guruprasad Murthy, Book Reviews, *'Inflation in India'* S L N Simha (ed) Bombay, Vora & Co Publishers Pvt. Ltd. – Prajnan – Volume IV, No. 3 – *The Quarterly Journal of the National Institute of Bank Management*, Bombay, July-September, 1975.

EXAMPLE

A company with a market capitalization of ₹ 100 crores and ₹ 5 crores in cash at bank would cost only ₹ 95 crores to acquire. The company's cash of ₹ 5 crores will be at the disposal of the acquirer to be adjusted against the purchase price. However a company with an identical market capitalisation of ₹ 100 crores and saddled with a debt of ₹ 15 crores would cost ₹ 115 crores to acquire. This is because debt is part of the purchase package and it is for the new acquirer to discharge the said obligation to the creditors.

EXHIBIT 41

ENTERPRISE VALUE (EV)

DEFINITIONS:

EV is equal to market capitalization plus preferred stock plus outstanding debt minus cash and cash equivalent.

Simplified version of the above formula is: EV = Market Capitalisation plus debt minus cash and cash equivalent.

Market Capitalisation = Prevailing market price per share × Total outstanding equity shares.

Debt = Long-term debt plus short-term debt.

Free cash flow = Cash flow from operations minus capital expenditures.

Another way of looking at enterprise value is as follows:

A company with a market capitalisation of ₹ 10 lakhs with no obligations and with ₹ 1 lakh as cash at bank and asset value of ₹ 2 lakhs would have an enterprise value of ₹ 7 lakhs (₹ 10 lakhs – ₹ 1 Lakh – ₹ 2 lakhs). Suppose 100 per cent stake of the company is purchased by using market capitalisation as the basis, the acquirer will have to pay ₹ 10 lakhs. If the acquirer wants to liquidate his stake in the company after 6 months (say) he will be left with ₹ 3 lakhs i.e., ₹ 1 lakh on account of cash plus ₹ 2 lakhs on account of asset value losing ₹ 7 lakhs on the ₹ 10 lakhs investment made in buying the company.

Thus, the imperfect role of market capitalization in providing a realistic value for acquisition is exposed. The P/E ratio which shows the market capitalization in the numerator and the earning power in the denominator is very popular and widely worshipped. Yet it looks at only earnings due to the equity shareholders. Hence, the need for an alternative metric/s to evaluate the financial prowess of a business.

Enterprise value is the risk taken in acquiring a company's shares. If a company's EV is zero the investment is a '***zero risk***' provided that future earnings are not negative. Hence, reputed companies with a steady stream of cash inflows would command higher enterprise value.

SATYAM

During the Satyam episode, Satyam shares dropped from ₹ 600 per share to ₹ 6 per share when the scam on accounting malpractices came to surface. However, there was strong buying even at ₹ 6 per share because EV was at or below zero. The purchase of Satyam shares at ₹ 6 per share was an attractive proposition, however bearish, the investment approach. Satyam shares rose to ₹ 20 per share even before the Government of India announced the merger acquisition plan. Thus, EV as a computation and value helps investors to take pragmatic and proactive investment decisions.

EXHIBIT 42

WARREN BUFFET

Warren Buffet known for his prudent buying invested in GEICO (Government Employees Insurance Company). The company made losses in 1976, due to the erroneous computations of insurance premiums. The share prices went down by 95 % from USD 42 to USD 2 per share. However, the company's core competencies and business were still well protected. Warrant Buffet started buying the GEICO share at USD 3 per share. In due course of time, GEICO progressed and Buffet continued to increase his stake in GEICO. Once again, the business started dropping off in the 80s and share prices fell drastically in 1994, Buffet managed to buy other shareholders for a song – for a price of 2.3 billion USD. Today, Buffet's investment in GEICO is valued at approx. 30 billion dollars.

RELIANCE INDUSTRIES LTD. (RIL)

In India, EV is used to articulate the company's future plans to shareholders. Reliance Industries Ltd. aspires to double its enterprise value and reach to be a ₹ 5 lakh crore company in the next decade. To quote, Mr. Mukesh Ambani "***I feel hopeful and confident that Reliance can accomplish value creation of similar magnitude in less than a decade.***" He also said it took RIL 30 years to create an enterprise value of ₹ 3,70,000 crores.

EV AGAIN

EV is a good substitute for the PE ratio. The PE ratio defined as market price per share / earning per shares captures only the valuation of the stake of the equity shareholders. However, debt holders (short and long-term), have to be brought within the valuation process. Hence, the free cash flows, as defined earlier available to a business has to find a place.

EV is an absolute monetary amount and hence has to be related to some other relevant parameter. Thus, the ratio to be used is:

$$\frac{\textit{Enterprise Value}}{\textit{Free Cash Flow}}$$

Where Free Cash Flow = NOPAT – Net investment in operating activities where NOPAT = EBIT (1-t).

Enterprise value represents the price which the acquirer has to pay to justify the purchase. The free cash flow of the firm is what the acquirer can enjoy over a period of time, all other things being equal. It's necessarily a ratio of resources invested to results likely to be obtained based on the historic data available from the financial statements of a business.

EV/EBITDA

Yet another measure is EV divided by Earning Before Interest, Tax and Depreciation and Amortization (EBITDA). If a company has considerable leverage (debt) in the capital structure, EV helps to arrive at the real worth of the enterprise by adjusting for debt in the formula. Once again, the numerator represents the resources to be invested by the acquirer and the denominator is the result the acquirer expects over a period of time all other things being equal. Hence, the EV/ EBITDA helps investors to get a clear picture of the whole business in relation to the prevailing obligation/s. Shareholders can then use enterprise value to look at the comparative returns that could be obtained from alternate business investments. In both the above formulae where free cash flow and EBITDA are used it should be noted that the relevant measure used to represent results is based on the cash flow concept. The P/E ratio uses earnings per share which is essentially an accounting measure of profit adjusted for depreciation and amortization. However, there are variations in business accounting policies. This results in variation in the reported profits intra company over a period of time and inter company or inter industry. Thus, the denominator of the PE ratio is suspect at least to that extent. Free cash flow and EBITDA are inputs which are bereft of the impact of the accounting treatment given to non cash items, *viz.*, depreciation and amortisation. Nevertheless accounting policies would influence several other items in the financial statements, *viz.*, inventory valuation, valuation of sundry debtors, valuation of fixed assets and valuation of liabilities. The evolution of international accounting standards and the progressive move towards International Financial Reporting Standards (IFRS)* would be a blessing for comparability of financial statements across the global network in the future.

Enterprise value is also preferred because it's a good tool which is capital structure neutral. Of course, EV alongwith EBITDA, free cash flow, leverage and weighted average cost of capital (WACC) and cash or near cash assets are alternative ways of looking at the economic health of an enterprise. These formulae and ratios can guide or influence investment decision making. Other relevant issues would include the competitive edge enjoyed by the company with respect to products and services along with its differential potential, the Government regulation, the ability to continuously earn rates of return which exceed the hurdle rate (modicum being WACC) which must be surpassed in order to justify the use of capital. Such an analysis helps to make informed, calculated and educated investment decisions, i.e., to say choosing from amongst alternate investment candidate proposals.

ENTERPRISE VALUE – A CASE STUDY

An alternative to the PE ratio: is a concept called enterprise value which, as mentioned earlier, measures how much capital it would take to buy an entire public company which is in vogue. Consider, two rivals J.C. Penny and Sears Roebuck. Penny's PE ratio was 19 and Sears was 9.5. One share of Penny was twice as costly as buying a share in Sears. This is what the P/E ratio would signal. Enterprise value is defined as the sum of the company's stock market capitalization plus its net debt. Stock market capitalization in turn is a company's total shares multiplied by its stock price and net debt is a company's total debt, minus its holdings of cash and marketable securities. Returning to Sears and Penny at 45 $ a share, Sears had a market capitalization of $13.4 billion and a P/E ratio of 9.5. However, Sears has a debt of 29 million. It's enterprise value works out to $ 42.4 billion. This is nearly 13 times the EBIP of 3.3 billion. Penny has a share valued at 23 $ and a market value of 6.2 billion with a PE ratio of 19. Penny owes only $ 3.2 billion to its creditors. Hence, its enterprise value is only 9.4 billion dollars. The enterprise value of Penny to its EBIT is 9.8.Penny therefore represents the better bargain. Another way of looking at the same figures is as follows: Divide EBIT by enterprise value indicating the percentage return that a potential buyer of the whole company may see. This percentage is called as cash return or capitalisation rate. Comparing Sears and Penny again.

**IFRS as a global norm seems to be a rather distant dream inasmuch as India has differed "the implementation of international financial reporting standards". The initial deadline was 31st March and from 1st April, 2011 IFRS reporting was to commence. The date of implementation of converged Indian accounting standards is to be notified at a later date. This postponement is withstanding the fact that Prime Minister Manmohan Singh had made a commitment towards the alignment of Indian accounting standards with IFRS at the G20 summit in 2009. (The Economic Time, 26th February, 2011, p. 13)*

Table 34

ENTERPRISE VALUE – A CASE STUDY

	SEARS (USD)	*PENNY (USD)*
Market Price Per Share	45	23
Stock Market Value	13.4 billion	6.2
PE ratio	9.5	19
EBIT	3.3 billion	958 billion
Debt	29 billion	3.2 billion

N.B.:

- EV is the input for the acquirer of an enterprise and represents the amounts (resources) to be invested for an acquisition.
- EBIT is the earning power of the company on a pre-interest and pre-tax basis and represents the anticipated benefits (results or output) which the acquirer can have access to over the tenure of the acquisition, all other things being equal.
- The relationship between EV and EBIT is essentially a resource (input) result (output) or result (output) resource respectively ratio depending on how the said two items are used as numerator denominator respectively.

Table 35

ENTERPRISE VALUE – SEARS AND PENNY

	SEARS 42.4 billion USD	PENNY 9.4 billion USD
Enterprise Value to EBIT ratio – input – output ratio	12.84	9.8
EBIT/Enterprise value – output – input ratio	3.3/42.4 = .07	.958 billion/9.4 = .10

Hence, though the enterprise value of Sears at 42.4 billion USD is greater than that of Penny which is valued at 9.4 billion USD, Penny seems to be a better buy than Sears because:

(a) The price of Penny (EV) is only 9 times its EBIT as against 12.84 times in the case of Sears. An investor is paying three times more for a unit of EBIT in the case of Sears. Thus, to capture a dollar of EBIT (result or output) in Penny the required investment (resources or input) in EV is only $ 9.8 as against $ 12.84.

(b) The EBIT is 0.1 times the enterprise value in the case of Penny as against only 0.07 times in the case of Sears. Thus, for a dollar of investment in Penny, a $ .1 (10%) is obtained in return by way of EBIT as against a $0.07 (7%) in case of Sears. The result – *resource or resource* – result ratio is clearly in favour of Penny *vis-à-vis* Sears.

⊙⊙⊙

14

GROUPS OF RATIOS – LEVERAGE

LEVERAGE DEFINED

The concept of lever originated in Physics. Leverage is a factor through which lever multiplies a force. It is related to the concept of mechanical advantage. The mathematics governing the principle of leverage was developed by Archimedes in the third century (B.C.). To quote the Wikipedia:

"***The simplest device for creating leverage is the lever. A lever is a stick which rests on a fulcrum near one end. When the long end of the stick is pushed down, the short end moves a small distance up with great force. With this device a man can easily lift several times his own weight. Other common devices that achieve leverage include the wrench, various pulley arrangements, a jack and hydraulic brakes***."

The application of the principle of leverage in finance arises in the context of capital structure management. Equity refers to the energy available. The question is with a given amount of equity (energy) how much debt (load) can be added on to the capital structure to enable a business to practice leverage? If with limited energy, a lot of debt can be absorbed, all other things being equal, business can reap financial advantages from the same in many ways.

WHAT IS LEVERAGE?

(1) Leverage refers to the presence of debt in the capital structure of any business.

(2) Debt is also known as borrowings or creditorship capital and can be

- short or long-term.
- local or foreign with arrangement for repayment either in specially designated foreign currency or local currency.
- various formats limited only by the variety of ways in which a contract can be made between a borrower and lender.

(3) Leverage in the context of the issue in this chapter is restricted to long-term borrowings.

(4) The capital structure, representing long-term funding, of any business therefore comprises:

- Equity Share Capital.
- Reserves and Surplus.
- Preference Share Capital.
- Debt (long-term) – Local or Foreign.

(5) The composition of a capital structure is an issue to be decided upon by the management of any business. Management have a choice between – zero debt, moderate debt or moderately levered and highly levered.

(6) Usually it is not possible to conceive of zero equity or zero owners contribution by design. However by default, businesses may encounter zero or rather limited owners funds due to consecutive years' of losses. Erosion of net worth is a situation where business may encounter zero owners contribution or negative net worth. Such a business is by definition a SICK UNIT requiring infusion of owners funds to bring the business back on track through a rehabilitation plan which includes, rescue package designed and managed usually by a consortium of lending bankers, financial institutions or any other stakeholder/s.

LEVERAGE RATIOS

DEBT: EQUITY

where DEBT = Long-term borrowings of a business.

EQUITY = Equity share capital plus reserves and surplus net worth.

N.B.: It needs to be known that debt is also employed in alternative forms. Thus, debt may include, as mentioned above, short-term borrowings too. However, debt: equity ratio normally refers to the capital structure or financial architecture of business from a medium and long-term perspective. Hence, to reiterate debt shall continue to refer to long-term borrowings.

Leverage is also understood as gearing of capital or trading on equity. If the proportion of debt is higher than usual, the business is said to be trading on thin equity. Where the presence of debt in the capital structure is relatively low, business is supposed to be trading on thick equity. High debt means top gear and *vice versa*. Hence to reiterate, another way of studying, leverage is by computing capital gearing ratios*, viz.,

$$\frac{\text{Preference Shares plus Long-term Liabilities}}{\text{Owner's Funds (Equity Share plus Reserves)}}$$

OR

$$\frac{\text{Capital Entitled to a Fixed, Predetermined Return (Interest or Dividends)*}}{\text{Capital not Entitled to a Fixed Predetermined Return}}$$

'DEBT EQUITY' ratio, while expressing the role of debt and its extent in the capital structure, also refers to the role and extent of proprietors' (equity shareholders) funds. In fact the debt: equity ratio and the proprietary ratio are complementary to each other. The debt: equity ratio also indicates the funding pattern of the assets of a business – ownership *vis-à-vis* creditorship capital.

**(Guruprasad Murthy, Financial Management, Seth Publishers, 1978, Vol. II, p. 102)*

Table 36

DEBT EQUITY AND PROPRIETARY RATIOS

Consider the data below:

				INR
	A	*B*	*C*	*D*
Total Capital	100	100	100	100
Equity Capital	100	50	33	25
Debt		50	67	75
Debt: Equity	0:1	1:1	2:1	3:1
Proprietary Ratio	100%	50%	33%	25%
Debt as % of Total Capital	0%	50%	67%	75%

Given the debt: equity ratio, the extent of equity shareholders (proprietors' funds) capital can be ascertained as follows:

Table 37

DEBT EQUITY AND PROPRIETARY RATIOS

DEBT: EQUITY RATIO	*WHAT IS THE PROPRIETARY RATIO?*
0%	100%
50%	50%
67%	33%
75%	25%

Table 38

DEBT EQUITY AND PROPRIETARY RATIOS

	Given the Proprietary Ratio	*What is the debt: equity ratio?*		
A	100%	$\frac{100-100}{100} = \frac{0}{100}$	=	0:1
B	50%	$\frac{100-50}{100} = \frac{50}{100}$	=	50%
C	33%	$\frac{100-33}{100} = \frac{66}{100}$	=	66%
D	25%	$\frac{100-25}{100} = \frac{75}{100}$	=	75%

If proprietary funds = x ₹, debt = y ₹ and total capital = $(x + y)$ ₹

Proprietary Ratio (Z – say) can be expressed as follows:

$$Z = \left\{\frac{x}{x+y} \times 100\right\}$$

Given the proprietary funds the debt: equity ratio (*D/E*) can be expressed as:

$$D/E = \left\{\frac{x+y-x}{x}\right\}$$

It can be observed that the debt: equity and proprietary ratios are complementary to each other and extremely important measures of leverage and stability respectively.

Table 39

IMPACT OF VARYING PROPORTIONS OF DEBT AND EQUITY IN THE CAPITAL STRUCTURE

(Figures in INR)

	A	B	C	D	E.	F	G	H	I
Debt: Equity	0:1	1:1	2:1	3:1	4:1	1:1	0:1	0:1	1:1
Total Capital	100	100	100	100	100	100	100	100	100
Debt	0	50	66	75	80	50	10	0	50
Equity	100	50	34	25	20	50	100	100	50
Profit before Interest and Tax	100	100	100	100	100	10	10	8	8
Interest @ 10%	0	5	6.6	7.5	8	5	0	0	5
Profit before Tax	100	95	93.4	92.5	92	5	10	8	3
Income Tax @ 30%	30	28.5	28.0	27.8	27.6	1.5	3	2.4	0.9
Profit after Tax	70	66.5	65.4	64.7	64.4	3	7	5.6	2.1
Return on Equity %	70	133	192	258	322	7	7	5.6	6.3

Given the data in Table 40 the following points emerge:

- In case **A** there is no debt capital, hence interest charges are zero and the return on equity without any leverage, is **70%.**
- In cases **B**, **C**, **D** and **E** the proportion of debt in the capital structure has progressively increased from a debt: equity ratio of 1:1. (Case **B**) to 4:1 (Case **E**).
- As business increases the leverage, the return on equity has increased from 70% (Case A) to 322% (Case E).
- As debt increases in the capital structure, ROE will increase; in fact ROE will catapult itself to higher and higher returns on equity as shown below:

Table 40

DEBT EQUITY RATIO AND ROE (%)

CASES	A	B	C	D	E
Debt: Equity (Times)	0:1	1:1	2:1	3:1	4:1
ROE (%)	70%	133%	192%	258%	322%

- The general principle is that as equity tends to zero, ROE will, algebraically, tend to infinity. Thus, leverage i.e. increasing borrowings which help to magnify gains and losses, is in operation.

How far should a business extend the use of debt in the capital structure**?**

- So long as the earning power of assets (return on total asset [capital]) exceeds the interest cost of debt, leverage will help to increase the return on equity. In cases **A** to **E** the earning power of assets (Profit before interest and tax divided by the total capital) is 100%. The interest cost of debt is only 10%. Hence leverage facilitates, (except case **A**), boosting returns on equity.
- If the earning power of assets (₹ 10) equals the interest cost of debt (₹ 10) (cases **F&G**) a business is indifferent to the presence of either debt or equity in the capital structure. Thus, in cases **F** & **G** it is clear that in case **G** where there is no debt, the ROE is 7% and in case **F** where there is debt the ROE is 7% again.
- The income level of ₹ 10, means an earning power of 10%, which equals the interest cost, is the break-even or indifference level. At this level of income of ₹ 10 a business is indifferent (or neutral) to the source of finance as the ROE is constant.
- If the earning power of assets is less than the interest cost of debt, the ROE is higher if debt is not employed and equity is used instead, *viz.*, cases **H** and **I**. The ROE is higher when equity is used at 6.3% (Case I) as against 5.6%. in case **H** where debt is present in the capital structure.
- The key to successful use of debt in the capital structure lies in the level of the earning power of assets in relation the interest cost of debt.

A general principle of financial management is that so long as marginal efficiency of capital is greater than marginal cost of capital, additional doses of debit (leverage) will help to boost return on equity, all other things being equal.

MAX. RETURN ON SHAREHOLDER'S EQUITY (ROSE) – FORMULAE

Consider the formula below:

ROSE *(R)*

$$R = \frac{(D-E)r - Di}{E} \quad \text{.......... Formula 1}$$

where D = Debt (₹)

E = Equity (₹)

r = Return on assets after tax (%)

i = Interest rate on debt after tax (%)

Formula 1 can be re-stated as follows:

$$R = r + \frac{D}{E}\{r-i\} \quad \text{.......... Formula 2}$$

COMMENT ON FORMULAE 1:

(a) So long as $r > i$, ROE is levered.

(b) If $r < i$, ROE is depressed and leverage is counter productive.

(c) If $r = i$, ROE is indifferent to the mix of finance or indifferent to the source of finance.

Formula 2 can be further re-arranged as follows:

$$r = \frac{ER + Di}{D + E} \quad \text{.......... } \textbf{Formula 3}$$

where D = Debt (₹)

E = Equity (₹)

r = Return on assets after tax (%)

i = Interest rate on debt after tax (%)

We can rewrite FORMULA 1 as follows:

$$(E \times R) = [D \times r - D \times i + E \times r]$$

$$\text{Again } E\,(R - r) = [D\,(r - i)]$$

$$\therefore \frac{D}{E} = \frac{(R - r)}{(r - i)} \quad \text{.......... } \textbf{Formula 4}$$

EXHIBIT 43

LEVERAGE (TIMES), RETURN ON ASSETS (%) AND RETURN ON EQUITY (%)

***Formula 1** helps to calculate Return on Equity (R) given the quantum of debt and equity in rupees and the rates of interest and the return on assets after tax in per cent.*

***Formula 2** is a re-statement of **Formula 1** where the debt : equity ratio and the gap between earning power of assets (r) and interest cost of debt (i) is visibly presented. The extent to which a given leverage and the differential between 'r' and 'i' can help to boost R for any business is easily seen.*

***Formula 3** puts '**r**' on the left hand side. Thus, the resultant earning power of assets for any given combinations of equity, debt, return on equity and interest cost can be ascertained through **Formula 3**.*

***Formula 4** puts D / E on the left hand side. Thus, the resultant D/E ratio which can hold a given combination of earning power of assets and interest cost of debt can be ascertained through **Formula 4**.*

Table 41

DEBT EQUITY RATIO, RETURN ON ASSETS (%) AND RETURN ON EQUITY (%)

THE FOLLOWING PROPORTIONS OF DEBT EQUITY GIVEN ROA = 100%, INTEREST COST OF DEBT = 10% AND

TAX RATE = 30% YIELD THE INDICATED ROE

(Figures in INR)

	B	*C*	*D*	*E*
D/E Ratio	0:1	1:1	2:1	3:1
Capital	100	100	100	100
Equity	100	50	34	25
Debt	0	50	66	75
PBIT	100	100	100	100
Interest @ 10%	0	5	6.6	7.5
PBT	100	95	93.4	92.5
Income Tax @ 30%	30	28.5	28.0	27.8
PAT	70	66.5	65.4	64.7
ROE	70%	133%	192%	258%
ROA	100%	100%	100%	100%

N.B.: Formula 1 or 2 can be used to ascertain the end result, *viz.*, ROE

Table 42

DEBT EQUITY RATIO, RETURN ON ASSETS (%) AND RETURN ON EQUITY (%)

GIVEN THAT THE EXPECTED RETURN ON EQUITY (R = 70%) AND r = INTEREST RATE AFTER TAX = 7%, WHAT SHOULD BE MINIMUM REQUIRED RETURN ON NET ASSET FOR ALTERNATE DEBT EQUITY RATIOS

Case	*Minimum Required ROE*	*Debt*	*Equity*
B	70%	D = 0	E = 100
C	38.5%	D = 50	E = 50
D	28.4%	D = 66	E = 34
E	22.75%	D = 75	E = 25

Proof to show that the above combinations of *R*, *i* and *r* result in the target *D/E* ratio.

CASE	(Using Formula 3)
B	$r = \frac{(ER + Di)}{D + E} = \frac{(100)(.7) + 0}{100} = \frac{70}{100} = 70\%$
C	$r = \frac{(ER + Di)}{D + E} = \frac{(50)(.7) + (50 \times .07)}{100} = \frac{35 + 3.5}{100} = 38.5\%$
D	$r = \frac{(ER + Di)}{D + E} = \frac{(34)(.7) + (66 \times .07)}{100} = \frac{23.8 + 4.2}{100} = 28.4\%$
E	$r = \frac{(ER + Di)}{D + E} = \frac{(25)(.7) + (75 \times .07)}{100} = \frac{175 + 5.25}{100} = 22.75\%$

PROOF TO SHOW THAT MINIMUM EXCEPTED "*r*" YIELDS TARGET $R = 70\%$

Table 43

DEBT EQUITY RATIO, RETURN ON ASSETS (%) AND RETURN ON EQUITY (%)

	A	B	C	D
Minimum "*r*" (%)	70%	38.5%	28.4%	22. 75%
Profit after Tax (₹)	70	38.5	28.4	22.75
Interest (Post Tax) (₹)	NIL	3.5	4.6	5.25
PAT (₹)	70	35	23.8	17.50
EQUITY (₹)	100	50	34	25
ROE (%)	70%	70%	70%	70%

Table 44

DEBT EQUITY RATIO (Times), RETURN ON ASSETS (%) AND RETURN ON EQUITY (%)

GIVEN THAT TARGET R = 133, 192, 258 AND 322 PER CENT FOR CASES *A, B, C, D* RESPECTIVELY i = INTEREST COST AFTER TAXES (%) AND RETURN ON TOTAL ASSET = r = 70%, WHAT SHOULD BE THE DEBT-EQUITY RATIO?

(Using Formula 4)

	R	"i"	"r"	DEBT-EQUITY RATIO
B	133%	7	70	1:1
C	192%	7	70	2:1
D	258%	7	70	3:1
E	322%	7	70	4:1

CASE	
B	$D/E = \frac{(R-r)}{r-i} = D/E = \frac{133\% - 70\%}{70\% - 7\%} = \frac{63}{63} = 1:1$
C	$D/E = \frac{(R-r)}{r-i} = D/E = \frac{192\% - 70\%}{70\% - 7\%} = \frac{122}{63} = 2:1$
D	$D/E = \frac{(R-r)}{r-i} = D/E = \frac{258\% - 70\%}{70\% - 7\%} = \frac{188}{63} = 3:1$
E	$D/E = \frac{(R-r)}{r-i} = D/E = \frac{322\% - 70\%}{70\% - 7\%} = \frac{252}{63} = 4:1$

USES OF LEVERAGE

(1) Leverage helps to broaden the quantum of capital that can be raised by a business by accessing debt capital in addition to equity shareholders funds.

(2) Leverage helps to provide business with an opportunity to increase, may be catapult, return on equity.

(3) Leverage requires the concurrence of top management because it includes amongst other things a strategic decision regarding levels of risks to be taken in the conduct of business. Risk takers will favour leverage and risk averters will tend to avoid debt in the capital structure by either employing equity share capital or internal generation or adjusting capital expenditures to available sources of ownership capital.

(4) Leverage ratios need to be studied and understood in a holistic manner alongwith its complementary ratios, *viz.*, proprietary and stability ratios.

(5) The use of leverage is not always by design. The presence or absence of debt in the capital structure could be attributed to situations, favourable or unfavourable, emerging in business. Thus,

- A business flushed with a lot of internal generation does not need debt. (example: companies in the I.T. industry)
- A business which is going through a difficult period due to '***losses in successive years***' may require support of debt.
- A business going through ambitious capital expenditures and aggressive acquisition programme. will necessarily like to inject debt in the capital structure. Thus, TATA Steel-Corus deal included debt and other costs of USD 13.7 bn. Similarly TATA Motors-Jaguar deal included a short-term debt of $ 3 billion.
- A capital intensive business like manufacturers of ships/aircrafts airlines, shipping companies and the like cannot survive without debt.

EXHIBIT 44

AIRLINE BUSINESS

Airline business is capital intensive. Initial funding runs into billions of US dollars. The capital structure is usually debt driven. It is humorously said that to venture into airline business one has to be a billionaire. A person is regarded as lucky if he can get out of the business as a millionaire.

(6) The study of leverage ratios is incomplete without bringing the '***cover***' and '***debt***' service coverage ratios within the scope of study.

(7)

$$\text{Cover Ratio (Times)} = \frac{\text{Profit Before Interest and Tax (PBIT)}}{\text{Interest}}$$

The cover ratio also known as the times interest-earned ratio, indicates the operating excellence as measured by PBIT, in relation to the fixed burden by way of interest expenses. This ratio relates the earnings of a business to the fixed charges that must be paid from the earnings defined as PBIT. From the creditors point of view, higher the ratio better the situation. A cover ratio of 2 means that every rupee of interest obligation is protected by a profit before interest and tax of ₹ 2 that is to say twice.

(8) **DEBT SERVICE COVERAGE RATIO** (**DSCR**) refers to the cash inflows generated to service the impending cash outflows viz. debt servicing towards interest, principal/lease payments. This ratio helps to assess the adequacy (or otherwise) of cash inflows to sustain the impending cash outflows. A lender - individual or institution, uses this ratio to facilitate lending decisions and measure the integrity of the cash flows of a loan proposal. The higher the ratio greater the chance that a loan can be successfully serviced. Hence, the loan is usually granted. The DSCR is also used by institutional lenders to establish a benchmark regarding the modicum level of the DSCR. The DSCR is defined in different ways as presented below:

In a very generic computation, DSCR is defined as:

$$\frac{\text{Net Operating Income}}{\text{Total Loans Amortisation Obligation}}$$

The DSCR in a typical investment proposal is defined as follows:

$$\text{DSCR} = \frac{\text{Profit after tax + Depreciation + Interest on term loans}}{\text{Interest on term loans + Annual instalment of term loans}}$$

$$\text{DSCR} = \frac{\text{Annual Net Income + Amortisation/ Depreciation + Other non cash discretionary items (non-contractual management bonuses)}}{\text{Principal Repayments + Interest Payments + Lease Payments}}$$

**In the real estate world, DSCR is defined as:

$$\frac{\text{Annual Net Operating Income}}{\text{Annual Debt Service}}$$

In Government finance,

DSCR is defined as: export earnings divided by annual interest on a country's external debts + instalments of loans of external borrowings.

$$DSCR = \frac{\text{Export Earnings}}{\text{Annual Interest on a Country's External Debts plus Instalments of Loans of External Borrowings}}$$

The DSCR can posit the following postures, *viz.*, unity or greater or less than unity. If DSCR equals unity, the cash inflows generated are just equal to the impending cash outflows. It is a risky situation because cash flow inadequacy looms large for a very small, adverse, variation in cash inflows. However, if DSCR is greater than unity, the cash inflows are greater than the impending cash outflows and the position of the lender is relatively safe. A DSCR which is less than unity indicates the inadequacy of the cash inflows in relation to the cash outflows. The usual benchmark for DSCR in commercial lending is 1.2 to 1.5. Every rupee of cash outflow should be supported by a cash inflow of ₹ 1.5 that is to say 50 per cent in excess of the maturing obligations.

In matters relating to personal finance like loans to individual, a DSCR of 1 is usually acceptable.

Debt-service coverage ratio gives a reliable picture of a firm's gearing capacity.

CAPITAL STRUCTURE

Managing a capital structure has many dimensions. Hence, developing a right balance between different sources of funds is indeed a dicey and dynamic task. The general tendency is to rely on capital structure to add intrinsic value via the benefits of leverage and make leverage work in favour of the corporate financial objective of continuous maximisation of shareholders equity alongwith business strategy. A delicate balance is implicit in the choice between the apparent economic advantages of debt and flexibility of equity. However, while financial leverage is an important component of the total leverage opportunities available to a business, enterprise must make efforts to create value primarily through excellence in operating management performance. This is lasting, durable and reliable. Capital structure *per se* does affect, to reiterate, a company's overall value by influencing operating cash flows as well as the cost of capital. Debt in the capital structure also increases the intrinsic value of businesses because of financial discipline associated with financial leverage. A company must be prepared to sustain the impact of amortisation obligations, *viz.*, interest payments and repayment of instalments. Hence, superfluous capital expenditures or other business decisions like acquisitions particularly opulent expenditures, may be avoided or postponed. A policy of caution and parsimony guides incremental outflows on revenue and capital accounts during the amortisation period. There is a fear syndrome of the bankers'/lenders' adverse response. Since, the main purpose of adding debt to the capital structure is to create value, frivolous investments and superfluous expenditures will run contrary to the laid down objective. The choice, between the options open, *viz.*, debt and equity is a trade-off between financial flexibility on the one hand and fiscal discipline on the other. Proponents of debt argue in favour of the benefits of leverage which include forced financial discipline, tax advantage and the value creation (productivity of every rupee invested by shareholders) through higher and higher returns on equity. Proponents of equity finance tend to place emphasis on the flexibility afforded by equity in terms of opportunities to retain debt capacity for various contingencies in the future, absence of forced discipline of amortisation plan by third parties and better internal control *vis-à-vis* the bankers. In fact, it is believed by the votaries of internal financing that the fiscal discipline and tax benefits of leverage are more than offset by the financial flexibility afforded by equity finance. Most important the business can operate *sans* the fetters of the lenders. Nevertheless, debt has its own role in the capital structure of a company. Companies which have stable and predictable cash flows should prefer debt because the discipline that debt inculcates in the company usually outweighs the advantages of financial flexibility. However, companies which face volatile cash flows are usually advised to carry less debt so that they can reap the benefits of equity financing as a flexible method and also take advantage of reinvestment opportunities in the future. In addition, they need not face the risks and uncertainties associated with the negative, opposite, impact of leverage when the marginal efficiency of capital goes below the marginal cost of capital.

Thus, rather than relying on capital structure to generate value on its own, a business should try to integrate the capital structure policies with their business strategies. This means striking a balance, as mentioned above, between the discipline and tax shield that debt can deliver and the greater freedom and flexibility of equity. It is believed that most industries can create more value by making their operations more effective and efficient rather than mere financial engineering that is to say employing leverage as a strategy to create value by using debt as an important or preponderant source of finance.

CONTRARIAN VIEW

In cyclical industries the general tendency is to wait for the recovery phase, allow profits to emerge and use internal generation to fund capital expenditures. This results in simultaneous additions to capacities and stimulates big gaps between demand and supply. Instead a contrarian view of making investments when others are silent may make more sense and wise use of debt. Counter cyclical capital structure posit on a contrarian basis may add more value to business. However, transition from one mix to another to meet the corporate financial objective through the targeted capital structure involves planning of timing of new borrowings, debt amortisation, dividend payments, repurchase or buyback of shares and issuance of fresh capital

Table 45

INDIA INC. – MANUFACTURING SECTOR

Debt – Equity Ratio

Year	*No.s of Companies*	*2:1 No.s of Companies (%)*	*3:1 No.s of Companies (%)*
Mar 1989	938	63.97%	83.26%
Mar 1990	1005	65.17%	82.79%
Mar 1991	1236	63.27%	82.77%
Mar 1992	1391	65.78%	83.11%
Mar 1993	1644	70.32%	85.10%
Mar 1994	2111	78.40%	89.48%
Mar 1995	2502	83.37%	92.45%
Mar 1996	2623	83.87%	92.95%
Mar 1997	2605	82.46%	91.40%
Mar 1998	2570	80.66%	90.82%
Mar 1999	2669	78.01%	88.46%
Mar 2000	2675	78.13%	87.93%
Mar 2001	2583	78.16%	87.80%
Mar 2002	2520	77.70%	87.30%
Mar 2003	2589	77.17%	86.87%
Mar 2004	2522	78.71%	88.22%
Mar 2005	2106	79.68%	89.03%.

COMMENT ON TABLE 45

Debt-Equity Ratio — After 1993, number of companies showed substantial increase upto 2004. In 1993, 85% of the companies were having a maximum debt-equity ratio of 3:1. Till 2004, the said per cent (85) increased to 88% indicating that more and more companies preferred reasonable and manageable debt-equity ratios not exceeding 3:1. In fact after 2005, better managed companies have shown preference for equity rather than debt in spite of tax advantage in debt finance.

The amount of debt depends on the policy governing leverage and its role in business. It also depends on the need for borrowings. There may be an intent to lever but no need to lever. There may be a need alright but availability and affordability are considerations which cannot be overlooked. Since leverage helps to boost ROE and an aggressive leverage helps to catapult ROE, enterprise should be interested in using their equity base to raise as much debt as possible. It is like speeding a car at a high or highest gear. In fact, leverage alternatively expressed is known as gearing of capital. Yet, borrowings do not take place as a routine perfunctory exercise. There are other considerations influencing capital structure decisions like, the attitude of borrowers, creditworthiness in the market, nature of industry, tax considerations, cash flow needs and ability, nature of industry, reinvestment plans, opportunities and government regulations (if any) and last but not the least autonomy desired by the entrepreneur *vis-à-vis* the omnipresence of lenders — banker and others in the event of leverage.

The presence of debt also means that creditors are always observing and the autonomy of the business could be limited to the mindset of the lenders. It is a truism to say that leverage *per se* helps to boost ROE and so long as the marginal efficiency of capital is greater than the marginal cost of capital the benefits of leverage can continue rather indefinitely — *ad infinitum*. However, the non-quantitative factors like controls exercised by lenders, covenants imposed by lending financial institutions and the fear of exposure to banks punitive action are factors which inhibit unfettered use of leverage. In addition to these qualitative considerations, business environment may see changes in fiscal, monetary and trade policies which require enterprise to revisit, periodically, the choice between debt and equity. Hence, the choice between debt and equity is one of evaluating, like all other decision choices, the quantitative and qualitative dimensions and assessing the combined impact of the same on corporate financial objectives in particular and corporate objectives in general. The choice finally boils down to risk-return matching and evaluation of the best option available and arrive at a possible solution given a set of circumstances in today's dynamic ever disequilibrated business situations. Financial leverage requires decision making with respect to interest management, nature, form, source, cost, currency, country from where debt is sourced, tax rates and the proportions between debt and equity subject to constraints (if any) imposed by the laws of the land in which business is transacted. Yet, borrowings need not necessarily happen. Companies which are not interested in expansion or diversification may not need funds and hence the question of borrowings does not arise. Companies which are not interested in using debt for expansion or diversification tend to restrict expansion and diversification plans to funds available from within through internal generations. Companies do tend to be conservative with respect to borrowings as a policy and also because they would not like to loose control – the presence of creditors, individuals or institutions, means loss of control to the extent of the restrictive covenants agreed upon. Invariably bankers impose covenants that tend to be harsh on borrowers. Moreover, bankers have a notorious reputation – "***offering an umbrella when there is sunshine and withdrawing it when it starts raining***". Hence the urge of enterprise in India for this and other valid reasons, to be out of the clutches of the banking system. Underutilization/overutilization, under trading/over trading and undercapitalization and overcapitalization of enterprise were, all driven by the motivation of entrepreneurs which was influenced in the main by licensing laws and controls prevailing during the permit raj (prior to 1991).

Corporates, as a policy, do not wish to entertain a fair weather cock. While conservative policies may result in low leverage, cash rich companies also need not borrow. Hence the leverage is rather low or maybe nil.

Reliance is a very good example of successful leveraging year on year basis. Perhaps this is the only example of its kind where leverage has been proactively employed to raise funds, pre-empt outflows on account of repayment and boost returns on equity through a series of conversions of debt into equity.

CHEAP MONEY POLICY AND FUNDING STRATEGIES OF ENTERPRISE

In India inflation control is a predominant *desiderata* of monetary policy. Hence, short-term interest rates were and may continue to be used as a lever to balance the demand for and supply of loanable funds. Infact, in monetary parlance, high powered money was a critical parameter to be watched and controlled. Therefore, even between 1991 to date interest rates have been inverted from time to time. In fact, unfettered expansion of credit through overdraft, cash credit and pledge resulted in flow of funds into hoarding of stocks giving vent to the profit motive, nay profiteering. By default or otherwise this fanned the fumes of inflation. Hence from time to time interest rates were raised to make hoarding less attractive. High interest rates increased the cost of hoarding and therefore hoarding became expensive making it uneconomical to practice profit motivation via hoarding. This was the Singapore experience too. As a strategy, interest rates were placed at levels twice the inflation rate to make hoarding an unattractive proposition. Hence inverted interest rates emerged and had to be accommodated and sometimes inducted as a part of planned policy. This seemed to be a '***fait accompli***' at least till 1998. However, since 1999, the inversion of interest rates stands corrected due to fall in inflation rates to levels below even the floor rate of four per cent. Though, generally short-term interest rates have to be lower than long-term interest rates, this relationship is deliberately distorted from time to time, because in India inflation management is the key consideration. Between 1991-1998, this was the main reason for which distortions between short and long-term interest rates were tolerated even though it defied the financial fundamentals. After 1998, the Government started using interest rate as an instrument relevant for enterprise investment decisions and cost of capital. Hence, short-term interest rates continuously lowered themselves from 1997 to 2004 as part of the new paradigm shift from dear money policy to cheap money policy and from inflation management to investment decisions. Now, the main objective was to encourage investment with a view to offer attractive returns to enterprise. The side effects of this effort was that short-term debt became cheaper than before. However, low tax rates and low interest rates made post-tax debt cost not very attractive. Thus, the impact of tax breaks demotivated use of debt. Further, low interest rates improved the bottom line and increased the dividend. The equity investors were happy because profit levels improved and dividends were tax free. They responded positively to new issues of equity through Initial Public Offers (IPO's). Hence equity became attractive and cheaper than debt. However, cheap money policy did not really interest many enterprises. Since banks were keeping industry on their tenterhooks, industry wanted to be as unfettered as possible by being outside the scope, ambit and purview of the stranglehold of banks. Enterprise wanted total freedom from the control of banks. Banks were putting a condition that the end purpose of term loans given should be strictly complied with. Moreover, using cash credit facilities from a particular bank was made compulsory, if the borrower had availed of term loans facility from that particular bank.

EXHIBIT 45

MEGA BIZ. DEALS NEED NO BANKERS

Piramal says, "I know my business better than a banker ever could."

Enam Securities Promoters fear leaks if bankers enter picture.

Even the $2 billion Holcim – ACC – Ambuja deal, done in phases and helmed by Anil Singhvi (then the CEO of Ambuja Cement), didn't involve bankers playing dealmaker.

We do our deals ourselves because we are able to move fast – Malvinder Singh.

SOURCE: "Mega biz deals need no bankers". *The Times of India,* 27th December, 2010.

ENTREPRENEURS – CHANGING MINDSET

Industry wanted autonomy with respect to investment decisions because daring entrepreneurial decision like acquisitions, mergers and demergers were in the offing. Hence, as a strategy many enterprises hived off certain strategic business units to augment cash flows and enjoy unfettered use of the same. Simultaneously they were outside the banking system. This upset the apple cart of the banking sector. In the anxiety of the banking system to retain their customers, the banks wanted to ensure that customers completed their tenure as borrowers. Hence, the concept of penalty clause for premature amortisation of loan was introduced. Companies like Imperial Chemical Industries (India) Ltd.(ICI), Nestle, Glaxo, Nicholas Piramal hived off their basic strategic businesses from 2001 onwards, generated a lot of cash and freed themselves from the yoke of the banks. This was a paradigm shift in the mindset of enterprise notwithstanding the cheap money policy. There was one more paradigm shift and that was relating to the mix of finance used to run business. Companies preferred equity to debt. This served their purpose inasmuch as falling interest rates, falling tax rates, improved dividends and a buoyant capital market, rendered equity cheaper than debt after 2002. As if this was not enough, entrepreneurs started giving vent to their ambition by seeking loans at cheaper rate from foreign countries in terms of external commercial borrowings, global depository receipts, American depository receipts and foreign currency convertible bonds, after 2002. Since the INR was continuously appreciating,* it became cheaper for entrepreneurs to borrow in foreign currencies now and repay at a later date taking full advantage of an appreciating local currency, *viz.*, INR. The paradigm shift that has taken place is the change in mindset towards the currency mix in the financial structure. In the past, there was a fear of foreign currency because of a falling INR and the adverse impact of devaluation on loan amortisation.** Now, enterprise wanted to ride at the crest of the wave of a rising INR. The appreciating INR had its own problems. Sales targets of export sector, as mentioned in Box was continuously disfigured. The loss in earnings due to receipt of relatively weak currency particularly the USD was feared by many. However, this loss was more than offset by the incremental volumes mopped up by a booming IT export sales in particular and other products too, *viz.*, gems and jewellery. Incidentally the payments for imports were reduced because of an appreciating INR and the favourable effects were reduced imports, improved balance of trade and a favourable current account balance.

**The reverse phenomenon is in operation if the rupee is depreciating.*

***Devaluation results in an increase in obligations (liabilities) to the foreign vendor and a simultaneous increase in asset value on the balance sheet. In the same vein, an appreciation (upvaluation) of the local currency (say INR) would result in a decrease in obligation (liabilities) and a simultaneous decrease in the asset value on the balance sheet. Even in recent times in 2011 the dollar was continuously appreciating against the rupee and the $ – INR Rate ranged from 1 $ = INR 39.41 (Dec. 2008) to 1$ = INR 54.3 (15th December, 2012).*

LOW INTEREST RATES – A NEW PARADIGM – LEADING TO NEWER PARADIGMS

High interest rates and high tax rates were complimentary and worked on many occasions to the advantage of enterprise. High tax rates mean an opportunity for leveraging the benefits of tax deductibility. Thus, if e = expense and t = tax rate, tax shelter = '$t \times e$' and tax adjusted expenses = (1-t) e. In the context of this formula, higher the tax rate, higher was the tax shelter. In the seventies, when the intensity of marginal tax rate was as high 95 per cent plus, (more than 100% including wealth tax) an incremental amount of ₹ 100 tax deductible expense meant that the Exchequer bore the burden to that extent namely at least 95% of the expense. Only the residual 5% or less was borne by the business. Enterprise was also motivated to boost the amount of expenses claimed for tax purposes.

DEBT AND EQUITY

When income tax rates were high and interest rates were also high the tax adjusted interest cost was reduced substantially. In 93-94, Reliance Capital and IDBI could price their shares at ₹ 130 per share (₹ 10 face value). The post issue price ruled around ₹ 55-60. The substantial premium of ₹ 120 per share(1200%) depressed the effective cost of equity to such an extent that equity was cheaper than debt even with the combination of double digit interest rate and tax rates placed above 50%.The post-issue price gave shock waves to many entrepreneurs who wanted to follow the Reliance Capital route. While Reliance Capital managed the show and so did Larsen and Toubro finance, Mahindra & Mahindra financial services and the Kotak group, a few others failed miserably, *viz.*, Lloyd Finance, Suman Motels and Mafatlal's finance. In 2006 the corporates raised a lot of money through IPO equity issues along with hefty premium. Sun TV raised ₹ 500 crores with equity shares of face value of ₹ 10 at a price of ₹ 730 to ₹ 875 per equity share giving a premium of at least 630%. Similarly D. S. Kulkarni builders raised ₹ 100 crores with an equity share face value of ₹ 10 and a premium of 230%. Plethico Pharmaceutical raised ₹ 110 crores with a face value of ₹ 10 and a premium of at least 240%. In the case of Sun TV the premium itself was substantial and would have helped the company to service the capital almost into perpetuity. In all such situations there is no such thing as a choice between debt and equity. Equity is bound to be preferred. Till recently since tax rates were low and interest rates were also falling, companies which managed to go to the primary market by issuing shares, at a premium preferred equity to debt. Thus, the theme that debt is cheaper than equity is not a dictum applicable universally *in vacuo*. The cost of debt and equity is driven by interest rates, tax rates and the ability of the companies to mop up surpluses by way of share premium at the time of issue of shares.

Capital Structure Policy has different dimensions in different industries. Within an industry, different companies may have different approaches to managing their respective capital structures. Further, within a company there can be policy variations from time to time, regarding the ways and means of a managing capital structure. In India over a period of time the theory and practice of financial management recommended a '***2:1***' debt:equity ratio as a benchmark. This was an understood, tacit, government norm. Industries therefore vow by 2:1. Many companies did not touch the perceived ceiling of 2:1 regarded as an immutable hurdle. Certain industries like tea, IT, toothpaste and certain companies, from time to time, enjoy surfeit cash and healthy internal accruals. In such situations, debt is conspicuous by its absence. Further the issue for such industries/companies is how to deploy the surplus cash before it is frittered away into unproductive end uses – maybe amongst other choices, superfluous, extravagant, consumption, either on revenue or capital accounts. Industries which vow by 2:1 evolve a capital expenditure policy which helps to sustain the sacrosanct ratio. Capital intensive units like shipping and aviation including shipbuilding and aircraft manufacture cannot just afford to use ceilings like the 2:1 ratio. Exigencies of business decide the debt:equity though broad guidelines from within the business emerge. Two clear mindsets emerge first, that business would not like to lever beyond perceived norms of '***2:1***'. Profit motivation is adjusted, *pro tanto,* to the benefits of leverage resulting from a ***2:1*** debt: equity ratio. Second, that profit motivation is key to enterprise. No projects which have a positive net present value should be rejected. Funds should be made available to such projects so that the objective of continuous profit maximisation, on a present value basis is well sustained.

Mindsets are undergoing a change in the business world in the post-liberalization area. Access to foreign capital markets and cheap money available outside India on the one hand and banking practices which have not undergone major paradigm shifts at home on the other have motivated enterprise to evolve their own indigenous approaches to managing debt:equity ratios.

DEBT EQUITY PROFILE OF INDIA INC

In India, the debt equity profile has been in favour of equity. The data for the last several years indicates ownership capital (retained profits plus depreciation plus fresh equity capital plus share premium) have always been much more than the long-term borrowings. The Table below bears testimony to the same: Even if current liabilities and provisions are included as part of creditorship capital it can be seen that ownership capital is preponderant in the capital structure. A look at the RBI database also provides with similar indications: The data below, once again, bears testimony to the role of ownership capital in the long-term funding of the enterprise. According to the RBI data, across the network of India Inc., the debt equity ratio is as shown below for 1526 large public limited companies the debt equity % ranges from 41 to 44, for 3114 for public limited companies it ranges from 44 to 48 and for 1475 private limited companies and it ranges from 21 to 28 per cent. This shows the rather limited role of leverage in the funding strategy of India Inc.

In recent times (2011) many Indian companies are facing serious financial problems. In view of their high debt equity ratios, two companies which are in serious trouble are Air India and Kingfisher. For the year ended 31st March, 2009 Air India has loan funds of ₹ 1,92,424 million with a shareholder funds of 2083.5 million. For the year ended 31st March, 2010, Air India has loan funds of ₹ 2,50,668.2 million as against shareholders funds of ₹ 10,074.8 million. The situation seems to be rather preposterous. The debt equity ratios for the respective years 2009-10 are 92.35 (times) and 24.89 (times) are mind boggling. Even the latter is absurd. One can imagine the status of a company with the former debt equity ratio. Incidentally, these ratios exclude the future lease obligations which are placed at ₹ 1,16,887.5 million (2009) and 1,33,559.6 million. A debt equity ratio which captures future lease obligations too is frightening. Again, Kingfisher Airlines has a staggering debt equity ratio of 17.58 times as on 31st March, 2010 and of course a reduced debt equity ratio of 2.94 times as on 31st March, 2011. In the meantime by November, 2011, the position of Kingfisher airlines has become a part of everyday news for the financial muddle which it is in. The same is true of Air India.

An analysis of the BSE 200 list shows that at least 9 other companies have debt-equity ratios in excess of two and interest coverage ratio which is less than two and a half times. A brief profile of their financials, with respect to the debt equity and related parameters, is presented below:

Table 46

KINGFISHER IS NOT ALONE

Nine companies that have debt-equity ratio of over two times and interest coverage under pressure

	Total debt (₹ crore)	*Debt-equity (x)*	*PBIDTA/ interest #*	*PBIDTA/ interest ##*
Aban Offshore	13,048	6.31	2.11	2.05
Dish TV*	1,076	4.85	2.66	2.07
Hind Construction*	7,382	4.52	1.46	0.84
Shree Renuka Sugars	8,612	4.15	1.59	-1.25
J P Associates*	44,758	3.53	2.14	1.99
Bhushan Steel*	16,593	2.81	3.43	2.4
Lanco Infratech	16,652	2.63	3.08	1.93
GMR Infra	24,457	2.27	0.82	1.46
Essar Oil*	14,547	2.22	2.4	0.82

PBIDTA: Profit before interest, tax, depreciation and amortisation

Total debt and debt-equity ratio as on March '11.

For Shree Renuka Sugars, it is for year ended Sept '11;

#Based on trailing 12 months to Sept '11;

##Based on the quarter ended Sept '11;

**Stand-alone trailing and quarter financials*

SOURCE: *Capitaline Plus*

SOURCE: *Gupta. J. K., and Chhabria. V, Business Standard, 2nd December, 2011.*

High debt equity ratios, as presented in **Table 46,** show the inability of companies to manage leverage successfully and also the failure of strategies. Hence the financial quagmire. Different companies have different reasons for the predicament posit. However, leverage ineffectively handled can lead to disaster a la Kingfisher or Air India or the Chapter 11 cases in the USA. The nine companies, presented in **Table 46** have different reasons for their respective financial muddle.

Aban Offshore is suffering from weak business fundamentals which have been bad for quite sometime. Again, HCC has seen its operating performance (PBIDT) going up but post interest the profits are low and the matters are going from bad to worse because increase in debt levels have crossed ₹ 4,000 crores (March, 2011) alongwith high interest cost and the repayment of zero coupon foreign currency convertible bonds. Operating performance is also adversely effected due to time and cost overruns in project management. In fact, steadily interest expenses are exceeding the PBIDT and simultaneously the PBIDT is slipping. This has resulted in dwindled net profit and erosion of net worth to that extent. Thus, every company would have its own tale but the fact remains that leverage, when it is in its negative trail, is a signal of impending, if not actual adversity.

Table 47

INDIA INC.: PROFILE OF DEBT: EQUITY RATIO (D/E)

D/E (Times)	*2010*	*2011*
>5	2	2
4-5	3	3
>2	2	1
>1	5	8
<1	28	26
	40	40

A study, based on the annual financial statements presents that the debt equity profile of 40 different industries. Industries which have high debt equity ratio are predominantly the service industries like housing, asset financing, automobile and other infrastructure financing services. All other industries including financial services, electricity distribution, transport services, food and beverages, wholesale and retail trading and the rest have a debt equity ratio which is less than two.

Bankers who practice financial prudence to the utmost in the case of individuals and insist that they will provide housing loans only to the extent of 80-85% of the value of property are now over board to fund highway projects equivalent to twice the project cost for whatever reasons. A recent news item in *The Times of India* (28th December, 2011) show that at least in three projects the developers project cost is more than twice the estimate of National Highways Authority of India (NHAI). This is likely to bring the banking industry into serious trouble and expose the financial institutions to a high risk. Moreover NHAI guarantees only 90% of the project cost estimated by the Government to the lenders. The risk is therefore exclusively that of the financial institutions. In short public funds, that is to say innocent depositors' money are put to great risk.

EXHIBIT 45 (A)

CAPITAL STRUCTURE – PRIVATE CORPORATE ENTERPRISES RESEARCH STUDY

A study on the capital structure policies of the private corporate sector in India presents some very interesting results viz.

(1) For the period under study and also for the periods of study by other authors viz. Brajkishor (1951-74), Raut and Swain (1992-97) Jain and other (1995-98) and Suresh Babu and P. K. Jain (1980-94) have all reported the preference for short-term debt in lieu of long-term financing.

(2) For the period of the study (1980-94), there is a shift towards preference for long-term debt in lieu of short-term debt.

(3) Historically the private corporate enterprise had aggressive debt equity ratio and therefore relatively poor debt service coverage ratio. This is indicative of the high risk profile of the private corporate enterprises ranging from liquidity shortages to extreme cases of bankruptcy.

(4) Managing a capital structure requires the retention of some unused debt capacity to accommodate the future mobilisation of capital. The private corporate enterprise do not have scope for further mobilisation of debt capital in view of the aggressive debt equity ratio. Hence, private corporate enterprises are likely to face problems with resource mobilisation.

(5) The above findings of different studies need to be kept in mind in understanding various dimensions of capital structure management.

SOURCE: *The Management Accountant, February, 1999 pp. 107-113*

15

RATIOS — DIFFERENT DATABASES

TYPICAL ANALYST APPROACH

LIQUIDITY RATIOS:

- Current Ratio, Acid Test Ratio (Quick Ratio)
- Cash Position Ratio

STABILITY RATIOS:

- Debt Equity Ratio
- Current Liabilities/Total Assets (%)
- Proprietary Ratio (%)
- Coverage Ratio = PBIT/Interest

VALUATION RATIOS:

- Dividend per Equity Share (₹)
- Payouts (%)
- Ploughback (%)

TURNOVER RATIOS:

- Debtors Turnover Ratio (in times)
- Creditors Turnover Ratio (in times)
- Debtors Turnover Period (in days)
- Creditors Turnover Period (in days)
- Net Operating Cycle = C-D (in days)
- Inventory Turnover Ratio (in times)
- Inventory Turnover Ratio (in days)

Table 48
RATIOS USED BY STOCK EXCHANGE DIRECTORY NON FINANCIAL COMPANIES

◆ **Stability Ratios:** ● Net Worth to Total Assets % ● Net Block to Net Worth % ● Total Liabilities to Net Worth %	◆ **Credit Ratios:** ● Current Assets to Current Liabilities ● Quick Assets to Current Liabilities
◆ **Turnover Ratios:** ● Net Sales to Total Assets ● Net Sales to (Net Worth + Debentures) ● Net Sales to Plant and Machinery at Cost ● Sundry Debtors to Average Daily Sales	◆ **Profitability Ratios:** ● Return on Total Capital Employed % ● (Net Profit + Debenture Interest) to (Net Worth + Debentures) % ● Net Profit to Total Assets ● Gross Profit to Net Sales % ● Pre-depreciation Operating Profit to Net Sales % ● Operating Profit to Net Sales % ● Pre-tax Profit to Net Sales % ● Net Profit to Net Sales %
◆ **Appropriation Ratios:** ● Depreciation Provision to Gross Block % ● Depreciation Provision to Written Down Value of Block % ● Tax Provision to Pre-tax Profit %	◆ **Capitalisation Ratios:** ● (Preference Capital + Debentures) to Equity Capital % ● Debentures to (Net Worth - Debentures) % ● Preference Capital to (Net Worth + Debentures) % ● (Equity Capital + Reserves) to (Net Worth + Debentures) % ● Coverage of Senior Chargers

RBI DATABASE

RBI conducts several studies and publishes the findings of the same in its monthly bulletin known as RBI. Of course there are other reports too, *viz.*, annual publications like RBI report on currency and finance, RBI's handbook of statistics of the Indian economy and a wide variety of other, regular and occasional publications brought out from time to time. RBI studies on the finances of India Inc., are a regular feature of RBI monthly bulletins. The finances of different categories of companies are studied in depth with quantitative data and supporting analysis and interpretation in prose, is presented in the RBI publication as shown in **Tables 49 to 52.**

The typical categories include public limited companies, large public limited companies, private limited companies, private corporate business sectors, financial investment companies and foreign direct investment companies. The public limited companies are non-government, non-financial public limited companies. The large public limited companies are non-government, non-financial, large pubic limited companies each with paid-up capital of ₹ 1 crore and above. The private limited companies include select non-government, non-financial, private limited companies. The private corporate business sector includes non-government public limited companies. The financial and investment companies include non-government, financial and investment companies other than banking, insurance and chit fund companies. Foreign direct investment companies are the non-government, non-financial Foreign Direct Investment (FDI) companies. The FDI companies include public limited companies and private limited companies.

The database uses the audited annual accounts as a key input in the development of vital and elaborate statistics relating to the financial performance of the sector, category or industry studied. A typical analysis usually includes, *inter alia*, the following:

(1) Growth rates and ratios of select items.
(2) The income expenditure pattern of the companies.
(3) The composition of liabilities and assets.
(4) The composition of sources and uses of funds.
(5) Performance of companies by size of sales.
(6) Industry-wise performance.
(7) The industry group includes the list presented in **Table 50** and the key indicators of financial performance are sales, gross profits, bank borrowings, gross profits to sales, debt: equity and tax provision to profits before tax.
(8) Growth rates of select items which include at least 26 items.
(9) Select financial ratios which include capital structure ratios, liquidity ratios, assets utilization and turnover ratios, sources and uses of funds ratio, profitability and profit allocation ratios. The list of ratios used by RBI across the network of groups and categories studied is presented in **Table 52** Combined income, value of production, expenditure and appropriation accounts which is a combine of profit and loss account and profit and loss appropriation account, combined balance sheet of the select number of companies studied.
(10) Earnings and expenditure in foreign currencies.

Table 49

RBI DATA – CATEGORY OF COMPANIES AND SCOPE OF COVERAGE

CATEGORY	*SCOPE OF COVERAGE*
(1) Public Limited Companies	Non-government, non-financial public limited companies
(2) Large Public Limited Companies	Non-government, non-financial large pubic limited companies each with paid-up capital of ₹ 1 crore and above
(3) Private Limited Companies	Select non-government, non-financial private limited companies
(4) Private Corporate Business Sectors	Non-government public limited companies
(5) Financial Investment Companies	Non-government, financial and investment companies other than banking, insurance and chit fund companies
(6) Foreign Direct Investment Companies	Non-government, non-financial Foreign Direct Investment (FDI) companies

Table 50

RBI DATA – COVERAGE OF INDUSTRIES

SR NO.	*INDUSTRY*	*SR NO.*	*INDUSTRY*
(1)	Tea Plantations	(15)	Tyres and Tubes
(2)	Mining and Quarrying	(16)	Plastic Products
(3)	Food Products and Beverages	(17)	Cement and Cement Products
(4)	Sugar	(18)	Iron and Steel
(5)	Edible Oils and Oil Cakes	(19)	Fabricated Metal Products
(6)	Cotton Textiles	(20)	Machinery and Machine Tools
(7)	Man-made Textiles	(21)	Electrical Machinery and Apparatus
(8)	Paper and Paper Products	(22)	Radio, Television and Communication Equipment and Apparatus
(9)	Chemicals and Chemical Products	(23)	Motor Vehicles and Other Transport Equipment
(10)	Basic Chemicals	(24)	Construction
(11)	Chemical Fertilisers and Pesticides	(25)	Wholesale and Retail Trade
(12)	Paints and Varnishes	(26)	Hotels and Restaurants
(13)	Pharmaceuticals and Medicines	(27)	Transport, Storage and Communications
(14)	Rubber and Plastic Products	(28)	Computer and Related Activities

The list of industries is fine-tuned, from time to time, to be as representative as possible.

Table 51

RBI DATA – CATEGORYWISE PROFILE

	CATEGORY	YEAR AND MONTH OF PUBLICATION OF STUDY	YEAR/S FOR WHICH DATA IS PUBLISHED	NO.S OF COMPANIES STUDIED	NO.S OF YEAR/S DATA AVAILABLE IN STUDY
(1)	Public Limited Companies	August, 2009	2006-07 and 2007-08 2005-06 to 2007-08	3114 (NOTE 1)	2 Years 3 Years
(2)	Large Public Limited Companies	June, 2007	2004-05 and 2005-06 2003-04 to 2005-06	1004(NOTE 2)	2 Years 3 Years
(3)	Private Limited Companies	October, 2009	2006-07 and 2007-08 2005-06 to 2007-08	1475(NOTE 3)	2 Years 3 Years
(4)	Private Corporate Business Sector	September, 2009	2007-08 and 2008-09 (quarterwise)	2549(NOTE 4)	2 Years
(5)	Financial Investment Companies	September, 2009	2006-07 and 2007-08 2005-06 to 2007-08	1175(NOTE 5)	2 Years 3 Years
(6)	Foreign Direct Investment Companies	February, 2009	2006-07 and 2007-08 2005-06 to 2007-08	502(NOTE 6)	2 Years 3 Years

NOTE 1: 3114 companies include non-government, non-financial public limited companies during 2007-08, based on their audited annual accounts closed during April, 2007 to March, 2008.

NOTE 2: 1004 companies include non-government, non-financial large public limited companies, each with paid-up capital of ₹ 1 crore and above during 2005-06, based on their audited annual accounts closed during April, 2005 to March, 2006.

NOTE 3: 1475 companies include non-government, non-financial private limited companies during the year 2007-08, based on the audited annual accounts which close their accounts during the period April, 2007 to March, 2008.

NOTE 4: 2549 companies include non-government public limited companies based on abridged financial results during 2008-09.

NOTE 5: 1175 companies include select non-government financial and investment companies, other than banking insurance and chit fund companies during the year 2007-08, based on their audited annual accounts which closed during the period April, 2007 to March, 2008.

NOTE 6: 502 companies include non-government, non-financial foreign direct investment companies for the year 2007-08, based on their audited annual accounts closed during the period April, 2007 to March, 2008.

Table 52

RBI DATABASE – FINANCIAL RATIOS

PRO FORMA

	CATEGORY		
	PERIOD OF STUDY 2005-06 TO 2007-08		
	2005-06	*2006-07*	*2007-08*
A. Capital Structure Ratios			
R1 = Net Fixed Assets to Total Assets			
R2 = Net Worth to Total Net Assets			
R3 = Debt to Equity			
B. Liquidity Ratios			
R4 = Current Assets to Current Liabilities			
R5 = Quick Assets to Current Liabilities			
R6 = Current Assets to Total Net Assets			
C. Asset Utilization and Turnover Ratios			
R7 = Sales to Total Net Assets			
R8 = Inventories to Sales			
R9 = Sundry Debtors to Sales			
D. Profitability and Profit Allocation Ratios			
R10 = Gross Profits to Total Net Assets			
R11 = Gross Profits to Sales			
R12 = Profit After Tax to Net Worth			
R13 = Products Retained to Profits After Tax			
R14 = Ordinary Dividends to Ordinary Paid-up Capital			

FINANCIAL DATABASES

There are a wide variety of financial databases available to users. These databases help in meeting a variety of needs of different stakeholders, *viz.*, the existing and potential shareholders (investors), management, Government, staff, lenders (individual and institutional), customers, competitors, foreign investors and interested parties desirous of establishing enterprise in any part of the World. A few data bases along with their functionality and the kind of financial information which users have access to are discussed below:

EXHIBIT 45 (B)

DATABASE: MYIRIS

SALIENT FEATURES: *Provides financial information relating to a wide variety of matters, viz., homes, shares, mutual funds, loans, credit cards, insurance, markets, companies and industries.*

Myiris.com is India's leading personal finance destination, where people research stocks and mutual funds before transacting in them through an intermediary of their choice.

IRIS seeks to be a strategic provider of information and research solutions to global customers through leading edge technology, people and processes. IRIS has many years of proven expertise in the financial information management space. The firm owns and manages one of India's most comprehensive financial information databases, covering the universe of publicly traded companies, mutual funds, markets reference data to a live news service on Indian business, markets and the economy.

Our expertise in the XBRL arena, the information standard for financial reporting, has led to several prestigious contracts from regulators and associations, including the Institute of Chartered Accountants of India to build the taxonomy for India.

EXHIBIT 45 (C)

DATABASE: COMPUSTAT/STANDARDS AND POOR'S

SALIENT FEATURES: *Compustat is a division of Standard and Poor's which is a division of the McGraw Hill Companies. It is a USA-based company in the financial services industry. Compustat is a database which includes financial statistical and market intelligence of active and inactive global companies throughout the World. This service which began in early sixties, targets users who are institutional investors, universities, bankers, management analysits, investment bankers and all those who are interested in corporate economic management. The coverage of the database includes nearly one hundred thousand global securities and the database is a universe (population) itself because it captures 99% of the World's total market capitalisation. The annual company data history is available for nearly 6 decades. A key financial application includes: a product called research insight which evaluates company performance in depth. Research insight is an analytical solution based on financial modelling which can help determine a company's true value and identify by sell opportunities. Similarly, another service known as the total return performance graph service provides for five year stock performance graphs as required by the Securities and Exchange Commission (SEC) of the USA.*

EXHIBIT 45 (D)

DATABASE: FINALAYA

SALIENT FEATURES: *Finalaya is first of its own kind SaaS (software as a service) architecture based '**Investor Communication**' Platform in India. It is a unique web based content management system which has revolutionized the existing investor communication channel and helps investors to connect to Public Companies, Market Experts, Brokerage Houses and Mutual Funds.*

Finalaya aims to bring Retail Investors, Institutional Investors, Brokers, Mutual Funds and Public Listed Companies all on a single platform. Finalaya addresses the financial data and information needs of stakeholders of the financial services industry.

The objective is to empower investors through this platform so that they can register their views or issues about Companies, Mutual Funds and Brokerage Houses or interact and discuss with Brokers or Market experts about their portfolio or investments.

In the Indian marketplace this platform acts as a centralized platform available for results of all public companies, public documents of stocks and mutual funds and information on all public companies.

Why Investors should use this Platform?

(1) Speak their mind and share their experience, opinion, views and issues about any Public Company Stocks, Mutual Funds or Brokerage Houses.

(2) Register the queries or directly raise the query with company's Investor Relations Officer.

(3) Take advice from Market Expert or Different Brokerage Houses about any stock or mutual fund.

(4) Availability of critical information about Public Companies and Mutual Funds at a single place.

(5) Know about companies and mutual funds which are good at Investor Relation Practices and keep their Retail Investors updated with latest happenings.

Why Corporates should use this Platform?

This platform opens an additional channel to reach retail investors for corporate. Finalaya is a web-based investor relations platform and aspires to help companies realize increased reach to investors and other stakeholders.

SALIENT FEATURES: *Finalaya is a complete Corporate Disclosure and Investor Communication Platform for Public Companies. The objective is to help Corporates to maximize shareholders value by improving efficiency of communication with investors. The idea is not to replace the existing practice of Investor Relation but to complement it by providing additional reach.*

Benefits: In the context of ratios Finalaya provides for 30 ratios categorised as follows:

Return Related: *Return on Total Assets (%); Return on Networth (%); Return on Capital Employed (%)*

Profitability: *Gross Margin (%), Operating Margin (%), Net Profit Margin (%), Adjusted Net Profit Margin (%); Asset Turnover (x)*

Leverage: *Debt/Equity Ratio (times); Total Debt/Total Assts (%); Long-term Debt/Networth (times); Interest Coverage (times)*

Liquidity: *Current Ratio (times); Quick Ratio (times); Cash Ratio (times)*

Working Capital: *Working Capital to Sales (times); Working Capital Days (days gross sales); Receivables (days gross sales); Creditors (days cost of sales); FG Inventory (days cost of sales); RM Inventory (days consumption)*

Cash Flow Indicator: *Operating Cash Flow/Sales (%)*

Per Share: *Book Value Per Share (₹); Earnings Per Share (₹); Dividend Per Share (₹)*

Growth (%): *Total Operating Income; EBITDA; EBIT; Net Profit; Total Assets*

EXHIBIT 45 (E)

DATABASE: FACTIVA

SALIENT FEATURES: *According to Wikipedia,* ***Factiva*** *is a business information and research tool owned by Dow Jones and Company. Factiva aggregates content from both licensed and free sources, and provides organizations with search, alerting, dissemination and other information management capabilities. Factiva.com facilitates informed business decisions. It claims to deliver the "****World's best news and business information with search tools that fit every need****" of an organisation. The characteristics of factiva.com include inter alia the following:*

- *More than 28,000 plus leading sources from 157 countries in 23 languages, including an unmatched collection of regional and industry publications, Web and blog content.*
- *Patented taxonomy and superior editorial processes so that user gets highly targeted and precise search results.*
- *Newsletter feature lets users share news across the organization in a professional, attractive and easy-to-use format.*
- *Advanced search tools that are built to the demanding requirements of information professionals so that research can be conducted effectively.*
- *Alerts for an individual or entire organization that can be easily created for general or sophisticated topics. Timely or continuous delivery to e-mail, RSS or mobile devices allows everyone to keep track of current news.*
- *More than just headlines, Factiva.com offers charts and graphs that provides the big picture around. From article timelines to themes and trends, users quickly understand what's going on without having to read every story.*
- *Flexible delivery and information integration options that range from simple Web tools that can be implemented by anyone to sophisticated technologies that can extract deep business intelligence from content.*

Favita provides the following key financial ratios viz.

Relative Valuations: *P/E Ratio, Price/Revenue, Price/Cash Flow, Price/Free Cash Flow, Price/ Book Value, Price/Tangible Book, Book Value Per Share.*

Financial Strength: *Current Ratio, Quick Ratio, Debt/Equity, Total Debt to Equity, Total Capital, Debt/Total Capital, Interest Coverage from Continuing Operations, Long-term Debt as per cent. Of Invested Capital.*

Profitability: *Pre-Tax Profit Margin, Post-Tax Profit Margin, Net Profit Margin, EBIT Margin, EBITDA Margin, Gross Margin, Effective Tax Rate.*

Effectiveness and Efficiency: *Total Return, Return on Equity, Return on Assets, Return on Invested Capital, Revenue/Employee, Net Income/Employee, Asset Turnover, Receivables Turnover, Inventory Turnover, Inventory as per cent of Revenue, Cost of Goods Sold as per cent of Revenue.*

EXHIBIT 45 (F)

DATABASE: REPORT JUNCTION

SALIENT FEATURES*: ReportJunction.com is a joint initiative of Sansco, Iden Investment Advisors Pvt. Ltd. and Intelgain Technologies Pvt. Ltd. Report Junction is a reputed vendor of annual reports to the top Research houses and Corporates in the country by virtue of the association of its partners.*

Sansco has leading clientele which includes top corporate honoures.

The value proposition of Report Junction is to be a one stop shop for annual reports for Indian companies in the electronic format. It has years of collection and transforming these physical copies into the electronic format.

The IT platform has been provided by Intelgain Technologies (Intelgain) which brought into existence, Wow-india.com, the pioneer in Independent research. Intelgain has marquee clients on technology in various geographies across USA, UK, Canada, Australia with its strengths in the Capital market domain displayed in various websites globally.

Iden Investment Advisors Pvt. Ltd., advises FII clients and other Institutional clients for their Investments into Equity.

EXHIBIT 45 (G)

DATABASE: MONEY CONTROL

SALIENT FEATURES*:*

Our Vision: *The foundation on which moneycontrol.com is built is best summarized by a quote from Robert Noyce, one of the founders of Intel:*

"Start with a growing market. Swim in a stream that becomes a river and ultimately an ocean. Be a leader in that market, not a follower and constantly build the best products possible." *We moneycontrol.com was conceived as a personal finance portal in February, 1999 and it took almost nine months to give it birth on November 5, 1999. This precocious child of the cyberworld has been growing at a breath taking rate ever since. On the way, we had another memorable date with destiny, when we were acquired by e-Eighteen.Com Limited on June 1, 2000 and became part of the Television Eighteen India Limited group. Today, moneycontrol.com is the premier end-to-end business and finance portal for Indian citizens everywhere. Come, be part of the journey as our valued member and leave it to us to make this relationship click....*

EXHIBIT 45 (H)

DATABASE: VALUE NOTES

SALIENT FEATURES: "The only "unbiased", online research aggregator focused on Indian financial markets"*. The research service includes providing information research intelligence which includes research support i.e. providing India based, cost effective solution to corporations, consultants, internal research firms and other interested parties, quality research services at affordable cost, consulting engagements for customised studies for India entry, partner selection and so on and published material providing inputs for informed decision making. Online research aggregator is focussed on Indian financial markets and specialised know-how about outsourcing industry.*

The corporate financial analysis of individual companies is also provided and the date base includes 501 companies. The contents of the report includes details regarding share prices and other ratios like earnings per share, price earnings ratio, price book value ratio, dividend yield and market capitalisation. In addition, profitability picture of the company is presented through various profit margin ratios, viz., operating gross and net.

EXHIBIT 45 (I)

DATABASE: BLOOMBERG BUSINESSES

SALIENT FEATURES: *Bloomberg BusinessWeek, understood and known as BusinessWeek is a weekly magazine published by Bloomberg L.P. (Headquarters: New York) Bloomberg also has two sites viz. BusinessWeek.com and the Bloomberg.com and is supposed to have "**more unique visitors than non-portal business and financial site**". The said site publishes information relating to the financial health of companies which captures various ratio, viz., profitability (return on assets and return on capital), margin analysis (gross margin and EBITDA margin), (levered free cash flow margin), SG&A margin, asset turnover (total asset turnover, fixed assets turnover, accounts receivables turnover and inventory turnover), credit ratios (current ratios and quick ratio), long-term solvency ratio (total debt / equity and total liabilities/total assets). In addition, the site also provides for growth (%) over prior year with respect to (EBITDA, receivables, diluted EPS before extra, cash from operations, tangible book value, gross profit, inventory, capital expenditure and levered free cash flow).*

EXHIBIT 45 (J)

DATABASE: REUTERS

SALIENT FEATURES: *Reuters is a United Kingdom based news service and a former financial market data provider. The main focus is on "**supplying the financial markets with information and trading products**". The financial services include providing market data, research and relevant analysis and computer based trading systems. The database of the company includes 40,000 companies, information on debt instruments and three million economic series. Reuters publish information about individual companies which includes consensus estimates analaysis. These estimates provide quarter ending and year ending mean, high and low figures with respect to shares, earnings per share, growth rate. They also publish several ratios which include: Valuation Ratios (P/E ratio, P/E high, P/E low), Beta (Prices to Sales, Price to Book, Price to Tangible Book, Price to Cash Flow, Price to Free Cash Flow), Dividends (Dividend Yield) Growth Rates (Sales, EPS)*

EXHIBIT 45 (K)

DATABASE: CHOLAWEALTHDIRECT

SALIENT FEATURES: *Cholawealthdirect is supposed to be an online adviser on financial matters. This site provides information on investment options, equity and IPOs and provides detailed company information which includes amongst other things, key financial ratios covering share price, debt-equity ratio, long-term debt-equity ratio, current ratio, interest cover ratio, PBIDTM (%), PBITM (%), PBDTM (%), CPM (%), APATM (%), ROCE (%) and RONW (%).*

EXHIBIT 45 (L)

DATABASE: INVESTMENTZ.COM

SALIENT FEATURES: *Investmentz.com is a investment intermediary which has a very specific corporate purpose viz. "**to reach appropriate financial products, services and solution to every Indian entity.**" The company also presents a page known as investmentz.com with key financial ratios for various companies. A typical page includes amongst other things, the following ratios viz. debt equity ratio, long-term debt equity ratio, interest cover ratio, PBIDTM (%), PBITM (%), PBDTM (%), CPM (%), APATM (%), ROCE (%) and RONW (%).*

EXHIBIT 45 (M)

DATABASE: CORPORATEINFORMATION.COM

SALIENT FEATURES: *CorporateInformation.com is a corporate database which provides information for more than 30,000 companies from nearly 60 countries. The Wright Investors' research has analysed company information since 1960. They have developed financial tools, which include quality rating system that is applied to companies where sufficient information is available, which form part of their database. The quantified information is well supported by detailed explanatory notes which supplements the process of interpretation of corporate results. In the mid 1980s, Wright Investors service developed Worldscope which is a premier global corporate financial database. The database includes information collected from primary source documents, viz., annual report, interim reports and former announcements made by competent authorities of a company. The corporate information database provides with a wide variety of information relating to the financial health of a company. It includes accounting ratios which reflect on assets utilization, employee efficiency, fixed charges coverage, leverage analysis, liquidity analysis, per share ratios and profitability growth. A sample report indicates that information is presented for a five year period. A wide variety of ratios are used. To start with asset utilization shows receivables turnover, inventory turnover, gross and net property plant and equipment turnover. Asset utilization is studied by presenting the data relating to individual assets as a percentage of net sales. Employee efficiency is studied through the concept of value per employee. The year to year percentage change per employee is compared with the percentage change in sales, net income, cash earnings, working capital, total debt, total capital and total assets. The next segment of analysis includes fixed charges coverage which include EBIT/Total Interest Expense, EBIT/Net Interest, EBIT/(Total Interest Exp + Preference Dividend), EBIT/Dividends on Equity Shares, EBIT/(Dividends on Common + Preference), EBITDA/Total Interest Expense, EBITDA/Net Interest, EBITDA/(Total Interest Exp + Preferred Div), E BITDA/Dividends on E Shares, EBITDA/(Dividends on Equity + Pfd).*

SALIENT FEATURES: *The database also provides for detailed leverage analysis for a period of five years and presents the following ratios: Long-term Debt % of EBIT, Long-term Debt % of EBITDA, Long-term Debt % of Total Assets, Long-term Debt % of Total Capital, Long-Term Debt % of Equity, Total Debt % of EBIT, Total Debt % of EBITDA, Total Debt % of Total Assets, Total Debt % of Total Capital, Total Debt % of Total Capital and Short-term Debt, Total Debt % of Common Equity, Minority Interest % of EBIT, Minority Interest % of EBITDA, Minority Interest % of Total Assets, Minority Interest % to Total Capital, Minority Interest % of Com Equity, Preferred Stock % of EBIT, Preferred Stock % of EBITDA, Preferred Stock % of Total Assets, Preferred Stock % of Total Capital, Preferred Stock % of Total Equity, Common Equity % of Total Assets, Common Equity % of Total Capital, Total Capital % of Total Assets, Capital Expenditure % of Sales, Fixed Assets % of Common Equity, Working Capital % of Total Capital, Dividend Payout, Funds from Operations % of Total Debt.*

EXHIBIT 45 (N)

DATABASE: FORBES.COM

SALIENT FEATURES: *Forbes.com is a homepage which provides with real time reporting, objective commentary, '**concise analysis**' and relevant tools. According to Forbes.com "**throughout the business day forbes.com publishes thousands of articles delivering the best of Forbes journalism.**" The nine editorial channels of the site covers business technology, markets, personal finance, entrepreneurship, leadership, Forbes life opinions and lists. Forbes.com also publishes subscription investment newsletter. The forbes.com provides company wise information which includes the latest 12 months data exploring gross profit margin, EBIT margin, EBITDA margin, pre tax profit margin, current ratio, quick ratio, leverage ratio, receivables turnover and assets turnover. The site also provides various other ratios which includes. Revenue to Assets, ROE from Total Operations, Return on Invested Capital, Return on Assets, Debt/Common Equity Ratio, Price/Book Ratio (Price/Equity), Book Value per Share, Total Debt/Equity, Long-term Debt to Total Capital, SG&A as % of Revenue, Receivables per Day Sales, Days CGS in Inventory, Working Capital per Share, Cash per Share, Cash Flow per Share, Free Cash Flow per Share, Tangible Book Value per Share, Price/Cash Flow Ratio, Price/Free Cash Flow Ratio and Price/Tangible Book Ratio.*

Further the site provides five year averages of: Return on Equity, Return on Assets, Return on Invested Capital, Gross Profit Margin, Pre Tax Profit Margin, Post Tax Profit Margin, Net Profit Margin (Total Operations), R&D as a %age of Sales, SG&A as a %age of Sales, Debt/Equity Ratio and Total Debt/ Equity Ratio. An unique feature of the site is that it provides multifaceted profile of the price earnings ratio. The site shows: Current P/E Ratio, P/E Ratio, High P/E Ratio, Low P/E Ratio, Current P/E as %age of Avg. P/E, Normalized P/E Ratio.

RATIOS FOR CREDIT RATING

Credit rating uses the outcomes of different ratios put together in a composite form, either in the aggregate or segment-wise to assess the ability of a business to sustain at least historic performance to meet its emerging obligations. There are many rating companies all over the World, *viz.*, Fitch, Moody's, S&P, FICO scores, ICRA, CRISIL which perform the credit rating, function. It is quite possible that different credit rating houses use different criteria to determine creditworthiness and different strengths and weaknesses in rating issuers of instruments of finance. However, most determinants of credit quality of an enterprise are related to liquidity ratios, debt-equity ratio, cash flow to debt ratio, return on assets, return on equity, interest coverage ratios, fixed charge coverage ratios. In short, financial ratios are a key dimension of credit risk analysis all over the World. Companies with strong competitive positions, favorable business projections and stable cash flows are in a better position to sustain additional financial risk for any given credit rating in relation to companies with relatively poor business performance, profiles and projections. Thus, key ratios help to measure the performance of a business as well as its risk exposure in some combination. The performance ratios are those which explore the ability of a company in terms of return on investment as well as the ability to absorb costs and sustain obligations to stakeholders. This is an indication of a company's performance as well as market standing. Risk on the other hand is measured by coverage ratios which indicate the pre tax income from ongoing operations in relation to the fixed obligations. Operating excellence, as measured by the return on capital employed and the profit margin ratio, is indicative of the cost competitiveness and market standing. The cash flows indicate the ability of a company to generate enough cash from operations to service amortisation obligations. Two Standard ratios used by credit rating agencies are Free Operating Cashflow (FOC) – to total debt and Funds From Operations (FFO) – to total debt. Leverage ratios indicate the risks facing various categories of creditorship capital. A brief, on the rating patterns and explanation of the ranges of grades/scores obtained by entities solicits rating services for their instruments of finance is presented below:

Table 53

CREDIT RATING AGENCIES: GRADING

MOODY'S RATING	*S&P*	*FITCH*	*FICO*	*ICRA*	*CRISIL*
Aaa, Aa1, Aa2, Aa3, A1, A2, A3, Baa1, Baa2, Baa3	Aaa, Aa, A, BBB	Aaa, Aa, A, BBB	A, B, C, D	LAAA, LAA, LA, LBBB, LBBB, LB, LC, LD	FAAA, FAA, FA

MOODY'S RATINGS:

- **Aaa:** highest quality with the "***smallest degree of risk***".
- **Aa1, Aa2, Aa3:** high quality, with "***very low credit risk***", but "***their susceptibility to long-term risks appears somewhat greater***".
- **A1, A2, A3:** as "***upper-medium grade***", subject to "***low credit risk***", but have elements present that suggest a "***susceptibility to impairment over the long-term***".
- **Baa1, Baa2, Baa3:** "***moderate credit risk***". *They are considered medium-grade and* as such "***protective elements may be lacking or may be characteristically unreliable.***"

S&P:

- **Aaa:** the best quality borrowers, reliable and stable (many of them governments).
- **Aa:** quality borrowers, a bit higher risk than AAA.
- **A:** economic situation can affect finance.
- **BBB:** medium class borrowers, which are satisfactory at the moment.

FITCH:

- **Aaa:** the best quality companies, reliable and stable.
- **Aa:** quality companies with a bit higher risk than AAA.
- **A:** economic situation can affect finance.
- **BBB:** medium class companies, which are satisfactory at the moment.

FICO SCORE

Generally, FICO (Fair Isaac Corporation) score is the most widely used credit rating model in the United States and ranges from 300 to 850. The exact formula for calculating FICO credit score is not disclosed but FICO has factored the following aspects of an enterprise for determining credit rating. The approximate weights assigned to the different aspects are as follows: 35% – pervious payment history; 30% – amount of debt owed; 15% – length of credit history; 10% – new credit obtained recently and 10% – types of credit used.

***ICRA*:**

- **LAAA:** The highest-credit-quality-rating assigned with the lowest credit risk.
- **LAA:** The high-credit-quality rating with a low credit risk.
- **LA:** Adequate-credit-quality rating with average credit risk.
- **LBBB:** A moderate-credit-quality rating with higher than average credit risk.
- **LBB:** An inadequate-credit-quality rating with high credit risk.

- **LB:** Risk-prone-credit-quality rating with very high credit risk.
- **LC:** Poor-credit-quality rating with limited prospects of recovery.
- **LD:** The lowest-credit-quality rating with very low prospects of recovery.

CRISIL:

- **FAAA: "*Highest Safety*"**: The degree of safety regarding timely payment of interest and principal is very strong.
- **FAA: "*High Safety*"**: The degree of safety regarding timely payment of interest and principal is strong. However, the relative degree of safety is not as high as FAAA rating.
- **FA: "*Adequate Safety*"**: The degree of safety regarding timely payment of interest and principal is satisfactory. Changes in circumstances can affect such issues more than those in the higher rated categories.

Moody's Ratings include long-term ratings (investment grades), speculative grade also knows as high yield of junk, short-term taxable ratings, short-term tax exempt ratings and individual bank ratings. The investment grade assesses the quality of the issuer and an exposure to risk (degree of risk). The speculative grade assesses credit quality and the extent of risk involved alongwith the potential recovery value of money in the event of crises. Short-term taxable ratings focus on ability (superior, strong, acceptable with respect to repayment of short-term obligation). Short-term tax exempts, focus again on the ability to repay short-term obligations. In the case of Moody's ratings, there is a separate category for short-term municipal bonds. Individual bank ratings focus on a bank's financial strength and offer a quantitative measure of the extent of assistance required from third parties *vis-à-vis* the intrinsic financial strength which is classified as superior, strong, adequate, modest or very modest.

Standard and Poor's provide grading in terms of investment grade which focuses again on the quality of the borrower and their reliability and ability to meet contractual obligation. Further, S&P includes non-investment grade, also known as junk bonds, which highlights the ability to sustain emerging obligations and the susceptibility for economic conditions. Short-term issue credit ratings again provide inputs on the issuers commitment to meet its obligations. In addition to the usual analysis of liquidity, profitability, capital structure, activity, valuation and cash flow, the rating factors in country risk and currency of repayment of the creditor. The rating ranges from strong, satisfactory and weak to uncertain, vulnerable and default.

Fitch grade provides for investment grade, non-investment grade (also known as junk bonds) and short-term credit ratings. The investment grade indicates the quality of companies, *viz.*, best quality, quality affected by economic situation and medium class companies. The non-investment grades expose the extent of vulnerability of the company to the economic conditions. The ratings range from more prone to changes, financial situation varies, currently vulnerable and dependent on favourable economic conditions, highly vulnerable and very speculative instrument, highly vulnerable perhaps in a state of bankruptcy but no default yet and defaulting on all obligations. The short-term credit ratings, which are usually for a 12 month period, grade the ability of the business to meet its financial commitment. The grades range from exceptionally strong capacity, strong capacity, satisfactory capacity, adequate capacity, minimal capacity, possibility of default.

FICO score assesses the trustworthiness of borrowers and provides a numerical score which translates into later grades with supporting tags in prose for the credit valuation as shown below:

Table 54

FICO SCORES: INTERPRETATION

FICO Score	*Credit Valuation*	*Letter Grades*
720+	excellent	A-credit
650+	good	B-credit
575+	average	C-credit
below 575	poor	D-credit

ICRA ratings include long-term rating scale of all bonds, non-convertible debentures, other debt instruments, excluding public deposits with original maturity exceeding one year. The focus is on rating, credit quality and the extent of risk involved in the instrument in question. ICRA's medium-term rating again focusing on credit quality and risk is applicable to all public deposits. ICRA's short-term rating scales applies to instruments with original maturity within one year. ICRA also provides rating scale for the following:

(a) Claims paying ability of insurance companies.
(b) Corporate governance rating scale.
(c) Stakeholder value and governance rating scale.
(d) Issuer rating scale.
(e) Mutual fund credit risk ratings.
(f) Short-term debt fund credit risk rating scale.
(g) NSIC's performance and credit rating scale.
(h) SME rating scale.
(i) Grading scale for initial public offer.
(j) Grading scale for microfinance institutions.
(k) Grading scale for real estate developers.
(l) Grading scale for real estate projects.
(m) Grading symbols for contractors and consultants.
(n) Grading scale for maritime trading institutions.
(o) Grading scale for healthcare.
(p) Rating of issuers in Nepal.

CRISIL ratings include the following:

- Long-term ratings indicating the ability to meet financial commitments ranging from very strong capacity, strong capacity, adequate capacity, less vulnerable but facing major on-going uncertainties.
- Short-term ratings.
- Assessing the ability of the obliger to meet the commitments.
- Ratings symbols for debentures which range from highest safety, high safety, adequate safety, moderate safety, inadequate safety, high risk, substantial risk and default.
- Rating for fixed deposits again ranging from highest safety, high safety, adequate safety, speculative grade, high risk and default.
- Rating symbols for short-term, instruments indicating the degree of safety as very strong, strong, adequate, minimal followed by expected default and actual default.
- Rating symbols for structured obligations exploring, once again, the ability to meet financial commitments and follow the same pattern of safety levels indicated above.
- Foreign structure.

Rating symbols carrying non-credit risk ranges from high investment grades, investment grades and speculative grades.

US SOVEREIGN CREDIT RATING

Sovereign credit rating: Standard and Poor an international credit rating agency downgraded the US sovereign rating from AAA to AA+. This is unparalleled in World history. The following questions need to be addressed:

What does sovereign credit rating mean?

For investors who plan to invest their savings abroad sovereign credit rating is an indictor of the risk involved in investing in that country.

What does sovereign debt rating mean?

Sovereign debt rating is an indicator of the risk involved in interest bearing financial instruments issued by the national Government of a country. It should be noted that, unlike corporates, Central or Federal Government of any country has the powers to mobilise financial resources through taxes and alter levels of money supply in their respective countries. Hence, government debt rating is a separate exercise and usually the ratings of the government of a particular country are pitched at a higher level than other sectors in the same rule of regime.

What does sovereign credit rating measure?

Sovereign credit rating measures the willingness and ability to successfully fulfil the existing and emerging amortisation obligations which include the payment of interest and repayment of the instalments due against the principal amounts borrowed.

What are the key factors affecting the measure?

The key factors included in the measure are:

(a) Countries' performance in the recent economic and political cycle

(b) The flexibility of fiscal, monetary and commercial policies to tackle the impending economic issues in future economic cycles.

Thus, the rating scale captures many factors like institutional effectiveness and political risk, economic structure and growth prospects, international investment position, debt burden and of course the flexibility of economic policies.

What is the *modus operandi* of the rating?

The *modus operandi* of the rating is based on a five criteria model to arrive at a composite index (score) which forms the basis on which ratings are assigned to a country. The five variables are ranked individually on a six point scale - one being the strongest and six being the weakest. Quantitative and qualitative aspects of economic health of any country influence the scoring of each of the five variables which include: political score, economic score, external score, fiscal score and monetary score. The first two factors indicate the political and economic profile of the country and the last three factors show the flexibility and performance profile. The sovereign rating level uses the scores of the five factors, just mentioned and provides for an adjustment to accommodate exceptional events, episodes and experiences to finally arrive at a country's sovereign rating.

Why did Standard and Poor downgrade the US?

The US economy has been in serious trouble ever since the real estate bubble in 2008. The US is suffering from several economic ills like rising public debt burden, policymaking uncertainty consistent with established criteria of rating agencies, inadequate fiscal consolidation and the general mood of gloom in the economy in terms of employment levels. Hence S&P has downgraded the US though the US dollar still remains the key international currency (Japanese Yen is a distant third),

US prices are more stable, US growth prospects are better and generally the US is perceived, in the World at large, as a mighty economic, social and military force to reckon with. Yet S&P thought equity and fairness requires that US rating should be downgraded from AAA to AA+. A similar downgrade was attributed to Japan when the debt to GDP ratio of Japan in 2001 was similar to that of the US (August, 2011). The US was clearly on the same trajectory in August, 2011.

What are the implications?

The implication of a downgrade of the US Sovereign rating are as follows:

(1) Reduced creditworthiness of assets linked to the United States, e.g., securities collateralised by loans backed by the US.

(2) Companies that must hold AAA securities will be forced to offload the downgraded securities.

(3) Increase in the borrowing cost to offset the risk associated with the downgrade – mainly Government borrowings.

Of course, such a downgrade may not affect corporates because many companies may be enjoying surfeit cash. The downgrade of the US in August, 2011 has taken place in the backdrop of a US corporate enjoying more reserves than the US Government itself. As reported in *The Hindustan Times, Indo-Asian News Service* (July, 2011), "***As of today, Apple boss Steve Jobs is richer than Uncle Sam. While the worlds most powerful government has just $73.76 billion***" in its reserves, the worlds top technology company has a neat cash pile of $75.87 billion.

How often have national Governments defaulted on their debt?

Normally governments don't default except in the case of dictators who tend to use their absolute political power to expropriate properties of foreign investors. Adolf Hitler's command economy and Idi Amin's rule in Africa reminds us of these events. In the normal course governments rarely default. When the economy is on the verge of a crises, the government in trouble is protected through a IMF rescue package which reschedules the amortisation plans to tide over the burning economic problems that have emerged. Of course, the market is driven by sentiments and suspicious investors may demand higher returns. Recently, Greece, Ireland and Portugal were engulfed by crises when the respective governments were unable to honour their amortisation obligations. Again, in the early eighties Latin American countries were caught in a debt crises because their foreign investments grew higher than the incomes and the governments were unable to mobilise resources to sustain repayment obligations. Mexico, Russia and Argentina have all gone through these situations. Similarly India in 1991, had faced a severe crises and the country had to face humiliation at the hands of international creditors (UK) who insisted that gold should be exported to honour their amortisation obligations.

Overseas Demand for U.S. Assets Climbed Amid Standard and Poor (S&P) Downgrade

US Sovereign Credit Rating was downgraded by S&P in August, 2011. Inspite of the said downgrading, "***the flows into Treasuries really prove that, despite S&P's ratings downgrade, the dollar and treasuries remain the global safe-haven asset of choice.***" (Guy LeBas). Thus, instead of erosion in the value of US Government debt, the sovereign downgrade of the US triggered off a financial market turmoil. As a result, the World reserve currency, namely the USD, became the darling among investors. The net buying of long-term equities, notes and bonds totalled US 57.9 billion the highest since December, 2010. Thus, the perceptions of investors matter more than the grades of credit rating agencies.

16

MERGERS AND ACQUISITIONS

MERGERS AND ACQUISITIONS – MEANING

A merger represents a fusion which results in one company absorbing another. Hence, the expression '***Merger***' is also used in the context of '***merger by absorption***'. In fact, merger normally refers to one company merging with another. However, even if the fusion involves more than two companies it is also called a merger.

The expression '***Amalgamation***' is unique to India and includes mergers and efforts towards consolidation. Thus, the expression '***Consolidation***' is broader in nature and comes into the picture even when several, small or medium sized, companies are ubiquitous in an industry and need to be brought together to avoid further subdivision and fragmentation.

An interesting example is that of ACC Ltd., which owes its origin and emergence mainly to the thoughts of leading entrepreneurs to unite and pre-empt a subdivided and fragmented industry from further degeneration. In fact, consolidation is a generic expression and includes, amongst other things, different ways and means or strategies or approaches adopted by business to consolidate its position from various perspectives, *viz.*, marketing, operations, finance, human resources, supply chain, information technology apparatus and prowess, unification of processes and methods and fusion of cultures.

ACC

Associated Cement Company Ltd. (ACCL) was formed on 1st August, 1936 as a result of 10 cement companies, again dispersed, decentralized, manufacturing companies coming together. The industry faced serious problems of viability of small and medium units. Unbridled competition had distorted the price-cost structure. With a view to rationalize operations and also ensure better yield to producers and prices to consumers, the said companies were brought under one umbrella. The outcome in terms of economies of scale and scope and sharing of facilities, including research and development facilities, was a key motivation for the creation, once again, of a monopoly organisation called ACCL. History will recall that four business houses, *viz.*, groups Tatas, Khatau, Killick and Nixon, F. E Dinshaw came together to form a cement giant of India, at a time when the thought and concept of mergers and acquisitions were unknown in Indian industry. The birth of ACCL was regarded as the birth of an institution of national pride.

Amalgamation means:

- The action or process of amalgamating and includes any combination of assets and liabilities, strengths and weaknesses, opportunities and threats.
- The coming together or combination, of two or more businesses, which merge, unite, consolidate or integrate into one entity.
- A voluntary action of two business entities to emerge as a new legal entity through the process of mergers or a combination of one or more corporation where only one firm survives and all other combining entities lose their identity.

Thus, a merger is a voluntary amalgamation of two or more business entities into one new legal entity. A merger is effected through a consideration which includes the exchange of the pre merger shares for the shares of the new entity. Owners of the pre merger firms continue as owners. However, the resources of the merging business entities are pooled together for the benefit of the newly created entity. The motivation is to reap synergistic effects with respect to all resources, *viz.*, men, machines, money, markets, materials, mindsets, management and technological process.

When an amalgamation takes place there are four expressions which are relevant: (1) Amalgamating Company, (2) Amalgamated Company, (3) Transferor Company and (4) Transferee Company.

Thus, if *X* Ltd. is amalgamating with *Y* Ltd. then *X* Ltd. is the amalgamating and transferor company and *Y* Ltd. is the amalgamated and transferee company. The transferee or amalgamated company continues to operate in business while the amalgamating or transferor company ceases to do business.

VERTICAL MERGERS

Vertical mergers take place between companies in a buyer-seller relationship, where backward or forward integration is possible. In case, one or more companies are the suppliers of some of the basic inputs for the final product to be manufactured by a company, then the latter company merges with the former company so that it is assured of supplies and is able to control the quality of production of supplies, effect economies of scale and improve the profitability of the final product. A car manufacturer merges with the suppliers of some of the essential parts. This ensures an assured source of supply and/or outlet for products or services and improvements in quantity, quality, cost, delivery schedules of operations and a command over the entire supply chain. The possible reasons for vertical merger are value chain management, technical and other economies like tax benefits, better control on the supply side and a stronger as well as a larger resource base.

EXAMPLE:

Reliance Industries Ltd. (RIL) was predominately a textile-oriented business, particularly synthetic textiles. There was another company known as Reliance Petrochemicals Ltd. (RPL) floated by the Ambanis for the purpose of carrying out business in the petrochemical industry mainly Vinyl Products. In December 1992, Reliance Petrochemicals Ltd. was absorbed by RIL. This was a vertical merger. Prior to the absorption, RIL was buying Purified Terephthalic Acid (PTA) from the open market, local and foreign. PTA is a raw material for the production of synthetic textiles. Reliance Petrochemicals Ltd., was a downstream company which went into the manufacture of other petrochemicals products from crude oil.

This unified the manufacturing process for the Reliance group and generated financial synergies in terms of

- replacing high cost debt with equity share capital.
- reducing interest cost and also cash outflows on account of repayment.
- tax benefits arising out of depreciation (Section 32 of Income Tax Act) on the new assets of RPC.
- benefits of Section 32(A) of Income Tax Act through investment allowance.

Thus, RIL profits were moderated by the losses and other tax deductible business expenditures of RPL and the post-tax profits were well protected.

The vertical merger between RIL and RPC was further followed by the mergers of Reliance Polypropylene Ltd. and Reliance Polyethylene Ltd., with RIL in the year 1995. The said two companies are downstream companies which enabled RIL to have control over the commanding heights of the Petrochemical Industry. The products RIL could manufacture included four important inputs used by downstream Petrochemical industry, *viz.*, PTA, Di-methyl Terephthalate (DMT), Polypropylene and Polyethylene.

The process did not stop at that. In 2002, RIL acquired 26% stake in IPCL. This enabled Reliance to get a further hold on the market — both factor market and output market. In factor market, they could command the production of DMT (input for textiles) and Caprolactium (input required for fertilizers production). Incidentally, a major buyer of DMT from IPCL was Bombay Dyeing, a competitor of RIL in the textile market. Thus, RIL could extend its command to almost all spheres of the industry. This acquisition was followed by increase in the stake to the extent of 55% through further buying of shares from the open market. According to Mr. Mukesh Ambani, Chairman RIL Group "***The merger will be earnings accretive for RIL shareholders and shall provide participation in RIL's diversified portfolio***". RIL absorbed IPCL and the merger by absorption was completed in October, 2007. IPCL ceased to exist from that date and of course in the meantime RIL itself was split into ADAG and RIL.

Following the split of the Reliance Group of Companies into RIL (Mr. Mukesh Ambani) and ADAG* (Mr. Anil Ambani – Coal-based, gas-based, financial services and telecommunications undertaking/businesses) there was one more event which is worth noting in the context of mergers. The split itself, in December, 2005, was a demerger. Following the same, RIL floated Reliance Petroleum Ltd. (RPL) and entered the capital market on 14th April, 2006 with a public issue of ₹ 135 crores equity share of ₹ 10 each for cash at a premium to be decided through 100% book building route. RIL was to subscribe to 90 crores share at the issue price and the public was to subscribe to the remaining 45 crores share. The issue was made to part finance the ₹ 27,000 crores export-oriented refinery set up in a Special Economic Zone (SEZ) at Jamnagar (Gujarat). This enabled RIL to get a hold on the petroleum industry which was just experiencing the benefits of liberalisation. The project was supposed to encourage the production of internal gas find (CNG). The petroleum refinery was located in Jamnagar because it was to process crude oil with petro products designated for exports. The gas project was to fund, process and distribute gas through pipelines to domestic consumers. If the Government permitted, the petro products designated for export market could be offered for local consumption too. The whole project was conceived in the wake of decontrol of petroleum and diesel prices and RIL launched a preemptive move to attain and maintain its competitive edge in the petroleum industry. The story ended, only thus far, with the merger of Reliance Petroleum with RIL. The terms of the merger is a lesson in strategic financial management to maximize owners interest. 29th September 2009 was set as the record date for amalgamation and swapping of shares in the ratio of 16 Reliance Petroleum stock for one Reliance Industries stock.

Reliance Industries Ltd., Annual Report 2009-10, p. 78

At the time of the public issue of RPL (14th April, 2006) Reliance had collected ₹ 2,700 crores from the public. ₹ 450 crores was the face value of the equity shares and the balance ₹ 2,250 crores was the share premium. When RPL was absorbed by RIL the swap ratio was 19 shares of RPL to be exchanged for 1 share of RIL which means RIL had to part with 2.37 crores of equity shares of ₹ 10 face value, i.e., say ₹ 23.70 crores only. Thus, RIL sacrificed ₹ 23.70, i.e., crores in order to get ₹ 2,700 – ₹ 23.7, i.e., ₹ 2,676.3 crores. This is reflected in the balance sheet of Reliance Industry Ltd., as on 31st March, 2010. Thus, the important message is how to use strategic benefits of merger, to generate financial synergies, in the post merger scenario.

HORIZONTAL MERGERS

Horizontal mergers take place between competing companies. A merger is horizontal if it involves the merger of two or more companies which are producing essentially the same products or rendering similar services which compete directly with each other — for example, sugar and artificial sweeteners. Horizontal mergers facilitate elimination of duplication of facilities and operations, broadening the product line, reduction in finance for working capital, widening the market area and reducing unhealthy competition. Care should be taken, while attempting horizontal mergers, to avoid impediments to competition that result in the creation of monopolistic organizations, as this would attract the attention of regulations like monopoly laws, anti-competition act or investigations which want to make sure that the operation of the industrial order is not to the detriment of the larger interests of society.

EXHIBIT 46

HORIZONTAL MERGERS - REASONS

- Achieving economies of scale.
- Shortening of gestation period for new businesses which would be complementary to the existing businesses of the company.
- Enabling and empowering the businesses to compete globally.
- Putting to use the liquidity available with the company for achieving growth through diversification.
- Exercising command over production and markets.
- Bargaining power.
- Maintaining complementarity between product and services.
- Improving management practices, processes and procedure launching of new products and brands.

In addition to the above reasons, there are a wide variety of other reasons limited only by the genius of the enterprise for identifying creative and innovative strategies.

HORIZONTAL MERGER - EXAMPLE

In November, 1999, HDFC Bank had acquired Times Bank, prompted, initiated and actioned by the owners of the country's largest publishing group, Bennett Coleman and Co., the owner of The Times of India and The Economic Times. It should be noted that Centurion Bank which in turn had a presence in the western part of the country previously merged with Bank of Punjab which in turn had a presence in the northern part of the country. The owners of Centurion bank were not interested in continuing with their investments in India any more. Around the same time (February, 2007-08). HDFC was looking for growth through horizontal merger and saw a great opportunity in Centurion Bank which had a presence in the western and northern parts of the country with established modern banking, state-of-art facilities. Hence, HDFC bank absorbed Centurion bank in February, 2008 with a swap ratio of 1:29. The economics of this merger is interesting. Centurion Bank had a share capital of ₹ 300 crores (approx.). With the said swap ratio HDFC would incur a liability in terms of incremental share capital of ₹ 10 crores only. This had its own positive implications for computation of earnings per share and the dividend policy of the company. Further, in return for an incremental liability of ₹ 10 crores, HDFC acquired a deposit base of Centurion Bank which was of the order of more than ₹ 15,000 crores as on 31st March, 2007 (Annual report of Centurion Bank of Punjab 2006-07). The effective ratio, of incremental liabilities incurred to incremental assets acquired, speaks for itself. In other words, income generating assets far exceeded the liabilities demanding periodic income distribution.

CONGLOMERATE MERGERS

Conglomerate mergers take place between entities which are neither competitors nor in buyer-seller relationship. The said entities operate in different businesses and are acquired/merged to diversify the products marketed. The companies may not be related to each other horizontally. In a '***pure conglomerate***' there are no important common factors between the companies in production, marketing, research and development or technology. Conglomerate merger is motivated by the need of management for rationalisation, simplification, ease of administration, minimal rather than multiple compliance requirements, economies of scale in the overall management of business, effective and efficient administration and greater and better management control and command over the resources of the business.

HLL – A CASE STUDY

HLL which had diversified itself into several product lines, viz., toothpaste, toiletries, beauty products, detergents, food, ice cream and so many other products wanted to consolidate all its multiple, widely spread, diversified businesses under a common umbrella identifiable through a common international brand, *viz.*, UNILEVER, Thus, they preferred one entity called Unilever and multiple divisions under that common parent brand rather than multiple entities in the same industry. HUL sought identification in an industry as a FMCG business. To quote the annual report, "***In mid 2006, the decision to create "One Corporate Office" for HLL in India was announced. In accordance with that the Foods Business was relocated from Bengaluru to Mumbai***"*. This enabled the company to enhance the functional capabilities of human resources particularly "***in the areas of marketing and customer development***". To quote the 2006 annual report of HLL again, "***Continuous communication and engagement led by the CEO directly, initiatives to drive recognition and celebration have all helped to embed the vitality culture.***"* The story of HLL (HUL since 2007), from 1.04.1993 is presented in **Exhibit 47**.

**Hindustan Lever Limited, Annual Report of 2006, p. 19*

EXHIBIT 47

THE STORY OF HINDUSTAN LEVER LTD (HLL) – HINDUSTAN UNILEVER LTD. (HUL) SINCE 2007

AMALGAMATIONS, MERGERS, TAKEOVERS AND DIVESTMENTS

- *On 1st April, 1993, Tata Oil Mills Co. Ltd., was merged with Hindustan Lever Ltd. (HLL).*
- *In 1995, HLL acquired quality and milk food 100% brand names and distribution assets. (Acquisition or Takeover).*
- *In 1996, Brooke Bond India Ltd., was amalgamated with HLL.*
- *In 1998, Ponds India Ltd. was amalgamated with HLL and both companies were subsidiaries of Unilever Plc which holds 51% equity in each.*
- *In 1998, HLL acquired Lakme brand factories and Lakme Ltd.'s 50% equity in Lakme Lever Ltd. (Acquisition or Takeover).*
- *In 1999, Industrial Perfumes Ltd., a subsidiary of HLL was merged with HLL. (Merger).*
- *In 1999, HLL sold its ₹ 80 crores dairy business to Nutricia International to the Dutch Dairy Products giant Koninklijke (Royal) Numico Envy Group. (Divestment).*
- *In 2001, HLL hived off the business of fragrances, flavors and food ingredients into a separate joint venture alongwith Quest International India. However, ICI India held a majority of shares in QII. In 2003, Dalda, one of HLL's oldest brands (introduced in 1937), was sold off. The transfer to Bunge, a US-based food company was structured as a slump sale/going concern. The divestment for HLL was in line with its focused business strategy and rationalisation of existing portfolio. "Value-added processed foods will continue to remain a key focus area for HLL's growth and it will seek to build and grow its portfolio of products and categories in this market with power brands such as Knorr, Kissan, Annapurna etc." Thus, the sale is part of HLL's strategy to exit from loss making business.*
- *In 2004, HLL sold Kissan factory premises in Bengaluru. (Divestment).*
- *In 2010, HUL exited from BPO firm Capgemini Business Services India by divesting the remaining 49% stake to IT consultancy firm Capgemini, SA. (Divestment).*

TYPES OF CONGLOMERATE MERGERS

There are two main types of conglomerate mergers – the pure conglomerate merger and the mixed conglomerate merger. The pure conglomerate merger is one where the merging companies are doing businesses that are totally unrelated to each other.

The mixed conglomerate mergers are ones where the companies that are merging with each other are doing so with the main purpose of gaining access to a wider market and client base or for expanding the range of products and services that are being provided by them.

There are also some other subdivisions of conglomerate mergers like the financial conglomerates, the concentric companies and the managerial conglomerates.

MIXED CONGLOMERATE MERGER – EXAMPLE

ITC

ITC regarded as a sin company is in the business of manufacturing cigarettes and was formerly known as Imperial Tobacco Company. Over the years, there have been several changes which included horizontal integration because they owned agricultural land which supplied raw tobacco for the manufacture of cigarettes, paper and paper board manufacturing facility (Bhadrachalam Paper Mills). Thus, as a cigarette manufacturing company most of the inputs required for the manufacture of cigarettes came from within the business wholly controlled by ITC. However, as part of an ambitious diversification plan and also with a view to get outside the tentacles of indirect taxes (excise duties) they started moving into other areas of business. Thus, they ventured into the hotel business and started luxurious hotels converting ancient heritage places (in fact, Palaces) into hotels. A chain of hotels was established all over the country. As of today, May, 2011, ITC group runs nearly 100 luxury hotels in 80 locations in India. ITC had started in 1975 as Welcome group and saw the merger of ITC Hotels into ITC Ltd. Incidentally, the swap ratio was 3 shares of ITC for 25 shares of ITC Hotels. ITC is also identified as a FMCG company and is in the business of spices, processed seafood, export of rice, apparels, personal care products, stationery, safety matches and agarbattis and last but not the least infotech.

EXAMPLE:

ENAM SECURITIES LTD.

Enam Securities Ltd. and Axis Bank, received RBI permission on 18th November, 2011 to merge. This is an example of Conglomeric Merger. Enam's business includes a wide range of financial products and services, *viz.*, investment banking, capital market services, broking services, *et al.*, Axis bank now offers a full range of financial products and services coming within the fold of commercial banking, investment banking, equity research, capital market services and broking services. Axis bank will use the outlets of Enam Securities Ltd., to offer their service. This deal is valued at ₹ 20.67 crores and it's an all stock deal.

Congeneric Merger refers to the fusion between two firms in the same general industry. The merging entities have no mutual customer or supplier relationship, such as a merger between a bank and a leasing company.

CIRCULAR MERGERS

Companies producing distinct products, within the same market, come together to share common distribution and research facilities to obtain economies by elimination of cost on duplication and promoting market enlargement. The acquiring company obtains benefits in the form of economies of resource sharing and diversification. A circular merger is understood to be one of the three types of mergers, the other two being vertical and horizontal mergers discussed earlier. The strategy is to diversify the products mix within a given generic market. Though the advantage of offering a diversified product mix are many, there is a risk attached to the proposition if the marketing expertise of the company does not come upto expectations. If there is a deviation from the core marketing competence the job may be ill done and rather than economies of scale the results may be rather counterproductive, apart from malfunctioning in the organisation.

ACCRETIVE MERGER

Accretive mergers occur when a company with a high price to earnings ratio purchases a company with a low price to earnings ratio. This helps the purchasing company's to increase its earnings per share. This type of merger is the opposite of a dilutive merger, discussed later.

Consider two companies – *A* and *B*. Company *A* has a high price earnings ratio and company *B* has a low price earnings ratio. Profile of the performance of their shares as on 1st April, 2011 is presented below:

Table 55

PRICE EARNINGS RATIOS: HIGH vs. LOW

	COMPANY A	COMPANY B
No.s of Equity Shares	1,000	500
Equity share capital (₹)	10,000	5,000
Face value per share (₹)	₹ 10	₹ 20
Profit After Tax	₹ 10,000	₹ 5,000
Market Price Per Equity Share (per quotation on 1st April, 2011)	₹ 100	₹ 60
Earnings Per Share (Profit After Tax/No.s of Equity Shares)	₹ 10	₹ 10
Price/Earnings Ratio = (Market Price Per Share/ Earnings Per Share)	10 (times)	6 (times)

Co.s A and B decided to merge. The combined profits after tax for company *A*, post merger, is ₹ 15,000. The swap ratio (say is 2:1) that is to say for every 2 equity shares of company *B*, Co. *A* will allot 1 equity share. Co. *A* takes over 50% of the shares of Co. *B*, i.e., 250 shares for which they will issue 125 shares of company *A*. The outsiders will hold the remaining 125 shares of company *A* issued in lieu of the remaining 250 shares of company *B*. Post merger Company *A* holds 1000 shares plus 125 shares newly issued, i.e., 1125 equity shares in all. Earnings per share for company *A*, post merger is the combined profits divided by the numbers of equity shares held, i.e., ₹ 15,000/1125 = ₹ 13.33. Thus, company A enjoys a 33% increase in its earnings per share and the market will factor the same for appropriate capitalization for the future.

EXAMPLE:

ICICI BANK ABSORBING BANK OF MADURA (BOM) FEBRUARY 2000

ICICI bank share had a book value of ₹ 60 per share as against a book value of BOM at ₹ 2.33 per share at the time of the absorption. The earnings per share of ICICI bank was ₹ 7 and that of BOM ₹ 44. ICICI bank and BOM had paid dividends of 15% and 55% respectively during that financial year. This merger is considered to be accretive, from the EPS perspective, for ICICI bank shareholders by 23%, i.e., to say an increase from the pre merger level of ₹ 7.10 per share annualized to ₹ 8.7 per share annualized based on September, 2000 data. The merger took place in February, 2000.

(SOURCE: Babu, Venu K. "ICICI or Bank of Madura: Who will benefit?" www.karvy.com <http://www.karvy.com/articles/icicibom.htm>)

DEMERGER

A "***demerger***" is a word sometimes used to describe a firm, that instead of merging with another firm, splits its original, parent company into two, creating a second company to be listed on the stock exchange.

Table 56

DEMERGER: EXAMPLE

COMPANY	*BUSINESS*
Hindustan Ciba Geigy (HCG) SANDOZ (S)	Pharma/Speciality Chemicals Pharma/Speciality Chemicals

Both the above companies were Swiss multinationals. The parent companies had gone through merger exercises and wanted to reorganise themselves with pharma as a core business and speciality chemicals as separate allied businesses. Keeping this segmentation in mind, the above two companies, operating in India were required to go through a merger demerger exercise. To start with, the pharma segments of HCG and S merged together which resulted in Novartis India Ltd. – a pharma company keeping in line with the global segmentation of the parent group. Again, the speciality chemical segment of Sandoz was demerged into Clariant Chemicals. HCG speciality chemicals was demerged into CIBA speciality chemicals. The above exercises took place between the years 1995-97. HCG with S became Novartis in 1995-96. Sandoz speciality chemical business became Clariant Chemicals in 1995. HCG speciality chemical business became CIBA speciality chemicals in the year 1996-97. Of course, eventually when CIBA was taken over by BASF in 2008, CIBA speciality chemical came within the fold of BASF a German chemical giant. Again in 1997, HOECHST Chemical merged with Clariant Chemicals. However, HOECHST pharma was combined with Marriott and Russell around the same time.

DILUTIVE MERGER

Dilutive mergers take place when a company with a low price to earnings ratio acquires a company with a high price to earnings ratio. This causes the purchasing company's earnings per share to decrease. This type of merger is opposite to that of an accretive merger, discussed earlier.

DILUTIVE MERGER – EXAMPLE:

Jet Airways Ltd. (JAL) with Sahara Airways Ltd. (SAL)

JAL initiated an IPO of ₹ 1899 crores in the year 2005. The face value of the share was ₹ 10 and the issue price, in March, 2005 was ₹ 1,100 per equity share. This was an all cash deal. The IPO was motivated to retire high cost debt to the International Finance Corporation and Infrastructure Development Finance Corporation to moderate the debt levels. Expansion plans were also on the anvil. Before the IPO, the debt equity ratio of JAL was 5.4:1. After the IPO, it was to be reduced to 1:1. The issue was a success and helped JAL to garner ₹ 1,899 crores. The company identified Sahara Airline for purposes of acquisition at a price of ₹ 2,300 crores in June, 2006. This was to make Jet-Sahara combination the biggest domestic airline with a 48% market share at that point of time. However, the deal was delayed due to delays in Government sanction for JAL. Sahara had other problems because of pressure from creditors. Realizing the situation, in April, 2007, the valuation of Sahara was reduced to ₹ 1950 crores because book debt equivalent to ₹ 350 crores were taken on board in the books of JAL. The final outcome of this cash deal was that Sahara was salvaged. Nevertheless, JAL had to pay its own price because the Jet share which was priced at ₹ 1,100 at the time of the IPO (March, 2005) lost its value. The JAL price fell to ₹ 359 per share in 2009 as against the said issue price of ₹ 1,100, i.e., a 67% fall. The price earnings ratio of JAL went down. Again, the business environment of the aviation industry was rather turbulent because of the continuous escalation in crude oil prices then ruling at $ 140 per barrel. This resulted in high aviation fuel prices which in turn affected the bottom line of the company resulting in lower earnings per share and further depression of the share prices of JAL in the share market.

Recently (4th May, 2011) the Bombay High Court in its judgement in Jet Airways vs. Sahara has said that JAL's liability in Sahara Air deal is ₹ 1,450 crores. The deal which was struck in June, 2006 was for ₹ 2,300 crores. After adjusting for the book debts of Sahara for ₹ 350 crores, the liability of Jet was reduced to 1,950 crores as the deal value. JAL had paid a token amount of ₹ 500 crores. Thus, JAL owed ₹ 1,450 crores to Sahara that which is now confirmed in the recent judgment of Bombay high court. At the time of filing the suit JAL had paid ₹ 900 crores. The dispute was with respect to the balance amount to be paid. Thus, JAL now owes SAL a balance of ₹ 550 crores out of which 107 crores have been deducted on account of income tax liability of Sahara which was collected from JAL. The bottom line bears testimony to the dilutive nature of this merger as reflected in the profits of JAL between 2007-10.

Table 57

JET AIRWAYS (INDIA) LTD. (JAL)

YEAR	*PROFIT AFTER TAX (₹ CRORES)*
2007	28
2008	– 253
2009	– 402
2010	– 468

REVERSE MERGER

Reverse merger occurs when a small company acquires or absorbs a large company. The result of a reverse merger is that a private company goes public.

REVERSE MERGER – EXAMPLE

ICICI Bank absorbing ICICI Ltd., in 2001, is an example of a reverse merger. ICICI Bank was a small business with a deposit base of ₹ 9728 crores and total assets of ₹ 12,763 crores (September, 2000) in relation to the parent company, ICICI Ltd., had developed an asset base over the years. ICICI Ltd., started in the year 1955, as an investment and development bank in the private sector. Its main role was to provide medium and long-term loans to facilitate the process of industrial development in the private sector. ICICI Ltd., *per se* would not be allowed to venture into commercial banking. However, a reverse merger paved the way for ICICI Bank to establish itself as a banking company with a much larger asset base and the opportunity to forge the entire network of ICICI Ltd., as a development bank, into commercial banking business. This advantage did not accrue to other competing commercial banks in the private sector in the post-liberalisation era.

Salient Features of the Reverse Merger ICICI Bank with ICICI Ltd. (31st March, 2002):

(1) This reverse merger is regarded as a landmark fusion of a child prodigy with a parent bringing the concept of universal banking to the forefront in India. It reshaped and redefined banking, following liberalisation in a new World order. With this merger, the merged entity became the second largest bank in India with an asset base of over 1 trillion rupees.

(2) The reverse merger came at a time when commercial banking was being redefined and development banking had almost reached a saturation point outliving its utility in the context of liberalisation, globalization, competition, improved foreign exchange position, cheap money policy all over the World and access of Indian enterprise to rather cheap funds across national frontiers. The channels for raising funds included many in addition to Government to Government transactions, *viz.*, external commercial borrowing, foreign currency convertible bonds, Global Depository Receipts, American Depository Receipts and a wide variety of other business to business transactions which made available funds at very low interest rates say around 4% including the transaction cost. LIBOR around March, 2002, a year of recession in India and none too rosy business environment abroad, was in the range of 1.84 to 2.00 per cent. The rupee dollar parity rate saw the dollar gaining strength *vis-à-vis* the INR at 1 USD = ₹ 49, the highest ever in recent times. The prime rate then in the US was around 1%. Since then the prime rate only saw successive declines under Allen Greenspan's cheap, cheaper and still cheaper money policy. The dollar was appreciating. Hence, the American lender wanted to cash on the differential between the exchange rate at the time of lending and receiving the money back. The American lender gave 1 dollar, and the Indian borrower got ₹ 49. However, in the meantime, the Indian rupee appreciated and in four years time stood at 1 USD = ₹ 45. This meant that the American lender parted with a strong USD (1 USD = ₹ 49) and got in return a relatively weak USD (1 USD = ₹ 45), at the time of repayment. The optimistic expectations of the American lender did not materalise, after all. On the contrary, fortunes in the market place swung in favour of the Indian borrower who gained by importing a strong dollar and repaying a weak dollar. In this scenario, the supply of cheap loanable funds was in plenty outside India, the role of development bank as a channel for bringing in foreign funds was lost to that extent. Hence, the redundance of ICICI Ltd., which had to be rejuvenated through this reverse merger. Thus, the reverse merger, well justified and timed as a strategic, almost, pre-emptive move.

"***On 31st March, 2002 under US GAAP, total impaired loans of ICICI Ltd., stood at ₹ 16,000 crores which included ₹ 7,500 crores of reported NPA's and ₹ 8,500 crores restructured loans.***" (*The Economic Times*, 17th September, 2002) The non-performing asset portfolio of ICICI Ltd. created many problems for ICICI bank and it was estimated that a provision of ₹ 10,000 to ₹ 10,500 crores was required of which the bank had already provided for about 70%. The balance was to emerge from profits by selling the stake of ICICI Ltd. Thus, ICICI bank was exposed to risk of non-performing assets and it had to identify innovative methods to ensure that the absorbed entity turned around and was not a toll or bane on the otherwise well performing, high profile, ICICI bank. Given the non-performing assets of ICICI Ltd., and the then annual performance of ICICI bank at ₹ 258 crores (2002) and ₹ 1,206 crores (2003) profit after tax per annum, it was projected that it would take about 3 years for ICICI bank to recoup the burden. To quote the Equitymaster.com (27/10/2001), "***Another concern is ICICI's escalating base of Non-Performing Assets (NPA). As on September, 30, 2001, the institution's net NPA to advances ratio stood at 5.2%, while for the bank it was just 1.4%. ICICI's net NPA outstanding at ₹ 32 billion is 12 times larger than ICICI Bank's net NPA outstanding of ₹ 2.7 billion. It would require the merged entity to write-off its entire profits as provisions for the next two years to clean its balance sheet.***" This reverse merger is an exercise in showing how trying to save a parent institution, the economics of the child prodigy can be adversely affected at least in the immediate context following the fusion. The valuations presented below are self-explanatory:

Table 58

REVERSE MERGER: ICICI BANK AND ICICI LTD.

PARTICULARS	*ICICI BANK*	*ICICI*	*MERGED ENTITY**
Market Price (₹)	106	53	106
Price Earnings Ratio (Times)	9	2	6
Dividend Yield	1.9%	10.4%	5.2%
Price/Book Value (PBV)	1.5	0.5	0.7

**Taking the current price of ICICI Bank at the time of reverse merger.*

ICICI bank merger by absorption of Bank of Madura was a good example of accretive merger. However, the reverse merger between ICICI bank and ICICI Ltd., is illustrative of a dilutive merger and establishes the rationale for mergers transcending beyond the fervor of profit motivation and also identifying innovative strategies, post merger, not to recoup or rehabilitate but to rejuvenate into a new format which can continue to sustain the winning edge. ICICI bank precisely did this.

As a financial restructuring process, ICICI bank, following the reverse merger, sold the said NPAs of ICICI to Asset Reconstruction Company (ARC). In effect, ICICI used ARC as a factor, generated cash to the extent of liquidation and also reaped the tax benefits under the provisions of Income Tax Act relating to set off of business losses against reported losses.

FORCED MERGER – EXAMPLE:

GLOBAL TRUST BANK (GTB) WITH ORIENTAL BANK OF COMMERCE (OBC)

A forced merger is a situation where the decision to merge is a result of a fiat issued by a competent authority, *viz.*, a regulator or the Government. Global Trust Bank was instructed to declare a moratorium by Reserve Bank of India on 24th July, 2004, to prevent the spread effects of the crises on the banking sector and also uphold the interest of the depositors of GTB. The Government stepped in and proclaimed an alliance of GTB with OBC. The new name of the combined entities was to be OBC which continues to date. An erstwhile private sector bank (GTB) thus went into the fold of a nationalised bank by virtue of a fiat. Of course, the failure of GTB and the helplessness of innocent depositors triggered the intervention. Incidentally, this was the first causality post 1994 liberalisation of banking sector.

ACQUISITION and TAKEOVER

The purchase of one business by another either through purchase of shares or through purchase of assets. Takeover is the act of assumption of control by one business (company) over another through ownership of assets or acquisition of equity shares. The expression acquisition and takeover are synonyms. Acquisition is an act or a strategy adopted by a business, say a company, to acquire control over another business say a company. The process of acquisition involves identifying the entity to be acquired which is known as '***Target Company***'. By acquiring the right to control the target company, the acquirer has the power to manage and take policy decisions in the target company. Since the governance of the company has its roots in the Board of Directors, the acquirer would have the power to appoint majority of the Directors of the Company. The right to appoint would also include the right to divest some Directors of their role in the acquired company as Directors. However, in any acquisition, the target company's identity remains intact. Of course, control over a target company can be exercised through acquisitions in many ways, *viz.*:

- Understanding between persons as to who will exercise decision making powers in the company.
- Control over an apex company, usually an investment or holding company, which holds a controlling interest in the target company.
- Acquiring voting rights in the target company either through power of attorney or through proxy voting arrangement.
- Outright purchase of a major portion of shares which entitle voting power in the target company.

Of course, the four approaches, indicated, are illustrative rather than exhaustive. There are various provisions in the Companies Act which lays down the ground rules regarding the voting rights and the process governing acquisition.

In the context of competition and need to grow fast to sustain the competitive edge in business, greenfield projects have lost their importance. Inorganic growth is the order of the day and hence acquisitions play a very important role in modern business in the twentyfirst century. Thus, the annual number of mergers and acquisitions has doubled in the last two decades which bear testimony to the popularity of acquisition, as a means to grow rapidly. The motivation for acquisition is business aggrandisement through improved market share, access to state-of-the-art technologies, benefits of symbiosis in operations management, as well as distribution arrangements, control of assets acquired at low price due to under valuation or '***slump sale***' of assets.

Acquisitions do pave the way for a fast growth track and reduce the gestation period between conception of an idea and commissioning of a plant, unlike greenfield projects which have a relatively long gestation period. Yet, acquisitions entail their own problems, *viz.*, clash of cultures, shock of a new order, turnover of key employees, synergistic effects not materializing, valuation process being erroneous because of the mismatch between purchase price and value benefits of assets acquired, employee motivation and morale post acquisition hitting a low and counterproductive cost management exercises causing cost escalations. Thus, mergers which promise value addition pre merger turn out to be a failure post merger thus putting aspirations of synergies to rest.

ACQUISITION LEADING TO A MERGER

In 1993, Coca-Cola paid around ₹ 175 crores to Parle to acquire its soft drinks brands like Thumps Up, Limca, Gold Spot to re-enter India after a gap of nearly two decades. Thumps Up, the brand taken over by Coca-Cola, was estimated at ₹ 1,400 crores, bigger than Coca-Cola itself in India. Thumps up and Limca, two key brands that Coke acquired from Parle, account for not less than ₹ 2000 crores in sales for Coke. The Coca-Cola company in India had ₹ 3,500 crores of sales of soft drinks, while Pepsi Co.s three main brands had nearly a sales of ₹ 2,500 crores. The motivation for the purchase was a quick entry into the then just liberalized Indian market and gain a foothold in the soft drinks market immediately. In fact for Coca-Cola it was, as mentioned above, regaining lost ground when they had to exit in 1977 due to the policy of the then Government in power. From the sellers point of view it was a bonanza sale price and also accepting the truth that withstanding competition from this global giant was not without potential difficulties. However, the Parle group retained their mother business manufacture and sale of biscuits, *viz.*, Parle-G, *et al.*

EXHIBIT 48*

TAILPIECE: ONE NATION ONE CORPORATION

Whenever a merger is scheduled to take place, in the public sector particularly, invariably there is opposition from labour and staff unions of the merging units. The Times of India report dated 17th April, 2011, provides some interesting reading in this behalf.

"Members of the General Insurance Employees Union, Southern Zone (Karnataka branch) affiliated to the General Insurance Employees All India Association have launched a campaign for merger of the four public sector general insurance companies." The theme of the State conference was "One Nation One Corporation." "Such a merger would help provide better service. A lot of money can be saved and the customers will definitely be benefitted." *Organised by the union here on Saturday, it focussed on the need for merger of United India, National, Oriental insurance companies and New India Assurance Co. Ltd. Inaugurating the conference, H.V. Anantha Subba Rao, general secretary of the All India Trade Union Congress (AITUC), said there is an urgent need to consolidate the four companies through merger and to create a corporation on the lines of Life Insurance Corporation (LIC) of India.*

SOURCE: *"Merger of four insurance firms mooted." The Hindu, 17th April, 2011. <http://www.hindu.com/2011/04/17/stories/2011041763420500.htm>*

**There is no Exhibit 49.*

OTHER EXAMPLES: Life Insurance Corporation (LIC) of India: The Government of India nationalised insurance business in 1956 and created a corporation known as LIC which started functioning 1st September, 1956 under a Special Act of Parliament called Life Insurance of India (19th June, 1956). LIC represents the fusion of many (245) private insurance companies which were in the life insurance business prior to 1956, i.e., to say on the eve of nationalisation. As part of the Government of India policy to protect and promote public good, life insurance was taken out of the private, dispersed and decentralized, sector to create a monolithic, monopoly corporation called LIC. This was a forced surrender for the private insurance companies to be combined into a state owned venture by the Government of India.

AMERICA ON LINE (AOL) AND TIME WARNER (TW)

The merger of AOL and TW was announced in January, 2000 when AOL acquired TW. The merger was regarded as a block buster merger and it stunned the financial markets and also sent shock waves throughout the American investment fraternity. It was described as a merger of equals. However, the nominees of AOL controlled the new Board and in the new combined company, AOL's name came first. At the time of the announcement, AOL's stock enjoyed a market capitalization of 160 billion USD against revenue of less then 5 billion USD. In contrast TW market capitalization was only 90 billion USD against revenue of 26.8 billion USD. AOL's much higher market capitalization reflected the confidence and expectations of existing and potential investors in AOL *vis-à-vis* TW. It is believed that AOL's valuation was driven by the price bubble that had boosted tech stocks and particularly internet stocks. The combined companies valuation, on a pre merger basis, was 250 million USD with AOL accounting for 64% of the total and TW the balance (36%). AOL shareholders received only 55% of the new companies stock. The market perceived this as an overvaluation of TW. As a result, immediately after the announcement of merger, TW's stock rose by more than 35% while AOL's stock fell by at least 30%, in fact more. The financial justification for the acquisition was TWs asset earnings, cash flows and the potential business that it could complementarily generate. Thus, the reasons for the merger were the perceived synergies. AOL had more than 30 million subscribers and was a dominant internet service provider. TW had a huge cable franchise and the services included internet, music, films, cable, magazines and TV as shown in **Table 59** below:

Table 59

TIME WARNER: PRODUCT LINES

INTERNET	*MUSIC*	*FILMS*	*CABLE*	*MAGAZINES*	*TV*
Compuserve AOL ICQ	EMI Warner Elektra Atlantic Virgin	Warner Brothers	Times Warner Cable	Time Fortune People Sports Illustrated	CNN Cartoon Network HBO TBS TNT

Further, TW also had the potential of bringing high speed broadband internet access to several millions of household as indicated above. It had high quality value providing services with famous brands like Warner Bros. Studios, Warner Music, *et al.* The idea was to use the cable system to sell TWs range of quality services to AOL subscribers. The mutual society between the two companies was projected as a symbiotic alliance, one feeding the other and triggering a cash throw-off of billions of dollars resulting from the incremental revenues and profits and consequent value addition to shareholders through higher market capitalisation. Of course, this did not happen. TW stock which was priced at 95 USD per share immediately after the merger (January, 2000) fell to nearly 9 USD and even below, i.e., to say a fall of more than 90%. The S&Ps 500 index had also declined but not to such an extent. It was apparent that the anticipated financial synergies were a miscalculation and the alliance had failed. Around this time the company was still trying to make up for the failure and were visualising a bright future. The reasons for the failure were: substantial variation in the work culture of the merged entities; atmosphere of arrogance of AOL managers *vis-à-vis* TW staff - The AOL staff considered their colleagues at TW as lower-class internet guys; conflict of interest; prevalence of hubris in every meeting; misunderstanding in using emails; accounting scandals and total incompatibility.

It was eventually described as an end of the mega merger of the century resulting in an annual loss of one billion dollars and one of the greatest debacle in the business history of USA.

DRESDNER BANK WITH ALLIANCE INSURANCE

These two German organisations were in the same general industry — the financial services sector. They came together and formed a new company called Dresdner Alliance AG. The fusion was motivated to meet the needs of an emerging market for a new product which was called '***Bancassurance***' in 2006. However, this alliance did not continue long. It failed and hence as part of the hindsight the said two entities separated themselves into their respective original businesses. The complementarities between banking and insurance, wherever they existed, were taken care of, post separation, through the networking at the right time and place for the right purpose with the right clientele. Viewing the global meltdown in 2008, where financial services activity (Lehman Bros) muddled with AIG (Insurance business), it would not be incorrect to say that a potential failure which awaited the two European organizations was rightly foretold. The alliance between Dresdner Bank and Alliance Insurance, during the tenure of the merger, did not show any signs of mutuality in day to day operations, except for the expression '***bancassurance***' which is just a fusion of two words, from the English dictionary '***bank***' and '***insurance***'. The incompatibility of the two entities was realised in good time and acted upon. However, these two organizations still maintain a mutual network of activities and relationships to give them the benefits of a symbiotic relationship without a formal fusion.

DIVESTMENT OR DIVESTITURE

According to Wikipedia, divestment or divestiture "***is the reduction of some kind of asset for either financial or ethical objectives or sale of an existing business by a firm. A divestment is the opposite of an investment.***" Thus in any divestment, there is an outright sale of most of the assets of a company or any of its clearly identifiable segments of business, *viz.*, product lines, subsidiary company, divisions, brands, distribution channels, *et al.*, The consideration for such a sale is usually cash or a debt with an understanding that the covenants of the debt agreement shall be met. Equity shares normally do not figure as a consideration for a divestment. From time to time, companies take stock of the performance of different segments of business. The performance of these segments of business are measured through criteria like return on investment or return on capital employed or economic value added or any other suitable similar or different measure. If certain segments of business do not meet the fundamental standards of financial performance laid down by enterprise as targets which must be surpassed, to justify continued use of funds, the company is inclined to sell off such segments which signal want of adequate performance. A divestment may also take place for other reasons. Thus, the history of Hindustan Unilever Ltd. (erstwhile HLL), as presented in **Exhibit 47,** shows a wide variety of business transactions which includes amongst other things divestment too.

⊙⊙⊙

17

DEFERRED TAX ASSET (DTA)

DEFERRED TAX ASSET (DTA)

DTA is the outcome, in the main, of the provisions of the Income Tax Act (I.T.A.) 1961 relating to Minimum Applicable Tax (MAT) under section 115 JB of ITA 1961, introduced *w.e.f.*, financial year 2005-06, that is to say assessment year 2006-07.

Salient features of S115 JB are as follows:

(I) "***Where the income tax payable on total income of a company computed under the Income tax Act, in respect of any previous year relevant to***

(a) assessment year 2007-08 and onwards is less than 10% of its book profit.

(b) assessment years 2001-02 to 2006-07 is less than 7.5% of its book profit, such book profit shall be deemed to be the total income of the company and the tax payable by the company on such total income shall be the amount of

(i) *income tax at the rate of 10% in relation to assessment year 2007-08 and onwards,*

(ii) *income tax at the rate of 7½% in relation to assessment years 2001-02 to 2006-07.*

The income tax so arrived at is to be increased by surcharge on income tax if any/ additional surcharge on income tax and surcharge if any [Section 115 JB (1)]."

In the context of MAT, the tax authorities intended to plug zero tax companies and ensure that such assessees are also liable to pay a minimum tax. Hence, the emergence of the item **DTA**. The concept of zero tax assessees was alien to the former fiscal policies which was committed to eliminate income inequalities and also facilitate transfer of wealth from the rich to the poor. Minimum tax also enables the authorities to ensure that there is no unfettered freedom for assessee to use tax incentives to be outside the tentacles of the fisc year on year basis. It also helps to keep a tab on the proportion of population paying taxes again year on year basis and also helps to sustain the revenue collection levels.

HOW THE DTA COMES INTO BEING?

As mentioned earlier DTA is the outcome of the provisions of the ITA relating to MAT (Section 115 JB). With the help of the data in **Table 60** the following points can be noted:

(1) Row 1 shows the book profits as per the Financial Accounts (FA) of a business for the seven years, assessment years, ending 2012-13. The book profit is computed in accordance with the generally accepted accounting principles and typical accounting concepts, conventions and principles governing the determination of profit or loss as well as values of assets and liabilities for a given accounting period.

(2) Using the book profit as a starting point and making adjustments for various deductions, tax free income and tax holidays and concessions, the taxable income is presented in row 2. In six of the seven assessment years ending 2012-13, there is a positive taxable income. However, the assessment year 2009-10 shows a loss of ₹ 40 crores.

(3) Row 3 shows the tax liability at 10% including Surcharge (SC) and Educational Cess (EC) on column 1. For the assessment year 2006-07, the relevant tax rate is 7.5%.

(4) Row 4 presents the tax at 30% plus surcharge plus educational cess on row 2 as the base.

(5) DTA analysis rests on a comparison of rows 3 and 4. If row 3 is greater than row 4 in a particular assessment year, then the higher amount shall be the tax liability of the business. Thus, MAT is, *ipso facto*, applicable. We can also say that if row 4, that is to say the actual tax liability on the taxable income, is lower than row 3 which is the perceived liability under section 115 JB, the higher amount of the two shall be the tax liability.

(6) Row 5 indicates the tax credit available or otherwise. In four of the seven years row 3 shows a tax liability which is higher than the figures indicated in row 4. Thus, the tax liability shall be the row 3 figures and of course a tax credit can be availed of by the assessee. The tax credit available is thus defined as row 3 minus row 4 and is shown in row 6. Under the provisions of Section 115 JB of the I.T.A., 1961, the tax credit available and quantified in row 6 can be carried forward for a period of seven years from the assessment year 2006-07. Thus, for the assessment year 2006-07 the tax credit of ₹ 15.99 crores can be carried forward upto the assessment year 2014-2015. Row 5 indicates the years upto which the quantified tax credit shown in row 6 can be carried forward for the respective assessment years 2007-08, 2009-10 and 2010-11.

(7) It is necessary to track and trace the tax credit available and eventually availed of. This is a separate tax exercise. Keeping in mind the number of years for which a particular assessment year's tax credit can be carried forward the cumulative tax credit can be known. However, if due to inadequacy of profits during the tenure of a particular assessment year's tax credit, i.e., seven years cannot be availed of the tax credit un-availed of till the said seventh year lapses.

(8) Row 7 shows the cumulative tax credit.

(9) Row 8 indicates the set off process of the tax credits which in this illustration can start from the assessment year 2007-08. A tax credit can be set off only if the tax liability on taxable income is greater than the tax liability under section 115 JB. It can be observed from row 8 that the set off process is inactive for the first assessment year (2007-08) in which the set off was possible. It is also inactive during the assessment years 2009-10 and

2010-11 due to a loss in the assessment year 2009-10 and inadequate profit in the assessment year 2010-11.

(10) Row 9 shows the maximum amount which can be set off in the year in which set off is possible. Thus, in the assessment year 2008-09 the maximum amount which can be set off is the difference between row 4 and row 3 where the amount indicated in row 4 is greater than the amount indicated in row 3. In the assessment year 2008-09, row 4 shows a tax liability of ₹ 129.93 crores as against a tax liability under Section 115 JB of ₹ 123.7 crores. The difference of ₹ 6.23 crores can be set off as indicated in row 9 (assessment year 2008-09). Using the same analogy, while no set off is possible in the subsequent two assessment years ending 2010-11, ₹ 2.53 crores can be set off in the assessment year 2011-12 and a relatively huge amount of ₹ 57.22 crores can be set off in the next assessment year 2012-13.

(11) Row 10 shows the credit which has lapsed. However, no tax credit has lapsed for the business in the illustration.

(12) Row 11 shows how much tax credit is carried forward. The amount carried forward is defined as follows: Opening balance of tax credit for the nth year plus added tax credit of the (n^{th}) year minus the credit availed of minus the tax credit lapsed (if any).

(13) Row 11 shows that prior to the first set off of the tax credit, the cumulative tax credit available is ₹ 49.65 crores. Further, ₹ 6.23 crores is the tax credit set off in the assessment year 2008-09 thus reducing the cumulative tax credit to ₹ 43.42 crores from ₹ 49.65 crores. Once again, assessment years 2009-10 and 2010-11 provide for tax credits of ₹ 17.67 and ₹ 8.42 crores respectively resulting in an increase in the carry forward amount of tax credit from ₹ 43.42 crores in 2008-09 to 69.51 in the year 2010-11. For the last two years ending 2012-13 no tax credit is created in the respective assessment years. However, cumulative tax credits have been used to set off a maximum of ₹ 2.53 crores in the assessment year 2011-12 and ₹ 57.22 crores in the assessment year 2012-13. The cumulative tax credit is reduced by the said amounts in the respective years. Thus, in the last assessment year 2012-13 the amount of tax credit carried forward is ₹ 9.76 crores. **Table 61** presents an overview of the '***modus operandi***' of the set off and carried forward of the tax credits.

(14) Row 12 indicates the tax liability of the business which is always the modicum indicated by row 3, of course, adjusted for set offs drawn from the cumulative tax credit created and unavailed of so far.

(15) **Table 60** row 6 shows the deferred tax asset created in the respective years. The cumulative tax credit row 7 shows the aggregate value of DTA which appears in the balance sheet. The cumulative tax credit is adjusted year on year basis for additions due to new tax credits and also for the set offs claimed and lapses of tax credit. DTA is thus a fiction of an accounting contrivance required to put Section 115 JB into action. In other words if section 115 JB is in operation and the rules governing the Section, including set offs and lapse apply, then DTA emerges.

Table 60
DTA: EXAMPLE

₹ in Crores

Sr. No.		*2006-07*	*2007-08*	*2008-09*	*2009-10*	*2010-11*	*2011-12*	*2012-13*
(1)	Book Profit	670	750	1102.50	157.5	1275	490.5	1275
(2)	Taxable Income (without 115 JB)	120	150	386	(-40) Loss	400	171	595
(3)	Tax @ 10% + S.C. + E.C. on Row 1 (7.5% for 2006-07) M.A.T.	56.38	84.15	123.70	17.67	143.06	55.03	143.06
(4)	Tax @ 30% + S.C. + E.C. on Row 2	40.39	50.49	129.93	NIL	134.64	57.56	200.28
(5)	Whether tax credit available (and upto which year)?	Yes (2013-14)	Yes (2014-15)	No	Yes (2016-17)	Yes (2017-18)	No	No
(6)	Tax credit available Row 3 – Row 4	15.99	33.66	NIL	17.67	8.42	N.A.	N.A.
(7)	Cumulative tax credit	15.99	49.65	49.65	61.09	69.51	69.51	66.98
(8)	Tax credit set off during current year [only if Row 4 > Row 3]	N.A.	N.A.	Yes	N.A.	N.A.	Yes	Yes
(9)	Maximum amount which can be set off during current year (excess of Row 4 over Row 3 upto Row 7 amount)	N.A.	N.A.	6.23	N.A.	N.A.	2.53	57.22
(10)	Tax credit which has lapsed	N.A.	N.A.	NIL	N.A.	N.A.	NIL	NIL
(11)	How much is carried forward Rows 7-9-10?	15.99	49.65	43.42	61.09	69.51	66.98	9.76
(12)	Tax payable for the current year = Row 3 M.A.T.	56.38	84.15	123.70	17.67	143.06	55.03	143.06

Table 61

TAX CREDIT CREATED (₹ CRORES)

Tax Credits of Respective Years set off between 2006-07 to 2012-13	*TAX CREDIT OF ASSESSMENT YEARS (AYs) ↓ 2006-07 TO 2012-13 DTA CREATED*					
↓ A	2006-07 15.99	2007-08 33.66	2008-09 —	2009-10 17.67	2010-11 8.42	2011-12 —
2006-07	—	—	—	—	—	—
2007-08	—	N.A.	—	—	—	—
2008-09	6.23	—	—	—	—	—
2009-10	—	—	—	—	—	—
2010-11	—	—	—	—	—	—
2011-12	2.53	—	—	—	—	—
2012-13	7.23	33.66	—	16.33	—	—
Set off DTA Utilised (B)	15.99	33.66	—	16.33	—	—
Balance C/Fd.(A-B)	NIL	NIL	—	1.34	8.42	—

The cumulative balance carried forward is ₹ 1.34 plus ₹ 8.42, i.e., ₹ 9.76 crores

Table 62

IMPACT OF DTA ON CASH FLOWS

₹ in Crores

Years	*A.Y.*	*IT Act (Row 3)*	*FA (Row 4)*	*Row 3 V/s. 4*	*Co's Tax Liability*	*DTA*	*Cum Tax Credit*	*Cash Flows*
1	06-07	56.38	40.39	3>4	56.38	15.99	15.99	↓
2	07-08	84.15	50.49	3>4	84.15	33.66	49.65	↓
3	08-09	123.70	129.93	3<4	129.93	(6.23)	43.42	↓
4	09-10	17.67	NIL	3>4	17.67	17.67	61.09	↓
5	10-11	143.06	134.64	3<4	134.64	8.42	69.51	↓
6	11-12	55.03	57.56	3<4	57.56	(2.53)	66.98	↓
7	12-13	143.06	200.28	3<4	200.28	(57.22)	9.76	↓

N.B.:

- Tax **increased cash outflow; reduction in cash outflow** liability is > M.A.T. i.e. Row 3 or Row 4 whichever is higher.
- If MAT in Row 3 is greater than tax on taxable income (Row 4), then, MAT shall be payable. Thus, tax credit (DTA) is defined as (MAT - tax on taxable income) that is to say (Row 3 - Row 4). If tax on taxable income is > MAT the tax to be paid is the former i.e. the usual tax liabiltiy. If there is carried forward DTA then to the extent tax on taxable income is > MAT set off of carry forward tax credit is permissible. In any case amount equivalent to MAT shall always be the modicum tax liability for the said FY /AY. Question of zero tax as such therefore does not arise.

MODUS OPERANDI OF DTA OVER THE YEARS AND SET OFFS OF TAX CREDIT

The DTA account has a tax credit of ₹ 49.65 (Table 60 – Row 7) crores at the beginning of AY 2008-09. No tax credit is due to the assessee in the said AY vide (**Table 60 – Row 6)**

Table 63

TAX CREDIT POSITION

₹ in Crores

Tax Liabilities	*AY 2006-07*	*AY 2007-08*	*Cumulative Tax Credit*
Per S 115 JB	56.38	84.15	140.53
Per book profit	40.39	50.49	90.88
Tax credit	15.99	33.66	49.65

In the AY 2008-09, the situation reverses. The tax payable per S 115 JB is ₹ 123.70 **(Table 60, Row 3)** crores is less than the tax liability of ₹ 129.93 **(Table 60 – Row 4)** arising out of the taxable income shown in Row 2 of **Table 60** for the AY 2008-09. The gap of ₹ 6.23 crores is thus a reduction in cash outflow and can be set off against the excess payments made in the past, stored and parked in an account called DTA.

At this stage the cumulative tax credit appears as follows:

Table 64

CUMULATIVE TAX CREDIT POSITION

₹ in Crores

	A.Y.	*Tax Credit of the Year*	*Cumulative Tax Credit*
Beginning	2008-09		49.65
End	2008-09	NIL	(6.23)
			43.42
Beginning	2009-10	17.67	61.09
End	2010-11	8.42	69.51

Again, extending the illustration in **Table 60** further into the assessment year 2009-10 another addition to tax credit of ₹ 17.67 increases the cumulative tax credit to ₹ 61.09 crores **(Table 60, Row 7)** and in 2010-11 yet another ₹ 8.42 crores get added to increase the DTA to ₹ 69.51 crores as on 31.03.2010 **(Table 60, Row 7)**. In both the said years, the MAT liability is greater than the income tax liability on taxable income – Row 3 *vis-à-vis* Row 4 respectively.

AY 2011-12 presents a MAT liability which is less than the income tax liability on taxable income **(Table 60)** (Row 3 – Row 4) of ₹ 2.53 and ₹ 57.22 crores for the two successive years ending 2012-2013. However, the maximum set off possible, in the respective AYs is the difference between Row 3 and Row 4 as shown below:

Table 65

TAX CREDIT BALANCES

₹ in Crores

	2011-12	*2012-13*
Opening balance	69.51	66.98
Tax Credit	NIL	NIL
Set Off	2.53	57.22
Closing balance	66.98	9.76

MESSAGE OF DTA – TAX CREDIT AND SET OFF:

- MAT shall be payable as the modicum tax liability
- Set off is limited to the amounts shown above in **Table 65**
- Even if the DTA amount expires for want of further continuity it lapses alright but cannot be used.

In the instant case, the DTA is still active for purposes of set off of the unused DTA of ₹ 9.76 crores so far in future years as shown in **Table 65** In all, over the seven years ending 12-13 the cash flow pattern are as follows:

- For the first two AYs ending 2007-08, an excess cash outflow on account of income tax of ₹ 49.65 crores **(Table 60 – Row 7)** would have adversely affected the cash flow per share and all other cash driven business activities.
- The third AY 2008-09 is a beneficiary of the DTA, for set off purpose but only to the extent of ₹ 6.23 crores **(Table 60 – Row 9)**.
- In the next two years the DTA account increases again to ₹ 61.09 and ₹ 69.57 crores thus causing further dent into the cash flows and adversely affecting the cash flow per share to that extent. However during the assessment cumulation of tax credit ceases and the peak of the DTA at ₹ 69.51 crores in the AY (2010-11) reduced marginally to ₹ 66.98 in 2011-12 and substantially to ₹ 9.76 crores in AY 2012-13 as shown in **(Table 60 – Row 7)** and **Table 65.** The assessee is able to avail of the set off facility against profits earned in the respective years. Since the set off can be claimed on a FIFO basis the residual of ₹ 9.76 crores is deemed to be from AY 2010-11 ₹ 8.42 crores and AY 2009-10 ₹ 1.34 crores respectively. Thus, (₹ 8.42 crores) can be carried forward upto AY 2017-18 and ₹ 1.34 crores can be carried forward upto AY 2016-17.

DEFERRED TAX LIABILITY (DTL)

Consider the data in **Table 66** which presents the profit after tax as per Section 32 of ITA and also as per the requirements of Section 205 Companies Act read alongwith Schedule XIV of the Companies Act (Financial Accounts). In Year 1, the income tax liability is ₹ 1200. For the same year as per financial accounts the reported Profit Before Tax (PBT) is ₹ 7500 and the tax liability in the financial accounts is ₹ 2250. This difference between the tax liability under the two sets of accounts is key to understanding of the concepts underlying deferred tax asset and liability.

If the provision for income tax as per the Income Tax Act is less than 10% of the book profit shown by financial accounts then the company shall pay tax of 10%. In the instant case, (year 1) the provision for income tax as per Section 32 of IT Act is ₹ 1200 on a reported book profit, as per financial accounts, of ₹ 7500. Thus, the tax provided for is 16%. The company is already meeting the provisions of MAT. Therefore, MAT does not apply. However, the difference between ₹ 1,200 and ₹ 2,250, i.e., ₹ 1,050 has to be reckoned with and is identified as a deferred tax liability. The reasoning is that in the normal course, if tax liability is computed on book profit of ₹ 7,500, the tax liability would be ₹ 2,250. However, the company provides for ₹ 1,200 only. Thus, a deferred tax liability (DTL) of ₹ 1,050 emerges and results in a journal entry as follows:

Profit & Loss A/c .... Dr. ₹ 1050

To Deferred Tax Liability .... ₹ 1050

Again in the second year it can be observed that the provision for income tax of ₹ 2,080 as per IT Act is 28.06% of the PBT of ₹ 8,125. This amounts to 28.06%. Once again MAT does not apply and a DTL is created for an amount of ₹ 157 (₹ 2,280 – 2,437). Thus, as and when the tax liability as per the income tax act is greater than the income tax liability, in the financial accounts, a DTL emerges. In the same vein, if the tax liability as per S32 of IT Act less than the income tax liability as per financial accounts, the (DTL stands written back). For year 3, a write back of ₹ 134 is created. The situation in years 4, 5 and 6 is similar and a write back is created as shown in **Table 67** The income tax as per the IT act is more than the income tax as per the financial accounts as shown in **Table 67** Hence, a write back emerges is created and this means that the deferred tax liability is being returned back in the four years ending year 6.

Table 66

DEFERRED TAX LIABILITY: EXAMPLE

₹ in Crores

AS PER S32 OF IT ACT	*YR. 1*	*YR. 2*	*YR. 3*	*YR. 4*	*YR. 5*	*YR. 6*
Income	10000	10000	10000	10000	10000	10000
Depreciation on IT Equipment @60% WDV p.a	(6000)	(2400)	(960)	(640)	(-)	(-)
Taxable Income	4000	7600	9040	9360	10000	10000
Income tax (IT) @30%	1200	2280	2712	2808	3000	3000
PAT	2800	5320	6328	6552	7000	7000
AS PER P&L (S205 SCH XIV)						
Income	10000	10000	10000	10000	10000	10000
Depreciation on IT Equipment @25% WDV	2500	1875	1406	1055	791	593
Book Profit	7500	8125	8594	8945	9209	9407
IT @30%	2250	2437	2578	2684	2763	2822
PAT	5250	5688	6016	6261	6446	6585

Table 67

DEFERRED TAX LIABILITY

	YR. 1	YR. 2	YR. 3	YR. 4	YR. 5	YR. 6
Provision for Income tax (as per S32 of IT Act)	1200	2280	2712	2808	3000	3000
Provision for Income tax as per Profit and Loss A/c. (per S. 205 of Companies Act)	2250	2437	2578	2684	2763	2822
DTL Created*/Reduced**	–1050*	–157*	134**	124**	237**	178**

N.B: DTL = (Taxable Difference × Tax Rate)

Table 68

DEFERRED TAX LIABILITY – CERTAIN COMPUTATIONS

	YR. 1	YR. 2	YR. 3	YR. 4	YR. 5	YR. 6
Provision for IT per IT Act	1200	2280	2712	2808	3000	3000
PBT per financial accounts	7500	8125	8594	8945	9209	9407
% age of Provision for IT to PBT per FA	16	28.06	31.55	31.39	32.57	31.89

N.B.: DTL created is a reduction in cash outflow and DTL reduction is an increase in cash outflow.

Table 69

DTA and DTL in ANNUAL REPORT

HINDUSTAN LEVER LIMITED

Balance Sheet as at 31st December, 2006

	2006 ₹ in Lakhs	2005 ₹ in Lakhs
SOURCES OF FUNDS		
Shareholders' funds	272348.27	230562.60
Loan Funds	7260.30	5694.07
	279608.57	**236256.67**
APPLICATION OF FUNDS		
Fixed Assets	151100.89	148353.03
Investments	241393.15	201419.84
Deferred Tax		
Deferred Tax Assets	38542.59	33868.17
Deferred Tax Liabilities	(16087.89)	(11853.71)
	22454.70	**22014.46**
Current Assets, Loans and Advances	**316965.51**	**277301.68**
Current Liabilities and Provisions	(452305.68)	(412832.34)
Net Current Assets	(135340.17)	(135530.66)
	279608.57	**236256.67**

Table 70

DTA and DTL in ANNUAL REPORT

HINDUSTAN LEVER LIMITED

Balance Sheet as at 31st December, 2006

(Relevant Schedule relating to DTA /DTL)

	2006 *₹ in Lakhs*	*2005* *₹ in Lakhs*
DEFERRED TAX ASSETS		
On employee separation and retirement	21126.28	18319.92
On other timing differences	12239.74	11670.44
On fiscal allowances on investments	53.50	529.68
Other items	5123.07	3348.13
NOTE: Deferred tax assets taken over consequent to the scheme of arrangement for amalgamation ₹ 1089.54 lakhs (Refer note 14 to Profit and Loss Account)		
	38542.59	**33868.17**

	2006 *₹ in Lakhs*	*2005* *₹ in Lakhs*
DEFERRED TAX LIABILITIES		
On fiscal allowances	16087.89	11853.71
Note: Deferred tax liabilities taken over consequent to the scheme of arrangement for amalgamation ₹ 629.74 lakhs (Refer note 14 to Profit and Loss account)		
	16087.89	**11853.71**

DEFERRED TAX ASSET (DTA)

(1) DTA indicates that a company has prepaid taxes relating to future accounting periods in the current accounting year itself.

(2) DTA is an asset on a company's balance sheet which can be used to reduce subsequent periods income tax liability.

(3) DTA is the result of extra income tax paid by a business in a particular assessment year/s. Such additional tax paid for, in advance, (due to S 115 JB not S 207 and other sections related to advance tax under the Income tax Act) is parked in an account called DTA for use at a later date to reduce tax liability if an opportunity arises.

(4) When a company bears an abnormal amount of tax liability in the present year it can save tax in the years when there is an opportunity to actually absorb the expenses or provisions.

DEFERRED TAX LIABILITY (DTL)

(1) A deferred tax liability shows that a company has postponed a portion of the tax liability of a particular year's transaction to future accounting periods.

(2) Deferred tax liability arises because of the difference between the amounts claimed for income tax purposes as against amounts charged to compute the book profits for financial accounting purposes. Examples, depreciation policies, rules regarding deduction of other expenses like advertisements, research and development expenditure alongwith weighted deduction. In the budget speech of 2011-12, the Finance Minister said "***In this Decade of Innovation, I enhanced the weighted deduction on payments made to national laboratories, universities and institute of technology, for scientific research, to 175 per cent in the last budget. I propose to further enhance this to 200 per cent***".

(3) DTL is just a recognition of a liability of the business to bear addition tax burden of S115J at a future date because of the gains enjoyed in the earlier years.

(4) The amount of deferred tax advantage shows the extent to which the business has relied on short-term tax shelters (DTL).

DTA AND DTL (GENERAL)

(1) Accounting for deferred tax assets or liabilities enables the presentation of a true and fair financial position of a company and helps to distinguish between profits from business operations as against accretion to reserves from fiscal savings. This aspect of true and fair picture emerges in due diligence in the event of mergers or acquisitions. In such cases, DTA/DTL are taken into account to ascertain the advantages (or otherwise) to the combined entity.

(2) In the case of DTA the cash flows are adversely affected and the earnings, per share, are also adversely affected.

The ICAI has given its pronouncement in this behalf through AS 22 which reads as follows:

Accounting Standards Interpretation (ASI) 7*

Disclosure of deterred tax assets and deferred tax liabilities in the balance sheet of a company

Accounting Standard (AS) 22, Accounting for Taxes on Income

ISSUE

(1) The issue is how should deferred tax assets and deferred tax liabilities be disclosed in the balance sheet of a company.

CONSENSUS

(2) In case of a company, deferred tax assets should be disclosed on the face of the balance sheet separately after the head '***Investments***' and deferred tax liabilities should be disclosed on the face of the balance sheet separately after the head '***Unsecured Loans***'.

BASIS FOR CONCLUSIONS

(3) Paragraph 30 of Accounting Standard (AS) 22, Accounting for Taxes on Income, provides as follows:

****SOURCE:*** *'The Chartered Accountant', November 2003, pp. 490. The authority of this ASI is the same as that of the Accounting Standard to which it relates. The contents of this ASI are intended for the limited purpose of the Accounting Standard to which it relates. ASI is intended to apply only to material items.*

"30. Deferred tax assets and liabilities should be distinguished from assets and liabilities representing current tax for the period. Deferred tax assets and liabilities should be disclosed under a separate heading in the balance sheet of the enterprise, separately from current assets and current liabilities."

From the above, it may be noted that the deferred tax assets and deferred tax liabilities should be disclosed separately from current assets and current liabilities

(4) Part I of Schedule VI to the Companies Act, 1956, does not contain a specific head for disclosure of deferred tax assets/liabilities. Section 21 1 (1) of the Companies Act, 1956, provides that every balance sheet of a company shall be prepared in the form set out is Part I of Schedule VI or as near thereto as circumstances admit. It is, therefore, clear that format of balance sheet as set out in Part I of Schedule VI to the Companies Act, 1956, has in-built flexibility to accommodate necessary modifications. A deferred tax asset is normally more liquid (realisable) as compared to fixed assets and investments and less liquid as compared to current assets. Therefore, in case of a company, it is appropriate to present the amount of the deferred tax assets after the head '***Investments***'. Similarly, keeping in view the nature of a '***deferred tax liability***', it is appropriate that the same presented in the balance sheet of a company after the head '***Unsecured Loans***'.

LEGAL VIEW OF DEFERRED TAX ASSET AND LIABILITY

In *CIT vs. Balarampur Chini Mills Ltd.* (297 ITR AT 15 Kolkata) the income tax appellate tribunal presented its directions on deferred tax. The question was whether a deferred tax charge debited to the profit and loss account is to be added back under explanation as income tax in computing the book profit for MAT purposes. The citation is presented below:

The Tribunal held that deferred tax charge is a provision for the tax effect of the difference between the taxable income and accounting income and is not a provision for income tax paid or payable. Deferred tax assets and liabilities are to be distinguished from current tax assets and liabilities. The Tribunal also found that deferred tax is not in the nature of reserve under clause (b) of the Explanation because it is an expense of the period in which it is charged and cannot be transferred to the P&L account or used for issue of bonus shares or declaration of dividend. The Tribunal also held that deferred tax is not an unascertained liability under clause (c) of the Explanation as deferred tax charges are measured scientifically and as per strict guideline of the ICAI and accepted globally. The Tribunal also observed that any withdrawal from the deferred tax provision would be taxable under the provision to Explanation 1. Consequently, the Tribunal held that the deferred tax charge is not to be added back in computing the book profit.

18

BUY-BACK OF SHARES, STOCK SPLIT AND REDUCTION OF CAPITAL

BUY-BACK OF SHARES

(1) S 77 (1) of Companies Act, prior to 1999, prohibited a company limited by shares or limited by guarantee, having a share capital from buying its own shares. The restriction was applicable to all companies having share capital, whether public or private.

(2) Post-liberalisation the amendment to the Companies Act introduced the concept of buy-back of shares. Thus, the Companies (Amendment) Act, 1999, *vide* sections 77A, 77AA and 77B and the guidelines issued by SEBI and the Department of Company Affairs, in this regard, allow companies to purchase their own shares or other securities subject to certain conditions.

(3) Companies wishing to buy-back shares had to meet certain conditions stipulated in Section 77 of the Companies Act, *viz., (a)* surfeit cash, *(b)* no unpaid creditors, *(c)* no objection from creditors and *(d)* no investment plans on the anvil in the same line of business to absorb the surplus cash.

(4) If the above conditions are satisfied a company could buy-back the shares. The shares so bought back have to be cancelled according to the provision of Section S 77 (G) of the Companies Act and to that extent the paid up capital and of course the issued share capital, also goes down.

(5) When shares are bought back the '***shareholder mix***' undergoes a change. The proportion of shares held by the public is reduced. The aggregate '***issued and paid up***' capital is also reduced. Hence, the proportion of shares held by promoters in relation to the new level of paid-up capital base increases. To that extent the promoters stake in the share capital of the company gets enhanced and they need not really buy the shares. Hence, there is no need for promoters to look for preferential allotments of shares or warrants to subscribe to fresh issues of share capital by the company rights issue or follow on offers to enhance their relative holding.

(6) Timely buy-back of shares prevents purchases of chunks of shares by various interested parties or predators interested in acquiring a company by virtue of their shareholdings. Buy-back therefore, enables promoters to consolidate their control over the management of the company and also pre-empt predators. Buy-back of shares reduces the supply of shares in the market and therefore there is a tendency for prices of shares to look northward.

(7) Further, since the number of shares is reduced to the extent of the shares bought back, the earnings per share increase automatically, all other things being equal. However the total earnings after tax remain the same. Sometimes buy-back is viewed by many as a management game, if not a gimmick, to shore up the market value of shares.

BUY-BACK OF SHARES – CASE STUDY:

GTL Ltd. announced buy-back of shares at ₹ 300 per share on 25th April, 2007. Of course this is subject to all the rules and regulations prescribed by the relevant provisions of the Companies Act and other regulatory authorities, *viz.*, Bombay Stock Exchange and Securities and Exchange Board of India (SEBI). The share price of GTL as on Friday, 30th March, 2007 was ₹ 135.20 and on the date of announcement of the buy-back, i.e., 25th April, 2007 the share price stood at ₹ 185.70 Post-buy-back the market price of shares of GTL - Market Prices of Shares as shown in **Table 71**:

Table 71

GTL – MARKET PRICES OF SHARES

Year	*PAT ₹ Crores*	*Market Price per share ₹*
30th June, 2006	72	148.70
30th March 2007	40	135.20
31st March 2008	121	260.00
31st March 2009	91	239.60
31st March 2010	158	420.00

The paid-up capital of the company as on 31st March, 2007 was ₹ 97.32 Crores (9,73,16,886 shares of ₹ 10 per share). The company was to buy-back 86,30,000 shares at a stipulated price of ₹ 300 per share, i.e., ₹ 259 crores. In the normal course when a buy-back is announced the ordinary investors are interested in surrendering their shares to take advantage of the attractive price at which the shares are bought back. The buy-back price of ₹ 300 per share (25th April, 2007) was higher than the market price which prevailed on the said date (₹ 185.20 per share). Shareholders benefitted to the extent of ₹ 114.80 per share which was a 61.98 % premium over the market price of the same date. Following the buy-back announcement, the market responded positively and between 25th April 2007 and 30th November, 2007 the market price of GTL share rose from ₹ 185.20 to ₹ 251.15 In fact, in January, 2008 the market price of GTL share crossed the buy-back price and reached the peak of ₹ 317, thanks to strong optimistic expectations in the market because of the favourable movement of the BSE index between 1st October, 2007 and 1st January, 2008 from 17,330 to 20,301, i.e., a 17.15% increase However, the response to the GTL buy-back presents a relatively queer situation. Normally FIIs do not necessarily respond positively to buy-back proposals. They hold on to their shares unlike individual retail investors. In the case of GTL, the FIIs sold nearly 6.7 million shares, in the buy-back offer of GTL at ₹ 300 per share. As a result the FII holding in GTL declined by nearly 5% to 21.08%. The major selling FIIs were Somerset India Fund and Citi Group Global Markets (Mauritius). Individual investors' response was relatively, rather, lukewarm. Out of 8.63 million shares which was bought back 6.7 million shares (circa 80%) belonged to FIIs, increased to 34.70% (32,518,022 shares) and 16.11% (15,090,661 shares), respectively, after the buyback offer which closed on November 19, 2007.

On hindsight, we may say that the FIIs were wise because they reaped the benefit of high buy-back price and did not hold on to their investments in GTL to face the decline in the price of GTL share from January, 2008 onwards when the share price fell from the peak of ₹ 317 (January, 2008) to ₹ 162 in September, 2008. Further, the stake of the promoters and individual investors remained intact. It is gratifying to note that shareholders who downloaded the shares in the buy-back of April, 2007 at the buy-back price of ₹ 300 per share benefited. However, the loyal investors who continued also found an opportunity to be rewarded in the second buy-back of GTL which was announced on 15th January, 2009. The buy-back was announced at ₹ 260 per share at the said date when the market price of the share was ₹ 220.75. Of course, the Board of Directors of GTL recommended a buy-back of GTL shares subject to fulfillment of all formalities prescribed by law and other regulatory agencies. The company announced the buy-back through the open market operations this time using stock exchange route. Further, the promoters were not to participate in this buy-back operation. In the financial year 2007-08 the Annual Report of GTL had said that "***in absence of any suitable acquisition opportunities in reasonable time, it would return the excess cash to the shareholders. In view of sufficient availability of cash reserves to meet future liquidity requirements of business operations, the Company has proposed to return excess cash to its shareholders by the way of buy-back of shares.***"

HUL BUY-BACK

HUL announced a buy-back of shares worth ₹ 630 crores on 11th June, 2010 at a market price of ₹ 280 per share on which date the market price of HUL share was ₹ 252.52 The motivation for the buy-back was again utilization of surplus cash and the company was to buy-back the shares from the Bombay Stock Exchange and National Stock Exchange through open market operations from time to time. HUL is a trusted brand and so is the share regarded by investors in general as a blue chip company. The profit performance and rate of dividend both have has been extraordinary as shown in **Table 72:**

Table 72

HUL: FINANCIALS

YEAR	*Paid-up Share Capital (₹ in Crores)*	*PAT Capital (₹ in Crores)*	*DIVIDEND (%)*	*Dividend Paid/ Paid-up Share Capital (₹ in Crores)*
December 06	221	1855	600%	1326
December 07	218	1925	900%	1962
March 09	218	2496	600%	1308
March 10	218	2202	650%	1417

Given the overall excellence of the company, shareholders are reluctant to divest themselves of their holdings in HUL. Hence, the response to the buy-back was rather poor and they could buy-back only ₹ 2.06 crores. The share capital as on 31st March, 2010 was ₹ 218 crores and as on 31st March, 2011 ₹ 215.94 crores. HUL could garner only ₹ 2.06 crores as against a planned ₹ 630 crores, i.e., a paltry .3%. The poor response to the buy-back, from the shareholders, is understandable. The speed of the wealth accumulation process at HUL measured by the value created for the shareholders, historically, exceeds the typical reinvestment opportunities available today, in the market, for an average retail investor. Hence, loyal investors holding shares in Blue Chip companies like HUL would be reluctant to divest. Thus, buy-back programs, however attractive, may not always entice investors or necessarily be a success.

DELHI LEASE AND FINANCE (DLF)

DLF which is in the construction business and regarded as the country's largest developer, announced a buy-back (1st October, 2008) of ₹ 1100 crores (11% of the original issue of ₹ 10,000 crores) at a price not exceeding ₹ 600 per share through open market operations. The market price of DLF at the time of the announcement was ₹ 329, a 52 week low (30th September, 2008). Following the news regarding the buy-back the share price recovered marginally and stood at ₹ 352 (1st October, 2008). The shareholders had responded to the DLF initial public offer of shares (face value ₹ 2 per share) at ₹ 525 per share in June, 2007. Therefore selling at ₹ 600 meant only a marginal gain of ₹ 75 per share, i.e., 14.29 % over the purchase price. Though DLF announced the buy-back price of ₹ 600 per share, actually the buy-back did not take place because the company did not have enough cash to sustain '***operation buy-back***'. **Apparently, the intent of the company was not consistent with the offer**. The cash collected in the public issue was meant for reducing the debt burden of the company. However, the buy-back was announced and *prima facie* the only source of cash with the company to sustain operation buy-back was what was collected in the public issue. According to the balance sheet the paid up capital of the company as on 31st March, 2008 and 2009 was ₹ 341 and ₹ 339 crores respectively representing less than 1% reduction in paid-up capital.

Clarifications made by the Finance Minister in his Budget Speech on buy-back are as follows: The Finance Minister clarified that:

- Buy-back cannot be treated as '***deemed dividend***' at the hands of the shareholders and therefore shall not be subject to income tax under the Income Tax Act, 1961.
- Buy-back shall not amount to reduction of share capital.
- Buy-back will not result in capital gains at the hands of the shareholders.

Table 73

DLF LTD.: FINANCIALS

	Capital ₹ in Crores	*PAT*	*Dividend %*	*Dividend ₹ in Crores*	*Current Ratio*	*Share Price in*
31st March, 2007	306	408	100	306	1.91	1225 (Jan., 08)
31st March, 2008	341	2575	200	682	1.93	329 (Sept., 08)
31st March, 2009	339	1548	100	339	2.34	325 (Nov., 09)
31st March, 2010	339	765	100	339	3.14	252 (May, 10)

NOTE: The following observations can be made from the above table:

(1) The impact of the ₹ 10,000 crores IPO resulted in a massive increase in share premiums account reflected in a massive net worth of ₹ 11,269 crores in 31st March, 2008.

(2) Profits increased between 2007 and 2008 by ₹ 2167 crores, i.e., 538% and dividend also increased to ₹ 682 crores by 123%. However, for the year ended 31st March, 2009, profits dwindled by ₹ 1027 crores to ₹ 1548 crores, i.e., 40% decrease. Dividend rate also dropped and dividend amount fell by ₹ 343 crores for the year ended 31st March, 2009. Profit after tax decreased to ₹ 765 crores by 50% for the year ended 31st March, 2010. The steep fall in share prices during this period shows that every buy-back dues not necessarily contribute to improvements in shareholders expectations regarding the price of shares. Market capitalisation is very sensitive and captures extraneous too.

MOTIVATION OF BUY-BACK

(1) Earnings of the company, i.e., profit after interest and tax, are shared by fewer number of shares, in the post buy-back period. Earnings Per Share (EPS) increases and cash flow per share also increases though the aggregates, of the said items for the business as a whole, remain the same.

(2) To the extent market prices of shares are driven by earnings per share, the company's share may command a higher market price with consequent increases in market capitalisation.

(3) Enhanced earnings per share or return on equity makes share valuation realistic if the shares are undervalued. The new enhanced EPS motivates enhanced market capitalization and hence, buy-back is a corrective response action to effectively tackle undervaluation of share prices.

(4) Cash deployment is effective particularly in situations where reinvestment opportunities are limited or the marginally efficiency of capital in new projects do not match the historic performance of the company. Cash rich companies loaded with financial assets, *viz.*, cash at bank and related money market instruments suffer from poor returns and confront rather uncomfortably, relatively tax inefficient situations.

(5) Cash rich companies are always an object of attraction for predators. Buy-back pre-empts predators' prowl.

(6) Buy-back helps to enrich the shareholders without altering the dividend policy. Dividend increases tend to soar expectations of shareholders to new levels on a perennial basis which may be difficult to sustain. Buy-back is a bonanza gain to shareholders resulting from an extraordinary or supernormal condition which is of an ephemeral (temporary) nature.

(7) Buy-back is preferred to dividends because dividends are paid out of profits after tax of the current year and/or undistributed profits. The book value of the shares go down and perhaps the market prices maybe, not necessarily, affected adversely.

(8) Top management compensation packages are invariably related to market capitalization. If share prices go up, the value of the compensation package goes up because compensation comes in the form of stock options, warrants and other related forms.

(9) Managers holding stock options do not benefit from dividends because stock options do not qualify for dividend payments or bonus issue.

(10) Buy-back signals that the company has adequate cash to successfully carry out the buy-back operation as well as maintain dividends per share. The average investor has to be alert to the '***cash ability***' of the company to benefit from the buy-back and stay on as a loyal investor if the divestment is not 100%.

(11) Frequent buy-backs are an early warning signal about the intentions of the company to reduce the aggregate supply of shares and thereby progressively withdraw from amongst the listed companies by reducing the free float. Examples: Cadbury, Philips, Altas Copco, CIBA Speciality, *et al.*

(12) If a buy-back is through open market operation the transactions must be routed through the BSE/NSE. Hence, all fiscal imposts, *viz.*, security transaction tax must be paid. Thus, such a buy-back arrangement qualifies for long-term capital gains tax exemption under Section 10 (38) of the Income Tax Act, 1961. If the buy-back is through tender (i.e., direct to the company) BSE is not in the picture because it's an off market transaction. STT does not get paid. Therefore such transactions do not qualify for the said long-term capital gains tax exemption under Section 10 (38) of the Income Tax Act, 1961.

(13) Buy-back participants are those who hold the shares at the time the buy-back is announced. Holders of stock options, warrants, outstanding GDRs, ADRs cannot participate in the operation buy-back. However, the buy-back announcement has a positive impact on the market prices of GDRs and ADRs. This is an externality of the buy-back.

BUY-BACK – LEGAL PROVISIONS

The buy-back of shares is governed by the provisions of the Companies Act and the conditions stipulated by SEBI.

COMPANY LAW: The Companies Act has a series of sections (Section 77, 77A, 77AA and 77B) under the heading "***Power of company to purchase its own securities***".

Section 77A Inserted by the Amendment Act 1999 (effective from 31st October, 1998). Section 77A prescribes the sources to buy-back and says that a company may purchase its own shares or other specified securities (hereinafter referred to as "**buy-back**") out of:

(1) its free reserves.

OR

(2) its securities premium account. Thus, premium collected from shares or debenture or other securities can also be used.

OR

(3) the proceeds of any share or other specified securities. However, buy-back shall not be made out of the proceeds of an earlier issue of the same kind of shares or some of other specified securities. Further, if the shares are bought back from free reserves section 77AA stipulates that a sum equal to the nominal value of share bought back shall be transferred to a reserve account to be called the Capital Redemption Reserve Account (*vide* section 80 (1) (d)). It is mandatory to disclose the details of such transfer in the balance sheet. According to SEBI guidelines, this account shall be account for the use of issuing fully paid bonus shares.

CONDITIONS FOR BUY-BACK

"***No company shall purchase its own share or other specified securities unless:***

(a) the buy-back is authorized by its articles of association.

(b) a special resolution has been passed in general meeting of the company authorising the buy-back".

Where a buy-back takes place through the resolution of the board the buy-back must not exceed ten per cent of the total paid-up equity capital and free reserves of the company. (S 77A and B). There cannot be more than one buy-back by the board within a period of 365 days.

Section 77A (c) Where the buy-back is through special resolution at a general meeting, the buy-back shall be less than 25% of the total paid-up capital and free reserves of the company purchasing its own shares or other specified security. In general buy-back of equity shares cannot exceed 25% of the total paid-up equity capital of a company in that financial year. The said percentage should be computed by referring to the amount of the paid-up equity capital at the time of decision making of the buy-back.

Section 77A (d) The ratio of debt owned by the company should not be more that twice the capital and its free reserves after such buy-back. However, the Central Government may prescribe a higher ratio of debt for a class or classes of companies. The expression debt includes secured and unsecured debts.

Section 77A (e) All shares or other specified securities are fully paid-up. Only fully paid securities can be bought back. Buy-back with respect to listed securities shall be in accordance with regulations made by SEBI in this behalf. Unlisted specified securities shall be governed by separate guidelines modified by Central Government and known as Private Ltd. Company and Unlisted Public Ltd. Company (Buy-back of Securities, Rules, 1999). There are other provisions in Section 77A which relate to secretarial details which need to be complied with, *viz.*, regulation to be passed alongwith explanatory statements, time limits prescribed for completing the buy-back which is 12 months, filing of documents with Registrar of Companies and SEBI, maintenance of Register where buy-back shall be prohibited Section 77 (B) provides for certain circumstances.

STOCK SPLIT

Stock split represents the division of stock with every share having a diminished nominal or face value. The number of share is increased depending upon the nature of the division. Assuming a company has 100 shares of ₹ 10 each on 31st March, 2011, the paid-up capital as of the said date is ₹ 1000. Assume that the company announces the stock split dividing the shares into a new reduced face value of ₹ 2 per share. A shareholder who had 1 share of ₹ 10 will now hold 5 shares of ₹ 2 each. The total number of shares for the company would be 500 shares of ₹ 2 each, i.e., a total paid-up capital of ₹ 1000. The number of share has gone up from 100 to 500 and the face value of the share has gone down from ₹ 10 per share to ₹ 2 per share. Such a stock split is known as a split in the ratio of 5:1. The market capitalization of the company does not undergo any change on account of the stock split *per se*. The price of each share gets adjusted on a *pro rata* basis. In our example, if the market price of the said share was ₹ 50 prior to the stock split, post stock split, the market price of the share would be ₹ 10 all other things being equal. The total capitalization therefore remains at ₹ 5,000. Prior to stock split market capitalsation was 100 shares x ₹ 50 per share and post stock split it is 500 shares @ ₹ 10 per share. Though it is perceived that stock split causes enhancement in market price of shares, research does not bear it out. The implication of the stock split is that the number of shares increases. Thus, the floating stock in the market, although at a reduced denomination per share increases. Trading can take place with lesser amount of initial investment and wider participation of retail investors is possible. This helps to broaden and deepen the market that is to say the investor base. If the pre stock split denomination was not in alignment with the usual nominal value of shares in the same industry in particular or in the corporate World in general, post stock split the market prices of shares can be comparable straight away. Since psychological impact of market prices of shares is a straight comparison without reference to the denomination of the face value of shares perceptions are misplaced regarding the good or bad performance of the company. Another advantage of lower denomination is that odd lots are minimized if not eliminated. Lower the denomination lesser the problems arising out of odd lots in the cases of rights and bonus issue. In the event of a company having outstanding '***GDRs/ADRs***' warrants and stock options *vis-à-vis* pre stock split denomination, suitable alteration has to be made in the terms and conditions governing conversion ratio and prices in the post stock split scenario. Further, historic data will have to be modified to suit the new post stock split denomination of face value of share. Earnings per share and dividend per share have to be deflated *pro rata* to make inter period and even inter firm comparison meaningful. Example: On 5th May, 2010 HDFC a leading housing finance company announced a stock split. The face value of the share was ₹ 10 which was to be split into 5 shares of ₹ 2 each. When HDFC started the face value of the share in 1978 was ₹ 100. In 1999, there was a first stock split which reduced the denomination from ₹ 100 to ₹ 10. Thus, 1 share of ₹ 100 became 10 shares of ₹ 10 each in 1999. In May, 2010, HDFC had 28.71 crore shares which would increase to 143.55 crore shares post split. The shares of HDFC closed at ₹ 2820 on 4th May, 2010. HDFCs competitors ICICI bank and SBI have shares with a face value of ₹ 10 per share. According to the CEO Keki Mistry "***Foreign institutional investors are very large holders of equity in HDFC. We would like to have more retail participation. The stock split will enable retail participation.***" The FIIs hold about 75% of shares in HDFC and retail investors a little more investment. The decision to split the shares was taken at the behest of several individual shareholders. The decision which was subject to the approval of shareholders in its annual general meeting of 14th July, 2010 was duly approved on the said date. The record date for the said stock split was 20th August, 2010. The HDFC share price movement, pre and post split, are presented below:

Table 74

HDFC SHARE PRICES - PRE-AND POST SPLIT

Date	*HDFC Share Price (₹)*
4th May, 2010	2820.30
5th May, 2010	2802.45
13th August, 2010	2997.85
17th August, 2010	3011.45
18th August, 2010	621.20
19th August, 2010	644.10
20th August, 2010	639.70
31st August, 2010	625.15

From the above it can be seen that in the market the cut-off point in change in price per share is 18th August, 2010. The ratio of old face value per share (₹ 10) to new face value per share (₹ 2) equals 5 and the ratio of the price per share on 17th August, 2010 to the price per share on 18th August, 2010 equals 3011.45 / 621.2 i.e. 4.8 (circa 5). Thus, as mentioned earlier the pre split and post split market price per share on the cut-off dates of 17th and 18th August, 2010 bear a relationship which is consistent with the ratio of the old face value to the new face value. The HDFC share price on 18th August, 2010 at ₹ 612.2 has fallen almost prorate to 1/5 th of the market price per share on 17th August, 2010.

Table 75

BUY-BACK vs. CAPITAL REDUCTION vs. STOCK SPLIT

	BUY-BACK	*CAPITAL REDUCTION*	*STOCK SPLIT*
LEGISLATION	Section 77 (1) of Companies Act, 1956 provides that a company limited by shares or by guarantee having a share capital cannot buy its own shares. This restriction is applicable to public and private companies. However, Sections 77A, 77AA, 77B of Companies Act, 1956, introduced with effect from 1999, allows a company to buy it own shares and other specified securities.	Sections 100 to 105 of Companies Act, 1956 provide for the reduction of share capital.	Section 13 (4) of Companies act, 1956 deals with requirements with respect to memorandum, which in turn deals with companies having a share capital. Section 12 (4) (a) of the Companies Act, 1956 says that, unless the company is an unlimited company, the memorandum shall also state the amount of share capital with which the company is to be registered and the division thereof into shares of a fixed amount. Thus, the division thereof into shares of a fixed amount show the financial sub-division of capital into a unit of denomination expressed as a face of share which is also known as the par value or nominal value of share. Hence, S2(46) of the Companies Act (1956) defines a share as a "share in the share capital of a company and includes stock ......"
SEBI'S ROLE	(a) SEBI (Buy-back of Securities) regulations 1998 as amended from time to time shall apply. These regulations are applicable to buy-back of shares or others specified securities of a company listed on a stock exchange. Buy-back with the intent of delisting of a	—	SEBI's guidelines 2000 provides for the requirements with respect to stock split. In the case of an initial IPO of unlisted companies, if the issue price is ₹ 500 or more the face value of a share may be less than ₹ 10 but not less than ₹ 1. However, if the issue price

	company's shares from a stock exchange is not allowed and (b) Private Ltd. Co. and unlisted Public Ltd. Co. (buy-back of securities) rules 1999 shall apply.		is less than ₹ 500 the face value shall be less than ₹ 10 per share.
SALIENT FEATURES	Buy-back of securities can take place out of free reserves or securities premium account or proceeds or issues of any shares or other specified securities. Proceeds out of issue of same kind of securities cannot be used. Buy-back can be of preference shares also. In case of buy-back through the resolution of the Board, the buy-back must not exceed 10% of the total paid-up equity capital and free reserves of the company. There cannot be more than one buy-back by the Board within a period of 365 days. Where the buy-back is through a special resolution it shall be upto or less than 25% of the total paid-up capital and free reserves and further the buy-back in a financial year shall not exceed, in a financial year 25% of total paid-up equity capital. Post buy-back the debt owed by the company shall not be more than twice the capital and free reserves, unless otherwise provided by the Central Government in this behalf. Only full paid securities can be bought back. Buy-back with respect to listed securities shall be in accordance with the regulations made by SEBI in this behalf. Separate guidelines shall be issued with respect to unlisted specified securities.	Sections 100 to 105 of Companies Act provides for reduction of capital in one or more of the following ways: by reducing or extinguishing the liability of members for uncalled capital, by paying off or returning capital which is in excess of the wants of the company, or pay-off paid-up capital on the understanding that it may be called up again or a combination of the preceding methods or write-off or cancel capital which has been lost or is not represented by available assets. A company can reduce its capital and pay the same partly in cash and partly in the form of non-convertible debentures. Reduction in capital in the case of a company limited by share must be authorised by its articles of association and by special resolution which is to be confirmed by a tribunal (Company's Amendment Act, 2002). The judiciary ensures that no stakeholders are being disadvantaged on account of the proposed reduction in capital. Specifically, the scheme shall not be prejudicial towards creditors and shall be fair and equitable between the different classes of shareholders. Interest of creditors must be safeguarded. Interests of	Stock split means an increase in the number of outstanding shares of a company's paid-up share capital such that proportionate equity of each shareholder remains the same. This requires approval from the Board of Directors and shareholders. A company whose stock is performing well may choose to split its shares, distributing additional shares to existing share-holders. The most common stock split is two-for-one, in which each share becomes two shares. The price per share immediately adjusts to reflect the stock split, since buyers and sellers of the stock all know about the stock split (in this example, the share price would be cut in half.) Some companies decide to split their stock if the price of the stock rises significantly and the prevailing price is perceived to be too expensive for small investors to buy. The major motives for issuing stock splits in India are: ◆ to improve liquidity of a firm's shares, ◆ to bring the share price down to a popular trading range and ◆ to attract new investors. Stock splits have gained popularity in the

		shareholder have to be considered in the event of opposition by any shareholder. The reduction of capital shall not be detrimental to public interest. In reduction of capital the number of shares remains the same with the nominal value of the investment undergoing a change.	Indian stock market only since 1999. In the past though the Companies Act empowered a limited company to alter it share capital using stock splits, these decisions were seldom taken. The face value of shares was either ₹ 100 or ₹ 10. Stock split gained currency following SEBIs initiative *vide* circular no. SMDRP/POLICY/CIR-16/99 dated June 14, 1999. Managers perceive stock split decisions to be a cosmetic corporate event. They believe that stock splits do not provide any possible signals about the firm's future prospects. Investors perceive the stock splits to be of import on account of the following: Attractive lower share price ◆ helps retail investors. ◆ improves marketability of shares. ◆ increases number of shareholders in a firm. ◆ brings share price within a popular trading range, increases liquidity because the number of shares traded after the stock split increases.
What happens to: ◆ **Authorised Capital**	Does not change	Does not change	Does not change
◆ **Issued Capital**	Changes provided the shares bought back have been subject to expiration as prescribed in Section 77 of the Companies Act. If the company instead plans	No change	No change

	to reissue the bought back shares, and actually does so, a *status quo* prevails with respect to issued capital.		
◆ **Paid-up Capital**	——DO——	Reduction takes place	No change
◆ **Subscribed Capital**	——DO——	——DO——	No change

⊙⊙⊙

19

WHAT IS PRODUCTIVITY?

EXHIBIT 50

WHAT IS PRODUCTIVITY?

In economics, productivity is the amount of output created (in terms of goods produced or services rendered) per unit input used.

—Wikipedia.com

Productivity is a measure relating a quantity or quality of output to the inputs required to produce it.

—From Econterms

A measure of the amount of output per unit of input. ***Investopedia says: For example, productivity in the auto industry might be measured by the number of hours of labor used per automobile produced.***

—Investopedia.com

Measured relationship of the quantity and quality of units produced and the labor per unit of time. For example, an increase in productivity is achieved through an increase in production per unit of labor overtime.

—Barron's Business Directory

*Productivity is the result or the sum of all efforts that it takes to deliver a product or service. Productivity is frequently referred to as output and, to some degree, can be measured. Productivity is the economic value of goods and services. It becomes the value or result of the "**price**" of a product or service minus all "**costs**" (supplies, materials, human labor, etc., which frequently are monetary) that go into the effort.*

—Answer.com

*"**Capital**" actually has two interrelated meanings: physical capital (machinery and buildings) and financial capital (stocks and bonds), which lays claim on physical capital and the income it generates. Capital productivity is the measure of how well physical capital is utilised in providing goods and services. Productivity of financial capital is measured, inter alia, by the yield or the internal rate of return of the capital investor in financial assets.*

*(**SOURCE:** Agrawal, Raj., Findley, Stephen., Greene, Sean., Huang, Kathryn., Jeddy, Aly., Lewis, William., Petry, Markus. Capital Productivity: Why the US leads and Why it Matters)*

Though **Exhibit 50** provides several definitions of productivity, it means many things in many other different fields. It depends upon the context and aspect that is studied. Of course, World over productivity is understood as a relationship between Output and Input to the systems under study. There are variables and other interrelationships within the elements which go to make a system. Productivity is also regarded as stimulus response model that an input causes an output. Hence, productivity is defined as output/input. In most studies, productivity is defined as a "a relationship between resources that come into an organizational system over a given period of time and outputs generated with those resources over the same period of time."* It is said that productivity measurements should have three objectives, *viz.*, identification of potential improvements, resource reallocation decision and assessment of the extent of conformance of actual productivity *vis-à-vis* target productivity. Different functional areas of management may establish different measurement indices to assess productivity and establish productivity norms for performance benchmarks. Since the primary objective of business is maximisation of profits, this objective has to be subjected to an acid test of productivity. In this context, an useful measure of productivity is once again output/input or profit/investment, i.e., to say return on investment (ROI) (%). Thus, ROI (%) is a measure of financial productivity and captures at least three dimensions as shown below:

$$\text{ROI}(\%) = \left[\frac{\text{Profit}}{\text{Total Assets}}\right] \times 100$$

$$\downarrow$$

$$\text{Profit Margin}(\%) = \left[\frac{\text{Profit}}{\text{Sales}}\right] \times 100 \qquad \text{Turnover of Assets} = \left[\frac{\text{Sales}}{\text{Total Assets}}\right] \text{Times}$$

(Profit/Total Assets (%)) measures the productivity of every rupee invested into business. (Profit/Sales (%)) measures the productivity of every rupee of sales and is referred to as profit margin. (Sales/Total Assets (%)) times indicate the productivity of assets with respect to utilization or the turnover of assets. The numerator in all the three ratios represents output or results and the denominator the input or resources. A study of financial productivity of India INC based on RBI's data is presented

---

***SOURCE:** *Baxi, Nishant. "Defining Productivity" 11th September, 2010, <http://expertscolumn.com/content/defining-productivity>*

EXHIBIT 51

ROI CHART – RBI DATA

1526 Large Public Limited Cos. (LPLC), 3114 Public Limited Cos. (PLC) and 1475 Private Limited Cos. (Pvt. LC) for the 3 years ending March, 2008

RETURN ON NET ASSETS (%)

GROSS PROFIT/TOTAL NET ASSETS (%)

	2006	2007	2008
LPLC	11	13	12
PLC	10	12	11
Pvt. LC	10	10	10

GROSS PROFIT/SALES (%)

	2006	2007	2008
LPLC	13	15	16
PLC	12	14	15
Pvt. LC	10	9	9

SALES/TOTAL NET ASSETS (TIMES)

	2006	2007	2008
LPLC	0.85	0.84	0.76
PLC	0.85	0.84	0.77
Pvt. LC	1.07	1.11	1.13

PRODUCTIVITY MODELS

A Productivity Conceptual Model (PCM) can be visualized, as mentioned earlier, through a typical output/input relationship with the conversion process being the link between the Input and the Output.

EXHIBIT 52

PRODUCTIVITY MODEL I

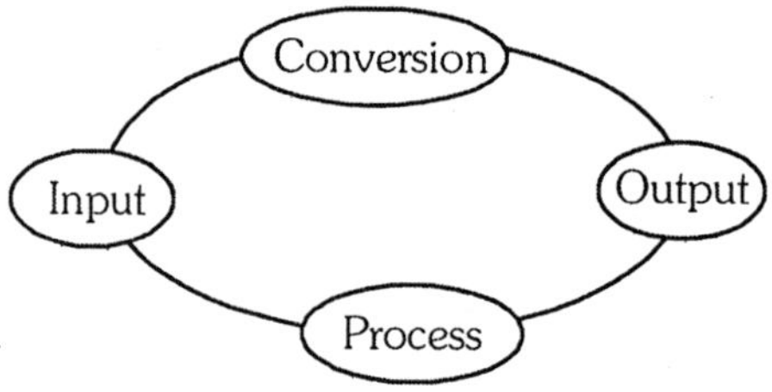

EXHIBIT 53

PRODUCTIVITY MODEL II

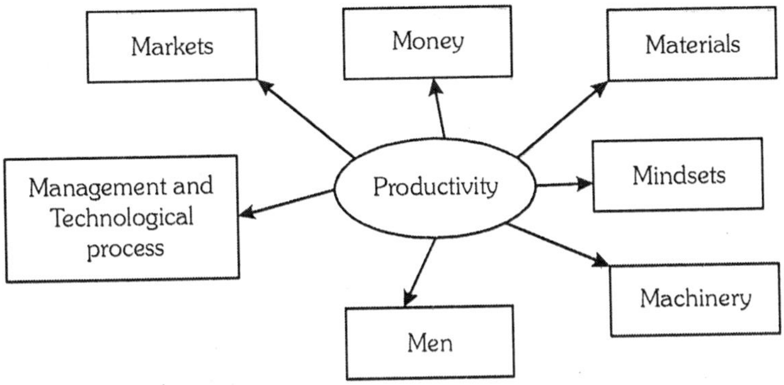

The aggregate productivity of a business as presented in **Exhibit 53** depends upon the productivity of all the seven M's taken together individually and jointly. A brief discussion on the 7Ms follows:

(1) ***MATERIALS AND OTHER INPUTS***: Raw material productivity (Inputs' productivity) is measured through the output-input relationship prescribed by mathematical (chemistry) equations in process industries or special engineering/technical studies in other industries. A given quantity of output, with a prescribed target input, is defined as a productivity norm with zero or limited spoilage or rejections.* In other words, production quantity increases which adversely affect quality is counterproductive and the cost of such increased production is more than the benefit. Improvements in productivity are also attempted through continuous research and development and value analysis which helps to improve the ratio of output to input. What is true of materials productivity is true of other inputs' productivity, *viz.*, labour, variable and fixed factory overheads.

(2) ***MONEY PRODUCTIVITY***: It is necessary that money is made to work for business rather than, as it often happens, business working for money. Hence, productivity of money depends upon how the key factors influencing the grand overall measure of economic performance, *viz.*, Return On Investment (ROI) is monitored. Given that ROI is defined as profit divided by investment, there are only three ways of improving the productivity of monies deployed in enterprise, *viz.*, improved sales, reduced cost and reduction in capital employed in business.

Improvement in sales refers to managing sales volume, mix, price and also sales currency (USD, GBP, INR, *et al.*). Improvement in costs refers to reduction in the variable cost per unit through various ways and means. Further, reduction in fixed cost levels and decrease in fixed cost per unit usually achieved through increased production also helps to boost financial productivity.

**Spoilage/rejects permitted will be zero, if the enterprise practises tight standards often referred to as theoretical standards. Where limited or normal spoilage is permitted standards are defined as theoretical standards adjusted for normal spoilage that is to say practical standards. Theoretical standard are performance levels which do not provide any interruptions to production due to rest period, fatigues and machine downtime. Practical standards refer to theoretical standards minus normal downtime due to unavoidable interruptions.*

Reduction in capital employed refers to elimination of redundant and idle assets and managing existing and potential investments effectively and efficiently using prudent decision rules governing investment decisions.

(3) *MARKETS*: Enterprise operates in three markets, *viz.*, factor market, output market and financial markets. Factor markets refer to the market in which enterprise procures input requirements like material, labour and other overheads. Inputs' procurement has to be at the right time, place, price, quantity and mix. Hence, line managements have to be very active in procurement and ensure the best possible deals for the company. In a competitive market where price is driven by customers and competition, cost intensity and maybe controls, profit margin depends upon factor productivity. Hence, factor market operations have to be managed effectively and efficiently.

Output markets refer to markets in which an enterprise sells its goods and services. The effectiveness of sales in turn depends on sales volume, price mix and currency. In the process of driving sales to meet sales targets, output market operations tend to be counter productive unless monitored at source. Management must explode the myth and illusory belief of marketing managers that '***more revenue means more profits***'. On the contrary, if the prices realized are not competitive enough in relation to cost per unit, more revenue may only add to the losses of a business. Hence, the '*caveat*'.

Financial markets are markets from where money is procured to fund the needs of business – both short and long-term. The money markets and the banking financial system contribute to the short-term financial needs of business and the capital markets/institutions facilitate the flow of long-term funds into business. The effort is to make effective and efficient use of the capital procured to fund the business. The interest paid on monies borrowed should be the best possible rates from the best possible markets in the best possible currency to suit the financial objective of minimization of cost of capital to the business with a view to maximise return on shareholders' equity.** Thus, the enterprise depends upon the spread, *viz.*, return on assets *vis-à-vis* the cost of capital deployed into such assets.

(4) *MANAGEMENT AND TECHNOLOGICAL PROCESS*: Productivity depends upon support and attitudes of top management in the conduct of business. The support has to be continuous rather than sporadic. In the pre 1991 era, it was observed that because of sellers' market conditions, companies could pass on inefficiencies to the customer. Hence, the cost of control was more than the benefit. Productivity improvements were then not a priority for enterprise in India. However, post 1991 thanks to liberalisation, productivity improvements are a top priority on the agenda of every enterprise. There is a paradigm shift in business because market conditions have altered the structure of the equations concerning profit, revenue and cost from: '***profit = revenue minus cost***' to '***cost = revenue minus profit***'.

Annual reports of companies are abound with various comments on how the company has explored ways and means of improving productivity for a given financial year. For example: as part of environment friendly policy, conservation of energy is a top priority. Profit motivation, in this behalf, may be an incidental externality. Companies are required to disclose information pursuant to section 217 (1) (e) of Companies Act (1956).

***If cost of capital is lowered, more investment proposals with a positive net present value will be accepted. Hence, shareholder value creation is enhanced to that extent.*

Management are compelled to disclose ways and means adopted for conservation of energy, research and development and technology absorption, adaption and innovation. The implications of all the three taken together on the bottom line of the company are also highlighted. For example, in the case of Bluestar Ltd., the benefits derived as a result of the efforts to improve productivity are expressed as follows: "***Availability of energy efficient, environment friendly air-conditioning systems and equipment, wider range of products, improved quality and product designs and cost reduction were amongst the benefits derived***" (Blue Star Limited, Annual Report 2005-06, p. 18). Again, the Annual Report 2008 of Siemens (p. 24) presents the following:

Table 76

SIEMENS 2008 – ANNUAL REPORT – EXCERPTS

BENEFITS DERIVED AS A RESULT OF R&D:	BENEFITS DERIVED AS A RESULT OF TECHNOLOGY ABSORPTION AND INNOVATION:
◆ Overall cost reduction ◆ Reduced time to market the product. ◆ Re-use of existing code and domain expertise. ◆ Increased market penetration through energy efficient products. ◆ In-house competency for higher capacity motors. ◆ Complement existing products and thereby increase in market share. ◆ Lower lifetime costs for customers.	◆ Better cost position. ◆ Plant-wide integrated solutions ◆ Increased market coverage. ◆ Offering the complete product basket to end-customers. ◆ Meeting the demand of Indian Railways ◆ Higher productivity of personnel. ◆ Higher precision in adjustment products. ◆ Reduced defect levels.

(5) ***MEN:*** Men, including women, represent the human resources at the disposal of an enterprise for converting all other resources into results. People potential is the greatest asset and represents the edifice of any organisation. Increases in productivity hinge upon the performance of people. It is believed that the performance of employees depends on skills, attitudes and motivation given a particular environment. It is therefore necessary to have a human resource management policy in place which has a clear focus on productivity by exploring and engaging people in the best possible manner across the network of the organisation. Different companies have different approaches to relate their human assets to the bottom line measured in terms of shareholder value creation. Of course, the fundamentals which govern human resource management include, once again, procurement of staff, required for different levels of management, in the right numbers, right time from the right markets with the right qualifications and competencies in terms of skills, attitudes and motivation and last but not the least at the right remuneration package. Following this, talent management and retention are serious challenges to attain, maintain and sustain enhanced, continuously improving productivity performance levels. The challenges of managing people are reflected in the attention given to the same in the annual reports of companies. "***More than capital, more than technology, it's our people who set us apart in a competitive business scenario. Jindal Steel and Power Ltd. (JSPL) is committed to create and sustain a high-performance work culture, with people at the heart of all strategy***". (JSPL – Annual Report

2010-11, p. 34). The mission of the company includes, amongst other things, "***hiring, developing and retaining the best people with a view to sustain shareholder value creation and maximizing return to stakeholders.***"
Similarly in Larsen and Toubro (L&T), talent management assumes special significance. Talent management include structured induction paths, capability building programs, differentiated reward systems, career progression plans and leadership developing programs including succession planning. (L&T, Annual Report -2008-09, p. 2)

To quote the Annual Report 2010-11 (p.03) of the same company, "***The Company recognizes that talent management is a constantly evolving discipline which needs to engage with a dynamic environment. Built on an entrenched set of core principles, the Company's HR policies are designed to ensure that it remains the employer of choice. Compensation packages have been revised to ensure that superior resources are sufficiently incentivized to join and stay with the company. The Company also offers an unmatched canvas of professional opportunity for growth and development***".

Again L&T in its Annual Report – 2008-09 (p. 2) had revamped its organization structure. As the report says, "***The new structure opens up opportunities for leadership development, provides a platform for nurturing internal resources and is expected to provide focus to businesses within each OC. The structure aims to enhance shareholder value creation***".

At Tata Steel, human resource development includes focus on recruitment, training and development, talent management and career planning, leadership development and compensation management and better synergy. The focus is on being a learning organisation and managing knowledge to the advantage of the business. To quote the Annual Report, "***The performance improvement committee has improved both the knowledge management and the adoption of best practices initiatives across the Tata Steel Group and this has benefitted TSE alongside the other operations of Tata Steel***". **(Tata Steel, Annual Report -2008-09, p. 77)**

(6) ***MACHINE PRODUCTIVITY:*** Machine is a part of fixed assets of an enterprise. Net Fixed assets constitute at least 40% of the total assets and machinery is an important constituent of the same. Hence, productivity of machines is extremely important because even a small percentage change in machine productivity can have a powerful, cascading, impact on the bottom line of the business. Machines represent the commitment of resources in business and enterprise is expected to generate results commensurate with the historic results-resources ratio or even better benchmarks. In the ultimate, shareholders wealth needs to be maximised.

Machine productivity depends upon the utilisation of fixed assets. The measure of productivity usually used is asset turnover ratio defined as (sales/fixed assets) or (cost of goods sold/fixed assets). If further classification of fixed assets is available, individual items of assets, in the fixed assets category, can be studied for its performance through the utilization ratio. The ability of management to make machines work without interruption is a challenge. If machines are in proper condition, their continued utilization should permit management to exceed normal expectations and even reach super normal levels of performance. Thus, machines should be able to perform to achieve and exceed practical standards by tending towards theoretical standards. Such an extraordinary efficiency and effectiveness assumes that all other cooperant resources are available in the right quantity, quality, mix and of course, on time. In pure assembly operations like TOYOTA, inventories get delivered twice a day and machine productivity is at its peak because of uninterrupted availability of cooperant resources – from vendor to the conveyor belts of the assembly line. Further, improvements in quantity of production should not be at the cost of quality. Even normal spoilages should be avoided and tend to zero. Practice of zero defects is of utmost importance.

EXHIBIT 54

SIX SIGMA

Motorola created the concept of Six Sigma in the mid-1980s to improve the performance of key processes, productivity and quality. Six sigma efforts target three main areas, viz., improving customer satisfaction, reducing cycle time and reducing defects. Typically, six sigma is perceived as a well-structured improvement approach with strong links to an organization's strategy, high level of management involvement, strong customer focus and strong links to financial results. A successful six sigma implementation generally build upon a number of quality management prerequisites such as an existing quality culture, certain level of quality maturity, et al.

A six sigma process is one in which 99.99966% of the products manufactured are statistically expected to be free of defects, that is, 3.4 defects per million is the tolerance level.

Note that the notion of zero defects is not at work here; six sigma recognizes that there is always some potential for defects, even in the best-run processes. However, six sigma sets a performance target where defects in many products and processes are almost non-existent.

In the past many businesses operated at 1, 2 or 3 sigma levels which translates to 690,000 defects/million, 308,537 defects/million and 66,807 defects/million respectively. Today, many companies have goal of moving from 3 sigma to 4 sigma which itself is impressive because it means moving from 66,807 defects/million to 6210 defects/million.

EXHIBIT 55

SIX SIGMA – PRACTICAL MEANING

99% Good (3.8 Sigma)		***99.99966% Good (6 Sigma)***
20,000 articles of mail lost per hour	→	***Seven articles of mail lost per hour***
Unsafe drinking water for almost 15 minutes each day	→	***One unsafe minute every seven months***
5,000 incorrect surgical operations per week	→	***1.7 incorrect operations per week***
Two short or long landings at most major airports each day	→	***One short or long landing every five years***
200,000 wrong drug prescriptions each year	→	***68 wrong prescriptions per year***
No electricity for almost seven hours each month	→	***One hour without electricity every 34 years***

SOURCE: *Chitanvis, Shreerang. A Presentation made at Dr. V. N. Bedekar Institute of Management Studies, Thane*

Machine productivity is also gauged by quantifying the utilization of machines through a formula, *viz.*, cost per unit. Thus, cost of a machine is usually accounted for through depreciation which is charged, in the normal course, as a function of time. Thus, depreciation becomes a fixed cost. Higher the utilization of machine, lower the depreciation per unit of activity because economies of scale and scope help improve productivity in terms of cost per unit. This enables business to aspire for and actually achieve cost leadership and also improve competitive edge. However, yet another way of managing machine productivity is to relate the cost of the product or service to consumption of machine time. Thus, depreciation is charged, in this case, on actual usage basis and is defined as cost of machine/machine hours resulting in cost per machine hour. An otherwise fixed cost is converted into a variable cost and the consumption of machine time is embedded in a unit of product. This facilitates better and accurate product costing, control and also decision making particularly pricing. In the aviation industry Cathay Pacific was using this method to assess the consumption of aircraft travel time per unit of seat (passenger mile or seat kilometre). Thus, the formula used for assessing the use of the aircraft is the cost of the aircraft/flying hours. Variable cost per unit or hour, as the case maybe, facilitates complete control over the machine cost and therefore its productivity.

(7) MINDSET: Productivity of an enterprise is greatly influenced, if not exclusively determined by the mindsets of human resources. A proactive, positive, purposeful and pragmatic frame of mindsets is a very powerful incentive for productivity improvement. Such mindsets represent the '***group think***' of an organisation and help to evolve and develop new paradigms and manage paradigm shifts concerning ways and means of doing a business. Of course, the flip side of this is the '***reactive group think***' which could be a very powerful, negative, inhibitor towards any change required or plan to set the business on a new creative, innovate trail.

Thus, productivity is a mindset and is driven by a set of attitudes which need to converge to producing, continuously, the best and most competitive end results. The expression '***best***' means an effectiveness outcome measure from the customers perspective and the expression '***most competitive***' refers to the competencies and process capabilities that drive effectiveness and efficiency outcome measures. Six sigma enables the practice of best and most competitive performance.

PROACTIVE 'GROUP THINK'

An example of a proactive frame of mindsets is Southwest Airlines. Group behaviour in Southwest Airlines permits successful managing one of the most creative airlines in the World. Southwest Airline is a living example of possessing '***only one non-replicable competitive advantage and i.e., intangible assets***'. No matter what other airlines do, Continental, United Airlines or others to mimic Southwest Airlines, the organizational capabilities of Southwest are inimitable because "***these exists in a complex web of social interactions and may even depend on particular individuals.***"

Again, in Southwest Airlines humour and capacity to work in a collegial environment is important. The Chairman Mr. Kelleher quotes "***We hire attitudes***". We look for "***listening, caring, smiling, saying thank you and being warm.***" Our people are result-oriented, not process-oriented. They don't focus on organisational hierarchy or position or title. Kelleher has created air travel's Greatest Show on Earth.

It is difficult for any airline to reproduce Southwest culture of fun, family, frugality and focus. The '***group think***' in Southwest Airlines is expressed through its camaraderie and goal-directed behaviour is conspicuous across the network of the company at all levels of responsibilities. Individuals' and organisational goals are well blended and promote congruence. Contrariwise, a reactive '***group***

think' in General Motors' Buick Division, presented in **Exhibit 56** shows the extent to which divisional and overall organisational objectives are at loggerheads. This is a classic case of incongruent behaviour.

EXHIBIT 56

REACTIVE 'GROUP THINK'

"I remember that Buick, for example, at that time was very loath to give up its cash. This profitable division was, of course, the most prolific source of cash for the corporation, and long experience had made Buick's financial staff highly adept at delaying its report of the cash they had on hand. Buick made a practice of maintaining large cash balances in its factory sales branches. The amounts of these balances were not ascertainable at headquarters until Buick had submitted its monthly financial statement for the division as a whole — and this was usually a month or two after the fact. When the corporation needed cash, the treasurer, Meyer Prentis, would try to guess how much Buick actually had and how much of it he could probably get from them. Then he would go to Flint, discuss whatever other questions might be outstanding between Buick and headquarters and at last casually bring up the subject of cash. Buick's financial people would invariably express surprise at the size of Mr. Prentis' request and occasionally would try to resist the transfer of such a large amount. Naturally, this cat-and-mouse game did not result in the most efficient utilization of funds, especially when some divisions had more operating cash than they needed, at the same time that other divisions were short of operating cash." *(Sloan, Alfred. My Years with General Motors. New York: DoubleDay and Company, INC., 1990, pp. 122-123)*

The diagram presented below shows the value creating zone for a successful organisation or any product or service. Southwest Airlines is one of the rare examples whose services satisfies all the three requirements of value education year on year basis.

EXHIBIT 57

VALUE CREATING ZONE: SUCCESSFUL ORGANISATIONS/ PRODUCT/SERVICE

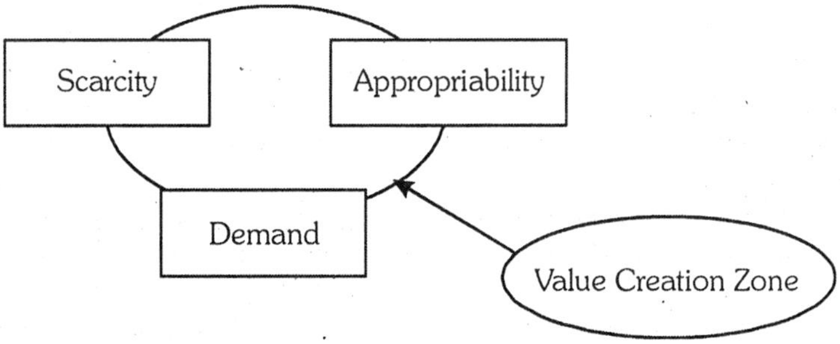

Thus, the 7Ms represent the fundamental factors around which productivity of an enterprise depends. All the 7Ms are interrelated, so a change in one does have a ripple effect on all others. It is not possible to progress one without simultaneously making progress on all. Therefore, enterprise has to posit and master a systems thinking approach and pay attention to all of 7Ms at the same time. There is no initial step or any understood hierarchy which defines the sequence of the 7Ms and the order in which they drive the enterprise. When all the 7Ms are simultaneously in action, proactively, in the same direction enterprise is at its best and positioned to attain performance levels which transcend above and beyond excellence.

In the final analysis, mindsets play an important role and tend to converge in favour of super-ordinate goals or shared values which spell out the aspirations of people and along with that the aspiration of the organisation itself. Productivity is one way of attaining and sustaining enterprise excellence which in turn is functionally related to shared values which give individuals and groups of an organisation the passion, the sense of integrity, ownership and belonging. Shared values in favour of achieving and surpassing excellence enable active pursuit of goals with deep conviction and generates wellsprings of energy, enthusiasm, enterprise and last but not the least focus.

EXHIBIT 58

WHAT PROVOKES AND PROMOTES PRODUCTIVITY !!!!!

- *Work should be enjoyable, pleasant and optimistic*
- *Targets should meet levels of practical, preferably, theoretical standards*
- *Creativity and innovation*
- *Risk taking*
- *Committing mistakes should not entail punishment*
- *Attention to detail*
- *Focus on people - with fraternity assuring the dignity of the individual*
- *Provision of superior quality goods and services*
- *Organisational structure should permit informality for free communication*
- *Economic surpluses are important*
- *Managers should be obsessed by action, because action is key to management*
- *Recognise shared values*

EXHIBIT 59

FACTORS AFFECTING PRODUCTVITY

(1) *Jung's definition of attitude is a "**readiness of the psyche to act or react in a certain way**" (Attitude is one of Jung's 57 definitions in Chapter XI of Psychological Types)*
SOURCE: *http://en.wikipedia.org/wiki/Attitude_(psychology)*

(2) *Proctor, R.W. and Dutta, A. (1995), define skill as '**goal-directed, well organised behavior that is acquired through practice and performed with economy of effort.**'-*
SOURCE: *(Skill acquisition and human performance. Thousand Oaks, CA: Sage.)*

(3) *Competency: '**the specification of knowledge and skill and the application of that knowledge and skill to the standards of performance required in the workplace.**' (definition in Learning and Assessment Strategies (2003) ANTA)*
SOURCE: *http://www.qasa.com.au/media/4894/assessment%20of%20ability%20-%20knowledge,%20skills%20and%20competence.pdf*

(4) *In decision theory and general systems theory, a mindset is a set of assumptions, methods or notations held by one or more people or groups of people which is so established that it creates a powerful incentive within these people or groups to continue to adopt or accept prior behaviors, choices, or tools. This phenomenon of cognitive bias is also sometimes described as mental inertia, "**groupthink**", or a "**paradigm**", and it is often difficult to counteract its effects upon analysis and decision making processes.*
SOURCE: *http://en.wikipedia.org/wiki/Mindset*

WAYS AND MEANS OF IMPROVING PRODUCTIVITY – POST 1991

- Aviation industry: use of leased instead of owned aircrafts to keep the asset base lean and augment ROI. This is true for many other industries too.
- Hero Honda, Colgate, Nestle, HLL and many others operating with negative networking capital from time to time enjoy improved financial productivity (ROI) (%).
- Benefits of outsourcing resulted in flexibility and dispersal of production facility, lower labour cost and better control over operating cost. E.g., pharma industry, Piramal Healthcare, Lupin Laboratories.
- Better negotiating skills and strengths particularly with respect to labour and pricing of products. This is again an externality of outsourcing.
- Use of technology, improved and safer communication methods encouraged Western Countries to outsource from India (banking, insurance and related financial service industry), e.g., in the banking industry voluntary retirement, technology upgradation and ATM, facilitated and contributed to higher productivity.
- Retail chain outlets experienced better (effective) utilization of capital through improved velocity of money that is to say fast moving cash sales.
- Using interest free capital, i.e., suppliers' credit-by cash rich FMCG companies and better managed auto giants in India like Maruti and Hero Honda. This reduced the cost of capital and improved the bottom line of business.
- Improved logistics and transport facilities reduced transport cost which was as high as 30% of raw material cost in international business. The industries which benefitted were steel, cement, fertilizers and oil industry.
- Productivity of India Inc., also improved because of lower import duties (tariffs), dismantling of quantitative restrictions (quotas) and an appreciating INR against the USD and EURO (post-liberalisation).
- Cheap and cheaper cost of capital through use of preference shares – (convertible and redeemable), e.g., Infosys and Citi Group in 2001 to 2006. Infosys consolidated its financial position without borrowing and by re-investing profits in its own business, to enjoy financial independence in 2006 and reduced onerous, may be unconscionable, covenants of lenders.
- Use of External Commercial Borrowing (ECB) and Foreign Currency Convertible Bonds (FCCB) to take advantage of interest rate differential between interest rates in India and other countries. In addition, if exchange rate position happened to be favourable to the Indian entrepreneur, productivity of capital improved. Further, the funds so raised were meant to finance imports of raw materials/machinery. The items imported were paid for by the loans raised in the debt market in foreign land. Productivity was sustained because imports became relatively very cheap, particularly in 2006.
- Use of Equity capital with high premium (e.g., Sun TV – February, 2007, Jet Air – 2004, Sahara deal – 2006, DLF – June, 2007, ICICI – June, 2007, DS Kulkarni – February, 2007, SBI Rights Issue – February, 2008).
- Lehman Bros's case – Higher dependence on short-term capital for long-term use led to credit default. Maturity mis-match led to collapse. Renewal of short-term funds is in creditors hands. If credit is withheld then company has to file Chapter 11 protection in the US. The message is "***excess of anything is an unmitigated nuisance***". Productivity improvement *sans* financial wisdom and prudence can be counterproductive.

Table 77
OPTIONS OPEN FOR IMPROVING PRODUCTIVITY

	Sales	Contribution	Profits	Productivity
(1)	k = constant	↑ (less cost)	↑	↑
(2)	↓	k (by amount)	↑	↑
(3)	↑ (quantity and value)	↑	↑	↑
(4)	k	↑	↑	↑

In the cases above it is assumed that the capital employed is constant (except 4). If the above improvements in productivity can be achieved with the same capital, productivity, of course, improves. However, if the capital can be reduced through improved management of assets used for business or reduction in capital through buy-back or other methods of reducing capital, productivity can improve further. The above four options are by no means exhaustive. They are illustrative. Several myriads of permutation and combinations of sales, contribution (sales minus variable cost), profit (contribution minus fixed cost) are possible to identify viable option/s. Enterprise normally put a simulation model into action to explore viable options open to improve productivity.

EXHIBIT 60

PRODUCTIVITY OF LEADING ECONOMIC POWERS – USA, GERMANY AND JAPAN

There are significant differences in capital productivity across nations. At one time it was believed that Japanese productivity was one of the highest in the World. However, a recent study has shown that productivity in Germany and Japan is just about two thirds of US levels. US achieve higher productivity in both labour as well capital utilization. Japan's productivity is low due to poor performance on account of both labour and capital. Germany's productivity is low because of capital intensity and the relatively less efficient use of capital. Higher capital productivity in the US has increased the return on financial investments which in turn have offset the lower savings and investment rates. Further, higher returns have contributed to more capital income. Overall productivity level in Germany is 20% below US level which accounts for the relatively low GDP per capita in Germany which is 26% below the US level. Since capital productivity depends upon the ratio of output to input, productivity is affected if either the output is low or the input is in excess. Thus, managerial decisions need to give attention to increased, productive, capital utilization so that the numerator and denominator in the capital productivity ratio are well managed and monitored to sustain the levels of effectiveness and efficiency in the economy.

SOURCE: *Agrawal, Raj. and others "Capital Productivity: Why the US leads and why it matters". Mckinsey Quarterly <http://mkqpreview1.qdweb.net/article_print.aspx?L2=5&L3=2&ar=167>*

DEVELOPING A COMPOSITE PRODUCTIVITY INDEX (CPI)

CPI is a measure developed by using a combination of factors concerning and affecting the performance of an enterprise.

A CPI helps to

(a) develop an objective standard of productivity performance against which performance of an enterprise can be assayed.

(b) develop suitable benchmarks using the performance measures developed in (a) above and continuously sustain historic performance and also revised, new, quantified benchmarks.

(*c*) perform an inter firm, inter period, performance assessment.
(*d*) evolve a quantified enterprise rating mechanism on account of productivity.

CPI requires reliable database of enterprises which are to be rated. Before the rating, available data has to be converted into meaningful information to add to the knowledge of the information evaluators and decision makers.

The major quantified information available in any organisation, in any part of the world, is the financial and accounting information. Thus, every enterprise has its historic financial data and information in place in terms of financial statements, *viz.*, profit and loss account or income statement, balance sheet and cash flow statement. In addition, there would be several other supporting schedules and statements throwing light on the nuances which govern the preparation of the main financial statements.

Given the financial statements, the key financial factors which can be identified amongst others, are sales, operating and net profit (book basis), cash profit, total assets (or capital employed) net worth, market capitalisation, *et al.* These are absolute measures expressed in monetary terms and by themselves they may not convey much particularly from the perspective of measuring productivity *per se* and developing a CPI. These absolute measures can indicate only the size of the enterprise (sales, total assets/net worth) and performance in terms of operating, cash and net profit and market capitalisation. Information related to these indicators, for a period of time, of course, signal the variation between the indicators *inter se*. Thus, variations in size and performance, based on absolute measures expressed in monetary terms, can be gauged through such information. They may also indicate the role played by the key factors (sales, total assets and net worth) in influencing certain performance-related absolute measures such as operating profit, net profit and perhaps market capitalisation to the extent that market perceptions are guided by fundamentals. However, absolute measures of financial performance, drawn from the financial statements, are not of direct use in developing a CPI. The absolute measures have to be deployed into appropriate productivity statistics.

Productivity by definition, as presented in **Exhibit 50** is a relative measure and therefore, an evolving and developing a CPI must use relative measures of performance. Given the data in **Table 81** the following points may be noted:

(1) The data in **Table 80** based on Business Standard 1000 for 2009 and presents the top twenty companies in sales (ranks 1 to 20) and their ranks with respect to other measures, *viz.*, operating profit, net profit, cash profit, total assets, net worth and market capitalisation. Rank 1 is the best performer and rank 20 the worst performer.
(2) Nine Companies have single digit rank in sales. These are companies of India Inc., with the highest turnover (sales) figures ranging from ₹ 2,88,227 crores (IOC) to ₹ 26,082 crores (Suzlon). However, companies which are top in sales need not necessarily have top ranking with respect to other key measures.
(3) Eight companies have single digit rank in total assets and six companies have single digit rank in net worth as seen in **Table 80.**
(4) Given the profile of the said top companies, with single digit rank in sales, total assets and net worth, it can be observed, from **Table 80** that seven companies have single digit rank in operating profit and net profit and six companies have single digit rank in market capitalisation. Of course, not all the nine companies having single digit rank in sales and the eight and six companies having single digit rank in total assets and net worth respectively, figure in the class of single digit ranks with respect to absolute financial performance measures, *viz.*, operating profit, net profit and market capitalisation.

Table 78

TOP 9 COMPANIES IN SALES HAVING SINGLE DIGIT RANK IN OTHER FINANCIAL INDICATORS

SALES	*TOTAL ASSETS*	*NET WORTH*	*OPERATING PROFIT*	*NET PROFIT*	*MARKET CAPITALISATION*
IOC	Reliance Industries	Reliance Industries	ONGC	ONGC	Reliance Industries
Reliance Industries	ONGC	ONGC	Reliance Industries	Reliance Industries	ONGC
Tata Steel	IOC	NTPC	Bharati Airtel	NTPC	NTPC
BPCL	Tata Steel	IOC	Tata Steel	Bharati Airtel	MMTC
HPCL	NTPC	Bharati Airtel	NTPC	SAIL	TCS
ONGC	Tata Motors	SAIL	SAIL	TCS	Bharati Airtel
Tata Motors	Hindalco		IOC	Tata Steel	
Hindalco	Bharati Airtel				
NTPC					

N.B: There are fiftyfour cells in all. Nine companies top in sales occupy only thirtytwo cells in all, that is to say twentythree cells other than sales. Four companies, *viz.*, TCS, Bharati Airtel, SAIL and MMTC occupy eleven cells other than sales and eleven cells are vacant.

A further incisive analysis presented **Table 79** shows the frequency with which the top nine companies in sales enjoy recurring occurrences in twentythree cells in categories other than sales:

Table 79

FREQUENCY OF RECURRENCES OF TOP 9 COMPANIES

	SALES	*TOTAL ASSETS*	*NET WORTH*	*OPERATING PROFIT*	*NET PROFIT*	*MARKET CAPITALISATION*
IOC	✓	✓	✓	✓	×	×
Rel. Inds.	✓	✓	✓	✓	✓	✓
Tata Steel	✓	✓	×	✓	✓	×
BPCL	✓	×	×	×	×	×
HPCL	✓	×	×	×	×	×
ONGC	✓	✓	✓	✓	✓	✓
Tata Motors	✓	✓	×	×	×	×
Hindalco	✓	✓	×	×	×	×
NTPC	✓	✓	✓	✓	✓	✓

N.B. ✓ = Nine companies top in Sales = 32 cells; × = Twentytwo cells of which eleven cells are occupied by four companies (TCS, Bharati Airtel, SAIL and MMTC) and eleven cells are vacant.

The following observations are in order with respect to the nine companies top in sales:

- Reliance, ONGC and NTPC are the only three companies which enjoy single digit rank in all the six cells.
- Tata Steel and IOC have recurrence in four cells, Tata Motors and Hindalco have a presence in two cells.
- BPCL and HPCL have single digit ranking only in one cell namely sales.

Thus, the above analysis shows that companies which are top in sales (nine) total assets (seven) and some cases (four) net worth need not necessarily enjoy excellence with respect to absolute performance measures like operating profit, net profit and market capitalisation. Hence, the inconsistency of the frequency of recurrence of companies in the different cells.

RELATIVE MEASURES OF PERFORMANCE FOR CPI

The top twenty companies in sales have been studied by identifying productivity measures of financial performance, *viz.*, return on sales or profit margin (%), assets turnover (times), return on total assets (%), return on net worth (%) and market capitalisation as percentage of net worth. A brief on the different indicators used for developing the CPI, in this example, is presented in **Table 80**

Table 80

FINANCIAL INDICATORS FOR DEVELOPING CPI

Ratio Code	*Title of the Ratio*	*Ratio*
R_1	Operating profit margin ratio (%)	(Operating Profit/Sales) × 100
R_2	Assets turnover ratio (times)	(Sales/Total Assets)
R_3	Return on total assets (%)	Operating Profit/Total Assets × 100
R_4	Return on net worth (%)	Net Profit/Net Worth × 100
R_5	Market capitalisation as percentage of net worth	Market Capitalisation/Net Worth × 100

Table 81

BUSINESS STANDARD

1000 COMPANIES - 2009

INDIA INC., FINAL RANKING USING ABSOLUTE MEASURES OF PERFORMANCE

SR. NO.	CO. NAME	SALES	OP	CP	NP	TA	NW	MCAP	GRAND TOTAL	RANK
1	REL. IND.	2	2	1	2	1	1	1	10	1
2	ONGC	6	1	2	1	2	2	2	16	2
3	NTPC	9	5	6	3	5	3	3	34	3
4	BHARTI AIRTEL	15	3	4	4	9	7	9	51	4
5	SAIL	10	6	7	5	10	8	11	57	5
6	IOC	1	7	5	20	3	4	18	58	6
7	TATA STEEL	3	4	3	9	4	11	24	58	7
8	LARSEN and TOUBRO	11	11	10	13	11	22	13	91	8
9	TCS	17	12	8	8	33	16	7	101	9
10	BHEL	18	20	11	16	16	25	10	116	10
11	HINDALCO	8	27	9	74	8	15	41	182	11
12	BPCL	4	21	12	57	13	24	55	186	12
13	HPCL	5	23	14	50	14	29	93	228	13
14	MAN. REF. PET. (MRPL)	12	38	15	38	58	52	90	303	14
15	ADANI ENT	19	61	17	71	41	73	57	339	15
16	SUZLON ENERGY	20	37	16	124	20	35	88	340	16
17	MMTC	14	78	18	139	61	140	4	454	17
18	TATA MOTORS	7	34	13	1000	7	45	29	1135	18
19	ESSAR OIL	13	58	19	989	31	64	71	1245	19
20	CHENNAI PETROLEUM	16	983	20	984	88	72	233	2396	20

Legend: OP = Operating Profit, CP = Cash Profit, NP = Net Profit, TA = Total Asset, NW = Net Worth, MCAP = Market Capitalisation

Table 81 (A)

INDIA INC., TOP 20 COMPANIES FINAL RANKING – 2009
USING COMPOSITIE FINANCIAL PRODUCTIVITY INDEX - RELATIVE MEASURES OF PERFORMANCE

Sr. No.	CO. NAME	OP/ SALES* 100	Sales/ TA	OP/TA* 100	NP/NW* 100	MCAP/ NW* 100	Grand Total	Rank
1	BHARTI AIRTEL	5	19	1	1	2	28	1
2	TCS	6	9	6	5	3	29	2
3	ONGC	1	16	2	3	8	30	3
4	MAN. REF. PET. (MRPL)	3	3	7	12	11	36	4
5	SAIL	4	13	5	7	9	38	5
6	BHEL	7	18	8	2	6	41	6
7	LARSEN and TOUBRO	2	15	4	8	13	42	7
8	TATA STEEL	9	10	9	6	14	48	8
9	NTPC	11	20	3	4	12	50	9
10	HINDALCO	8	11	10	11	10	50	9
11	SUZLON ENERGY	13	14	16	9	5	57	11
12	REL. IND.	19	17	12	10	1	59	12
13	MMTC	10	2	15	17	18	62	13
14	IOC	14	6	14	14	17	65	14
15	ESSAR OIL	15	7	19	20	4	65	14
16	HPCL	12	4	18	16	15	65	14
17	ADANI ENT	16	8	11	15	16	66	17
18	BPCL	18	S5	13	13	19	68	18
19	TATA MOTORS	17	12	17	19	7	72	19
20	CHENNAI PETROLEUM	20	1	20	18	20	79	20

LEGEND: OP = Operating Profit, NP = Net Profit, TA = Total Assets, NW = Net Worth, MCAP = Market Capitalisation

SOURCE: Compendium of Business Standard Top 1000 Companies in India 2009 – India Inc., Ranks based on Key Financial Indicators

The procedure for developing an aggregate score to quantify the CPI is as follows:

(1) For all the above ratios the interpretations is higher the ratio better the performance and further higher the ratio lower the numerical scores given to the performance - the best performer starting with rank one and the worst performer having a rank of twenty.

(2) **Table 81 (A)** compiles the rank of twenty companies (top in sales) on account of the five measures of financial productivity indicated in **Table 80.**

(3) Thus, as can be seen from the **Table 81 (A)** Bharati Airtel has a fifth rank in profit margin, nineteenth rank on account of asset utilisation, first rank on account of two measures viz. return on total assets and net worth and second rank on account of market capitalisation as % of net worth. Bharati Airtel therefore has a scorecard, in terms of ranks, as shown in **Table 81 (A)**

Table 82

BEST AND WORST COMPANY – BHARATI AIRTEL vs. CHENNAI PETROLEUM

		Scores (based on ranks)	
Ratio Code	*RATIOS*	*Bharati Airtel*	*Chennai Petroleum*
R_1	Profit Margin (%)	5	20
R_2	Asset Turnover (Times)	19	1.
R_3	Return on Total Assets (%)	01	20
R_4	Return on Net Worth (%)	01	18
R_5	Market Capitalisation as % of net worth	01	20
	TOTAL	27	79

(4) Bharati Airtel score of 27 is the lowest score obtained by any company among the 20 companies studied and stands out as the best performing company (Rank One).

(5) Chennai Petroleum on the other hand is the last in the rank of the 20 companies studied with a score of 79 as shown above. All other companies apparently fall in-between as shown in **Table 81(A)**

(6) The methodology adopted to develop the CPI can be algebraically captured as follows:

- R_1, R_2, R_3, R_4 and R_5 are the respective relevant ratios for measuring financial productivity.
- Ranks assigned to individual companies are based on the theme higher the value of the ratio better the performance and lower the numerical score attached to the top performers.
- Scores range from 1 to 20 – 1 being the best performer and 20 being the worst performer.
- The companies are then arranged in ascending order of scores based on ranks.
- The rank-based score of any company is the Composite Financial Productivity Index (CFPI).
- If there are five ratios used for developing a CFPI, every company will have five scores one on account of each ratio.
- The CFPI score of any company can be defined as:

$$\overset{5}{\underset{i=1}{}} Si$$

- It is assumed that the ratios R_1 to R_5 have equal weightage and therefore, there is no need for weighting as such.
- If weights are to be assigned the formula will undergo a change as shown below:

Let R_1, R_2, R_3, R_4 and R_5 be the relevant five ratios; S_1, S_2, S_3, S_4 and S_5 be the scores of individual companies with respect to each one of the respective ratios and W_1, W_2, W_3, W_4 and W_5

be the weightages of the respective ratios from R_1 to R_5. The formula to define FCPI is thus presented:

$$FCPI = \{(S_1 \times W_1) + (S_2 \times W_2) + (S_3 \times W_3) + (S_4 \times W_4) + (S_5 \times W_5)\}$$

$$= \sum_{i=1}^{5} Si\, Wi$$

The following points need to be noted:

- There could be more than five ratios and the set of ratios could be different.
- Depending upon the accessibility to information the groups of ratios studied could capture liquidity, profitability, asset utilisation, capital structure, valuation and any other relevant facet of an enterprise.
- Weights may or may not be assigned. When no weights are assigned it is assumed that all the ratios, among the chosen set of ratios, are equally important and therefore, weightages are deemed to be equal.
- The weights used could be different by different persons for different sets of ratios depending on the end purpose, mindset of the analysts and a host of other factors.
- The ranking process in this illustration is based on the theme higher the ratios better the performance.
- There can be ratios which have to be understood through alternate themes like lower the ratio better the performance, *viz.*, cost as percentage of sales or individual elements of cost as percentage of total cost.

There could be ratios like debt equity which needs to be tackled in a totally different way depending on the schools of thought. One school of thought may prescribe that 'higher the ratio better the performance'. A second school of thought may vow by an opposite theme 'lower the debt equity ratio better the performance'. A third variety may develop a benchmark say a rule of thumb of 2:1 which was regarded as an ideal and almost a sacrosanct ceiling not to be exceeded except in certain cases. Anything above 2:1 may be risky and entail a lower score. Anything below 2:1 may also entail a lower score. Between risky situations (higher debt equity ratio) and unrisky situations (lower debt equity ratio) the latter may be given a better score than the former. There may be analysts who perceive the same risk/unrisky situation in a diametrically opposite manner.

Different companies develop different versions of CPI. The extract from the annual report of Wisconsin Energy shown below in **Exhibit 61** develops and discloses a financial productivity index known as Total Shareholder Return (%) and allows stakeholders to assay the performance of the company *vis-à-vis* different indices.

EXHIBIT 61

WISCONSIN ENERGY: FINANCIAL PERFORMANCE INDEX: TOTAL SHAREHOLDER RETURN

On virtually every meaningful measure – the company made great strides during the year. We reduced our costs, improved productivity and posted record financial results. In fact, on virtually every meaningful measure – from customer satisfaction to network reliability to progress on our Power the Future plan – the company made great strides during the year. Here are some of the highlights of 2009.

SOLID FINANCIAL PERFORMANCE

Earnings from continuing operations rose to $337 million or $3.20 a share, the highest in company history. During the year, we invested $818 million to expand and improve the energy infrastructure of the region. Cash flow was strong, and we ended 2009 with our debt to total capital at 55.2 per cent – better than year-end 2008 and better than plan.

The market value of the company continued to grow during the year. The price of Wisconsin Energy stock increased by 18.7 per cent, trading at a new all-time high of $50.62 a share on December, 30. And our total shareholder return continued to outspace the return you would have earned in the Dow Jones Industrials, the S&P 500, the NASADAQ or the major utility indexes. The table below, which provides you with information for the past five years, tells the story.

TOTAL SHAREHOLDER RETURN (2005-09)*	
Wisconsin Energy	67.01%
Dow Jones Industrial Average	10.11%
S&P 500 Index	2.10%
NASDAQ Composite Index	8.83%
S&P 500 Electric Utility Index	36.74%
Philadelphia Utility Index	35.09%

**Stock price appreciation plus reinvested dividends.*

SOURCE: *Wisconsin Energy, Annual Report 2009*

⊙⊙⊙

20

MANAGING PRODUCTIVITY OF CAPITAL

MANAGING PRODUCTIVITY OF CAPITAL – INDIA INC. ILLUSTRATED

P/V ratio, also known as profit-volume ratio, indicates the speed with which a business is able to generate surplus (selling price per unit minus variable cost per unit) to initially recoup the fixed costs and eventually start earning profit. Once the fixed costs are fully recouped, that is to say after the break-even point is reached, a business starts earning profit at the PV Ratio. Higher the volume of sales above the break-even point, greater the cushion which an enterprise enjoys *vis-à-vis* break-even sales. This cushion is known as margin of safety which indicates the gap between prevailing sales (actual or budgeted) in relation to break-even sales. The margin of safety is also indicative of the extent to which sales can fall before losses start. Thus, the product of PV Ratio and margin of safety results in operating profit divided by sales, indicating the operating margin (%). Higher the operating margin (%) greater the productivity of every rupee of sales. The operating margin (%) multiplied by capital turnover ratio (times) results in operating profit divided by capital employed, *viz.*, return on capital employed (%). The ROCE is an overall measure of the productivity of capital employed in business. The interrelationships between the different parameters concerning operating performance is shown in **Exhibit 64.**

EXAMPLE 1:

BANKING INDUSTRY

In the nineties banking industry had to face large number of customers within the banking hours and had to offer service in decreasing response time. Banks had to manually keep the records of individual customer bank accounts (current, savings and others), record this in the ledger and also communicate to the customer through the passbook. Further, information had to be retrieved as and when required. Providing services to the satisfaction of the customer was becoming a difficult proposition. The cost of every unit of service provided in terms of time, effort and money was becoming disproportionate to the returns.

The productivity of banks suffered both in operations due to high unit cost of service and in marketing too because of poor service and the consequent dissatisfaction and disgruntlement among customers. However, there was a paradigm shift in the banking industry through the introduction of the Automated Teller Machine (ATM) since 2001. Following the wave of voluntary retirement scheme in the banking industry, the introduction of ATM was inevitable. The unions also agreed to this. ATMs revolutionized the services in the banking industry. Services were available on a '**24 x 7**' basis unlike the four to five hours of banking in the course of the day. This resulted in higher all round productivity through: increased duration of service, higher usage of facilities (space and manpower) and reduced space requirements (600 sq. ft. plus skeleton staff for branch with ATM operation as against 1200 sq. ft., in prime location and elaborate staffing pattern based on union agreements and banking bureaucracy). Thus, historically in the pre ATM days whereas the bank could service only 100 customers through cash deposits, withdrawals, passbook updates, the post ATM saw at least 300 customers per day, that is to say an increase in the total volume of business. As a result, the contribution per unit of revenue earned increased. Banks were able to generate higher surplus per rupee of revenue and also break-even faster and also enjoy improved margin of safety due to larger volumes of business. The banking industry saw new opportunities in this scenario and the staff could pay attention to customers by focusing on value added services which brought about more and more numbers of customers and quality of customers (high net worth individuals). The three principal areas which were focused upon included wealth management services, insurance products and treasury management services for corporate clients. Thus, technological innovation enabled the bank to bring about a paradigm shift in its mode of operation and reap full benefits through increased volume and quality of business, increased revenue and also reduced variable cost per unit of service offered.

EXHIBIT 62

BANKING INDUSTRY – IMPACT OF TECHNOLOGICAL INNOVATIONS

The net effect was visible in certain performance measures, viz., the numbers of customers per employee, revenue per employee and profit per employee. In short, employee productivity improved on two counts: thanks to VRS, numbers of persons in the banking industry were reduced (fixed costs were reduced), existing/fixed costs (staff costs) could be recouped faster to break-even with a lower volume of business and relatively higher profit levels provided for satisfactory margin of safety. As a result overall operating excellence improved resulting in a favorable return on capital employed.

Banking industry was thus the prime mover in visualizing the benefits of leveraging technology in service operations to improve return on capital employed. Prior to 2001, banks were investing in premises, people and physical assets. Post 2001, saw the redundancy of the said assets and investments were made in technology which facilitated divestment from physical, unproductive, sterile and agitating (union), animate, assets.

EXAMPLE 2:

BANKING INDUSTRY MANAGEMENT OF PRODUCTS AND INCOME MIXES

One-way of improving productivity of capital is to keep a continuous and constant tab on the product mix. This ensures that maximum return per unit of resources (materials, machines, labour hours and others) is obtained and the objective function of maximization of profit defined as: Max $P = [(S\text{-}V) - F]$ is well sustained. In manufacturing processes and even in service industries like

P = Profit (in ₹), S = Sales (in ₹), V = Variable Cost (in ₹), F = Fixed Cost (in ₹)

banks, mathematical tools ranging from simple to the complicated – simultaneous equations and linear programming to mathematical programming were and continue to be employed to achieve the optimal product mix.

In the banking industry, constant use is made of '***product/service mix***' planning to sustain the revenue line. The following aspects need to be kept in mind:

DEPOSIT MIX: Banks prefer a deposit mix in favour of current and savings bank accounts and less of term deposits. The choice of the said mix is apparent because of the interest cost associated with the savings mobilised by the banks. The bank intent is to maintain its spread intact.

ADVANCE MIX: Banks prefer short-term to long-term advances. This is also consistent with their tenure of the deposits. Banks are benefited on all counts – interest income, rolling over of money and the risk factor. Shorter the tenure of the loan, lower the risk and relatively higher the interest rate. Cash realisation of income (margin) is also very fast. In fact, banks charge highest interest rate on credit card and the least on bill discount (3 months period). Banks have to follow this tenure of advance mix because the pressure of depositors for withdrawal from time to time and maturity portion of term deposits are always an impending toll on the cash outflows. Thus, banks give 1% more on deposits of 1 year (or less duration). At the same time, deposits for longer term periods are not in favour of the banks' taste. Hence, interest rates tend to be relatively low.

INCOME MIX: Banks prefer more fee-based income than interest on loans. Fee-based income includes bank guarantees, buying and selling of foreign exchange, letter of credit and money transfer.

Professional approach to managing the asset and liability mix of banks is in the domain of quantitative techniques which many banks use. Foreign banks have invested heavily in information technology so that they are enabled with the right information and inputs for decision making. They are thus empowered to take informed decisions so that they can enact themselves effectively and efficiently to meet the objective function of maximization of profit. The above matrix of mix of assets and liabilities, within the framework of the guidelines provided by the Reserve Bank of India, has helped foreign banks to maintain all-round productivity on a sustained basis. Thus, foreign banks enjoy higher profit, volume of business and income per employee apart from having relatively low unit cost per service and per employee. However, one point should be remembered. Foreign banks are in India to make money only and they are a part of class banking rather than mass banking. To quote a report on Foreign banks in India "***One peculiar feature of .... foreign bank is that they concentrate on the corporate clientele***".... "***They also charge excessive commission for the currencies of those countries which do not have their own bank branches in India***". The report continues "***These banks may be having a small number of branches, but they enjoy a sizeable presence in the non-fund business and are earning huge profits. Because of the nature of their operation their productivity on resources invested and consequently return on investment also very high.***"

EXAMPLE 3:

MANUFACTURING COMPANY – Production for Mass versus Class markets

Manufacturing companies have a choice, once again, between Producing for masses versus Producing for classes. A product mix therefore has to balance between Mass and Class production. In mass production the selling price has to be competitive because of the relatively limited ability, of target customers, to pay. Whatever is lost in the margin per unit has to be offset in the volume. However, mass production by global standards can result in very low unit cost and maintain the spread between selling price and cost price per unit. The assumption is that whatever is produced can be sold. Production for class provides several USPs for the product albeit at a higher price. A niche market is created, sales volume is low and profit margin per unit of product is high. Different companies adopt different approaches to maximize their profits over a period of time.

HENRY FORD:The philosophy of Henry Ford was totally different. In fact he is credited with a principle called Fordism which means "***mass production of large number of inexpensive automobiles using the assembly line***". Further he believed in the manufacture of one type of a car and just in one color, *viz.*, Black. This resulted in mass production at lowest possible unit cost and hence permitted competitive pricing with controlled margins. As a marketing proposition it created a well identified product with a USP accepted by the Americans.

EXAMPLE 4:

MARUTI UDYOG

Thus, Maruti Udyog started with two products Omni and Maruti 800 priced around ₹ 55,000 in the early eighties (1983). The profit realisation per unit of sale was relatively low. Over a period of time, the company has progressively shifted from producing for mass markets to niche markets, i.e., to say cars with several USPs, relatively highly priced with a low volume sale and high profit margin per car. The product mix ratio between Mass and Class products is 1:1. There is another side to the operation of Maruti Suzuki. Insofar as small cars are concerned Maruti is very competitive though the competition is gathering momentum. To quote the Chairman, Mr. R. C. Bhargava "***This issue is for bigger cars where the volumes are small and it doesn't matter to us because small cars are our bread and butter. I think although there will be growth in sedans, the volumes won't be very large even 10 years from now. We will remain a small car market.***"

EXAMPLE 5:

HUL: RATIONALISATION OF BRANDS

Rationalisation of brands. From time to time corporates take a look at the number of brands that they market to bring about a rationalisation in the productivity of brands. Its often found that the 80:20 principle is in motion and that a large number of products are marketed under a variety of brands. Just a few brands contribute to a major portion of the profit contribution. Disproportion amount of time, money and effort is invested in the other brands which are not productive enough and contribute poorly to profit contribution. A typical example of a company which was marketing nearly 20 products is presented below:

Table 83

EFFECT OF MARGINAL CONTRIBUTION ON SALES

Figures in (₹)

Nos. of Products	*% to Total Nos. of Products*	*Contribution Margin*	*% to Total Contribution*	*Sales*	*% to Total Sales*
First 3	15%	10,850	52%	30,000	27%
Next 7	35%	8,565	41%	45,000	41%
Next 10	50%	1,366	7%	36,000	32%
Total 20	**100%**	**20,781**	**100%**	**1,11,000**	**100%**

Table 83 speaks for itself and shows the disproportionality between % to total sales and % to total contribution. Hindustan Lever (now HUL) also carried out a rationalisation programme of their brands. From the 110 brands that they had at one point of time, they decided to keep 30 power brands which contribute to 75% of sales and more than 100% of their profit. Apparently, some brands were contributing to the losses. Such an exercise is carried out from time to time to maintain the productivity of capital intact.

EXAMPLE 6:
HOTEL INDUSTRY

In the hotel industry we find ITC, Hotel Leela and Indian Hotels all cater to the classes with high quality service, 5 star or 7 star, mostly catering to foreign tourists, business class travellers and honchos of the corporate World. Thus, the focus is on high profit margin and if demand materializes, high volume too. In the case of hotel industry the volume is expressed as '***room utilisation***'.

EXAMPLE 7:
RETAIL CHAIN OUTLETS

The retail chain outlets were dependent upon the chain of distributors to reach the ultimate customers. This disturbed the logistics because the retail outlets could not exercise effective control either on procurement of goods or distribution of final products. The retail outlets were only a perfunctory '***link in***' the chain with responsibility to deliver quality goods and services to suppliers, distributors and remotely to final customers. The method of reaching out to the final customers underwent, again, a paradigm shift. Distribution formats had to move away from traditional chain logistics to a more effective and direct link with the final customer. Thus, the retail outlets identified at least two innovative ways of breaking away from the shackles of the past: First, concept of one-stop-shop emerged, *viz.*, Stoppers Shop, Crossroads and Big Bazaar. These shops also found it necessary, wherever possible, to replicate their outlets in different parts of cities. This was limited though. Second, manufacturers came into retail business maybe by default. For example, shopkeepers did not wholeheartedly cooperate to stock Vimal fabrics (1972). Reliance established a chain of retail outlets dedicated to the procurement and sale of Vimal fabrics. Thus, the concept of Vimal showroom gained momentum and the expression '***Only Vimal***' became a household cliché. This concept was applied to other segments of business perishable (Monginis cake shops), Godrej (Furniture and Lock showrooms), Ice Cream parlours (Amul). Further, RIL saw a great opportunity in retail business in recent times (2006). RIL entered into retail business through several outlets all over the subcontinent – a plan of 700 retail outlets in 700 cities. The outlets would market fresh vegetables and fruits, grocery products and other related items. As part of the extended supply chain the latest addition of items in some of these retail outlets includes exclusively branded jewellery (gold and silver). Thus the range is from farm fresh products to high value bullion items.

The principles governing the above scenario in distribution management was

- high ratio of sales upon capital, i.e., to say high velocity of capital.
- improved logistics because transport cost and warehousing cost were minimized by following principles of scientific management like just-in-time. Incidentally, transport cost is as high as 30% of raw material cost in international business.
- suppliers credit was used to lever return on investment. Of course, muscle power did play its usual role in the market place.

Table 84

REDUCING COST OF CAPITAL

SR. NO.	INSTRUMENT	COMPANY	PURPOSE
(1)	Redeemable Convertible Preference Shares	Infosys, Citi Group Financer (2001-2006)	To avoid control by lenders.
(2)	External Commercial Borrowing (ECB)/FCCB	Piramal, Bharat Forge	Cheaper cost of funds and appreciating rupee.
(3)	Equity issues	Sun TV – 500 Crores; Premium – 630% DS Kulkarni – 100 Crores; Premium – 230% Plethic Pharmaceuticals – 110 Crores; Premium – 110 Crores – 240%	To raise equity share capital on extraordinarily favourable terms.

EXAMPLE 8:
BUY-BACK OF SHARES

Section 77 of the Companies Act permits buy-back of shares (since 31st October, 1998). Buy-back of shares is defined as a company offering to take back the shares from interested shareholders at an announced price. Companies resort to buy-back of shares as a strategy to restructure their capital and improve productivity of resources. Thus, when shares are bought back the financial impact on the company is an outflow of cash (asset side) and reduction in the equity share capital of the company (liabilities side - capital section). Companies which enjoy surfeit cash, from time to time, use the same to buy-back shares, reduce the capital and improve the return on capital employed. Surplus cash adversely affects return on investment in the immediate context if adequate reinvestment opportunities are not available through pipeline projects which can absorb funds. Hence, the motivation for cash rich companies to use buy-back as a powerful strategy to increase return on equity and return on capital employed *ab initio*. Undoubtedly, it also serves the purpose of increasing the proportion of promoters share to the new equity capital base which is diluted to the extent of the buy-back. Promoters need not buy shares in the market to protect their controlling interest post buy-back. Dividend policies are also not put to question because of the limited circulation of equity share capital and reduced number of shareholders.[1]

[1]RIL has bought back shares worth more than ₹ 500 crores in just 10 trading sessions between 11th May and 24th May (2012). The company has purchased 7.78 million shares. As on 24th May, 2012, the company had purchased more than 19 million shares. The company had a target of buy-back of ₹ 10,440 crores. As on 24th May, 2012 RIL had acquired shares valued at 13% of the said target. This buy-back programme is regarded as the largest ever in the history of corporates in India. According to the new rules the company must pick-up at least 25 per cent of the maximum buy-back stipulated. However, the buying has not helped to stimulate the sagging price of RIL in the share market. The share price fell to its lowest in the last three years at ₹ 673 on 16th May, 2012.

EXAMPLE 9:
NEGATIVE NET WORKING CAPITAL

Many companies manage productivity of capital by leveraging their goodwill in all the markets in which they operate, *viz.*, factor market (procurements of inputs required for business), financial markets (procurement of loanable funds) and output market (sale of goods to customers with best profit realisation per unit per rupee of sales). Companies which can lever their goodwill in the said markets, particularly factor market and output market, tend to use suppliers credit as a powerful medium to fund the day to day financial needs of business. Depending upon the structure of the market in which they sell their products and services, they are in a position to command premium price, cash sales in lieu of credit sales and in some cases advances from customers. Thus, such companies tend to have a negative networking capital as a planned financial strategy. Examples are many - Dell, an American computer manufacturer, really speaking, was amongst the forerunners to identify negative net working capital as a financial strategy to maximize return on investment and augment productivity of capital. Similarly, in India, HLL (now HUL), Nestle (2004 to 2006) and at least a few other leading, well performing companies (SAIL and Tata Motors - 2004 and 2005) are into the same game. Of course, negative working capital could also mean that a company is desperate and using short-term funds for long-term uses. Nevertheless, these companies deployed the concept of negative net working capital as a strategy and were able to maximize return on investment to that extent. Finally the relationship between Current assets and Current liabilities has to converge to the advantage of business in terms of return on investment. **Table 85** presents the impact of positive and negative working capital:

Table 85

IMPACT OF POSITIVE AND NEGATIVE WORKING CAPITAL

(1)	Current Assets Greater than Current Liabilities.	Net Working Capital is Positive.	◆ Long-term funding of Short-term uses. ◆ Low Risk ◆ Low Return ◆ Long-term funding relatively more expensive. ◆ Cost of funding therefore increases and R.O.I. decreases.
(2)	Current Assets Lower than Current Liabilities.	Net Working Capital is Negative.	◆ Short-term Funding of Long-term uses ◆ High risk. ◆ Cost of funding decreases and R.O.I. increases.

EXAMPLE 10:
LEASING

In the aviation industry, airlines use leasing as a strategy to maximize return on investment. Airline business is capital, cost, competition and control intensive. As a result returns on investment are relatively poor except in the case of few airlines like Singapore Airlines, British Airways, Cathay Pacific which are regarded as profit paragons of the airline business. Even theses airlines face problems from time to time. Hence, to keep the organization lean and mean, the entrepreneurs in airline business prefer to lease aircrafts rather than buy them. In airline business and in other businesses too, productivity of capital is well sustained not by ownership of assets (fixed or current) but by intense operation (active utilisation) of assets. In India, for a very long period Jet Airways continued to be in business through a fleet of leased aircrafts. The annual report of Jet Airways for the period ending 31st March, 2010 indicates various kinds of arrangements for having control over use of aircrafts, *viz.*, finance leases, hire purchases, operating leases (dry and wet leases).

Similarly Kingfisher Airlines is into several lease and hire purchase agreements. This bear testimony to the role of leasing as a financial strategy.

From time to time globally, airlines fall into a debt trap and face a severe cash crunch. In such a distress situation to salvage the business and also sustain the return on investment, airlines venture into what is known as a '***sale and lease back***' agreement. Sale of aircraft/s eases the liquidity position while lease back ensures continuity of business. Thus, businesses adopt different approaches to sustain the productivity of capital and protect their competitive edge as far as possible.

In the above cited cases the concerned airlines enjoyed the benefits of leased assets and were in a position to raise, on a relative basis, the productivity of business. Since the denominator in the formula of return on capital employed was diluted *ab initio*, the question of bearing the burden of capital intensive denominator *per se* in the ROCE did not arise. The said companies levered the benefits of leasing, as a financial strategy, to keep the ROCE under control.

EXAMPLE 11:

Table 86

COLGATE-PALMOLIVE

COLGATE-PALMOLIVE (INDIA) LIMITED – FINANCIALS			
	2000-01 *Base Year*	*2004-05*	*2009-10*
Sales (%)	100	91	172
Net Profit After Tax (%)	100	179	671
Total Assets (%)	100	101	131
Share Capital (%)	100	100	10
Reserves and Surplus (%)	100	111	304

Considering the financial health of Colgate Palmolive India Ltd. for the three years shown above and using 2000-01 as a base year, it can be seen that upto 2004-05 though sales have declined by 9% profit after tax has gone up by 79%. Again, total assets and share capital have remained static, the reserves and surplus have increased by 11%. Thus, productivity of capital is maintained by reduction in sales and increase in net profit after tax. Extending the analysis to the year 2009-10, sales have increased by 72% while net profit after tax has gone up by 571% with total assets increasing only marginally by 31%. For the said same years 2000-01 Vs. 2009-10, the reserves and surplus have increased by 204% as against a mind boggling decline in share capital of 90%. Thus, we have a dynamic return on equity model where the rate of increase in profit after tax outstrips the rate of increase in sales by leaps and bounds and the rate of decline in share capital from the index of 100 in 2000-01 to 10 in 2009-10. is rather mind-boggling. In the same period reserves have increased from an index of 100 in the base year to 304 in the year 2009-10. In 2009-10, the all-round productivity of Colgate-Palmolive India includes the following increases:

Sales to ₹ 2025 crores by 15%; net profit after tax to ₹ 423 crores by 46%; total assets to ₹ 331 crores by 50% and reserves to ₹ 313 crores by 54.2%. These increases were in the wake of a massive decrease in share capital by 90%.

Certain Myths about Productivity:

(1) More sales do not mean more profit. According to 2009 Fortune 100 companies General Motors and Ford enjoyed a 3rd and 7th rank respectively for sales. However both the companies had huge losses and they are placed at rank 98 and 100 respectively in the profit ranking.

(2) More sales are not required to make more profit. Thus, Pfizer which has a 39th rank in sales is ranked as 5th in profit and Microsoft which has a 49th rank in sales enjoys a 10th rank in profit.

(3) Some companies are able to match their prowess in sales with their rank in profits. In the said year Exxon mobile was ranked 2nd in sales and first in profit. Similarly Citi Group could get 8th rank in revenues and an elevated 2nd rank in profits.

Productivity of Pfizer and Exxon mobil make interesting reading as shown in **Table 87**:

Table 87

PFIZER vs. EXXON

		USD Mn.
	REVENUE	*PROFIT*
Pfizer *(A)*	52415	19337
Exxon Mobile *(B)*	347254	39500
A as % of *B*	15	48

Pfizer is able to make 48% of profit with just 15% of revenue of Exxon.

EXAMPLE 12:

IMPERIAL CHEMICAL INDUSTRIES (INDIA) LTD. (ICI)

A look into the Annual Report of ICI gives insights into the business strategies and their financial implications, as reflected through financial statements shown in Table 88:

Table 88

ICI – FINANCIALS

6 yrs. ending 2004	*(₹ in Crores)*
Profit before Tax	301
Exceptional Items Profit	298
Provision for Tax	107
Post Tax Profit	492
Dividend	200
Loan Amortisation	109
Cash Surplus even after Loan Amortisation (since 2000)	229
Debt (since 1999)	NIL
Debt/Equity (since 2000)	Negative
Working Capital (since 2003)	Negative

The picture is very clear. The company enjoyed a debt free situation since 1999. The debt-equity was reported negative. Further the working capital defined as current assets minus current liabilities was also negative and placed at ₹ 48 crores for the year 2003. The negative working capital continued to be negative for the years 2004-2006. As a result of the above the assets profile of the company underwent change in 2006 as against 2003 as shown below:

Table 89

ICI – FINANCIALS

	2003	*%*	*2006*	*%*
	(₹ in Crores)	*In Total Assets*	*(₹ in Crores)*	*In Total Assets*
Net Fixed Assets	187	30	145	21
Investments	200	33	253	36
Current Asset	228	37	296	43
Total	**615**	**100**	**694**	**100**

It can be seen that investment as a % of Total Assets has gone up to 36%, while that of Net Fixed Assets reduced to 21%. The rate of increase in investment is 27% for a company which had reasonably high Net Fixed Assets in 1999. The business strategy was to increase investment outside the company *per se* but within the umbrella of ICI group. This strategy helped the company to become lean and mean. VRS was the key to this and the substantial reduction in staff due to the hiving off of divisions bear testimony to the same. Inspite of the hiving off of divisions, the sales of ICI have shown a 20% increase while reaching to ₹ 993 crores over the 8 years ending 2006. The long-term liabilities on account of obligations towards employees were funded through long-term one time cash flows made possible through sale of divisions. The extinction of obligations was ₹ 294 crores and the funding of the same order came, to reiterate, from sale of divisions. In the same period though increase in sales was meagre 20%, the extent of increase in profit was mindboggling 95% over the said 8 years ending 2006. The surplus which emerged on account of sale of divisions was used to extinguish obligations to employees and repayment of debt. Further cash surpluses were used to pay 325% dividend for the 3 years ending 2004. This amounted to ₹ 41 crores in 2002 and 2003 each year and ₹ 51 crores in 2004. The total dividend paid is of the order ₹ 133 crores. ICI situation is interesting – today it has no debt to be paid, minimal staff, initial capital of ₹ 41 crores more than fully recouped-3 times; in fact recouped umpteen times. The company is totally free of any responsibility whatsoever. The company is mean and lean in the true sense of the term. Thus ICI as a foreign investor can walk away with their realizations at market prices as soon as possible.

EXAMPLE 13:

BHARAT FORGE LTD.

Annual Report 2005-06 presents the financial structure of the company as shown in Table 90:

Table 90

BHARAT FORGE LTD. – FINANCIAL STRUCTURE

Loans Repaid (Long-Term)	*₹ in Millions*
9.25% Redeemable secured Non-Convertible Debentures	100
Foreign Currency Term Loan (secured loan)	112
Rupee Term Loan (secured loan) from Banks	53
Public Deposits (unsecured loans)	77
Foreign Currency/Rupee Demand Loans from Banks	628
TOTAL	**970**
Unsecured Loans Raised	
0.5% Convertible Foreign Currency Bonds (CFCB)	4,752
Short-term finance for import of goods by buyers line of credit	111
Pre-shipment Packing Credit from Banks	68
TOTAL	**4,931**

This obviously reduced the cost of finance for the company but more than that it released charge on assets of the company because it repaid "***secured loans***" whereas Foreign Currency Convertible Bonds was an unsecured loan. Taking a step further, it repaid 0% Interest Sales Tax Package Loan of ₹ 43.86 millions and obtained a discount on early repayment of loan which was a "***capital profit***"

Even on the share capital side company used three different instruments to generate huge funds (though not immediately required for business operations, but certainly keeping in mind future business acquisitions) by taking advantage of a booming capital market.

(1) Global Depository Receipts (GDR).
(2) Right issue at substantial Premium in October 2004.
(3) Conversion of Detachable Warrants which were issued alongwith rights shares at hefty premiums, i.e., ₹ 266/- per share of ₹ 2/-.

In this manner company generated ₹ 6946 million extra money by way of share premium for increase in share capital of ₹ 49 million only! No wonder at first it repaid 9.5% Redeemable Cumulative Non-convertible Preference shares of ₹ 100 million.

To top it up the company converted **Foreign Currency Convertible Bonds (FCCB)** at a premium of ₹ 334/- per share of ₹ 2/- face value into equity capital with almost negligible cost of finance for ever. This *modus operandi* of the company clearly indicates strategic approach to funding decisions with least constraints.

EXAMPLE 14:

NICHOLAS PIRAMAL INDUSTRIES LTD. (NPIL)

Financial strength was created by disposing off landed property of some of the acquired pharma companies and that money was pumped into the flagship company Nicholas Piramal India Ltd. But many of the subsequent acquisitions were carried out by issuance of equity shares, without losing control over the business. NPIL has sizable Redeemable Preference Share capital of ₹ 53.37 crores (even more than equity share capital of the company) at just 5%-6% rate of dividend.

NPIL used convertible share warrants as well as right shares that it alloted in Sept.'05 at hefty premium of ₹ 173 for ₹ 2 face value equity share. NPIL also raised USD 15 million (Rupee equivalent 67 crores) as External Commercial Borrowing (ECB) from two foreign banks at cheap rate and repaid unsecured loans, totalling ₹ 115 crores, which were costly domestic loans.

EXHIBIT 63

VALUE DRIVERS ECONOMIC ROAD MAP

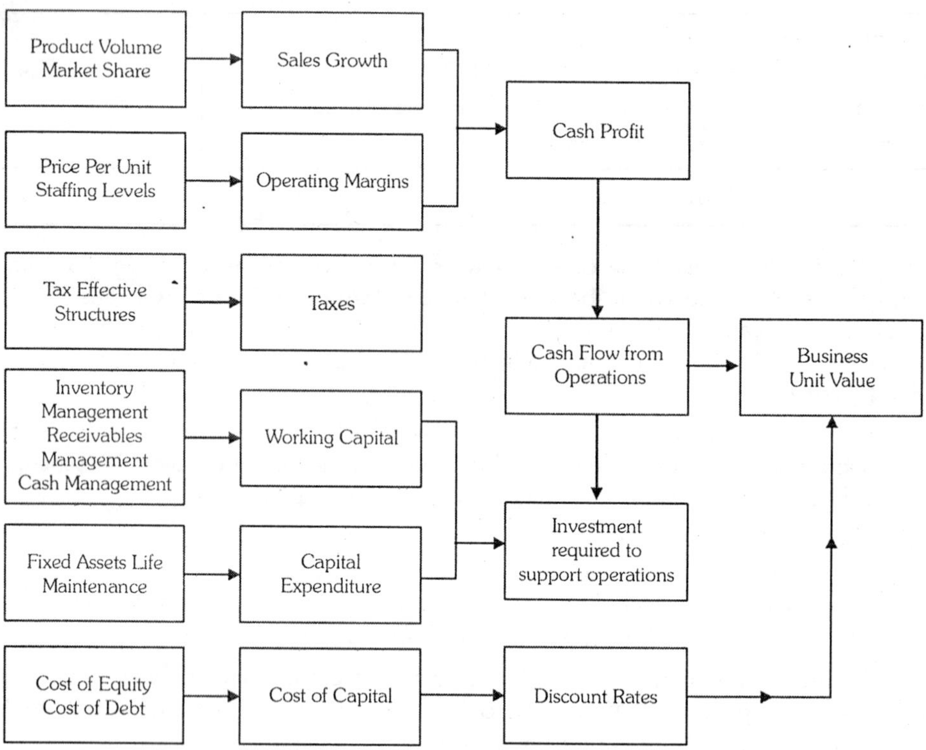

***Exhibit 63** presents the value drivers map for any business the end objective to continuously improve the value of the business through continuous maximisation of the result resource ratio. In financial parlance this amounts to return on investments defined as profit divided by investment. The numerator is derived from the income statement and the denominator from the balance sheet. The objective of business can be achieved by maximising ROI on a book profit or cash profit basis. Both are tenable, viable and acceptable as a reliable measure of performance. Most of the options listed above have been explored in the course of of this work. Another road map showing the components which drive the value of any organisation, in terms of a specific brand of ROI, viz., ROE, is presented in **Exhibit 64**.*

Right issue resulted in ₹ 3.8 crores increase in equity share capital and added ₹ 328.9 crores to Reserves. Right shares issued in F.Y. 05-06 at high premium brought down Weighted Average Cost of capital (both Debt as well as Equity taken together) substantially. At the same time the company invested a fresh ₹ 460 crore in Fixed Assets that gave an advantage to the company in tax saving through depreciation on assets. Company also part financed additional requirement of working capital of ₹ 88 crores necessitated by growth in business.

EXHIBIT 64

VALUE DRIVERS OF ROE (%)

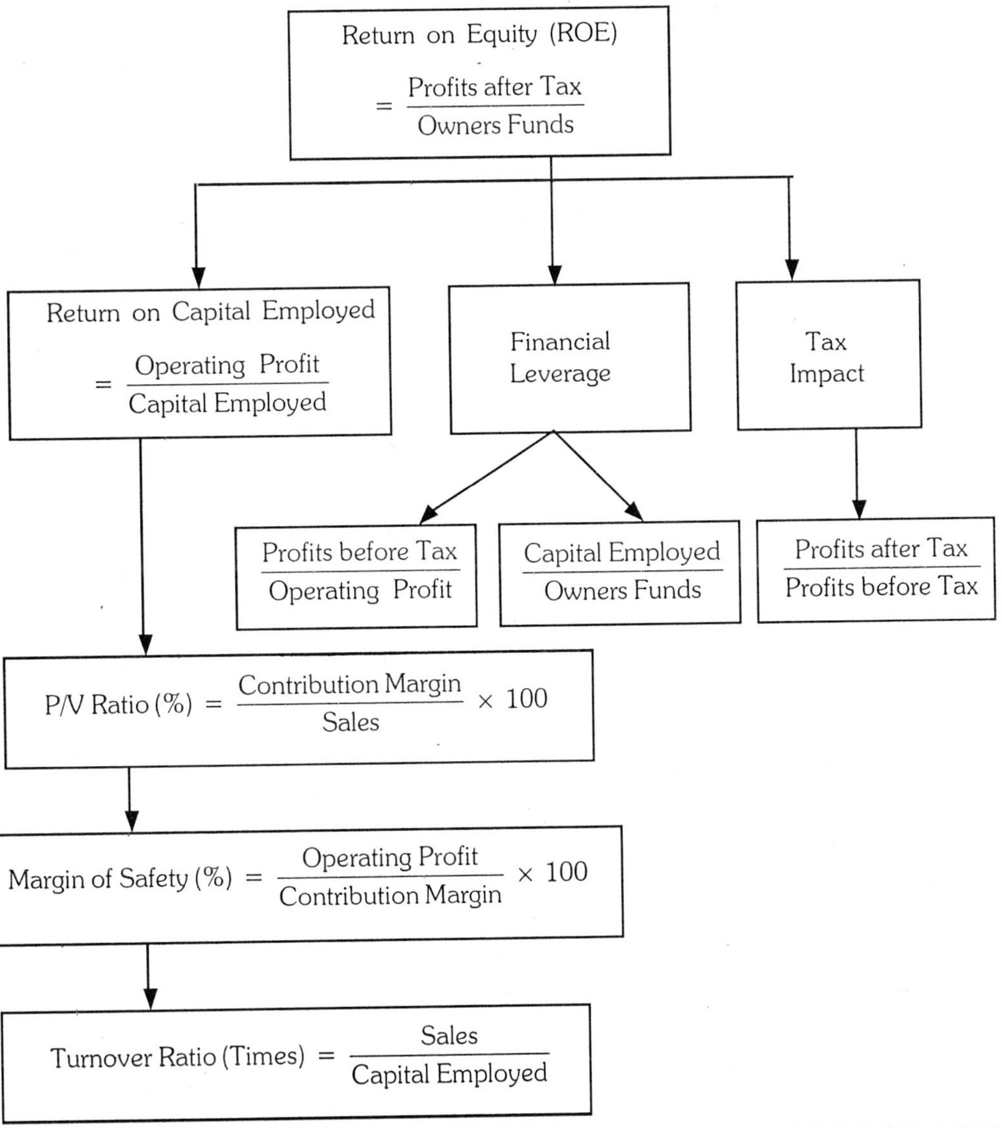

Table 91

MANAGEMENT OF PRODUCTIVITY

MARUTI SUZUKI LTD. – FINANCIALS

TABLE A

	Sales Volume Nos.	*Sales ₹ (Cr.)*	*PAT ₹ (Cr.)*	*Total Assets ₹ (Cr.)*	*Profit Margin %*	*Assets Turnover Ratio (Times)*	*Return on Total Assets %*
2007-08	764842	17860	1731	9486	9.69	1.88	18.24
2008-09	792167	20358	1219	10199	5.99	2.00	11.95
2009-10	1018365	28958	2498	12793	8.63	2.26	19.52

SOURCE: *Maruti Suzuki Ltd. – Annual Reports 2007-08 to 2009-10*

TABLE B

INDEX NOS. USING 2007-08=100

	Sales Volume Nos.	*Sales*	*PAT*	*Realisation per Vehicle*
2007-08	100	100	100	100
2008-09	104	114	.70	110
2009-10	133	160	144	121

TABLE C

AS % TO NET SALES	*2007-08*	*2008-09*	*2009-10*
Total Manufacturing Cost	91.3	97.1	91.6
Other Income (Cost recovery)	(–) 5.0	(–) 4.9	(–) 4.0
NET COST	86.3	92.2	87.6
PBT	14.0	8.2	12.40
PAT	9.7	6.0	8.60

TABLE D

	% increase in Volume	*% increase in small car segment (A2 – Class)*	*% increase in high value car segment (C – Class)*	*% increase in Sales*	*% increase in PAT*
2008-09	4			14	(–)30
2009-10	29	23.8	30.8	60	74
2010-11	24.8	27.7	45	24.6	(–)8.4

The Tables alongside about Maruti Suzuki Ltd. (MSL) provides useful insights into the management of the productivity of capital.

TABLE A: Return On Total Assets (ROTA) has gone up from 18.24% in 2007-08 to 19.52% in 2009-10. 2008-09 which was the year of global meltdown, an international recession of the worst type, since 1930, saw ROTA decline to 11.95%. The ROTA at MSL is well balanced between the two key parameters, *viz.*, profit margin (%) and the assets turnover ratio (times). The margins which reflect the productivity of every rupee of sales was high at 9.69% in 2007-08 and dropped to 8.63% in 2009-10. 2008-09 saw margins decline substantially to 5.99%. The company has managed to improve its utilization of assets steadily over the years from 1.88 times (2007-08) to 2.26 times (2009-10), though during the same period the total assets have increased from ₹ 9,486 crores to ₹ 12,793 crores, i.e., by 34%. Automobile industry is capital intensive and yet such an increase in asset turnover speaks volume about the management of market shares of different products by MSL. It may be pointed out that for the three years ending 2009-10. Tata Motors Ltd., had a turnover ratio (Sales/Capital Employed) of 2.33, 1.12 and 1.22 times only. Considering that capital employed excludes current liabilities this ratio of sales/total assets or total liabilities for Tata Motors for the said period would have been lower. Thus, managing the productivity of total assets in MSL, is reasonably well balanced between Profit margin and Assets turnover ratio.

TABLE B: For the three years indicated in Table B which shows 2007-08 as the base year the sales volume has gone up by 33% for the three years ending 2009-10 and the sales realization (value) has gone up by 60% for the same period. Further, the profit after tax has increased by 44% during the three years ending 2009-10. Even during the abnormal year 2008-09 sales volume went up by 4% and sales value increased by 14%. However, the profit after tax went down by 30%. Table B also shows realization per vehicle which is increasing steadily at 10% per annum for the three years ending 2009-10. The productivity of MSL is interesting because in 2008-09, a 4% increase in sales volume brings in a 14% increase in sales value coupled with a 10% increase in realization (₹) per vehicle. Further in 2009-10, a 29% increase in sales volume brings about a 46% increase in sales and once again a 10% increase in realization (₹) per vehicle. This shows the marketing productivity of MSL, thanks to the product mix strategy quantified and presented in Table D.

TABLE C: shows the cost productivity at MSL. Over the three years ending 2009-10, manufacturing cost has gone up marginally by 0.8%. Of course, during the year 2008-09 the cost productivity has not shown much improvement. In fact the cost as a % of net sales has gone up by more than 5%.

TABLE D: The company has gradually increased the share of high value cars in total sales, i.e., more than the overall average growth in per cent in number of vehicles sold which were giving higher profit per vehicle thus leading to higher average realisation (₹) per vehicle.

The four Tables read in conjunction with each other and one another *inter se* shows the relationship between sales volume (vehicles), sales value (₹), product mix strategy and the profits using resource productivity management as a tool. Resources include different niche markets, selling price management, sales volume, cost productivity and capital utilization and levels of capital deployed into business. Thus in financial management parlance the tables show the cost, volume, profit and product mix and assets relationship and their impact on the bottom line of the business.

⊙⊙⊙

21

ECONOMIC VALUE ADDED (EVA)

***N.B.:** EVA had been marketed by Stern Steward and Company. In fact, they have acquired the patent on the expression EVA and its modus operandi.*

EXHIBIT 65

EVA AT QUAKER OATS

In Quaker Oats business segments were evaluated on the basis of quarterly profits. The managers developed a myopic view of reporting profit performance and therefore, started offering sharp discounts to boost quarterly sales. In response, retailers placed huge orders and there was a sudden, sharp, surge in quarterly production. This resulted in trade loading which in turn blocked funds in current assets (working capital). In anticipation of huge orders, purchase department bought large quantity of boxes, plastic wrappers, granola and chocolate chips. Fifteen Quaker warehouses were full. The overheads associated with purchase and storage of packing materials were borne by headquarters making segment managers feel that the service of buying and storage was bereft of any cost. However, the hidden cost of holding huge packing materials had a toll on the bottom line of Quaker Oats.

Enter EVA - many things happened: trade loading was cancelled; production was smoothened and linked with sales and inventory build-up was monitored. Thus, Quaker's Danville plant reduced inventories from 15 USD million to 9 USD million. Quaker's has closed one-third of it's 15 warehouses, saving 6 USD million annually in salaries and capital costs.

EVA, which is not a new discovery, is an estimate of true economic profit after making corrective adjustments to GAAP accounting, including deducting the opportunity cost of equity capital. EVA can be measured as Net Operating Profit After Taxes but before interest (NOPAT) less the cost of capital. NOPAT thus represents the total pool of profits available on an ungeared basis to provide a return to lenders and shareholders. EVA can also be viewed as a variant of an accounting performance measure called residual income which is defined as 'operating profit subtracted with capital charge.' The recognition of a charge for equity capital transforms traditional accounting earnings into residual income. General Electric coined the term residual income in the 1950s and David Solomons (1965) later popularised it when he argued for the measure as a divisional

EXHIBIT 66

EVA DEFINED

As defined by ***Alfred Marshall,***

"EVA is a measure of economic profit. It is wealth created by a firm after accounting for the cost of capital employed in business."

*Again, Alfred Marshall defined economic profit as "**What remains of his (the owners or managers) profits after deducting interest on his capital at the current rate may be called his earnings undertaking or management.**"*

SOURCE: Principles of Economics, Volume – I, New York, Macmillan and Company, 1890, p. 142.

*EVA is defined by Peter Drucker as "**Until a business returns a profit that is greater than its cost of capital, it operates at a loss. Never mind that it pay taxes as if it had a genuine profit. The enterprise still returns less to the economy than it devours in resources .... Until then it does not create wealth; it destroys it.**"*

Traditional approaches to measuring "Shareholders' Value Creation" have used parameters such as earnings capitalization, market capitalization and present value of estimated future cash flows. Extensive equity research has now established that it is not earnings per se, but VALUE which is important. A new measure called 'Economic Value Added" (EVA) is increasingly being applied to understand and evaluate financial performance. (HUL, Annual report, 2010-11, p. 111)

performance measure. The concept, however, has been around much longer. Hamilton (1777) recognised as far back as the 1770s that one could calculate a merchant's gain only after deducting from his gross profits an interest charge on his stock. Alfred Sloan, the legendary leader of General Motors, implemented an EVA like system in 1920s. Finnish academics and finance experts identified residual income as a complementary tool to ROI. EVA can be termed as the quest for value where value is defined as the excess of operating excellence after adjusting for opportunity cost (interest cost) of resources (capital) employed to produce those results. The amortization of goodwill or capitalization of brand advertising and other similar adjustments are the translations that occur to 'Economic Profit' to make it EVA. EVA is the wealth created by a business over and above the cost of capital deployed in business and represents Real profit versus Paper profit. Since economic wealth created is the operating excellence after accounting for interest on capital employed, EVA trains managers not to think of capital entrusted as a free resource. EVA underlies shareholder value and is increasingly the main target of leading companies' strategies. Shareholders are players who provide the firm with its capital; they invest to gain a return on that capital. The concept of EVA is well established in economic theory, as elucidated by Alfred Marshall, but only recently has the term moved into the mainstream of corporate finance, as more and more firms adopt it as the base for business planning and performance monitoring. There is growing evidence that EVA, not earnings, determines the value of a firm. Effective use of capital is the key to value - this message applies to business processes, too.

EVA – SALIENT FEATURES

- EVA measures the status of the wealth of shareholders. So long as the earnings are greater than the cost of capital there is value addition to the stock of wealth of a business and *vice versa*.

- For companies which are listed on the stock exchange, the market prices for shares are readily available. Hence, there is another concept known as Market Value Added (MVA). If the total market value of a company is greater than the amount of capital invested in it, the company has managed to create wealth for the shareholders. In the same vein, if the market value of the shares of a company is less than the capital employed the company has destroyed shareholders wealth to that extent. Thus, MVA is the difference between companies market value of shares and book value of shares or market value added equals company's total market value – capital invested.
- There is a strong correlation between EVA and market prices of shares and further with market capitalisation, e.g., AT & T, Coca-Cola, Godrej *et al.* In the eighties when Coca-Cola introduced EVA in its business, the Coca-Cola stock prices increased from \$3 to over \$60. Again, in 1995, Coca-Cola investors received \$8.63 wealth for every dollar they invested.
- EVA is a single value-based measure and helps to evaluate the performance of an enterprise and provides early warning signals regarding wealth creation or wealth destruction in the business.
- EVA helps managers to divest value decreasing activity and redeploy capital so released into activities that can contribute to the shareholders wealth.
- Every activity of an enterprise need not necessarily contribute to shareholders wealth directly. For example, investments in high-tech apparatus to ensure that the environment is not polluted may not add to shareholders value immediately. However, the image of the company and its long run sustainability is ensured. Hence, shareholders worth creation is hemmed in the short run, by such apparent constraints.
- EVA sets managerial performance targets and helps to develop reward system. Rewards are driven by the ability of managers to convert capital invested into profits in an effective and efficient manner.
- EVA provides better direction and motivation to avoid dysfunctional behavior and incongruent decision making in comparison with return on investment.
- EVA unlike budgeting focuses on ends and not means. Managers usually have the discretion and a free hand to employ creative and innovative methods to improve the long run economic health of a business. EVA does help in avoiding potential dysfunctional short-term behavior.
- EVA rewards – bonuses, promotions, incentives are usually give at the end of stipulated periods, three years or so. This helps to ensure consistent medium/long-term approach to value addition and value creation management processes. It certainly avoids myopic short-term profit making approaches and facilitates development of positive mindsets among employees toward long run sustainable value addition and wealth creation.
- EVA is not without flaws. EVA may also lead to a parochial interest of individuals or segments to dominate over other important considerations like customer satisfaction or overall organizational interest.

EXHIBIT 67

HOW EVA PROMOTES VALUE MAXIMISING BEHAVIOUR?

Consider an IT investment which requires a ₹ 50,000 investment with return of ₹ 8,000 in non-quantifiable benefits. The ROI is 16% {8,000/50,000} and is above the cost of capital say (12%). The EVA is Net Benefits minus the cost of the capital employed, i.e., ₹ 8,000 – {12% of ₹ 50,000} = ₹ 2,000. Another way of calculating EVA in this case is the excess of the efficiency over the cost of capital employed multiplied by the capital employed. Thus,

(ROI % – Cost of Capital %) × Capital Employed

= (16% – 12%) × ₹ 50,000 = 4% × ₹ 50,000 = ₹ 2,000

Thus, EVA promotes value maximising behaviour among corporate managers. It's a single value brand measure that is intended to evaluate the actions of management leading to maximising long-term wealth.

DRIVERS OF EVA – 4Ms

As a mnemonic device, Stern Stewart describes four main applications of EVA with four words beginning with the letter 'M', *viz.*, Measurement, Management System, Motivation and Mindset.

MEASUREMENT

EVA is regarded as a measure of corporate performance over any given period. Fortune Magazine had called it "today's hot financial idea". EVA reflects the demands of an emerging changing knowledge society.

MANAGEMENT SYSTEM

EVA is a holistic measure embracing all segments of business and the drivers of those segments including planning, organizing and control. EVA as a measure gives companies a better focus on how they are performing. However, it's true value comes by using it as the basis of a comprehensive financial management system that encompasses all the policies, procedures, methods and measures that guide management operations and strategy. EVA system covers the entire gamut of managerial decisions, including strategic management, allocating capital, pricing, acquisitions or divestitures, setting annual goals and even day to day operating decisions. Continuous maximisation of EVA is one of the important objectives of modern business.

MOTIVATION

To instil both a sense of urgency and also a long-term perspective of an owner, Stern Stewart designs cash bonus plans that cause managers to blend their goals with those of the organisation. Bonuses are functionally related to EVA. This is the greatest motivation in the EVA system. Under an EVA bonus plan, the only way managers can make more money for themselves is by creating, continuously, greater value for shareholders. Bonuses then have no ceilings as such. Shareholders wealth maximisation coincides with managers' maximisation of their total take home pay kit (personal wealth maximisation).

MINDSET

EVA financial management and incentive compensation system inducts a new corporate culture with an overriding common interest with confluence of goals between stakeholders (owners and managers) and also between managers *inter se*. EVA becomes a common language across the network of business. Thus, through EVA communication and cooperation among divisions and departments is facilitated. Further, it links strategic planning with the operating divisions and leaves little room for mistrust between line management and the finance function. The EVA model is a governance framework within which all employees are adequately provoked in favour of self-actualisation and also enacting themselves in the best interest of the business. In addition, EVA is a tool which facilitates decentralisation and helps to evolve organisational structures which act as 'key to performance'. The resources, initiatives and capabilities of people are unleashed to propel individuals and groups to higher and higher levels of performance.

Thus, in the EVA system, there are four ways to increase value, *viz.*:

(1) OPERATE: Improve the returns earned on existing capital.

(2) BUILD: Invest so long as returns exceed the minimum acceptable rate of return (cost of capital).

(3) HARVEST: Divest capital when returns fail to meet minimum acceptable rate of return.

(4) OPTIMIZE: Reduce cost of capital by evolving an optimal capital structure.

STRATEGIES FOR INCREASING EVA

- Increase the return on existing projects – improve operating performance – one level of excellence to another, higher level, through '***stretch goals***'.
- Invest in new projects that have a return greater than the minimum acceptable rate of return.
- Use less capital to achieve the same return – improve ratio of output to input or input to output or manage to increase output and reduce input.
- Continuous reduction in cost of capital by ingenious management of the financing mix.*
- Divest from activities where inadequate returns are being earned.

ADVANTAGES OF EVA

EVA is also positioned and used as a motivational tool with focus on compensation-based reward penalty system that stimulates business activity. In addition it creates a sense of responsibility and accountability across the echelons of management. It is reported by the Stern Stewart group that companies which have adopted EVA have a higher market capitalisation than those who have not adopted EVA.

Several advantages claimed for EVA are:

- EVA eliminates economic distortions due to GAAP and focuses on real economic results.
- EVA provides for better assessment of decisions that affect financial statements.
- EVA bonus plans are not unitised with budgetary targets.
- EVA covers all aspects of the business cycle.
- EVA promotes goal directed behaviour and provides for better alignment and quick decision making. Team work and communication are relatively more effective.

DIFFERENCE BETWEEN EVA AND OTHER TOOLS

- The main differences between EVA, earnings per share, return on assets and discounted cash flow, the most common calculations, as measures of performance are as follows: Earnings per share tells nothing about the cost of generating those profits. If the cost of

---

**See Reliance Industries Ltd. explained as a role model in this behalf in Dr. Prasanna Chandra, Financial Management Theory and Practice, Fifth Edition, Tata McGraw Hill Publishing Company, pp. 466-467.*

capital (loans, bonds, equity) is, say, 15 per cent, then a 14 per cent earning is actually a reduction, not a gain, in economic value. Profits also increase taxes, thereby reducing cash flow. Renowned investor Warren Buffett calls these "owner's earnings": real cash flow after all taxes, interest and other obligations have been paid.

- Return on assets is a more realistic measure of economic performance, but it ignores the cost of capital. In its most profitable year, for instance, IBM's return on assets was over 11 per cent, but its cost of capital was almost 13 per cent. Leading firms can obtain capital at low costs, via favourable interest rates and high stock prices, which they can then invest in their operations at decent rates of return on assets. That tempts them to expand without paying attention to the real return, economic value added.
- EVA takes into account the cost of capital employed and hence it can be said that discounted cash flow is very close to economic value added, with the discount rate being the cost of capital.

LIMITATIONS OF EVA

EVA also has its critics. Stern Stewart study is the only public study available. Similar studies are required to justify the use (or otherwise) of EVA as a powerful financial management system it is claimed to be. In particular,

- EVA does not account for plants or divisions on the basis of size.
- EVA is based on financial accounting which is a game tool with which accountants always play.
- EVA can be myopic and pay attention to short run rather than medium and long-term welfare of business. Creativity and innovation can take a backseat.
- EVA does not add value beyond the historic financial information.
- Given the emphasis of EVA on segment performance, it may not always contribute to the paramount interest of the organisation and all its subsets evenly.

EXHIBIT 68

EVA: DEFINITION

=	The financial benefits accruing to a business out of the capital invested, *viz.*, Net Operating Profit After Tax. (NOPAT)	LESS	The charge on capital, i.e., ($k_o \times c$), where, k_o = Cost of Capital c = Capital Invested in Business, i.e., Owners Funds PLUS Long-term Debt

EVA FORMULA

EVA	=	NOPAT (A)	—	Capital Employed (B) × Weighted Average Cost of Capital (C)
EVA	= {	A	—	(B × C) }

(A) After Tax Operating Profit is referred to as NOPAT, i.e., Net Operating Profit After Tax.

- Profit concept tries to capture operating excellence [EBIT] on a post-tax basis.
- Taxes have to be measured with respect to operating profit [EBIT].

(B) Capital Employed (CE) = Either Owners Funds + Long-term Liabilities OR = Net Fixed Assets + Net Working Capital.

(C) Weighted Average Cost of Capital (Simple Computation)

$(k_o) = k_e (W_1) + k_i (W_2)$

Where, k_e = Cost of Equity

K_i = Tax Adjusted Cost of Debt

W_1 = Proportion of Equity to Total Capital

W_2 Proportion of Debt to Total Capital

$W_1 + W_2$ = 100% or unity OR

(D) Weighted Average Cost of Capital (WACC) using Capital Asset Pricing Model (CAPM) with details regarding Beta computation.

If WACC using CAPM is used then the formula is as follows:

Weighted Average Cost of Capital (k_o)

$= k_e (W_1) + k_i (W_2)$

Where k_e = Required return on the equity of the company

$= R_f + b_e (R_m - R_f)$

and R_f = Risk Free Rate

β_e = Beta of the Equity of a Company*

R_m = Expected return on the Market Portfolio

K_i = Tax adjusted cost of debt = $(1\text{-}t)\ i$

$= (1\text{-}t)\ i$

W_1 = Proportion of equity capital to total capital

W_2 = Proportion of debt capital to total capital

$W_1 + W_2$ = 1 (unity) = 100%

WHAT IS BETA (β)

β is a quantified measure of the risk of investing in a share. Risk refers to hazard, peril, exposure to loss or injury, a chance that some unfavourable event may occur (may not occur too). Equity returns tend to be volatile. Hence their standard deviations are also high. Treasury Bills rate have a relatively low rate of return and hence a low standard deviation. However, risk and uncertainty are different. Risk means possibility of loss or injury and uncertainty means the quality or state of mind of being uncertain or in doubt. Risks in the context of Beta include two types of risks, *viz.*, diversifiable risks and market risks.

Diversifiable risks are those which can be handled through alteration in portfolio patterns. This is within the domain of the investor *per se* and controllable to that extent. Diversifiable Risks are also known as company specific or unsystematic risks. CAPM establishes the relationship between Risks and Return. Diversifiable risks can be eliminated. Hence, it is not of much concern.

β of the equity of a company is available on* ***www.bseindia.com/about/abindices/betavalues.asp**. The site provides the β, for the 30 scrips that are BSE index. Annual reports of companies which compute EVA provides all details regarding the computation of EVA alongwith the details of inputs required which includes, inter alia, the company specific, financial year specific, beta.*

Market risks reflect the risk of a general stock market decline and cannot be managed through diversification. Market risks are of great concern. However, assets which have market risks require a higher rate of return to compensate for the extra risks associated. Risk aversion has to be adequately subsidized to motivate risk averters and also keep risk takers adequately compensated for the risks taken.

BETA

β reflects a coefficient of correlation/variation which quantifies the tendency of stock to move up or down with the market.

β can have a value as shown in **Table 92**

Table 92
INTERPRETATION OF BETA

β	*Nature of Risk*	*Interpretation*
1	Average	Market ↑ by 10 % Stocks ↑ by 10 % and Market ↓ by 10% Stocks ↓ by 10%
2	Above Average	Market ↑ by 10% Stocks ↑ by 20% and further if Market ↓ by 10% Stocks ↓ by 20%
0.5	Less than Average	Market ↑ by 10% Stocks ↓ by 5% Stock is only half as volatile, compared to average stock volatility

An average risk stock is defined as "one that tends to move up and down in line with the general market as measured by some index Dow Jones Industrials or S & P 500. Such a stock will, *by definition*, be assigned a beta, β, of 1.0, which indicates that, in general, if the market moves up by 10 per cent, the stock will also move up by 10 per cent, while if the market falls by 10 per cent, the stock will likewise fall by 10 per cent. A portfolio of such β = 1.0 stocks will move up and down with the broad market averages and it will be just as risky as the averages.*

E. F. Brigham and J. K. Houston, Fundamentals of Financial Management Thomson, Third Edition, 2004, pp. 189-190

Table 93

ILLUSTRATIVE LIST OF β COEFFICIENTS

STOCK	*BETA*
Merrill Lynch	1.85
AOL Time Warner	1.65
General Electric	1.30
Microsoft Corp.	1.20
IBM	1.05
Coca-Cola	0.85
Energen Corp.	0.75
Procter and Gamble	0.65
Heinz	0.55
FPL Group	0.45

SOURCE: *Adapted from Value Line 2002 (See-Fundamentals of Financial Management, E. Brigham and J. Houstan, Thompson South Western, 2004, p. 191).*

In India the beta values are computed and duly disclosed through the database of the BSE. **Table 94** titled as Beta, R^2, Volatility and Returns of SENSEX Scrips presents the data for One Year Period (October 2010 to September 2011). The Beta values are available for the 30 scrips which comprise the BSE Index. The beta, for the period October, 2010 to September 2011 ranges from 1.81 (JAI PRA) to .60 (CIPLA). Of the 30 scrips 15 scrips have a b of greater than 1. The remaining 15 scrips have a β of less than 1, the lowest being 6. Thus, in computing the CAPM driven weighted average cost of capital b values from the published data can be used. The format of the data is illustrated below in **Table 94**:

Table 94

BSE – SENSEX SCRIPS – β AND OTHER VALUES

Scrip Code	*Company*	*Beta Values*	*Coefficient of Determination (R^2)*	*Avg. Daily Volatility (%)*	*Returns (1 Year) (%)*	*Weightage (%) in SENSEX as on 30/08/2011*	*Free-float Adj. Factor as on 30/08/2001*
500325	RELIANCE	1.05	0.56	1.73	–18.05%	10.76%	0.55
500209	ICICI Bank	1.31	0.63	2.04	–21.16%	7.46%	1
500209	INFOSYSLTD.	0.96	0.46	1.75	–16.68%	9.14%	0.85
500182	HEROMOTOCO	0.45	0.06	2.28	4.86%	1.43%	0.5

HOW TO CALCULATE WACC

(1) Calculate the cost of equity and debt.

(2) Market, as a whole, would demand an extra income to invest in risky non-contractual residual claims to corporate cash flows. This is the market premium.

(3) Company's specific risks over and above the market risk premium measuring the risk of company's stock relative to the market average is captured by the leveraged beta (β),

which is the ratio of the coefficient of variation of a company's stock prices compared to the market as a whole.

(4) The cost of equity, which is the risk free return R_f plus a company premium *(pxb)* is multiplied by beta to get the cost of equity. Thus, the cost of equity adjusted for beta is defined as

$$k_e = R_f + \beta\ (R_m - R_f)$$

Where k_e = Required return on the equity of the company

= $R_f + \beta_e\ (R_m - R_f)$

and R_f = Risk Free Rate

R_m = Expected return on the Market Portfolio

β_e = Beta of the Equity of a Company*

(5) The weighted cost of equity is thus defined as $(w_1 \times k_e)$ where w_1 = proportion of equity capital to total capital and k_e = cost of equity.

(6) Multiplying the cost of pre-tax cost of borrowing (1) with the retention rate (1-tax rate) gives tax-adjusted cost of debt. This is the weighted cost of debt.

(7) WACC is the sum of the weighted cost of equity plus the weighted cost of debt.

EVA IN H.L.L – A CASE STUDY

What does EVA show?

EVA is residual income after charging the company for the cost of capital provided by lenders and shareholders. It represents the value added to the shareholders by generating operating profits in excess of the cost of capital employed in the business.

When will EVA increase? EVA will increase if:

(a) Operating profits can be made to grow without employing more capital, i.e., greater efficiency.

(b) Additional capital is invested in projects that return more than the cost of obtaining new capital, i.e., profitable growth.

(c) Capital is curtailed in activities that do not cover the cost of capital, i.e., liquidation of unproductive capital assets.

(d) Operating leverage improves through capacity utilisation which is in excess of break-even capacity resulting in high margin of safety (sales much in excess of break-even point) Examples – electricity companies, hotels, shipping, steel, cement.

(e) Improved financial leverage which lowers the cost of capital to maximise investment opportunities – more and more of incremental investments with a positive Net Present Value when cash flows are discounted at the minimum acceptable rate of return.

(f) Price escalation is higher than cost increase – example – monopolistic situations when it prevailed – HUL, Glaxo. These companies enjoyed high market capitalisation and net profit with very low sales.

(g) Capital employed is low due to efficient use of current assets, leasing of fixed assets instead of owning them and extended credit facilities.

(h) Hiving off low profit or loss making businesses and reducing labour cost through voluntary retirement scheme.

β of the equity of a company is available on* ***www.bseindia.com/about/abindices/betavalues.asp**. The site provides the β, for the 30 scrips that are BSE index. Annual reports of companies which compute EVA provides all details regarding the computation of EVA alongwith the details of inputs required which includes, inter alia, the company specific, financial year specific, beta.*

Table 95

EVA in HUL 2005-06 to 2010-11

The relevant data for the above years is presented below:

					₹ *in Crores*
	2006	*2007*	*2008-09*	*2009-10*	*2010-11*
Average Debt	163	382	342	119	2
Average Equity	2515	2402	1928	2497	3118
Profit after tax, before exceptional items	1540	1743	2501	2103	2153
Interest	10	24	24	7	0

Other Information pertaining to 2006:

(1) Cost of debt is taken at the effective rate of interest applicable to an "AAA" rated company like HLL with an appropriate mix of short, medium and long-term debt, net of taxes. A pre tax rate of 8.90% for 2006 (5.10% for 2005) is considered after taking into account the trends over the years and market situations.

(2) Cost of Equity is the return expected by the investors to compensate them for the variability in returns caused by fluctuating earnings and share prices.

(3) Cost of Equity = Risk free return equivalent to yield on long-term Government Bonds (taken at 7.65% for 2006)

(+)

Market risk premium (taken at 9%) *(x)* Beta variant for the Company, (taken at 0.97) where Beta is a relative measure of risk association with the Company's shares as against the market as a whole. Thus HLL's cost of equity = 7.65% + 9% *(x)* 0.97 = 16.38%

(4) The profit before tax ₹ 1862 crores and provision for income tax ₹ 322 crores.

(5) Income Tax rate is 33%.

Given the above data compute the EVA for HUL for the year ended 31.03.2006.

N.B.: HUL uses the WACC based on the Capital Asset Pricing Model as shown in the following pages:

HOW TO COMPUTE NOPAT?* – ILLUSTRATION

Given the data in **Table 95** compute NOPAT.

Table 96

	₹
Earnings Before Interest and Tax (EBIT)	10
Less: Interest	(1)
Earnings After Interest and Before Tax (EAIBT)	9
Less: Income-Tax @ 30%	2.7
Earnings After Tax (EAT)	6.3

**NOPAT means Net Operating Profit After Tax. NOPAT is also expressed NOPLAT which means Net Operating Profit ot Loss After Tax*

Table 97

ALTERNATE METHODS OF COMPUTING NOPAT

Method 1

	₹
Earnings Before Interest and Tax	10
Less: Income-Tax @30%	3
Net Operating Profit After Tax (NOPAT)	7
NOPAT = EBIT (1-t)	

Table 98

Method 2

	₹
Earnings After Tax (EAT)	6.3
Add: Interest After Tax	+.7
NOPAT	7
NOPAT = EAT + Tax Adjusted Interest = EAT + (1 – *t*) *i*	

Table 101

Method 3

	₹
Earnings After Tax	6.3
Add: Interest	1.0
Less: Tax on Interest	(.3)
NOPAT	7.0
NOPAT = EAT + Tax Adjusted Interest* = EAT + (1-*t*) *i*	

**Tax Adjusted interest = Interest less tax on interest*

Table 100

Method 4

	₹
Earnings After Interest Before Tax	9.0
Add: Interest	1.0
Earnings Before Interest and Tax	10.00
Less: Tax on EBT	(2.7)
Less: Tax on Interest	(.3)
NOPAT	7
NOPAT = EAIBT + Interest = EBT NOPAT = EBIT less Tax on EBT and Tax on Interest	

Table 101

Method 5

	₹
Earnings Before Tax	9.0
Less: Income-Tax	(2.7)
Earnings After Tax	6.3
Add: Interest	1.0
Less: Tax on Interest	(.3)
NOPAT	7.0
NOPAT = EBT – Income-Tax + Interest – Tax on Interest OR NOPAT - EAT plus tax adjusted interest	

***N.B.**: The above methods are presented to illustrate the many ways in which NOPAT can be computed for purposes of arriving at EVA. These methods are mutually related. Students may remember a standard formula viz. NOPAT = EBIT (1-t). HUL – EVA – 2005-06*

Table 102

STEP 1: COMPUTATION OF NOPAT

METHOD 1: Computing NOPAT for HUL for the year ended 31-03-06.

	₹ *in Crores*
Profit After Tax	1540
Add: Interest	10
Less: Tax on Interest	3
Net Operating Profit After Tax	1547

Table 103

METHOD 2: Computing NOPAT for HUL for the year ended 31-03-06.

	₹ *in Crores*
Profit Before Tax	1862
Provision for Income Tax	322
Profit After Tax	1540
Add: Interest	10
Less: Tax on Interest	3
Net Operating Profit After Tax	1547

N.B.: There can be other methods of arriving at NOPAT as presented earlier in **Tables 95** to **97** and **Table 99.**

Table 104

STEP 2: COMPUTATION OF WEIGHTED AVERAGE COST OF CAPITAL (K_o) FOR HUL FOR THE YEAR ENDED 31.03.2006

DATA FOR COMPUTING COST OF EQUITY (k_e):

R_f	=	risk free rate	=	.076
β_e	=	Beta of the equity of the company	=	.97
R_m	=	Expected return on the market portfolio	=	.166
W_1	=	Proportion of the equity capital to capital employed	=	.94
ke	=	$Rf+\beta e\ (Rm\text{-}Rf)$	=	[.076 + .97 (.166 – .076) = 16.33%
	=	(Ke × W1) = (.94 × 16.33%)	=	15.35%
Debt	=	*i*	=	.089
Tax rate	=	*t*	=	.33
W_2	=	Proportion of debt to total capital employed	=	.06
Ki	=	(1-*t*)*i* × W2	=	.06 (1-.33) .089 = 0.36%
WACC	=	*ke*(W1) + *ki*(W2)	=	15.35% + 0.36% = 15.71%

Table 105

STEP 3: CAPITAL EMPLOYED: HUL 2005-06

	₹ *in Crores*	*Per Cent*
Equity	2515	94%
Debt	163	6%
Total Capital Employed	2678	100%

Table 106

STEP 4: COMPUTATION OF EVA : HUL 2005-06

	₹ *in Crores*
NOPAT	1547
K_o	15.71
TCE	2678
K_o × TCE	421
EVA	1126

Table 107
HUL – 2006-11
COMPUTATION OF EVA – 2010-11
EVA TRENDS

₹ *in Crores*

Name	*2006*	*2007*	*2008-09*	*2009-10*	*2010-2011*
Cost Of Capital Employed (COCE)					
(1) Average Capital Employed: Average Debt + Average Equity**	**2678**	**2784**	**2270**	**2616**	**3120**
(2) Cost of Debt, post-tax %	5.9	6.24	3.91	3.95	5.36
(3) Cost of Equity %	16.38	17.59	14.47	12.51	12.93
(4) Weighted Average Cost of Capital % (WACC)	15.74	16.03	12.88	12.12	12.92
(5) COCE: (3) × (6)	**421**	**446**	***365**	**317**	**403**
Economic Value Added (EVA)					
(6) Profit after tax, before exceptional items	1540	1743	2501	2103	2153
(7) *Add:* Interest, after taxes	7	17	17	5	0
(8) Net Operating Profits After Taxes (NOPAT)	1547	1760	2518	2108	2153
(9) COCE, as per (7) above	421	446	365	317	403
(10) EVA: (10) – (11)	**1126**	**1314**	**2154**	**1791**	**1750**

*COCE computed for 15 months.

SOURCE: HUL Annual Report 2010-11 Page No. 111.

Based on **Table 94.

HUL – 2010-11

Other Information pertaining to 2010-11.

*Cost of debt is taken at the effective rate of interest applicable to an "AAA" rated company like HUL for a short term debt, net of taxes. We have considered a pre-tax of 8.02% for 2010-11 (5.99% for 2009-10).

*Cost of equity is the return expected by the investors to compensate then for the variability in returns caused by fluctuating earning and share prices.

Cost of Equity = Risk free return equivalent to yield on long-term Government Bonds (taken at 7.91% for 20010-11) **(plus)**

Market-risk premium (taken at 11%) (x) Beta variant for the Company, (taken at 0.456) where Beta is a relative measure of risk associated with the Company's shares as against the market as a whole.

The provision for income-tax for the year ended 31.3.2011 is ₹ 440 crores.

REQUIRED:

With the help of the above data of HUL for the financial year 2010-11 and the earlier data 'EVA in HUL 2005-06 to 2010-11 (Tables **94** and **106**), compute the EVA of HUL for 2010-11'.

STEP 1:

HUL – EVA – 2010-2011 – COMPUTATION OF NOPAT

The Net Operating Profit After Tax or NOPAT for the Hindustan Unilever Ltd. for 2010-11 is calculated by two methods in the following ways:

Table 108

METHOD 1: Computing NOPAT for HUL For the year ended 31-03-2011.

	₹ *in Crores*
Profit After Tax	2153
Add: Interest	0
Less: Tax On Interest	0
Net Operating Profit After Tax	2153

Table 109

METHOD 2: Computing NOPAT for HUL For the year ended 31-03-2011.

	₹ *Crores*
Profit Before Tax	2593
Provision For Income Tax	440
Profit After Tax	2153
Add: Interest	0
Less: Tax On Interest	0
Net Operating Profit After Tax	2153

N.B.: The above two methods are only illustrative methods of computation. There are other methods too. **STEP 2:**

Table 110

COMPUTATION OF WEIGHTED AVERAGE COST OF CAPITAL *(êï)* FOR HUL FOR THE YEAR ENDED 31.03.2011

DATA FOR COMPUTING (ko):

Equity *Rf*	=	Risk free rate	= .079
βe	=	Beta of the equity of the company	= 0.456
R_m	=	Expected return on the market portfolio	= .189
W1	=	Proportion of the equity capital to capital employed	= .97
ke	=	$Rf + \beta e\ (Rm\text{-}Rf)$	= [.079 + .456 (.189 – .079) = 12.92%
(*Ke* × *W1*)	=	(.1292 × .99) = 12.79%	
Debt	=	*i*	= .08
Tax rate	=	*t*	= .33
W2	=	Proportion of debt to total capital employed	= .01
Ki	=	$(1\text{-}t)i \times W2$	= .01 (1–.33) .08 = 0.5%
WACC	=	$ke(W1) + ki(W2)$	= 12.79% + .05% =12.84%

Table 111

STEP 3: HUL – EVA – 2010-11 CAPITAL EMPLOYED

	₹ in Crores	Per Cent
Equity	3118	.99%
Debt	2	.01%
Total Capital Employed	3120	100%

Table 112

STEP 4: HUL – EVA – 2010-11 COMPUTATION OF EVA

	₹ in Crores
NOPAT	2153
K_o	12.84%
TCE	3120
$K_o \times$ TCE	401
EVA	1752

COMPUTATION OF EVA

GODREJ CONSUMER PRODUCTS LTD. (GCPL)

Table 113

GCPL – EVA – DATA FOR CALCULATING NOPAT

	2001-02 (₹ in Crores)
Earnings before interest and tax	65.7
Interest	2.5
Earnings before tax	63.2
Provision for Income Tax	15.4
Earnings after tax	47.8

Table 114

GCPL – EVA – DATA FOR CALCULATING WACC

	2001-02
Leverage beta () β	0.63
Market risk premium (*P*)	10%
Equity risk premium (*Px*)β	6.3%
Risk free return (*r*)	11.5%
Pretax cost of borrowing (*I*)	14%
Tax rate	35%
Average Equity (₹ in Crores)	102-768
Average Debt (₹ in Crores)	4.282

Table 115

GCPL – EVA – COMPUTATION OF NOPAT – 2001-02

	₹ *in Crores*
Profit after Tax	47.80
Add: Interest after Taxes	(1.6)
	49.4
Profit before Tax	63.2
Provision for IT	(15.4)
Profit after Tax	47.8
+ Interest	2.5
	50.3
– Tax on Interest	.9
	49.4

COMPUTATION OF COST OF CAPITAL EMPLOYED:

COST OF EQUITY (R_e): = R_f + β E = R_m = 11.5%+ 6.3% (10%) = 17.8%

WEIGHTED AVERAGE COST OF EQUITY: = $(R_e \times W_1)$ = 17.8% × 96% = 17.1%

COST OF DEBT: = $(1 - t)\ i$ = (1-.35) 14% = 9.1%

WEIGHTED AVERAGE COST OF DEBT: = 9.1% × 4% = .4%

WACC: = 17.1 + .4 = 17.5% = 18%

STEP 2:

Table 116

COMPUTATION OF WEIGHTED AVERGE COST OF CAPITAL (ko) FOR FOR THE YEAR ENDED 2001-02

GCPL DATA FOR COMPUTING (ko)

Equity R_f	=	Risk free rate	=	11.5%
βe	=	Beta of the equity of the company	=	0.63%
R_m	=	Expected return on the market portfolio	=	21.5%
W_1	=	Proportion of the equity capital to capital employed		=96%
k_e	=	$R_f + \beta_e (R_m - R_f)$	=	[.115 + .63 (.215 - .115)] = 17.8%
$(k_e \times w_1)$	=	[(.96 (.178)] = 17.1%		
Debt	=	i	=	14%
Tax rate	=	t	=	35%
w_2	=	Proportion of debt to total capital employed	=	4%
K_i	=	$(1\text{-}t)i \times W_2$	=	.04 [(1-.35) .14] = 0.4%
WACC	=	$ke(W_1) + ki(W_2)$	=	17.8% + .04% = 18.2%

Table 117

STEP 3: GCPL – EVA – CAPITAL EMPLOYED 2001-02

	₹ *in Crores*	*Per Cent*
Equity	102.768	96%
Debt	4.282	4%
Total Capital Employed	107.050	100%

Table 118

STEP 4: GCPL – COMPUTATION OF EVA – 2001-02

	₹ *in Crores*
NOPAT	49.4
K_o	18.2%
TCE	107.05
$K_o \times$ TCE	19.48
EVA = 30 (circa)	**29.98**

⊙⊙⊙

22

CASE STUDIES

CASE STUDY NO.	TITLE OF THE CASE STUDY
(1)	Bluestone Manufacturing Company
(2)	J. Company
(3)	5 Agents
(4)	Ratio Company Ltd.
(5)	Om Shree Mahalaxmi Ltd.
(6)	4 Pharma Companies
(7)	Sources and Uses
(8)	Colgate Palmolive Ltd. (CPL) – Reduction in Capital
(9)	Colgate Palmolive Ltd. (CPL) – Analysis and Interpretation
(10)	100 Airlines – The Top Five
(11)	Andrews Company Ltd.
(12)	Nestle Company Ltd.
(13)	A Manufacturing Company
(14)	Yogesh Company Ltd.
(15)	Mark Waugh Company
(16)	Ace Company Ltd.
(17)	Farmer Company
(18)	Allied Food Products
(19)	Infosys
(20)	Dell – Working Capital Management – Negative Working Capital

CASE STUDY 1: (PROBLEM)

BLUESTONE MANUFACTURING COMPANY

Table 1.1

TRIAL BALANCE AS ON 31 MARCH 2011

	Debit (₹)	Credit (₹)
Cash	100	—
Accounts Receivable	80	—
Allowance for Doubtful Debts	—	10
Raw Materials	24	—
Work-in-Process	30	—
Finished Goods	50	—
Buildings	400	—
Allowance for Depreciation on Building	—	160
Equipment	180	—
Allowance for Depreciation on Equipment	—	90
Prepaid Insurance	4	—
Accounts Payable	—	33
Bills Payable	—	48
Loans	—	120
Preference Shares	—	140
Equity Shares	—	182
Retained Earnings	—	85
Total	**868**	**868**

Table 1.2

TRANSACTIONS – APRIL 2011

The following transactions occurred during the month of April 2011:

		₹
(1)	Purchased Materials on Account	100
(2)	Issued Materials to the Factory	
	◆ Direct	80
	◆ Indirect	10
(3)	Accrued Factory Payroll	
	◆ Direct	45
	◆ Indirect	15
(4)	Paid Accrued Payroll	40
(5)	The following items of factory overheads were incurred:	

	₹
Depreciation of Building	8
Depreciation of Equipment	10
Heat, Light and Power Paid	5
Repairs Paid	30
Insurance Expired	1

(6)	Product completed and transferred to finished goods	145
(7)	Finished goods costing ₹ 190 were sold for	300
(8)	Cash receipts on account for the month were	200
(9)	Cash payments on account for the month were	90
(10)	Selling and administrative expenses paid during the month were	100

REQUIRED:

(a) Prepare an Income Statement for the month ending 30th April 2011.

(b) Prepare a Statement of Cost of Goods manufactured and Sold for the month ending April, 2011.

(c) Prepare a Balance Sheet as on 30th April, 2011.

CASE STUDY 2: (PROBLEM)

J. COMPANY.

M/s. J. Co. presents the following ratios based on an earlier Balance Sheet (1.4.2010). Using the data given project the Balance Sheet of M/s. J. Co. as on 31.03.2011. State your assumptions clearly.

Current ratio 2.5; quick ratio 1.75; fixed assets to net worth 0.8; equity share capital to preference share capital 5:1; networking capital ₹ 75,000, reserves and surplus ₹ 55,000, bank overdraft ₹ 10,000.

CASE STUDY 3: (PROBLEM)

5 AGENTS

Table 3.1

FINANCIAL STATEMENTS BALANCE SHEET AS ON

₹ in Crores

	Agent 1 *31.10.01*	*Agent 2* *31.03.00*	*Agent 3* *31.03.01*	*Agent 4* *31.03.01*	*Agent 5* *31.03.01*
ASSETS					
Tangible Fixed Assets	45.0	96.23	3.30	0.19	0.93
Other Fixed Assets	0.6	NIL	NIL	NIL	NIL
Investments	—	7.36	6.22	NIL	NIL
Current Assets	116.5	154.73	12.46	2.30	2.89
Miscellaneous Expenditure (to the extent not written-off)	0.5	4.06	0.35	NIL	NIL
Total	**162.6**	**262.38**	**22.33**	**2.49**	**3.82**

	Agent 1 31.10.01	*Agent 2* 31.03.00	*Agent 3* 31.03.01	*Agent 4* 31.03.01	*Agent 5* 31.03.01
LIABILITIES					
Current Liabilities and Provisions	44.9	89.86	4	.82	1.63
Long-term Debt	25.5	73.24	0.35	1.24	1.11
Owners Funds	92.2	99.28	17.98	0.43	1.08
Share Capital	14.6	11.10	1.46	0.40	0.84
Reserves and Surplus	77.6	88.18	16.52	0.03	0.24
Total	**162.6**	**262.38**	**22.33**	**2.49**	**3.82**

Table 3.2

FINANCIAL STATEMENTS

PROFIT and LOSS STATEMENT FOR THE YEARS ENDING

₹ in Crores

	Agent1 31.10.01	*Agent 2* 31.03.00	*Agent 3* 31.03.01	*Agent 4* 31.03.01	*Agent 5* 31.03.01
Turnover (Revenue)	75	399	3.32	.57	.84
Operating profit before depreciation	23	29	1.20	.18	.18
Depreciation	5	9	.14	.04	.09
Operating Profit	18	20	1.06	.14	.09
Interest Charges	1	9	.60	.19	.05
Other Income	3	2	1	.06	.26
Profit before Tax	20	13	1.46	.01	.30
Profit after Tax	9	7	.50	*	.18

**Very Negligible Amount ₹ 14,000 or ₹ .0014 crores*

NOTES TO FINANCIAL STATEMENTS

AGENT 1: Other fixed assets include goodwill valued at ₹ 6 crores. Other income includes interest profit on sale of fixed assets, rent and exchange rate gain.

AGENT 2: Other income includes profit on sale of investment/assets and dividend income and debtors recovered.

AGENT 3: Other income includes profit on sale of fixed assets.

AGENT 4: Other income includes various service charges.

AGENT 5: Other income includes miscellaneous income; interest on fixed deposit receipts and rent received.

LIST OF RATIOS

(1) Profit Margin (%) $= \dfrac{\text{Operating Profit}}{\text{Revenue}}$

(2) Profit Margin Before Depreciation (%) $= \dfrac{[\text{Operating Profit plus Depreciation}]}{\text{Revenue}}$

(3) Return on Owners Funds (%) $= \dfrac{\text{Profit After Tax}}{\text{Owners Funds}}$

(4) Return on Assets (%) $= \dfrac{\text{Profit Before Interest and Tax}}{[\text{Debt plus Owners Funds}]}$

(5) Debt/Equity Ratio (Times) Use Your Discretion

(6) Interest Cover Ratio (Times) $= \dfrac{\text{Profit Before Interest and Tax}}{\text{Net Interest}}$

(7) Current Ratio $= \dfrac{\text{Current Assets}}{\text{Current Liabilities}}$

Table 3.3

FINANCIAL STATEMENTS EXERCISE

WORKSHEET 1

Financial Ratio	*Agent 1*	*Agent 2*	*Agent 3*	*Agent 4*	*Agent 5*	*Weight %*
Profit Margin (%) (1)						
Profit Margin before depreciation (%) (2)						
Return on Owners Funds (%) (3)						
Return on assets (%) (4)						
Debt/Owners Funds (TIMES) (5)						
Interest Cover (TIMES) (6)						

Table 3.4

FINANCIAL STATEMENTS EXERCISE

WORKSHEET 2

Financial Ratio	*Agent 1*	*Agent 2*	*Agent 3*	*Agent 4*	*Agent 5*	*Weight %*
Profit Margin %						
Rank						
Profit Margin before depreciation (%)						
Rank						
Return on Owners 'Funds' (%)						
Rank						
Return on assets (%)						
Rank						
Debt / Equity Ratio (TIMES)						
Rank						
Interest Cover (TIMES)						
Rank						
Current Ratio						
Rank						
TOTAL SCORE						

CASE STUDY 4: (PROBLEM)

RATIO COMPANY LTD.

M/s Ratio Company has a Net worth of ₹ 50,00,000 (50 Laks). The company's principal ratios for the year ending 31.12.2011 are as follows:

(1) Inventory Turnover = 8 times

(2) Quick Ratio = 1

(3) Long-term Debt to Networking Capital = 4 times

(4) Gross Operating Profit = 20 per cent of sales

(5) Current Liabilities (Short-term debt) to Net worth = 1/3 (one-third)

(6) Total Debt to Net Worth = 1

(7) Selling expenses are 60 per cent of the gross operating profit.

(8) Income Tax rate = 30 per cent

REQUIRED:

(a) Prepare projected Balance Sheet as on 31.12.2012 and income statement for the ensuing year ending 31.12.2012.

(b) What is the Company's return to Total Investment?

Case Study 5: (PROBLEM)

Om Shree Mahalaxmi Ltd.

The Balance Sheet of Om Shree Mahalaxmi Ltd. consist of only the following items:

Table 5

AS AT 31ST MARCH 2001

PARTICULARS	*LIABILITIES ₹ in LAKHS*
Equity Share Capital	———
Reserves	———
Long-term Loans	———
Bank Borrowings	———
Short-term Public Deposits	———
Sundry Creditors	———
Other Current Liabilities	———
TOTAL	———

PARTICULARS	*ASSETS ₹ in LAKHS*
Gross Fixed Assets	———
Less: Accumulated Depreciation	———
Net Fixed Assets	———
Inventory	———
Accounts Receivables	———
Sundry Creditors	———
Other current assets	———
TOTAL	———

(1) Total Debt (excluding current liabilities) to net worth 2:1.
(2) Working capital gap ₹ 210 Lakhs.
(3) 100,000 equity shares of ₹ 100 each fully paid-up.
(4) Public Deposits are 25% of Net worth.
(5) Long-term Debt to Net worth 0.8 : 1.
(6) The company gets73 days credit against purchases of materials and the company gives 36.5 days credit against sales.
(7) Book value per share ₹ 200.
(8) Current Ratio 1.5:1.
(9) Quick Ratio 1:1.
(10) Material consumption is 60% of sales. Material consumption is equal to purchases.
(11) Inventory turnover (on sales) 5 times.
(12) 80% of the Company's sales are credit sales.

(13) Accumulated depreciation upto 31st March 2000 (including current depreciation) ₹ 140 lakhs.
(14) Profit before tax, interest and depreciation, 20% of sales.
(15) Interest to be charged @ 12% on long-term loans, 15% on bank borrowings and 15% on Public Deposits.
(16) Depreciation is charged on a straight-line basis @ 10% on Gross Fixed Assets.
(17) Tax rate 30%.

REQUIRED:

From the data given above:

(a) Complete the Balance Sheet.

(b) Calculate the Return on Investment, Return on Shareholder's Equity and Earnings Per Share for the company.

Show all calculations in support of your answer:

CASE STUDY 6: (PROBLEM)

4 PHARMA COMPANIES

The following data relates to four Pharma companies, viz., Co. 1, Co. 2, Co. 3 and Co. 4 for three years (Year 1, Year 2 and Year 3)

Table 6.1

DATA - FOUR PHARMA COMPANIES

₹ in Lakhs

	COMPANY 1			*COMPANY 2*			*COMPANY 3*			*COMPANY 4*		
	Yr. 1	*Yr. 2*	*Yr. 3*	*Yr. 1*	*Yr. 2*	*Yr. 3*	*Yr. 1*	*Yr. 2*	*Yr. 3*	*Yr. 1*	*Yr. 2*	*Yr. 3*
CA	206	221	252	178	192	194	120	127	129	115	118	139
CL	125	130	172	53	79	73	99	91	91	58	61	75
INV	154	168	188	100	112	92	77	76	81	79	72	88
CASH	2.5	3.5	5.7	28	20.0	13.6	1.8	1.0	0.6	5.8	8.3	9.1
ESC	72	72	108	56	56	101	15	19	19	34	34	34
PSC	8	8	8	NIL	NIL	NIL	NIL	NIL	NIL	NIL	NIL	NIL
RES	92	107	64	114	104	77	32	36	45	37	41	48
LTL	NIL	NIL	NIL	NIL	NIL	NIL	16	22	20	35	35	38

LEGEND:

CA = Current Assets
CL = Current Liabilities
INV = Inventory
ESC = Equity Share Capital
PSC = Preference Share Capital
RES = Reserves
LTL = Long-term Liabilities

REQUIRED:

Given the data in Tables 6.1 and 6.2:

(a) Develop and compute a set of ratios to evaluate the financial health of the four Pharma companies.

(b) Briefly explain your views on the financial health of the four companies.

Table 6.2

4 PHARMA COMPANIES – FINANCIAL RATIOS

	COMPANY 1			*COMPANY 2*			*COMPANY 3*			*COMPANY 4*		
	Yr. 1	*Yr. 2*	*Yr. 3*	*Yr. 1*	*Yr. 2*	*Yr. 3*	*Yr. 1*	*Yr. 2*	*Yr. 3*	*Yr. 1*	*Yr. 2*	*Yr. 3*
ROE%	8.59	11.11	17.52	9.81	14.87	14.33	14.58	14.7	16.5	9	12	15
ROCE%	13.56	24.53	35.41	28	37.96	37.54	37.4	38.3	51	21	22	24
PAIT/OP%	64	45	48	34	.39	40	29	27	25	29	39	45
CE/OF (Times)	1	1	1	1	1	1	1.3	1.4	1.3	1.4	1.4	1.4
OP/S%	5.5	9.5	11.3	14.12	15.32	15.21	10	11	12	8	8	9
S/CE (Times)	2.4	2.6	3.1	1.9	2.5	2.5	3.7	3.9	4.3	2.6	2.8	2.8

LEGEND:

ROE = Return On Equity
ROCE = Return On Capital Employed
PAIT = Profit After Interest and Tax
OP = Operating Profit
CE = Capital Employed
OF = Owners Funds = Equity Share Capital + Reserves
S = Sales

Table 6.3

CAPITAL STRUCTURE

₹ in Lakhs

	COMPANY 1			*COMPANY 2*			*COMPANY 3*			*COMPANY 4*		
	Yr. 1	*Yr. 2*	*Yr. 3*	*Yr. 1*	*Yr. 2*	*Yr. 3*	*Yr. 1*	*Yr. 2*	*Yr. 3*	*Yr. 1*	*Yr. 2*	*Yr. 3*
OF	172	187	180	170	160	178	47	55	64	71	75	82
LTL	NIL	0	0	0	0	0	16	22	20	35	35	38
CE	172	187	180	170	160	178	63	77	84	106	110	120

Case Study 7: (PROBLEM)

Sources and Uses

Source and Uses of Funds: 935 Private Ltd. Manufacturing Companies 1998-2002

Table 7

	97-98	*98-99*	*99-00*	*00-01*	*01-02*
SOURCES OF FUNDS:					
Internal Sources	32.1	42.9	50.6	48.3	25.8
External Sources	67.9	57.1	49.4	51.7	74.2
Capital Markets	20.2	17.0	17.4	20.7	–3.2
Borrowings*	30.8	18.3	9.6	11.2	–4.1
Current Liabilities and Provision	16.8	21.7	22.4	19.8	81.6
USES OF FUNDS:					
Gross Fixed Assets	63.8	73.5	53.9	53.6	48.9
Investments	9.6	4.2	17.3	20.9	16.9
Current Assets	26.7	22.3	28.8	25.5	34.2
Cash and Bank Balance	5.4	0.8	5.5	-2.1	11.7

*Excluding Fixed Deposits and Debentures

REQUIRED:

Given the above table, explain what the sources and uses of funds indicate for the five years ending 2002.

Case Study 8: (PROBLEM)

Colgate Palmolive Ltd. (CPL) – Reduction in Capital

Colgate Palmolive Ltd. (CPL) has presented the following financial information, for the four years (2003-04 to 2006-07) and also the period ending June, 2007) shown in **Table 8**.

Table 8

OWNERS FUNDS

₹ in Crores

	2003-04	*2004-05*	*2005-06*	*2006-07*	*Jun - 07*
Share Capital	136.0	136.0	136.0	136.0	136.0
Reserves and Surplus	108.3	113.8	135.1	144.5	205.4
Net Worth	244.3	249.8	271.1	280.5	341.4

	2003-04	*2004-05*	*2005-06*	*2006-07*	*Jun - 07*
Dividend Per Share (₹)	6.00	7.00	7.50	9.50	.....
Dividend Payout (%)	85.2	95.2	84.5	92.5	.....
Cash and Miscellaneous Investments	309.3	270.7	305.6	313.2	355.7

The company is presently overcapitalised and is planning to reduce the share capital which is in excess of the operational requirements of the company.

(1) Reduction in the face value of the shares from ₹ 10 per share to ₹ 1 per share.
(2) Return of ₹ 9/= per share to each shareholder uniformly.
(3) ₹ 9 per share will be a tax-free "***deemed dividend***"; CP will pay the dividend distribution tax.
(4) The number of shares held by each shareholder will not change and further there will be no change in the shareholding pattern of the company.

REQUIRED:

(a) Evaluate the proposal for reduction in capital by listing the benefits of the same.
(b) Is the proposal of M/s. CP a split of shares? How is a split of shares different from reduction in capital?
(c) If M/s. CP were to buy-back shares, what is your evaluation.
(d) Will the reduction of capital impact future dividends?
(e) What is the likely impact of the share price?

CASE STUDY 9: (PROBLEM)

COLGATE PALMOLIVE LTD. (CPL) – ANALYSIS AND INTERPRETATION

Table 9.1
FINANCIALS

₹ in Crores

	2001-02	*2002-03*	*2003-04*	*2004-05*	*2005-06*
A. Operating Results:					
Sales	1,160.9	1,056.9	1,042.08	1,072.6	1,217.6
Other Income	31	36	30	34	46#
Net Profit After Tax	70	89	108	113	138
Cash Profits	92	108	132	136	169
B. Financial Position:					
Fixed Assets (Net)	172	158	94	147	169
Current Assets (Net)	57	30	37	(63)	(50)
Others (Net)	28	90	116	169	156
TOTAL ASSETS	**257**	**277**	**246**	**254**	**275**
Share Capital	136	136	136	136	136
Reserves and Surplus	112	139	108	114	135
Shareholders' Funds	248	275	244	250	271
Loan Funds	9	2	2	4	4
Total Capital Employed	**257**	**277**	**246**	**254**	**275**
C. Equity Share Data:					
Earnings Per Share (₹)	5	7	8	8.33	10
Dividend Per Share (₹)	4	4	6.00*	7	8
Number of Shares (in Lakhs.)	14	14	14	14	14
Number of Shareholders (in '000s)	2	2	2	2	1

Re-grouped.

*Including one-time special 25th Anniversary Dividend (since becoming public in 1978) of ₹ 1.25 per share.

Table 9.2

FINANCIALS WITH RECLASSIFICATION

Previous year's figures have been re-classified to conform with current year's presentation, wherever applicable.

₹ in Crores

	2006-07	*2007-08*	*2008-09*	*2009-10*	*2010-11*
A. Operating Results:					
Sales	1385	1553	1758	2025	2317
Other Income	67	85	108	98	107
Net Profit After Tax	160	232	290	423	403
Cash Profits	175	252	313	461	437
B. Financial Position:					
Fixed Assets (Net)	192	199	179	253	267
Current Assets (Net)	(66)	(133)	(14)	39	61
Others (Net)	159	100	56	39	56
TOTAL ASSETS	**285**	**167**	**221**	**331**	**384**
Share Capital	136	14	14	14	14
Reserves and Surplus	145	147	203	313	370
Shareholders' Funds	281	162	216	326	384
Loan Funds	4	5	5	5	5
Total Capital Employed	**285**	**167**	**221**	**331**	**384**
C. Equity Share Data:					
EarningsPer Share (₹)	12	17	21	31	30
Dividend Per Share (₹)	10**	13	15	20	22
Number of Shares (in Lakhs)	14	14	14	14	14
Number of Shareholders (in '000s)	1	1	1	1	1

**Including one-time special 70th Anniversary Dividend of ₹ 2.00 per share

Previous year's figures have been re-classified to conform with current year's presentation, wherever applicable.

With the help of the above financial data of Colgate Palmolive Ltd. (CPL) evaluate the financial health of the company for the 10 years ending 2010-11.

Case Study 10: (PROBLEM)

100 Airlines – The Top Five

With the help of the data shown in **Tables 10.1 to 10.3**, fill in the worksheet shown in **Table 10.4** by finding out the nos. of appearances of different airlines, in each category, over the last 6 years.

Table 10.1

THE TOP 5 AIRLINES IN SALES

US$ million
In Profit

1993	*1994*	*1995*	*1996*	*1997*	*1998*
15816AA	16137AA	16910AA	17753AA	18570AA	19205AA
14511UA	13950UA	15026JL	16362UA	17378UA	17561UA
12376DL	12062DL	14943UA	13917JL	15872FX	14743BA
10723LH	11162LH	13903LH	13841LH	14184BA	14402DL
9732AF	10436BA	12194DL	13247BA	13590DL	13979FX

Table 10.2

THE TOP 5 AIRLINES IN OPERATING PROFIT

US$ million
In Profit

1993	*1994*	*1995*	*1996*	*1997*	*1998*
745BA	1006AA	1139BA	1839AA	1926AA	2338AA
690AA	961BA	1014AA	1123UA	1530DL	1803DL
530FX	830NW	901NW	1067BA	1259UA	1754BA
522SQ	657SQ	828UA	1054NW	1157NW	1478UA
384KR	591FX	740SQ	699FX	1011FX	1617LH

Table 10.3

THE TOP 5 AIRLINES IN NET PROFIT

US$ million
In Profit

1993	*1994*	*1995*	*1996*	*1997*	*1998*
2602CO	648SQ	1031LH	1016AA	1025US	1314AA
624TW	389BA	739BA	875BA	985AA	1018DL
511SQ	309CX	726SQ	730SQ	949UA	821UA
430BA	298FX	384CX	535NW	845DL	813LH
296CX	296NW	356SK	532UA	755BA	616SQ

Table 10.4

WORKSHEET

Frequency Distribution of the Nos. of appearances in each category			*USD$ million*
	Sales	*Operating Profit*	*Net Profit*
American Airlines (AA)			
United Airlines (UA)			
Delta Airlines (DA)			
Lufthansa (LH)			
Air France (AF)			
British Airways (BA)			
Federal Express (FE)			
North-west Airlines (NA)			
Singapore Airlines (SA)			
Korean Air (KA)			
Continental Airlines (CA)			
Transworld Airlines (TA)			
Cathy Pacific (CP)			
Scandinavian Airlines (SA)			
Japan Airlines (JA)			
US Airways (US)			

Case Study 11: (PROBLEM)

Andrews Company Ltd.

(A) **Andrews Company Ltd.** makes a loss of ₹ 100 after providing for depreciation of ₹ 20. Assuming everything else remains the same, what will be the effect of this loss on:

(1) The company's net worth.

(2) The company's networking capital.

(B) **X Co. Ltd.,**

Table 11.1

PARTICULARS	*1998*	*1999*	*2000*	*2001*
Current Ratio	1.67	1.50	1.21	1.23
Net-Working Capital	40	50	30	28

Comment on the liquidity of X Co. Ltd.

(C) **Y Co. Ltd.,**

Table 11.2

PARTICULARS	*2001*
Leverage (overall)	2.9
Long-Term Leverage	0.4
Current ratio	0.9

Comment on the financial strength of Y Company Ltd. What steps would you recommend it to take to improve its financial position?

(D) *Z* Co. Ltd.,

Table 11.3

PARTICULARS	*1998*	*1999*	*2000*	*2001*
Net Income/Net Worth (%)	20%	29.2%	27.5%	18%
Net Income/Profit Before Interest and Tax (PBIT) (%)	33	39	37	26
PBIT/Sales	12%	15%	15%	14%
Sales/Total Assets	2	2	2	1.67
Total Assets/Net worth	2.5	2.5	2.5	3
Days Debtors	36	36	36	36
Days stocks	41	39	39	93
Fixed Assets/Sales	0.2	0.2	0.2	0.3

Comment on the trend in the return on Net Worth of *Z* Company Ltd.

(E) What is meant by sustainable growth? Which ratios would you use to measure a firm's potential for growth over a period of time?

CASE STUDY 12: (PROBLEM)

NESTLE COMPANY LTD.

Table 12.1

FINANCIALS

			₹ Million
	1998	*1999*	*2000*
Profit after Interest and Tax	862	985	1186
Share Capital	964	964	964
Free Reserves	1,797	1,923	1,616
Face value per Share	10	10	10
Market Price per Share (High)	477	654	549
Market Price per Share (Low)	272	425	292
Depreciation	302	319	379
Dividends per share	6.5	8.0	14

REQUIRED:

With the help of the above, compute the following:

(a) Earnings per Share.
(b) Book Value per Share.
(c) Cash Flow per Share.
(d) Dividend per share.
(e) Price - Earnings Ratio.
(f) Price per Share to Cash Flow per Share.
(g) Price per Share to Book value per Share.
(h) Payout Ratio.

(i) Plough back Ratio.
(j) Market Capitalization.
(k) Earning Price Ratio.

Table 12.2

GLOSSARY

(1)	Market Price per Share	=	Price as per Quotation
(2)	Nos. of Shares	=	$\frac{\text{Equity Share Capital (₹)}}{\text{No. of Equity Shares}}$
(3)	Price Earnings Ratio (Times)	=	$\frac{\text{Price Per Share}}{\text{Earnings Per Shares}}$
(4)	Earnings per Share (₹)	=	$\frac{\text{Profit After Interest Tax and Dividend on Preference Share (if any)}}{\text{No. of Equity Shares}}$
(5)	Book Value per Share	=	$\frac{\text{Net Worth or Owners Funds}}{\text{No. of Equity Shares}}$
	[N.B. Net Worth = Equity Shares Capital plus Reserves and Surplus]		
(6)	Cash Flow per Share (₹)	=	$\frac{\text{Profit After Interest and Tax and Dividend on Preference Shares + Depreciation + other non – cash write - offs}}{\text{No. of Equity Shares}}$
(7)	Dividends per Equity Shares (₹)	=	$\frac{\text{Dividends Distributed}}{\text{No. of Equity Shares}}$
(8)	Payout Ratio (%)	=	$\frac{\text{Dividends Per Share}}{\text{Earnings Per Shares}} \times 100$ OR $\frac{\text{Dividends Distributed}}{\text{Profit after Interest and Tax and Dividend on Preference Shares}} \times 100$
(9)	Dividend Yield (%)	=	$\frac{\text{Dividends Per Share}}{\text{Market Price Per Share}} \times 100$
(10)	Earnings Yield (%)	=	$\frac{\text{Earnings Per Shares}}{\text{Market Price Per Share}} \times 100$
(11)	Plough back Ratio (%)	=	[100% – Payout Ratio (%)] OR [1 – Payout Ratio]

CASE STUDY 13: (PROBLEM)

A MANUFACTURING COMPANY

Below are the factory account data for A manufacturing Company for the year 2011

Table 13

FINANCIALS

Inventories	*Beginning* ₹	*Ending* ₹
Raw Materials	1,35,000	1,12,000
Work-in-Process	2,18,000	1,98,000
Finished Goods	1,76,000	1,83,000
Factory supplies	23,000	33,000
Raw Materials Purchased		2,37,000
Factory Supplies purchased		27,000
Depreciation – Factory Building		18,000
Depreciation – Factory Equipment		12,000
Indirect Labour		38,000
Direct Labour		1,26,000
Heat, Light and Power		28,000
Factory Insurance		2,000
Accounts Payable	1,25,000	1,00,000
Accounts Receivable	2,50,000	2,00,000
Sales		7,30,000

REQUIRED:

With the help of the above data:

(a) Calculate the Operating cycle.

(b) Project the Working Capital.

CASE STUDY 14: (PROBLEM)

YOGESH COMPANY LTD.

PERCENT OF SALES METHOD

Table 14.1

YOGESH CO. LTD.

Balance Sheet as on 31 March 2001

	₹ in Lakhs	₹ in Lakhs
Assets:		
Fixed Assets:		
Land and Building	40	
Plant and Machinery	120	160
Current Assets:		
Inventories	100	
Accounts receivables	120	
Cash and Bank balances	20	240
		400
Capital and Liabilities:		
Share Capital	150	
Reserves	100	250
Long-term loans		75
Accounts payable	50	
Provision for Income Tax	25	75
		400

The Profit after tax was 10% of the total assets of ₹ 400 lakhs. The ensuing year is likely to experience a substantial jump in activity and sales. One estimate is a 40% increase in sales and another estimate is 80% increase in sales. The profit-sales ratio of 10% is likely to continue for the ensuing budget period too. Further the relationship between individual items in the balance sheet and sales will continue to hold for items, which continue to be driven by sales. The relationship between individual items in the balance sheet and sales can be expressed as:

Table 14.2

ASSET VALUE AND SALES

(1)	Nos. of days sales	=	$\frac{\text{Asset Value}}{\text{Sales Per Day}}$
(2)	Turnover times	=	$\frac{\text{Sales}}{\text{Asset Value}}$
(3)	Per cent of sales	=	$\frac{\text{Asset Value}}{\text{Sales}} \times 100$

REQUIRED:

With the above data, you are required to:

(a) Identify the balance sheet values in items of sales using the above three methods.
(b) Project the Working Capital requirements.

CASE STUDY 15: (PROBLEM)

MARK WAUGH COMPANY

Table 15

MARK WAUGH COMPANY – OPERATING CYCLE

(1)	Number of days Raw Material held	30
(2)	Number of days work-in-progress	15
(3)	Number of days Finished Goods held	30
(4)	Number of days for Collection	60
		135
(5)	Credit Sales	₹ 3,600
(6)	Cost of Goods Sold	₹ 2,400
(7)	Depreciation	₹ 365

N.B.: Figures in Rupees are in Crores

REQUIRED:

Estimate the working capital.

CASE STUDY 16: (PROBLEM)

ACE COMPANY LTD.

Table – 16.1 represents the abridged Balance Sheet of ACE Company Limited as on 31st December 2011. The company reported a sale of ₹ 600 lakhs for the year 2011. The after tax profit for the year was ₹ 300 lakhs.

Table 16.1

BALANCE SHEET AS ON 31ST DECEMBER 2011

Capital and Liabilities	*₹ in Lakhs*	*Assets*	*₹ in Lakhs*
Share Capital	100	Land and Building	30
Reserves and Surplus	80	Plant and Machinery	100
Term Loans	80	Inventories	100
Sundry Creditors	60	Sundry Debtors	110
Tax Liability	30	Cash and Bank	10
Total	**350**		**350**

The management is considering substantial increase in activity and sales, in 2012. Two proposals have come up, one suggesting 50 per cent increases in sales and the other a 100 per cent increases in sales. A quick assessment of the additional funds will have to be found, for the two alternatives.

Additional level of activity and sales will involve corresponding increase in investment in plant and machinery. A study of the company trends supports the assumption of a fixed relationship between Sales and Current assets and also between Sales and Current Liabilities, including Sundry debtors and Tax liabilities. The after tax profit rate of 5 per cent on sales is expected to persist.

The relationship between Sales and the Relevant balance sheet items can be expressed in 3 ways:

(1) As number of days sales.
(2) As turnover.
(3) As percentage of sales.

For ACE Company limited, Table – B highlights these relationships. The per cent of sales relationship has been set out in Table – B, only for such of the Balance Sheet items as are expected to vary in sympathy with changes in sales. The current assets constitute 37% of sales and the current liabilities, 15 per cent of sales. The net working capital thus forms 22 per cent of sales.

REQUIRED:

Using the above information project the Balance Sheet and other relevant inputs to estimate the working capital needs and the sources of finance to meet those needs for the ensuing budget period 2012.

Table 16.2

SHOWING RELATIONSHIP BETWEEN SALES AND BALANCE SHEET FOR 2011

Particulars	*₹ in Lakhs*	*Number of Sales Days*	*Turnover times*	*Percentage of sales*
Land and Building	30.00	18	20.0	NA
Plant and Machinery	100.00	61	6.0	17
Fixed Assets	**130.00**	**79**	**5.6**	**NA**
Inventories	100.00	61	6.0	17
Sundry Debtors	110.00	67	5.4	18
Cash and Bank	10.00	6	60.0	2
Current Assets	**220.00**	**134**	**2.7**	**37**
Total Assets	**350.00**	**213**	**1.7**	**NA**
Share Capital	100.00	61	6.0	NA
Reserves and Surplus	80.00	49	7.5	NA
Term Loans	80.00	49	7.5	NA
Equity and Long-Term Loans	**260.00**	**159**	**2.3**	**NA**
Sundry Creditors	60.00	36	10.0	10
Tax Liability	30.00	18	20.0	5
Current Liabilities	**90.00**	**54**	**6.7**	**15**
Total Capital and Liabilities	**350.00**	**213**	**1.7**	**NA**
Profit after Tax	30.00			5
Sales	600.00			100

NA – Not Applicable.

CASE STUDY 17: (PROBLEM)

FARMER COMPANY

Farmer was in the dairy business. They produced and bottled powdered milk. In 2003 Farmer sold 5,00,000 Litres of milk in 6,00,000 bottles. The capacity of Farmer was 6,75,000 bottles. They bought milk powder to which they added some other ingredients costing ₹ 0.10 per bottle. Of recent years pure milk was demanded by customers due to the sustainable increase in purchasing power and change of tastes. Farmer had to take a decision to change over product line from powdered milk to pure milk. Access to the later product line would, in addition to providing a total saving of ₹ 0.25 per bottle, necessitate capital expenditures (livestock and equipment) to the tune of ₹ 1,00,000. The economic life of these assets is 10 years. Because of an agreement with the trade union no rise in wages is contemplated.

Farmer has 50 employees who are paid on a negotiated wage of ₹ 2 per hour. The annual working hours per employee was ₹ 2,800. The controller said that approximately 35% of the labour cost was variable. It varied proportionately with increases or decreases in production activity. In 2003 production had required 7,50,000 kilograms of milk powder purchased at an imported rate of ₹ 2,466 per kilogram. The other overheads (variable) are approximately ₹ 0.25 per bottle. The projected price of powdered milk is ₹ 1 per bottle whereas projected sales price of pure milk was ₹ 0.97 bottle. In the past the latter was ₹ 1.22 per bottle.

Assume maximum capacity of 6,75,000 bottles and targeted profit of ₹ 3,75,000. The income statement for the year ended 31st December 2003 is shown in Exhibit – I.

Table 17

Income statement for the year ended 31st December 2003

Particulars	₹	₹
Sales – 60,000 bottles @ ₹ 1.25		750000
Manufacturing Costs		
Labour Costs	280000	
Material Costs	185000	
Other Overheads	150000	
Depreciation	5000	620000
Manufacturing Margin		**130000**
Interest	5000	
Depreciation	5000	
Sales Promotion	2000	
Administration Expenses	4000	
Non-Manufacturing Expenses		16000
Total Costs		**636000**
Operating Profit		114000

REQUIRED:

(a) What is the breakeven point of Farmer in bottles?
(b) Is the targeted return attainable at capacity?
(c) How much should Selling price increases to earn the desired profit at capacity?
(d) How much should Variable cost decreases to earn the desired profit at capacity?
(e) How much should fixed costs decreases to achieve the desired profits at capacity?

CASE STUDY 18: (PROBLEM)

ALLIED FOOD PRODUCTS

Table 18.1

BALANCE SHEET AS ON 2001 AND 2002

		US$ million
Particulars	*Amt(2001)*	*Amt(2002)*
Current Assets		
Cash and Marketable Securities	80	10
Accounts Receivables	315	375
Inventories	415	615
	810	**1000**
Current Liabilities		
Accounts Payable	30	60
Accruals	130	140
Notes Payable	60	110
	220	**310**
Networking Capital	**590**	**690**
Net Fixed Assets	870	1000
Total Net Assets	1460	1690
Long-term Bonds	580	754
Total Common Equity	840	896
Preferred stock	40	40
Capital employed	1690	1460

*Here current liabilities include only accounts payable and accruals. In other words Current liability exclude all interest bearing obligation.

Table 18.2

ALLIED FOOD PRODUCTS YEAR 2001 AND 2002

Relevant income statement data

		USD Million
	2001	*2002*
(A) EBIT =	$263	$284
(B) Income-tax	$105	$114
(C) Net operating profit after tax	$158	$170
(D) Current depreciation	$90	$100
Operating cash flows	$248	$270

Income Tax is computed at 40% of EBIT.

REQUIRED:

Compute Gross Operating Working Capital, Net Working Capital or Net Current Assets, Current Assets - Current Liabilities, Total Operating Capital (Net Basis), Gross Investment in Capital (Gross Basis), Net Operating Profit After Taxes (NOPAT), Operating Cash Flows (OCF) and Free Cash Flows (FCF).

Case Study 19: Infosys Ltd.

INFOSYS Ltd. is part of Chapter 9 – Measuring, Operating, Financing and Investing Cash Flows. For the year 2007 solution is built into the Chapter itself. However, for the years 2008 and 2009 the case poses problems for students to address. Solutions are accessible through softcopy.

Case Study 20: (PROBLEM)

Dell – Working Capital Management – Negative Working Capital

Dell Computer Corporation was founded in 1984 by the then 19 year old Michael Dell.

The company designed, manufactured, sold and serviced high performance Personal Computers (PC's) compatible with industry standards. Initially, the company purchased IBM compatible personal computers, upgraded them and then sold the upgraded PC's directly to businesses by mail order. Subsequently, Dell began to market and sells its own brand personal computer, taking orders over a toll free telephone line and shipping directly to customers.

Dell preferred to sell directly to customers. This was dell's core strategy. This build to order model helped Dell to deliver a customized order within a few days. Something the competitors could not do. The salient features of Dell's approach to management are brought out in **Exhibit 20.1.**

EXHIBIT 20.1

DELL'S APPROACH TO MANAGEMENT

- *Direct to customer model of delivery reduced the intermediaries and the need to keep inventory to supply to the intermediary.*
- *This also helped in proper forecasting that helped in avoiding unnecessary inventory.*
- *Build to order manufacturing system which reduced the finished goods inventory balances as compared to its competition.*
- *WIP and Finished goods inventory, as a per cent of total inventory was only 10 to 20 % as compared to competitor's inventory of 50 to 70 %.*
- *Just in time supply from all key component suppliers and factories of suppliers near to Dell's plants at Austin, Texas and Ireland.*
- *It sourced its requirements from 80 suppliers to minimize dependence on any one.*
- *During 1993 to 1996, it focused on Cash conversion Cycles and ROIC. It instituted metrics to control inventory and forecast appropriately.*
- *High efficiency in bringing new products to markets in around average of 35 days. This helped in reducing the obsolescence and increasing the market share.*

For the three years ending 1995 Dell's day's Supply of Inventory (DSI) is shown in **Table 20.1**:

Table 20.1

Days Supply of Inventory (DSI)*

	1993#	*1994#*	*1995#*
Dell Computer	55	33	32
Apple Computer	52	85	54
Compaq Computer	72	60	73
IBM	64	57	48

Source: Dell Computer Corporation Fiscal 1993-1995 Annual Reports; case writer estimates from Apple Computer, Compaq Computer and IBM Fiscal 1992-1994 Annual Reports.

*DSI=(Net Ending Inventory)/(Quarterly COGS / 90 – Days).

#Dell's Fiscal calendar ends in January; Apple's in September, Compaq and IBM's in December. The DSI for 1995 represents Dell's DSI for the quarter ended on 1/29/95, Apple's on 9/30/94 and Compaq's and IBM's on 12/31/94.

Table 20.2

DELL's INC – DATA

US$ Million

ADDITIONAL FUND NEEDED:	*AMT. 1995*	*AMT. 1996*	*CURRENT ASSETS*	*AMT. 1995*	*AMT. 1996*
Current Liabilities:			Cash	43	55
Accounts Payable	403	466	Short-term investments	484	591
Accrued and Other Liabilities	349	473	Accounts Receivables, net	538	726
TOTAL CURRENT LIABILITIES	**752**	**939**	Inventories	293	429
Long-term Debt	113	113	Other	112	156
Other Liabilities	77	123	**TOTAL CURRENT ASSETS**	**1470**	**1957**
TOTAL LIABILITIES	**942**	**1175**	Property, Plant and Equipment	117	179
			Other	7	12
Put Options			**TOTAL ASSETS**	**1594**	**2148**
Stockholders' Equity					
Preferred Stock	120	6			
Common Stock	242	430			
Retained Earnings	311	570			
Other	(21)	(33)			
TOTAL STOCK HOLDERS EQUITY	652	973			
TOTAL LIABILITIES	**1594**	**2148**			

REQUIRED: Prepare a Cash Flow Statement for the year ended 1996.

EPILOGUE

In October 1929, Irving Fisher famously proclaimed that stock prices had reached "a permanently high plateau". Just days later, Wall Street crashed. Further, in November, a well-known Professor from Yale University issued a fresh prognosis - "the end of the decline of the stock market will probably not be long, only a few days more at most". Well, the Dow raced to hit its lowest of the century on July 8, 1932 not returning to the pre-1929 levels until two and a half decades. In recent times, there was a report by the IMF on Global Financial Stability in April, 2006 which read as follows: "There is growing recognition that the dispersion of credit risk by banks to a broader and more diverse group of investors ... has helped make the banking and overall financial system more resilient.... The improved resilience may be seen in fewer bank failures and more consistent credit provision. Consequently, the commercial banks may be less vulnerable today to credit or economic shocks." It is by now well-known that just two years later the global meltdown sent shockwaves across the globe, with the chain reaction, following the collapse of the Lehman brothers (September, 2008). The whole concept of dispersion of credit risk had not made the financial system more resilient. On the contrary, it has made it more vulnerable to the vagaries and vicissitudes of the business. There was a general mood of depression and uncertainty was the order of the day. In a book by Robert Skidelsky, he says, "intellectual failure of the economics profession"* is the main

Skidelsky. Robert, Keynes - The Return of the Master, Allen Lane, September, 2009.

cause of the crises. This is where Keynesian thought makes all the difference. He distinguished between Risk and Uncertainty. Risk is something which can be captured, in a quantified manner, by assigning probabilities through cardinal or ordinal values. If managing business was only about risk management, quantitaive measures alone could help. The cardinal and ordinal values could be addressed. However, life in general and business too, has to encounter uncertainty which is known as "unknown probability" or "irreducible uncertainty'. This uncertainty is intrinsic to capitalism. To that extent mankind is fatalistic and "none of us has a precise inkling of what the future has in store." Thus the main flaw in the new classic economics is the failure to capture uncertainty in financial modelling which is in vogue. The efficient market hypotheses looks only at risk and all the risks are assumed to eventually reflect a normal bell curve. The risk is then assumed to be distributed smoothly within the precincts of the bell curve. However, this is preposterous. Outcomes of events cannot be captured through a science (statistics) which assumes that most distributions, if not all, *viz.*, binomial, poisson, chi-square *f*, *t* and perhaps many other distributions all tend towards the normal distribution**. As mentioned by Harish Damodaran, "All the modern bank risk management models (including the disastrous Black-Scholes option pricing formula) based themselves on "normal distribution", ignoring the possibility of extreme events. Small wonder, they failed and landed us in the mess we are in, from which we are, hopefully, now emerging." Hence, it is necessary to remember that the learning of finance is not mere formulae driven. Such a learning would make information evaluators and decision-makers cogs in a wheel and compel 'opertaion robots'. Human assets are rendered defunct pro tanto. Thus, it is necessary to note that formulae are only a mariners compass providing direction. Tools and Techniques which facilitate analysis and interpretation of financial statements are necessary but not sufficient. At best these tools and techniques are like a star which helps to steer the ship of enterprise.

"And all I ask is a tall ship, And a star to steer her by" – John Masefield.

However the challenges of decision making have to be assumed by human beings. As well said by Dr. K. S. Basu.

"By its very definition decision making starts where formulae end and where judgement has to be exercised, the imponderable has to be evaluated the intangible has to be assessed."

This epilogue is thus a *caveat* to those who are belated, beguiled and even overawed by formulae. I hope the readers understand the contents of the book and keep in mind what is said both in the prologue and epilogue.

Dr. Guruprasad Murthy.

***Approximately normal distributions occur in many situations, as explained by the central limit theorem. When the outcome is produced by a large number of small effects acting additively and independently, its distribution will be close to normal. The normal approximation will not be valid if the effects act multiplicatively (instead of additively), or if there is a single external influence which has a considerably larger magnitude than the rest of the effects.*

I can only recognize the occurrence of the normal curve — the Laplacian curve of errors — as a very abnormal phenomenon. It is roughly approximated to in certain distributions; for this reason and on account for its beautiful simplicity, we may, perhaps, use it as a first approximation, particularly in theoretical investigations. — Pearson (1901)

Measurement errors in physical experiments are often modeled by a Normal distribution. This use of a Normal distribution does not imply that one is assuming the measurement errors are normally distributed, rather using the Normal distribution produces the most conservative predictions possible given only knowledge about the mean and variance of the errors.

BIBLIOGRAPHY

Dobbins, Richard, and Stephen F. Witt., *Practical Financial Management*. Bombay: Basil Blackwell Ltd. (India Book Distributors), 1988.

Targett, David., *Analytical Decision Making*. Delhi: Macmillan, 1997.

Ramu, Shiva S., *Strategic Alliances*. New Delhi: Response Books, 1997.

Ramu, Shiva S., *Corporate Growth Through Mergers and Acquisitions*. New Delhi: Response Books, 1998.

Van Horne, James C., *Financial Management and Policy*. New Delhi: Prentice Hall of India Private Limited, 2000.

Van Horne, James C., *Financial Management and Policy*. New Jersey: Prentice – Hall, 2002.

Bhatt, Bimal R. *Accounting and Financial Policies, Practices Standards and Reporting*. Snow White Publication Pvt. Ltd., August, 2004.

Warren, Carl S., James M. Reeve and Philip E. Fess. *Financial Accounting*. South-Western Thomson Learning, 2004.

Kothari, Rajesh, and Bobby Dutta. *Contemporary Financial Management*. New Delhi: Macmillan India Ltd., 2005.

Brigham, Eugene F., and Joel F. Houstan. *Fundamentals of Financial Management*. Thomson South-Western, 2006.

Horngren. Charles T., George Foster and Srikant M. Datar. *Cost Accounting Managerial Emphasis*. New Delhi: Prentice Hall of India Private Limited, 2006.

Reimers. Jane L., *Financial Accouting*. Pearson Education, 2007.

Berk. Jonathan, and Peter DeMarzo. *Financial Management*. Pearson Education, 2008.

Gupta, Ambrish. *Financial Accounting for Management An Analytical Perspective*. Pearson Education, 2008.

Chandra, Prasanna. *Financial Management*. New Delhi: Tata McGraw-Hill Publishing Company Limited, 2011.

Ramachandran, N. and Ram Kumar Kakani. *Financial Accounting for Management*. New Delhi: Tata McGraw-Hill Publishing Company Limited., 2011.

⊙⊙⊙

